Best Native Plants for Southern Gardens

UNIVERSITY PRESS OF FLORIDA

Florida A&M University, Tallahassee
Florida Atlantic University, Boca Raton
Florida Gulf Coast University, Ft. Myers
Florida International University, Miami
Florida State University, Tallahassee
New College of Florida, Sarasota
University of Central Florida, Orlando
University of Florida, Gainesville
University of North Florida, Jacksonville
University of South Florida, Tampa
University of West Florida, Pensacola

University Press of Florida

Gainesville Tallahassee Tampa Boca Raton Pensacola Orlando Miami Jacksonville Ft. Myers Sarasota

Best Native Plants
for Southern Gardens

A Handbook for Gardeners, Homeowners, and Professionals

Gil Nelson

15 14 13 12 11 10   6 5 4 3 2 1

Library of Congress Cataloging-in-Publication Data
Nelson, Gil, 1949–
Best native plants for Southern gardens: a handbook for gardeners, homeowners,
and professionals / Gil Nelson.
p. cm.
Includes bibliographical references and index.
ISBN 978-0-8130-3458-4 (alk. paper)
1. Native plant gardening—Southern States—Handbooks, manuals, etc. 2. Native
plants for cultivation—Southern States—Handbooks, manuals, etc. I. Title.
SB439.24.S66N45 2010
635.9'51759—dc22   2009041781

The University Press of Florida is the scholarly publishing agency for the State
University System of Florida, comprising Florida A&M University, Florida Atlantic
University, Florida Gulf Coast University, Florida International University, Florida
State University, New College of Florida, University of Central Florida, University
of Florida, University of North Florida, University of South Florida,
and University of West Florida.

University Press of Florida
15 Northwest 15th Street
Gainesville, FL 32611-2079
http://www.upf.com

Contents

To my grandmother
the late Bessie Pettus

Preface

My fascination with native plants did not originate with gardening. For me, native plants in native places have always taken precedence over those along the garden path. More than thirty years of tramping the captivating floral assemblages of the southern United States has left an indelible mark. These adventures have not been based on great sojourns to exotic lands, nor even extended trips outside a relatively small home domain. Familiar landscapes in which we immerse ourselves time and again are our best teachers. Occasional forays into the southern mountains, Fall Line Hills, Mississippi savannas, and New England forests aside, my most important lessons have largely come from repeated visits close to home.

This is not to say that I was unfamiliar with gardening, or that my preoccupation with field over neighborhood taught me nothing about the gardening process. I recall as a teenager my grandmother rushing to lift the boughs of her Asian azaleas to prevent the mower blades from damaging them as I cleaned her yard; and I remember my family's occasional Sunday drives in early spring to see the city's finest azalea collections, then returning home to compare them to our own. We even made a few family forays to officially designated azalea trails in Mobile and Pensacola to see the mixture of form, color, and texture that define the traditional southern azalea garden.

It should come as no surprise that when my wife and I bought our first home, and then our second, we decorated them with Asian azaleas. The first time, we planted only a handful; the second time, nearly two hundred. I admit to enjoying the spring-blooming Asian azaleas that grace so many yards in Thomasville's and Tallahassee's older neighborhoods. Mixed with dogwood, redbud, fringe tree, and camellias, they put on quite a show.

That I enjoy native plant gardening today is the sum of these field, family, and residential encounters. With increasing field experience, it occurred to me that my neighborhood azaleas connected my psyche only with suburbia. They were reminiscent of none of my favorite natural areas and were certainly not characteristic of the indigenous American landscape. I never encountered them in the wild. I knew nothing of their ecology or natural affinities, and I could not visit them in their native habitats. They taught me nothing about the history of America's dominant vegetative associations and did not add to my understanding of our native ecosystems. In short, they were ecological aliens; cultural artifacts.

With our third home, I wanted a garden that celebrated the endowments of the

American landscape. Mere remembrances of spring wildflowers in a boggy meadow, a wooded slope ablaze with wild azaleas, an expanse of saw palmetto under endless pines, or the sweet fragrance of native magnolias in dimly lit woodlands were no longer enough. I wanted my garden to connect me with the natural places I valued; to teach me something of the plants and their ecology; to help me identify them in all of their stages. I wanted to see what coralbean and scarlet hibiscus look like when they emerge from the ground; to learn how long it takes a red buckeye to grow from seed; to observe the flowers of native azaleas at every phase; to learn things that only captive plants and daily observations can allow. This is not to say that I gave up non-natives entirely. It wouldn't be fair to the hummingbirds and butterflies, and fully adorned evergreen azaleas and Japanese camellias are still among my most favored garden shrubs.

I reveal this bit of personal history at the outset not as a confession, but to set the tone and to make a point. The paths to native plant gardening are many and varied, and those who practice it are anything but one-dimensional. There is no single definition of the activity, no dogma, no dominant ethos. Gardeners who enjoy native plants do so in their own way, in their own gardens, as an expression of their own creative spirits— and often as a celebration of a distinctly American endowment. They come from many perspectives, represent infinite points of view, and encompass a wide range of gardening philosophies. You don't have to be a fanatic. You don't have to give up your non-native garden treasures. There is no code of ethics, no secret handshake. No oath is required to join the club.

Acknowledgments

Numerous people have participated in making this book a reality. First and foremost, I thank the several organizations without whose financial support the travel necessary to complete this book would not have been possible. These organizations include the Alabama Invasive Plant Council, Florida Exotic Pest Plant Council, Florida Native Plant Society, Georgia Native Plant Society, and Southeast Exotic Pest Plant Council. I am especially grateful in this regard to Karen Brown, Shirley Denton, Alison Fox, Doria Gordon, Nancy Loewenstein, Ed McDowell, Elaine Nash, Howard Peavey, and Tony Pernas.

I owe a special debt of gratitude to a cast of advisors who have given me feedback during the book's completion, some very regularly. Above all I appreciate the extensive assistance offered by Ron Lance. Ron freely shared his extensive knowledge of southeastern plants and their garden uses, as well as contributed numerous photographs. He is certainly one of the preeminent plantsmen of the southeastern United States. Donna Legare also deserves much gratitude. In addition to contributing several valuable photographs, she read and commented on sections of the manuscript (especially the sections on wildlife gardening), provided knowledge and inspiration, and was helpful and supportive in numerous other ways. Others who deserve sincere gratitude include Caroline Dean, the late Dan Dean, Bill Fontenot, Jack Johnston, Ernest Koone III, Bob McCartney, Jan Midgely, Dan Miller, Charlotte Seidenberg, and Jody Walthall. All of these individuals reviewed plant lists, added content, and were helpful throughout the book's development.

Others who provided help, feedback, reader reviews, images, garden and nursery tours, or helped in numerous other ways include Nancy Bissett, Kathleen Brady, Linda Chafin, Stewart Chandler, Tom Corley, Nancy Desmond, Shirley Denton, Kathryn Gable, Bob Greenleaf, Bobby Hattaway, Bill Head, Bob Head, Ray Head, Betty Jinright, Hew Joiner, Martha Joiner, Gary Knox, Jeff Lewis, Chris Liloia, Carol Lovell-Saas, Jeff Norcini, Leslie Pierpont, Paula Reith, George Sanko, Allen Webb, Amy Webb, Charles Webb, Wayne Webb, and Steve Yeatts. I am especially grateful to David Ellis and the American Horticultural Society for allowing use of the heat zone map and to the Arbor Day Foundation for the hardiness zone map shown in Chapter 1.

I also owe a special word of gratitude to Bill and Pam Anderson for letting me use their outstanding photographs to fill in where my own images were either lacking or nonexistent, and for many hours of delightful, enlightening, and entertaining gardening conversation.

I thank John Byram, editor-in-chief of University Press of Florida, for his patience and assistance in shepherding this book to fruition. His support and encouragement are much appreciated. I also gratefully thank and acknowledge Ginny Stibolt and Steve Christman for their outstanding reviews of the manuscript and for their very helpful edits and suggestions.

This book is dedicated to my late grandmother Bessie Pettus. Grandmother was the earliest inspiration for my lifelong appreciation of nature. Her love of birds and plants was contagious, and her wildlife-friendly garden and yard were enticing. I spent many enjoyable hours exploring the grounds around her and Granddad's home. Many of my most ardent interests stem from these early experiences.

Finally and always, I thank my wife, Brenda, for her continued love, patience, support, and encouragement. Her unparalleled tolerance of my admittedly compulsive and often overly intense work habits and her comments and criticisms on the manuscript certainly elevate her to the realm of angels.

Financial Sponsorship

The financial sponsorship provided by the following organizations is much appreciated.

 Alabama Invasive Plant Council

 Florida Exotic Pest Plant Council

 Florida Native Plant Society

 Georgia Native Plant Society

 Southeast Exotic Pest Plant Council

I

Gardening with Native Plants

1

Gardening with Native Plants

An Introduction

This book is a guide to the best native garden plants for the southeastern United States. Its region of coverage includes eight states from Virginia southward through the Carolinas and Georgia; the northern two-thirds of Florida; and westward to Alabama, Mississippi, and Louisiana. This is an expansive region that encompasses USDA Hardiness Zones 6–9 and American Horticultural Society (AHS) Heat Zones 11–3 (note that the zone ranges in this book are given in this sequence—hardiness zone, then heat zone). For the most part, the plants included have been selected due to availability, dependability, and ease of care, or—as Dan Miller of Trillium Gardens in Tallahassee, Florida, would say—because they are "good doers."

The book is divided into three parts. Part I puts the cultivation of native plants into context and accentuates the fascination inherent in using American plants for American gardens. The several chapters in this part address the history and use of native plants and native plant gardening; the scourge of invasive species, including their enormous environmental and economic costs, and how to avoid them in the garden; and some of the opportunities made possible by gardening with native species.

The ten chapters that make up Part II focus on popular native plant groups. Included are chapters on such specialties as native azaleas, magnolias, and hollies; favorite perennials; showy shrubs; climbing vines; outstanding groundcovers; and others.

Part III consists of a catalog of one hundred of the best native plants for southern gardens. The plants included were compiled with the help of numerous native plant experts and enthusiasts, nursery owners, and gardeners across the south, with particular attention given to plants with broad natural ranges, wide adaptability, and successful garden performance. Each account in Part III highlights the species' common and scientific names, native range and habitat, hardiness and heat zones, form and size, essential characteristics, preferred culture, typical garden use, best features, companion plants, and similar or related species.

Native Plants: A Gardener's Definition

The definition of "native plant" is a controversial topic. At its temporal and simplest level, the term refers to a plant that existed in the United States prior to 1513—the advent of European expansion to the New World. Inherent in the definition is the idea that the plant arrived here by natural processes, without the help of human conveyance. For many native plant gardeners, especially those driven primarily by a desire for cold hardiness, for heat tolerance, or simply to grow American plants, this definition seems good enough. To such gardeners, if a plant is distinctly American in provenance and can be grown in a particular climate, it belongs in the garden.

More precise definitions include information about a plant's natural distribution— often demarcated by arbitrary political boundaries—and preferred habitat. The assumption in these more sophisticated definitions is that a plant's true native range may be limited only to portions of a particular state, county, or region, and then only to one or more particular ecosystems or habitat types within that region. These more technical definitions are normally the purview of botanists and ecologists who seek a clearer, scientifically based understanding of a region's phytogeographic history. Mere dots on state and county maps, these scientists would argue, do not give an accurate picture of a species' true nativity. If strictly applied to gardening, the stuffiest of these definitions would suggest that a Piedmont plant cultivated in the coastal plains or mountains, or even a typically wetland tree planted in the uplands, is technically not native to its cultivated locale.

For gardeners, a precise definition of native plant gardening often boils down to personal choice and individual gardening interests. For some the definition is very restrictive and limits the choice of garden plants to a narrow, geographically and ecologically informed pallet. Others choose to include plants native only to their state, or perhaps to a nearby portion of their state. Still others take the more expansive approach, allowing themselves broad geographical and ecological latitude. Most importantly, no matter where one's definition falls within these rather wide extremes, as long as the plants they choose originated in North America, the definition will not be incorrect.

Weedy, Non-native, and Invasive Species

Although the definition of "native plant" is in direct opposition to that of "non-native" or "alien plant," it should not be counterbalanced with the definition of "weed." The concepts of "native" and "weedy" are not mutually exclusive. It cannot be assumed that because a plant is native, it cannot also be weedy. Nor can it be assumed that all weeds are invasive, or that all non-native species are either weedy or invasive.

The classic definition of *weed* is as cultural as it is scientific and usually refers to plants that are growing where they are not wanted. Provenance is not operative in the equation. In contrast, invasive plants are usually those that have been introduced into the United States from abroad—either purposefully or accidentally—and that have subsequently spread into and substantially disrupted the natural processes of healthy ecosystems. Well-known southeastern invasive plants include Chinese privet (*Ligustrum sinense*), kudzu (*Pueraria montana*), Japanese honeysuckle (*Lonicera japonica*), nandina (*Nandina domestica*), Chinese tallow (*Triadica sebifera*), Japanese climbing fern (*Lygodium japonicum*), and oriental bittersweet (*Celastrus orbiculatus*). The common and scientific names of many of these species suggest their alien origins.

Invasive species often have few or no natural environmental enemies in the United States, leaving their control and containment to an assortment of biologists, land managers, and a growing cadre of professional invasive plant control specialists. The burgeoning demands of invasive plant management costs U.S. taxpayers millions of dollars annually and invasive plant infestations in natural areas have destroyed innumerable acres of otherwise healthy forests and native plant communities. Personnel at some public parks and forests report that they spend the bulk of their management time and money combating the problem.

Some of our worst invasive species have found their way to the United States for management use, especially for erosion control and wetland reclamation. Others have been introduced for horticultural purposes but have spread far beyond the garden. Environmentally sensitive gardeners at all levels, regardless of their interest in native plants, should be aware of the negative and costly impacts of invasive species and should make every effort to avoid them in their gardens. Chapter 3 addresses in depth the issue of non-native invasive species, with special emphasis on the roles gardeners can play in avoiding their use and reducing their impact.

That non-native species are neither universally weedy nor universally invasive is supported by the hundreds of well-behaved non-native shrubs, annuals, and perennials that grow in gardens throughout the United States. Many of these species have not become naturalized—meaning that they are not reproducing on their own by seed or, in many cases, even by vegetative reproduction—and remain confined to the gardens in which they have been planted. Of those that have become naturalized, the majority have not become pests.

The American Horticultural Society's *A–Z Encyclopedia of Garden Plants* includes more than 15,000 entries, many of which are not indigenous to the United States. Florida's flora alone includes just over 1,300 nonindigenous, naturalized plants, about one-third of the state's combined total of native and naturalized flora. Currently, about 150 of these non-natives—about 11 percent—are included on the Florida Exotic Pest Plant Council's list of known invasive species, with another 150 or so included on an unofficial watch list of potentially invasive species.

The key question is whether newly introduced plants, or even non-native species that have been present in the American landscape for a long time, will remain well behaved. Not all alien plants are like Asian azaleas and Japanese camellias. Some introductions show their invasive or weedy tendencies almost immediately, readily escaping into natural areas soon after becoming established in the garden. Others remain well behaved for many years before finally escaping and following an increasingly rapid pathway to invasiveness.

The difficulty for gardeners and weed scientists alike lies in accurately predicting into which category a new introduction is likely to fall. The invasive plant councils in all southeastern states maintain official or unofficial watch lists precisely for this reason. Many of the plants on these lists are known to be invasive in neighboring or nearby states, or are regularly observed in natural areas and are suspected of developing invasive tendencies. Monitoring the official and unofficial lists of invasive species will help gardeners keep their creations free of problem plants.

Cultivars, Selections, and Hybrids

The word *cultivar* literally means "cultivated variety." Cultivars represent plants that have been selected from wild populations or nursery stock, or that have been produced through an intentional organized breeding program. Once selected, cultivars are generally propagated vegetatively to ensure the persistence of one or more desirable traits, resulting in offspring that are essentially genetic clones of a single individual. (However, some cultivars, such as some garden vegetables, are propagated by seed; these are called "seed cultivars.") Cultivars that do not result from organized breeding are often also called "selections" because they are first noticed by keen-eyed horticulturalists who see unique—and hopefully marketable—features in a particular individual, then reproduce the individual from cuttings.

Hybrids often display larger or showier flowers, altered fruit color, unique foliage, abnormal flowering times, a smaller or larger form, or increased fruit production. Some native plant enthusiasts consider these modifications to be nonnatural and unacceptable. Others seek them out for their purportedly "improved" features. Numerous hybrids are commercially available in the garden trade, some of which have become very popular.

Strict native plant enthusiasts sometimes argue against the use of human-induced hybrids on several grounds. One commonly expressed concern is that hybrids might be sterile and produce neither nectar nor fruit, limiting the ecological services they provide

Cultivar Names

Named cultivars are selections that have been introduced into the trade using a registered or nonregistered cultivar name, such as *Ilex vomitoria* 'Nana.' Enclosing the cultivar name within single quotation marks is the accepted practice today. Previously, cultivars were designated by inserting the abbreviation "cv." prior to the cultivar name, as *Ilex vomitoria* cv. 'Nana,' but this method is no longer promoted by the *International Code of Nomenclature of Cultivated Plants*.

Some selections are the result of natural hybridization while others are the result of intentional crosses. The parents of natural hybrids can only be assumed, whereas the lineage of an intentional cross is often meticulously documented so that the resulting offspring can be used in further hybridization attempts. Hybrid plants include a multiplication sign (×) in their name to indicate the cross. Normally, the "×" is pronounced as "times" or "by" but is also sometimes replaced in speech with the phrase "the hybrid species." The name *Rhododendron alabamense* × *Rhododendron canescens* indicates a cross between two known species where the species names are given. In other instances, as with the name *Abelia* ×*grandiflora*, a hybrid between *A. chinensis* and *A. uniflora*, the names of the parent species are omitted and the hybrid taxon is given its own name. Several natural hybrids are well-known and often-used garden plants. The several forms of the so-called topal hollies (*Ilex* ×*attenuata*)—including the 'East Palatka' and 'Savannah' cultivars—that purportedly originated as natural hybrids of the dahoon and American hollies are excellent examples.

to insects, birds, and other wildlife. Another argument suggests that hybrids bred to flower out of season, even if fertile, might well be out of sync with insect and bird life cycles and migration habits, making any resources the plants might provide unavailable to wildlife at the appropriate time. Exactly how plants interact with their environment is still not well understood. As Sara Stein points out in *Noah's Garden*, "there is no plant in all the world that scientists can claim to have unraveled in all its multifarious connections." Those opposed to the use of human-engineered hybrids would argue that tinkering with systems about which we are not fully informed is likely to lead to unintended, hidden, and perhaps negative consequences. In addition to these more or less scientific reasons for avoiding artificial hybrids, strict native plant enthusiasts also argue that human-induced crosses do not derive from natural processes and therefore cannot be considered native. Including them in the garden, they reason, does not meet the strictest definition of native plant gardening.

Despite the arguments for and against the use of cultivars, the chapters and accounts in this book make frequent reference to some of the better-known named selections. Many of these were made by expert plants people and have subsequently proven to be popular and worthy garden plants. Some are selected from field collected plants; others from nursery stock. A few are of hybrid origin. The purpose of this book is not to rebuke, admonish, or pass judgment, but to assist southern gardeners in selecting the best native plants to incorporate into their landscapes.

Types of Native Plant Gardeners

Like the varying definitions of *native*—and largely because of them—there are also several types of native plant gardeners. At one extreme are native plant purists whose goal it is to restore their landscape to some preexisting natural condition. Purists are more closely aligned to restorationists than to gardeners, relying on the narrowest of definitions to inform garden design. They reconstruct regional ecological histories and diligently study the plants that would have occurred in their landscapes prior to human intervention. Plantings are meticulously scrutinized to ensure that provenance and placement are historically accurate and ecologically defensible, and that the chosen palette is representative of the specific region, ecosystem, and habitat being restored. Although astute restoration ecologists will find much useful information in this book, the challenge of recreating natural landscapes far exceeds the skills, knowledge, and interest of most of us average gardeners. As might be expected, native plant purists constitute an exceedingly small and specialized contingent of native plant enthusiasts.

Typical native plant gardeners are well to the right of purists, often relying on a much broader definition of what is meant by *native*. They tend to limit their choices to indigenous species but do so with less precision. Some restrict their choices to plants that grow naturally within a narrow geographical area, such as a handful of nearby counties or parishes. Others base their selections on ecoregion boundaries, either narrowly defined or broadly expansive in geographic extent. Some populate their gardens with species that are representative of a specific region, but not necessarily to a specific habitat. Others include plants that are representative of an entire state, a group of states, or even an entire section of the country. The most forgiving gardeners may be more concerned that a plant is native to the United States than to whether it is native to their own locale. Such gardeners are committed to native plants, but not necessarily to narrow boundaries.

By far the largest group of native plant gardeners is composed of those who incorporate both native and non-native species in their gardens. Many in this category consider themselves to be primarily native plant gardeners but with strong affinities to selected non-native plants with inherent attractions or that serve specific garden purposes. Especially good butterfly and wildlife plants are included among these favorite non-natives, as are plants that have extended blooming and fruiting cycles, serve well as groundcovers or grassy borders, display unique foliage or flower characteristics, or represent non-native species of a collector's favorite plant group, family, or genus.

Native plant incorporators also include collectors whose enthusiasm for a specific genus or family leads them to stray beyond the confines of local geography. Gardeners who are fascinated with magnolias, native azaleas, trilliums, irises, ferns, tickseeds, and carnivorous plants fall into this category, as do many others.

Acquiring and growing plants from remote locales derives from a long and colorful history and serves as the foundation for most of the world's botanical and display gardens. Modern gardeners who build impressive collections of specific plant groups epitomize this legacy.

Most gardeners who incorporate both native and non-native species readily accept cultivars and selections, especially if they enhance the flowering period, flower size, foliage characteristics, hardiness, heat tolerance, or robustness of native species. Few, however, are accepting of known invasive species. Native plant incorporators are typically environmentally sensitive gardeners who diligently avoid invasive and weedy species. They also regularly remove overly aggressive introductions from their landscapes.

Hardiness, Heat, and Floristic Regions

Selecting native plants for the garden depends at least partly on knowing something about a species' provenance, cold hardiness, heat tolerance, and soil preferences. While some plants are generalists and seemingly perform well throughout much of the southeast, others are more specific in their requirements.

For the purposes here, the southeastern United States can be divided into three major floristic regions, each of which is roughly parallel to one of three physiographic provinces. The smallest of these, at least within the geographical extent of this book, encompasses portions of the southern Cumberland Plateau, Southern Appalachians, and Blue Ridge and extends from extreme western Virginia southwesterly through the western portions of North Carolina, extreme north Georgia, and northeastern and north-central Alabama. For simplicity, this area is referred to in this guide as "the mountains," although much of north-central Alabama actually falls within the Cumberland Plateau and does not encompass much in the way of true mountainous terrain. The Piedmont lies south and east of the Appalachians in a distinct band that stretches from extreme southeastern New York southwestward to east-central Alabama. The Piedmont is bordered on its southeastern edge by the Fall Line Hills, a narrow boundary separating it from the Southeastern Coastal Plains.

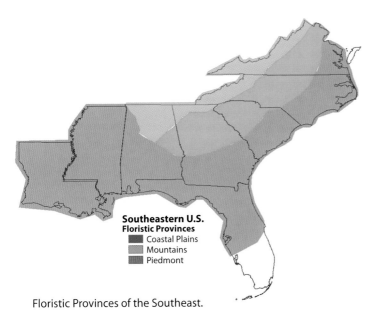

Southeastern U.S. Floristic Provinces
- Coastal Plains
- Mountains
- Piedmont

Floristic Provinces of the Southeast.

In this book I have chosen to cast the Southeastern Coastal Plains in the plural rather than singular. This is because the region constitutes a mosaic of smaller provinces, including the Atlantic Coastal Plain and the East Gulf Coastal Plain. Some experts further divide the Atlantic Coastal Plain into two or more sections. Others divide the entire coastal plains region into the Outer Coastal Plain, which includes the area within about two hundred miles of the coast, and the Upper or Inner Coastal Plain, which encompasses the more inland areas, especially portions of northwestern Alabama and northern Mississippi and Louisiana.

Ecologists, botanists, and field naturalists differentiate these regions on ecological processes, community structure, plant distribution, and phytogeographical origins. Native plant gardeners differentiate them on how well native species tolerate or adapt to their climates, soils, humidity, and maximum and minimum temperatures. Plants that do well in the mountains might find the summer temperatures and high humidity of the Outer Coastal Plain too demanding, and coastal plains endemics might lack the hardiness necessary to survive the sometimes severe cold of higher elevations or more northern climes.

The mountain region is characterized by much colder average winter temperatures, comparatively moderate summer temperatures, greater elevation and relief, and typically rich, humus-laden soils. Most of the region lies within zones 6B and 7A on the USDA hardiness map, although higher elevations are sometimes included within zone 6A. Plants grown in these zones must be able to tolerate low temperatures ranging from -5° to 5° F. Not only are such species typically cold hardy, but also their roots often require cooler daytime and evening soils and their seeds need sufficient winter cold to ensure that they break dormancy and germinate in the spring.

Most of the mountain region also falls within the range of the American Horticultural Society's (AHS) heat zones 7–3. AHS heat zones are based on the average number of days per year that the temperature exceeds 86° F. Zone 3 locations average 7–14 days, whereas those in zone 7 average 60–90. Given its varying elevations and transitional

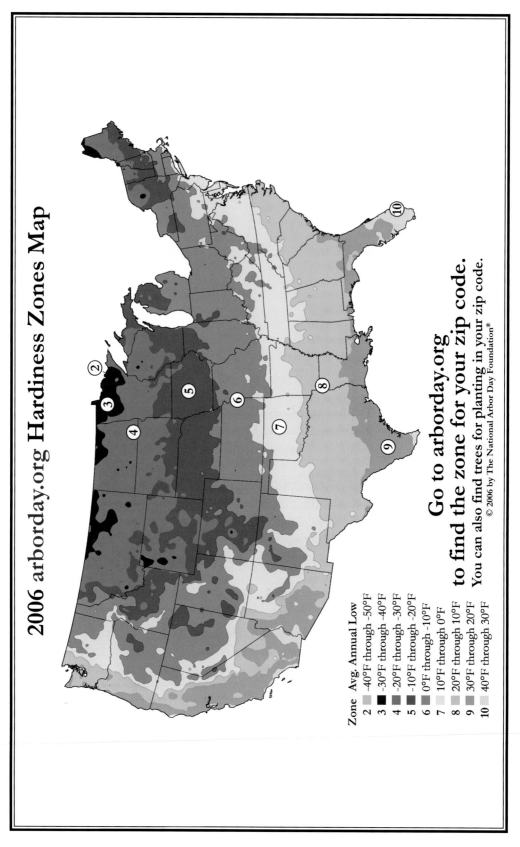

2006 arborday.org Hardiness Zones Map

Zone Avg. Annual Low
2   -40°F through -50°F
3   -30°F through -40°F
4   -20°F through -30°F
5   -10°F through -20°F
6   0°F through -10°F
7   10°F through 0°F
8   20°F through 10°F
9   30°F through 20°F
10 40°F through 30°F

Go to arborday.org
to find the zone for your zip code.
You can also find trees for planting in your zip code.

© 2006 by The National Arbor Day Foundation®

Hardiness Zones. Courtesy of Arbor Day Foundation.

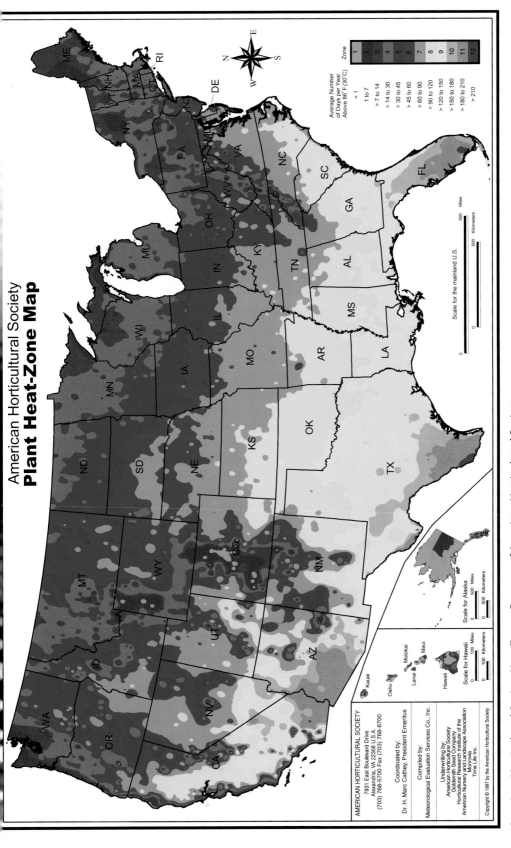

American Horticultural Society Heat Zones. Courtesy of American Horticultural Society.

juxtaposition to the Piedmont, it is not surprising that the northwesternmost portions of the southeast have the broadest ranges of cold hardiness and heat tolerance.

The name Piedmont means "foot of the mountains" or "foothills," an appellation that reflects the mountainous hint of its rolling topography. Although generally considered to extend northward to at least the Hudson River in New York, the area covered in this book includes an approximately six-hundred-mile swath that is bounded on the east by a gently curving line passing from Washington, D.C., through Richmond, Columbia, Augusta, Macon, Columbus, and Auburn. Like much of the eastern United States, the Piedmont has been severely altered by human intervention. It is generally thought to have been covered during presettlement times by oak–hickory–pine forests, the remnants of which are evident today in only a very few places. The climate is mostly warm–humid and the soils are mostly fertile loam—a varying mixture of clay, silt, and sand—and rocky clay, as evidenced by the multihued earth-toned layers that decorate many of the region's highway road cuts. Its position in USDA zone 7B, with minimum temperatures ranging 5–10° F, indicates its cold, and AHS zone 8, with 90–120 days a year above 86° F, its heat.

The Piedmont is probably best developed along its two-hundred-mile stretch through the Carolinas and Georgia. Here it straddles the transitional divide between majestic uplands and gently sloping lowlands, resulting in a flora that is partly unique and partly an intermingling of the mountains and the coastal plains. Piedmont gardeners take advantage of this unparalleled opportunity by filling their creations with an array of native species that is often unavailable to gardeners in either the deeper or shallower south.

South and west of the Piedmont, the younger sediments of the Southeastern Coastal Plains, left behind by retreating Ice Age seas, form a gently sloping plain that falls away to the Atlantic Ocean and Gulf of Mexico with an almost imperceptible gradient. Lucy Braun, in her classic 1950 work, *Deciduous Forests of Eastern North America*, tagged this region the Southeastern Evergreen Forest, a moniker reflective of the vast historical expanse of longleaf pine uplands and slash pine lowlands interspersed within by mixed evergreen and deciduous hammocks and ravines, and bordered on its seaward edge by evergreen maritime forests. Botanists Bruce Sorrie and Alan Weakley imply that this fascinating landscape can be thought of as exposed ancient sea bottom that over the past million years has become clothed with a diverse and luxuriant carpet of nearly 8,000 native species, about 1,600 of which occur nowhere else in the world. A number of these coastal plains specialties enjoy restricted natural ranges and are known only from a relatively few botanical hot spots that also serve as well-known field trip destinations for a variety of professional and amateur plant lovers. These hot spots notwithstanding, much of the region is naturally and horticulturally homogenous, supporting numerous native species with widespread distributions. For botanists, ecologists, and biologists, this means ample opportunity for floristic and systematic study. For gardeners, it means a seemingly endless array of new plants to introduce to the garden.

When extended to the southern tip of the Florida peninsula, the Southeastern Coastal Plains encompass about 450,000 square miles—about 8 percent of the North American landmass—and constitute a mosaic of natural communities, many of which offer fascinating studies in natural symmetry and garden design. Upland and lowland pine communities, from a distance seemingly all trees and a few shrubs, support several hundred showy native herbaceous plants, many of which have found their ways into gardening circles. Bogs, meadows, and wetland savannas support sun-loving carnivorous plants, orchids, and a fascinating array of showy wildflowers.

The climate of the Southeastern Coastal Plains is hot, humid, and sometimes described as subtropical, though the last assessment is probably a gross overstatement as there is little similarity between coastal plains flora and that of tropical climes. A more accurate description might be that the various habitats of the Southeastern Coastal Plains represent a transitional stage from the temperate to tropical biomes.

The portion of the coastal plains included in this book lies predominately within USDA zones 8 and 9, extending southward to about the latitude of Lake Okeechobee, Florida. Minimum temperatures seldom fall below 10° F, and the number of days with temperatures above 86° F ranges from 120 to 180. Cold tolerance is seldom an issue, except when rare, very late-season cold fronts in the northern parts of zone 9A freeze young leaves and early flowers. Heat tolerance, on the other hand, is essential.

Soils in the Southeastern Coastal Plains vary widely, from very acidic to alkaline. According to Sorrie and Weakley, eight of the ten recognized soil orders occur here, with pH values ranging 3.0–9.0. Soil type can vary considerably, even over very short distances, a feature that can probably be attributed to diversity of origin, variation in parent soil material, hydrological processes, and the diversity of freshwater wetlands. Gardeners who desire to have their soil tested should probably not rely on a single sample from just one location.

Benefits of Using Native Plants

The benefit of using native plants is more often expressed as an impassioned plea than a reasoned supposition; the zeal of committed native plant gardeners is often hard to suppress. But, impassioned pleas aside, there are some excellent reasons for including natives in the garden.

First, native plants tend to thrive well under local conditions. They are generally tailored to local environments and are well suited to regional climates, native soils, and annual precipitation regimes. If appropriately sited, they perform well with minimum care, little fertilizer, and no pest control. This, of course, applies more consistently to plants from nearby habitats than those from habitats far away. Plants limited to a mountainous distribution are not likely to survive the summer heat of the coastal plains, and strictly coastal plains plants may not be sufficiently cold hardy to withstand a mountain winter. Likewise, plants from xeric habitats may be intolerant of wetland gardens, shade-tolerant perennials of sunny borders, and acid-loving shrubs of limey soils.

Nevertheless, as a general rule most regionally native species are at least well adapted. They are appropriately hardy, require less in the way of soil amendment, and often survive with less, or in some cases no, supplemental irrigation (at least once they are established). More importantly, they typically, but by no means always, tend to be nonaggressive and well behaved. Most stay where they are planted, do not spread into neighboring habitats, and are not particularly weedy.

The second reason to use native plants is because of their inherent attractiveness to wildlife. Native plants benefit native wildlife in subtle ways that are often difficult to observe and by no means obvious. Plants, insects, mammals, and reptiles that have evolved together interact in ways that easily evade normal observation. Insects, for example, often rely solely on specific groups, genera, or species of native plants and sometimes depend upon them for the completion of their life cycles. For many insects, there are simply no substitutes for their favorite food or reproductive preferences. When the plants are absent, so are the bugs; and so too the wildlife that depends on the bugs. The innocent and seemingly innocuous elimination of particular plant species from a geographic area can result in the unanticipated, often unnoticed, and seemingly inexplicable loss or reduction of a suite of associated wildlife. Not only are insects displaced, but also the birds, mammals, frogs, and toads that depend on them disappear. From a purely selfish perspective, providing for wildlife ensures our personal enjoyment. More altruistically, it contributes to environmental integrity.

The third reason to use native plants has to do with availability. Increased interest has enhanced the quantity, diversity, and selection of native species, making it much easier and advantageous to include them in suburban landscapes. Natives are no longer available only at specialty nurseries. Large retail nurseries, big-box home stores, and several of the larger wholesale growers now stock them, often noting them as native but intermingling them with regular inventory. This has led to a greater assortment of plants from which to choose, including improved selections and cultivars as well as high-performing hybrids. Although some native plant enthusiasts lament the introductions of hybrids and cultivars, the fact that propagators and growers are paying attention to so-called "improved" native species suggests that the use of native garden plants is becoming well established in the mainstream nursery trade.

There are also more growers and nurseries specializing in popular groups of plants, such as magnolias, native azaleas, showy native shrubs, and native perennials. The greatest advances to date have been made with woody plants; availability now includes a wide range of native trees and shrubs. And, while there is still much work to be done with native perennials and wildflowers, even here the options continue to grow.

The purported benefits of native plants should not be taken to mean that in all cases native plants thrive better or are better adapted to local conditions than alien plants. Despite the fact that overzealous native plant enthusiasts sometimes make this claim, it is simply not true. Were natives always to outperform aliens, plants like kudzu, oriental bittersweet, Japanese climbing fern, and Chinese privet would not be invading natural areas or outcompeting native species. Nor would southern gardens dominated by Asian azaleas be so common, widespread, and healthy. Inflated claims about the value and cultivation of native species does a disservice to native plant gardening and runs the risk of casting those who encourage their use as environmental fanatics rather than fundamental gardeners.

Claims are also sometimes made that native species are invariably easy to grow and trouble free. Such tenets are often overstatements, promulgated by those of us who cherish native plants, enjoy them in our gardens, and wish to share our enthusiasm. Imbibing passion with unsupported idealism is a common human frailty. However, purveyors of the native plant ethos should not be disingenuous; the use of native plants is not a gardening panacea. I have certainly lost my share of plants to typical gardening woes: inexperience, improper placement, inappropriate drainage, inadequate attention, too much or too little irrigation, and poor judgment. I've also had plants die for what appeared—at least to me—to be no apparent reason. To be sure, there is certainly a suite of tough native species that tend to be relatively independent of care and that have found excellent use in situations where attention is lacking, conditions are stressful, and only a strong constitution ensures survival. Such species as wax myrtle, American beautyberry, muhly grass, and a number of the species included in Part III of this book tend to survive no matter what you do. However, for others it is not so easy just to plant them, water them in, and leave them alone. As later chapters make clear, some natives have exacting demands that are difficult to replicate and that require diligent attention. Most require at least some care.

The truth of the matter is that being pressed into caring for plants is probably of little consequence to the readers of this book. Most are already likely to be gardeners. Digging in the dirt is what we do. If we didn't have to tend the plants in our planted landscapes, just how much fun would gardening be?

2

Gardening with Native Plants

Historical Highlights

The use of native plants in gardening and landscaping is not a recent development. While it is easy to assume that the current fascination with native gardens is rooted in the environmental movement of the 1960s and '70s, and was founded originally on the dual tenets of conservation and sustainability, this is simply not the case. The use of indigenous plants in naturalistic landscapes began in the United States at least as early as the middle 1800s and initially had much more to do with regional authenticity and the informal style of landscape architecture than with conservation, preservation, or restoration. The earliest—and perhaps most eloquent—proponents of native plant landscaping appeared in the middle 1800s and included a select group of notable landscape architects—as opposed to gardeners and environmentalists—whose visions were grounded largely in favoring the indigenous over the exotic and the American over the European or Asian. These early adopters valued regionalism and a sense of place and sought to create signature landscapes that were unmistakably local in origin, sentiment, aspect, and appeal. Perhaps surprising to those of us who came of age in the latter half of the 1900s, all things environmentally sensitive—including populating our gardens with native plants—did not originate with the first Earth Day.

If I were asked to create a list of books that best espouse the emotions, virtues, and spirit of native plant gardening—the "why," not the "how to"—only two would have copyright dates in the last quarter century: Sarah Stein's *Noah's Garden* and Doug Tallamy's *Bringing Nature Home*. The others, by such writers as Jens Jensen, Frank Waugh, Wilhelm Miller, Caroline Dorman, Elsa Rehmann, and Edith Roberts, appeared much earlier, most well before 1950, and focused primarily on celebrating the American flora.

Siftings, one of the most persuasive treatises on respect for indigenous American landscapes, is the work of Jens Jensen, a Danish immigrant who was born on a farm near Dybbol, Denmark, in 1860 and came to the United States in 1884. Jensen was a landscape architect probably best known for his work in Chicago and the Midwest, especially with public parks and large estates. When he died in 1951 at the age of ninety-one, the *New York Times* heralded him the "dean of landscape architecture."

Jensen was aligned with the so-called Prairie School of architecture, whose most famous representatives included Louis Sullivan and his apprentice Frank Lloyd Wright.

Like these influential architects, Jensen's creations were guided by the desire to express ideas rather than merely to decorate landscapes. He valued the integration of structure with environment and the indigenous over the imported. He was fascinated with what he called the primitive landscape and its power to inform the structure of our gardens, the placement of our dwellings, and the strength of our sense of place. He regarded landscaping as art informed by native culture, native material, and the interaction between the two; his ultimate goal was to create gardens that reflected, celebrated, and validated the uniqueness and natural beauty of the aboriginal landscape.

Aspiring garden designers could not do better than a thorough reading and full understanding of Jensen's small but powerful book. Essentially a philosophical memoir, it distills an essence of native plant landscaping that is made even more remarkable by its 1939 copyright date. Reprinted in 1990 as part of the Johns Hopkins University Press American Land Classics series, it evokes elemental respect for the power, beauty, and history of the indigenous American landscape.

American Plants for American Gardens, published ten years before *Siftings*, must certainly have been influenced by Jensen's work as well as by the then-prevailing philosophy of integrated landscapes. The book was coauthored by plant ecologist Edith Roberts and landscape architect Elsa Rehmann, both of whom were professors at Vassar College in Poughkeepsie, New York. Roberts and Rehmann advocated using the natural composition of indigenous communities as inspiration for the design of ecologically sound and aesthetically pleasing gardens. "The beauty and variety of plants native to America have ever been recognized and have made a deep impression upon the plant lover," they write in their introduction. "Plant ecology, a comparatively new study of plants in relation to their environment, contributes toward a keener understanding of this natural vegetation and its use in garden making. It draws attention to the native plants as they appear in the landscape and suggests their inherent appropriateness to grounds and gardens. It is almost unbelievable that the native plants should ever have been overlooked."

Prevailing theories in the early days of the science of ecology recognized a natural progression of vegetative assemblages. Native communities were thought to pass through a predictable series, or sere, of ecological stages that eventually reclaimed open fields and turned them into luxuriant climax forests. Each stage in the progression could be characterized by a combination of its community structure and the collection—or association—of plants it supported. Roberts learned the fundamentals of ecological succession and plant community dynamics from botanist and pioneer ecologist Henry Cowles, her major professor at the University of Chicago. Encouraging gardeners to model their gardens after ecological processes and natural vegetative groupings formed the precepts of *American Plants for American Gardens* and made it the first practical handbook of ecologically based garden design.

These two books are the culmination of an interest in using native plants in landscape design that probably began in earnest in 1890 with the work of Frederick Law Olmsted Sr. at the Biltmore Estate near Asheville, North Carolina. Olmsted, born in Connecticut in 1822 and arguably the best known of America's landscape architects, was by then famous for his designs of public parks. He and collaborator Calvert Vaux had won the opportunity in 1858 to design New York City's Central Park, the first of many parks to which he would lend his expertise and vision. Olmsted and Vaux's design of Central

Park was in honor of Andrew Jackson Downing, Olmsted's friend and mentor. According to Linda McClelland, whose voluminous 1993 report for the National Park Service traces the history of landscape design, as early as the 1840s "Downing urged American gardeners to heed the beauty and potential of American plants for landscape gardening." Olmsted's mass plantings of native plants at the Biltmore Estate reflected Downing's early appreciation of indigenous species. Olmsted essentially returned the cut-over forests surrounding the newly constructed mansion to a natural landscape, augmenting its interior with plantings and curving paths. The naturalness of the Biltmore forests today show little hint of the massive reforestation and restoration efforts required to create them.

Olmsted's mass plantings were championed by Frank Waugh, a midwesterner strongly influenced by the ideas of both Jensen and the Prairie School. In 1917 Waugh wrote *The Natural Style in Landscape Gardening*, in which he not only proposed the use of indigenous species in a distinctly American style of natural gardening, but also recommended grouping plants into ecologically authentic units reflective of nature. Waugh wrote of native plants: "Practically every one is associated habitually with certain other species. Thus they form set clubs or societies. And these friendly associations, based upon similarity of tastes and complementary habits of growth, should not be broken up. If we as landscape gardeners desire to preserve the whole aspect of nature, with all its forms intact, we will keep all plants in their proper social groupings." As an introduction to these ideas, Waugh wrote that "the ideas, motives, and methods must come mainly from nature," and he encouraged gardeners to develop "a critical understanding of nature's landscape and a love of the native landscape at once ardent, sane, discriminating, and balanced."

Waugh recognized the importance of patterns in the grouping of native plants in garden settings. For grouping trees and shrubs, the most important of these patterns included groupings of three in irregular arrangements, groupings of five or more, and mass plantings. Waugh cautioned that the execution of these groupings should not be made haphazardly. As noted by McClelland, "Waugh cited several simple rules for grouping five or more trees: The law of simplicity cautioned against using too many species; the law of dominance called for one species to dominate the group; the law of harmony said that species must harmonize in color, form, and habit of growth; the law of ecology required that plants 'be socially compatible'; and the law of adaptation meant that all plants were to be adapted to the local conditions such as soil, drainage, and light."

Waugh's ideas were influenced by another midwesterner, Wilhelm Miller, whose 1915 publication, *The Prairie Spirit in Landscape Gardening*, offered a succinct and impassioned plea for preserving native landscapes. Miller was a horticultural writer and editor who had earlier published *What England Can Teach Us about Gardening*, a book that had grown out of a trip to England during which he visited the home of William Robinson. In 1870, Robinson had published *The Wild Garden*, in which he advocated "naturalizing or making wild innumerable beautiful natives of many regions of the earth in our woods, wild and semi-wild places, rougher parts of pleasure grounds, etc., and in unoccupied places in almost every kind of garden." Robinson's fascination with American plants reinforced Miller's belief in the garden uses of native species. However, in sharp contrast to Robinson, Miller coined the phrase "American style of gardening" and recommended that "every country use chiefly its own native trees, shrubs, vines and other permanent material, and let the style of gardening grow naturally out of necessity, the soil and the new conditions."

Ecological garden design and the fascination with native plants declined sharply in the middle 1900s, interrupted largely by the advent of two World Wars, the Great Depression, and a turn toward a modernistic approach to architecture and landscape design that valued homogenization over variation, composition over content, and industrialism over natural features. During this period, the idea of native plant gardening was carried forward by only a handful of enthusiasts, represented best by Caroline Dormon and Mary Gibson Henry.

Dormon was a native Louisianan who grew up near Saline, Louisiana, and became enamored with plants, nature, and the out-of-doors very early in life. Born in 1888 at Briarwood, her family's summer home, Dormon was the sixth child of James and Trotti Dormon. Her father was an attorney by profession, but as Caroline would later reflect, he was a naturalist by heart. James Dormon spent considerable time with his daughter, teaching her about nature's endowments on numerous outdoor excursions and fishing trips. Dormon's parents placed high value on education and enthusiastically encouraged their children's interests and natural inclinations. For Caroline, the inclination was what she was fond of calling "the gift of the wild things."

Dormon was heavily influenced by the work of Jens Jensen and credits him profusely in the second of her two wildflower books, *Natives Preferred*, published in 1965. Dormon was well-known and well connected in botanical circles. The acknowledgments in her first wildflower book, *Flowers Native to the Deep South* (1958), recounts among her friendships and field companions John K. Small, W. W. Ashe, Francis Pennell, Clair Brown, Edgar Wherry, Lloyd Shinners, and K. K. MacKenzie. Her books feature not only her extensive knowledge of recognizing and growing native species, but also an impressive collection of her original watercolor and line art.

Dormon traveled widely and consulted regularly about the use of native plants in landscaping, particularly for roadside and architectural beautification. "Perfect landscaping," she wrote in the circular *Roadside Beauty in Louisiana*, "is doing the work in such an artfully-natural way that it appears as if no planting has been done. The finished project closely approximates Nature at her best. Nowhere is this more true as in the landscaping of roadsides."

Indeed, roadside improvement was one of Dormon's lifetime pursuits. She lobbied the Louisiana highway department heavily, encouraging it to preserve and plant native trees and shrubs along the state's roadways. Her lobbying was so successful that in 1940 she was hired by the department to direct a program targeted at conserving roadside vegetation, using natural plantings to reduce roadside erosion, and enlisting the support of community organizations in the effort.

She was extremely interested in trees and forestry and for a period headed forestry education for the Louisiana Forestry Division. She visited schools, developed public education material about Louisiana trees, and oversaw the distribution of forty thousand trees to schools and clubs for planting on Arbor Day.

At least part of her motivation for educating the public about healthy forests stemmed

Caroline Dormon received much of her inspiration from Briarwood, the Louisiana summer retreat where she was born, spent many of her most enjoyable childhood days, and lived for much of her adult life. Briarwood served as the springboard for Dormon's love of nature, native plants, and native plant gardening, and in later years provided the testing grounds for her horticultural experimentation. The solace she cherished there still pervades its woodlands, and the whisper of her spirit is still sensed along its trails.

A few months before her death, Dormon willed Briarwood to the Foundation for Preservation of the Caroline Dormon Nature Preserve, which established and now operates the preserve to continue the commitment to conservation education that defined much of Dormon's life. Located on the northern edge of the 600,000-acre Kisatchie National Forest that Dormon helped to establish, the preserve is open to the public and has become a destination for horticulturists, botanists, and conservationists from all over the world.

from an intense desire for the establishment of a designated national forest in Louisiana. She worked diligently toward this dream, and in June 1930 she was rewarded with the purchase of more than seventy-six thousand acres for the state's first nationally designated forest. Given the opportunity to name the new acquisition, she christened it Kisatchie, after its first inhabitants. Today the Caroline Dormon Nature Preserve at Briarwood sits on the northern edge of the national forest that she was privileged to name.

Mary Gibson Henry was born in 1884 in Jenkinstown, Pennsylvania. Like Dormon she developed her interest in nature early in life and largely from her father, although interest in horticulture and gardening had long histories on both sides of her family. In her 1950 autobiography for *Plant Life*, she recalled becoming enamored with native plants as early as age seven when she saw her first northern twinflower, *Linnaea borealis* subsp. *americana*, a delicate and creeping herb with numerous short, upright stems topped with a pair of fragrant pink flowers. "It awoke in me not only a love for and an appreciation of the absolute perfection of the flower itself," she wrote, "but also for the dark silent forest that shelters such treasures."

She was fortunate to marry a kindred spirit in Dr. Norman Henry, a well-known physician and community figure who later served as Philadelphia's director of public health. "My husband loved the outdoors even as I did," she wrote in her autobiography, "and a tent and canoe were important factors of our wedding trip." The couple quickly had five children and the demands of motherhood kept Henry busy and close to home for the first two decades of her marriage.

In 1926 the Henrys bought Gladwyne, a ninety-acre farm a few miles from the center of the city. They built a home and greenhouse, and the surrounding grounds became the foundation for Henry's first extended garden. Although she studied plants intently in her limited available time, it was not until after her children had left home that she began in earnest her career in botany and horticulture. With the support and urging of her husband, she embarked on numerous trips to locations across North America, collecting live plants to grow at Gladwyne and scientific specimens to deposit in the collections at the Philadelphia Academy of Sciences.

Although her travels and collecting trips carried her throughout much of the United States, she seemed to have a special affinity for the southeast and made numerous trips into the Southeastern Coastal Plains and Piedmont. She reports that her first real collecting trip was to the coastal plains in search of *Rhododendron speciosum* (now *R. flammeum*). "My journey of approximately 2,500 miles in a car, and many on foot, was eminently successful," she reported, adding that "for some years I traveled down and up the Atlantic Coastal Plain at various seasons, always of course in the less frequented areas, usually as far as Florida." She was the first to discover what we now call the panhandle lily (*Lilium iridollae*), and in 1947 she described it as a new species in the pages of *Bartonia*, remarking in the descriptive material that it was "the 'pot of gold' at the end of my rainbow," in reference to the meaning of its Latin epithet.

This lily and many of the other plants she grew at Gladwyne were coastal plains species that proved to be hardy beyond their typical ranges, and a number were successfully introduced into the trade for use in public and private gardens. "Many of [my] new

---

Mary Gibson Henry

My first knowledge of Mary Gibson Henry came by way of a conversation with my good friend and field companion, Angus K. Gholson Jr., a respected field botanist and plantsman from Chattahoochee, Florida. We were on an outing to Jackson County, Florida, to look for early spring ephemeral wildflowers when Gholson told me about Henry's discovery of a small population of *Silene regia*, the royal catchfly. I knew of this species as a more northern inhabitant, only sparsely distributed in a few counties of Georgia and Alabama and nowhere common in its natural range. Like a number of plants in the central parts of the Florida panhandle, it was considered a northern disjunct, well separated from the center of its distribution. It seemed amazing that Mary Henry, a Pennsylvania botanist with many fewer opportunities to botanize in the Florida panhandle than more local plantsmen, could have made such a rare find, and even more amazing that no one had been able to reconfirm her discovery.

A succeeding visit to the herbarium at Florida State University turned up a single, photocopied duplicate of Henry's original collection. On the label of the specimen, which constituted her 2,312th collection, she noted: "18 in.–3 ft. tall. Plentiful. Growing in half-shade on stony grassy bank in sun, (small outcrop of porous limestone rocks). 6 miles northwest of Marianna."

Gholson also told me that Henry had been an expert botanist who traveled in a chauffeured Lincoln Continental that had been specially adapted for botanizing by the addition of a lighted desk, bookcase, and storage area. She had botanized extensively in the Florida panhandle, had described and named what we now call the panhandle lily, had a species of *Hymenocallis* (spider lily) named for her, and was responsible for numerous rare finds and discoveries. It was enough to pique a plant lover's interest.

---

plants have 'stepped out' in the world," she wrote in her autobiography, "for I have placed over 100 in the hands of propagators and commercial growers." Plants such as *Itea virginica* 'Henry's Garnet,' listed by the Missouri Botanical Garden as a Plant of Merit, underscore the importance of her name to modern native plant enthusiasts; indeed, her garden at Gladwyne is still considered to be among the best displays of cultivated southeastern natives.

Dorman's and Henry's dual passions for gardening and the American flora capture the spirit of many modern-day native plant enthusiasts. For those enamored with exploring natural vegetative assemblages, gardening that reflects and commemorates the indigenous landscape is strongly alluring. Nothing is more rewarding than recreating at home what one finds so appealing in the field.

Things have a way of coming full circle. Henry died in 1967 and Dormon in 1971, on the threshold of the first Earth Day and a resurgence in the use of native plants. Since their deaths, many new voices have been added to the native gardening chorus, some in the vein of "how to," others in the tradition of philosophical underpinnings. Voices in the "how to" category, especially for the southeast, include such authors as Richard Bir (*Growing and Propagating Showy Native Woody Plants*), Bill Cullina (*Native Trees, Shrubs, and Vines*), Bill Fontenot (*Native Gardening in the South*), Samuel Jones and Leonard Foote (*Gardening with Native Wildflowers*), Peter Loewer (*Native Perennials for the Southeast*), Gil Nelson (*Florida's Best Native Landscape Plants*), Rufino Osorio (*A Gardener's Guide to Florida's Native Plants*), Sally Wasowski (*Gardening with Native Plants of the South*), and, more recently, Allan Armitage (*Armitage's Native Plants for North American Gardens*).

For philosophical underpinnings there are probably no recent voices more eloquent than those of Sara Stein and Douglas Tallamy. Stein's first book, *My Weeds*, published in 1988, helped rejuvenate interest in native plants. It was followed in 1993 with *Noah's Garden: Restoring the Ecology of Our Own Backyards*, in which she encourages gardeners to view their suburban yards in terms of ecological processes rather than as artificial landscapes. *Noah's Garden*, in particular, inspires average homeowners with doable possibilities and is a must-read for environmentally sensitive garden enthusiasts. Tallamy's *Bringing Nature Home* (2009) reinforces many of the concepts presented by Stein but extends the message by adding significant scientific support for converting backyards into healthy, functioning ecosystems. No gardener should be without it.

3

Weeds, Aliens, and Invasive Plants

If there is environmental altruism to be had from gardening with native plants, it may well be in reducing the number of invasive species that are assaulting and destroying our most precious natural areas. Recent estimates suggest that at least fifty thousand non-native organisms of all kinds—plants, animals, insects, and microscopic pathogens—are present in the United States. Many of these were introduced intentionally and are utilized for all sorts of worthwhile purposes ranging from agricultural food crops to medicine, pest control, and ornamental horticulture. Others, however, have become extraordinary pests, invading natural areas, destroying or displacing native flora, endangering native wildlife, and resulting in huge economic losses to the American taxpayer. A recent review by David Pimentel and colleagues at Cornell University estimates that the environmental damage wrought by non-native species of all kinds now approaches $120 billion per year, more than $34.5 billion of which results from the loss, damage, and control of invasive plants, including crop weeds. And a 1998 estimate by Bruce Babbit, then Secretary of the Interior, reported that nonindigenous weeds were at that time invading approximately 1.7 million acres of United States wildlife habitat annually. These numbers are likely to grow even larger as the expanding global economy hastens the intentional and unintentional movement of organisms from one part of the earth to another.

Non-native, Naturalized, and Invasive Species

It is important to define terms at the outset of any discussion of invasive species, and to distinguish between what is meant by *non-native*, *naturalized*, and *invasive*, especially as related to plants. The three labels are often confused, but are not synonymous.

Non-native plants are those growing outside of their natural ranges. Typically, they arrived in a particular locale by nonnatural means and usually with human assistance, whether intentional or inadvertent. European and Asian plants that were imported into the United States for food production or ornamental gardening are the archetypal examples. However, western North American species that grow naturally only in California but are cultivated along the eastern seaboard also qualify, as do plants grown ornamentally in North Carolina but with natural ranges restricted to Alabama. Under the strictest definitions, plants may even be considered to be native to one part of a state—or even a single county or parish—but not to another. Subtropical plants native to southern Florida but introduced to north Florida gardens are examples.

Non-native species have been part of gardening for centuries. From the earliest historical record, explorers have moved food, medicinal, and horticultural plants from one place to another. Some, like the biblical fig and olive, have been so widely distributed that their precise nativity is uncertain. Although the vast majority of these non-native plants stay where they are planted and do not spread beyond their agricultural or ornamental setting, others are not so well behaved and are often called weedy or invasive.

Invasive plants constitute a select group of non-native species that colonize undisturbed habitat and spread into natural areas where they are not wanted. The word *invasive* is applied to these plants because they tend to invade and disrupt functioning ecosystems, displacing native flora and interfering with normal ecological processes. Invasive plants share several important features. They usually lack natural enemies in their newfound homes, often display vigorous vegetative reproduction, and typically produce seeds that germinate readily, often year-round, without the need for cold or scarification.

Invasive species can be native or non-native to the United States, although most are non-native. Many of the invasive species that have become established in the southeastern United States are native to Asia. This is likely due to latitudinal similarities of climate and habitat that probably begin with the ancient geomorphic connections that existed prior to the breakup of the earth's continents. The similarities between plant species of Asia and the southeastern United States is a long-studied and well-documented phenomenon.

Invasive species make up a relatively small fraction of imported non-native plants. There are more than 18,000 species of native plants in the United States; easily twice this many have been imported for agricultural and ornamental use. Estimates suggest that about 5,000 of these non-natives have become naturalized—meaning that they are now established and reproducing on their own—and up to 20 percent of the naturalized species have become invasive, or have at least expressed dangerously weedy tendencies. Although it is possible for virtually any non-native species to develop invasive tendencies, most non-native ornamentals remain well behaved and don't stray beyond the garden. Those that do can become serious pests with costly outcomes.

The Role of Horticulture

It is certainly true that horticulture bears a disproportionate responsibility for the dissemination and spread of invasive plant species, and for the insects that often arrive with them. Even with the increased use of American plants for all sorts of purposes —including such divergent applications as commercial landscaping, roadside and public area beautification, botanical garden displays, and residential gardening—two facts remain. Well over half of the plants used for horticulture in the United States today are of alien origin, and a large proportion of our most troublesome invasive species—more than 80 percent for some woody plant groups—were introduced to the United States primarily for horticultural purposes, many of which continue to be used in gardening.

This contrasts sharply with the popular assumption that most invasive plants arrived

Horticultural Pathways for Invasive Species

Gardening interests have long played a major role in the establishment and spread of invasive species. For several centuries our fascination with the rare and exotic has fueled a worldwide horticultural trade that has grown into a multinational industry that now exceeds $40 billion per year.

In the earliest days, American plantsmen were primarily exporters, sending seeds, fruits, and living plants to an expanding cadre of Old World collectors. Wealthy English and European gardeners lusted after newly discovered American species, sometimes coming in person to sample the New World flora but more often funding extensive collecting expeditions or retaining the services of American botanists like John and William Bartram to collect, pack, and ship new plants to their continental benefactors.

By the 1900s the United States had become a major importer of exotic species. Collectors from botanical gardens across the country were traveling the world, especially China and other Asian destinations, to find and bring home new introductions. The explorations and discoveries of such notable explorers as the U.S. Department of Agriculture's David Fairchild and the Arnold Arboretum's E. H. Wilson are legendary. Wilson alone is credited with the introduction of more than one thousand plants, and many of the now problematic species in south Florida may be escapes from Fairchild's collections.

---

here inadvertently as accidental stowaways in packing material, ship's ballasts, poorly processed agricultural seed lots, or, as in the cases of the infamous kudzu vine and Brazilian pepper, due to severely misguided and now nearly impossible-to-rectify governmental decisions. In contrast to most nonindigenous insects and microbes that arrived to the United States accidentally, the majority of non-native plants were imported on purpose.

The United States continues to be a major horticultural market. More than two billion plants are imported into the country every year, nearly five times as many as in the early 1990s. This figure is likely to increase exponentially in the coming years as China—home to as many as twenty thousand species of ornamental plants—implements plans to expand its exports. Given the well-known environmental and ecological similarities that exist between eastern Asia and the southeastern United States, it is likely that many of these new imports will be directed to southern gardens and landscapes. At least some will become naturalized; a few will become the next generation of aggressive weeds. As one south Florida biologist remarked, our worst invasive species has probably not yet arrived.

However, to assume that all non-natives behave alike is to deny an important fact. As representatives of the nursery industry often assert, only a small portion of foreign plants introduced into the southeast actually escape cultivation or create environmental problems. A few basic statistics about the region's native and naturalized flora help make their point.

There are nearly 9,000 species of spontaneously occurring plants in the eight states included in this book. These are plants that reproduce on their own, in the wild, without

Native and Naturalized Plants of the Southeastern United States

State	Native Species	Percent of Total	Naturalized Species	Percent of Total	Total
Alabama	3,884	84.14	732	15.86	4,616
Florida	4,010	77.37	1173	22.63	5,183
Georgia	4,066	84.39	752	15.61	4,818
Louisiana	3,261	80.08	811	19.92	4,072
Mississippi	3,220	84.23	603	15.77	3,823
North Carolina	3,892	81.30	895	18.70	4,787
South Carolina	3,603	82.73	752	17.27	4,355
Virginia	3,636	80.02	908	19.98	4,544

Source: USDA Plants National Database, http://plants.nrcs.usda.gov/.

human assistance. Nonnaturalized garden plants, those that do not reproduce or that have not escaped cultivation, are not included in this number. Of these 9,000, a little more than 2,000, or about 22 percent, are non-native, meaning that they arrived here by nonnatural means within the last five hundred years, sometimes only very recently. In some states the proportion of non-native species is lower than this average. In Mississippi, for example, the proportion is closer to 15 percent, and in Virginia 20 percent. In Florida, whose subtropical climate and extended growing season serve as magnets for introduced species, the proportion is nearly 23 percent as measured by the USDA Plants National Database. Other authorities suggest that the non-native component of Florida's flora may be closer to 32 percent.

Across the southeast, about 430 of the total number of naturalized non-natives—about 20 percent—are currently known to be invasive, meaning that they have spread into undisturbed natural areas and are displacing or successfully competing with native vegetation. Perhaps another 200 species are included on unofficial "watch lists" of species with presumed invasive tendencies, increasing the total proportion of problem naturalized species to about 30 percent. However, what might at first seem like a relatively large proportion is actually somewhat misleading. In Florida, for example, at least 25,000 nonindigenous species, varieties, and subspecies have been imported mainly for ornamental use (some experts estimate the number exceeds 50,000). Only about 1,100, a little more than 4 percent, have become naturalized. When the number of Florida's nearly 300 known and suspected invasive species is calculated against this larger total, the ratio of invasives to non-natives shrinks to less than 2 percent.

None of this should be taken to dismiss or minimize the debilitating impact even a single invasive species can have on natural systems and government pocketbooks. Nor should it absolve us of our responsibility for due diligence gardening. If this book has any message beyond a fascination with native plants, it is that all of us should avoid the use of invasive species in our gardens and be assiduous to the weedy potential of any non-native species that we plant. Continued importation, dissemination, and careless use of invasive species are major environmental problems. The costs are enormous.

The Costs of Invasive Species

The most visible cost of alien plant invasions is the lost scenic beauty of healthy ecosystems. Parks, preserves, and woodlands overrun with non-native invaders become weedy, unattractive blights on natural landscapes. Ornamental species like Chinese privet (*Ligustrum sinense*), coral ardisia (*Ardisia crenata*), silverthorn (*Elaeagnus pungens*), English ivy (*Hedera helix*), and Japanese honeysuckle (*Lonicera japonica*) tend to form dense monocultures, smothering native plants and leaving little room for wildlife. Heavy infestations result in reduced biodiversity, habitat loss, and the destruction, displacement, and fragmentation of our native biota.

The distress is particularly severe on imperiled species—plants and animals that are already struggling to survive. In a 1998 study, David Wilcove and fellow researchers determined that the contribution of invasive organisms to the obliteration of endangered species is second in severity only to habitat loss, and that given the current rate of new invasions, the situation may become even worse than we can now imagine. Fifty-seven percent of the 1,055 endangered plants that Wilcove's team surveyed, and 69 percent of 98 endangered birds, were imperiled by the advent of alien species of all kinds.

Worse, some studies have shown that the advance of nonindigenous plants may actually precipitate the decline of relatively stable native species, potentially contributing to their becoming endangered. When faced with the competition for resources and intensity of disturbance brought on by invading plants, native species of all types typically lose.

Coral ardisia.

This has led to a huge annual outlay of tax dollars directed mainly at control and elimination. Some experts estimate that hundreds of millions of dollars per year are spent nationwide on invasive plant management, virtually all of which is funded by taxpayers. Accurate calculations are difficult to derive given the number and types of agencies and organizations involved in the effort. A 1991 study of nonindigenous species by the Congressional Office of Technology Assessment estimated that the cumulative costs for controlling only fifteen invasive species from 1906 to 1991 totaled at least $603 million, but cautions that this figure may be significantly understated. In August 2000 the Governmental Accounting Office reported more than $70 million in annual expenditures for the ten federal agencies it surveyed—almost certainly an underestimation—but estimated that at least some individual states spend in excess of $50 million a year on invasive plant management activities. Biologists often report spending most of their time battling invasives instead of tending to the chores of habitat enhancement, ecosystem management, and public recreation services.

Examples of costly control projects abound. Purple loosestrife (*Lythrum salicaria*), a European species that is now invasive in forty-eight states (including at least four of those represented in this book), alone consumes an estimated $45 million annually, and Florida spends in excess of $15 million per year just to control the aquatic weed hydrilla (*Hydrilla verticillata*). When combined with the associated costs of lost recreational opportunities, neglected biological management activities, and increased expenditures for endangered species protection, the budgetary picture seems inordinately grave.

The Challenge for Gardeners

The difficulty for gardeners is determining which plants are already known to be invasive, which might become invasive, and what to replace them with. The expedient, broad-brush approach is to select natives only and to remove all existing non-natives from your garden, an approach that is neither desirable nor feasible for most of us. And even if this approach were feasible, it does not eliminate the introduction of potentially weedy native species from nearby regions or ecosystems. Florida betony (*Stachys floridana*), native and once thought to be endemic to Florida, is weedy and considered introduced in the Carolinas. It is nowhere listed as invasive, but given the opportunity it may well overrun lowland woods.

Predicting which plants are likely to remain well behaved and which might be destined for invasiveness is neither easy nor simple, and it is probably beyond the skills of the average gardener. Invasive plant specialists across the southeastern United States struggle continuously with the issue. Some species remain well behaved for many years, only to become invasive when environmental conditions change or some new, alien pollinator is introduced that helps it germinate and expand. Others are weedy from their first arrival, often due to a lack of natural predators. Still others appear weedy in the garden but may actually pose no threat in the wild. The powder puff (*Mimosa strigillosa*) that provides color and groundcover along the borders of my perennial bed certainly does not stay where it is put and is spreading in all directions. It is native to eastern Georgia and portions of the Florida peninsula in the eastern part of our region, and to Louisiana in the western part, but it is used in landscaping in both Alabama and

Invasive and Exotic Pest Plant Councils of the Southeast

The environmental and economic costs associated with troublesome alien plants has given rise to a number of state and regional organizations whose joint mission is to monitor, manage, control, and educate about the introduction and spread of invasive plant species. The several state and regional councils are membership organizations composed of biologists, invasive plant specialists, gardeners, homeowners, scientists, and others interested in invasive plant issues. Most important for gardeners and landscapers, these organizations produce lists of invasive species that are invaluable for determining which plants should be avoided in home and commercial landscapes. In addition, membership in any of the organizations affiliated with the Southeastern Exotic Pest Plant Council includes a subscription to the magazine *Wildland Weeds*, which provides excellent updates on invasive species problems and resources throughout the southeast.

Several of the state councils are linked by regional umbrella organizations. The Southeastern Exotic Pest Plant Council and the Mid-Atlantic Pest Plant Council include most of the states represented in this book. In addition, the Internet resource www.invasive.org—a joint project of the Bugwood Network, USDA Forest Service, USDA Animal and Plant Health Inspection Service (APHIS), and the University of Georgia—provides nationwide tracking and information about invasive species of all kinds.

Exotic and Invasive Plant Councils and Resources

Regional Organizations and Resources

Invasive.org	http://www.invasive.org/
Invasive Species Specialist Group	http://issg.org/
Mid-Atlantic Exotic Pest Plant Council	http://www.ma-eppc.org/
Southeastern Exotic Pest Plant Council	http://www.se-eppc.org/

State Organizations

Alabama Invasive Plant Council	http://www.se-eppc.org/alabama/
Florida Exotic Pest Plant Council	http://www.fleppc.org/
Georgia Exotic Pest Plant Council	http://www.gaeppc.org/
Mississippi Exotic Pest Plant Council	http://www.se-eppc.org/mississippi/
North Carolina Exotic Pest Plant Council	http://www.se-eppc.org/northcarolina/
South Carolina Exotic Pest Plant Council	http://www.se-eppc.org/southcarolina/

Mississippi. Although it sometimes requires control in the garden, it has not shown a tendency to invade or disrupt natural areas.

A better approach is to learn which plants are already known to be invading natural areas and to avoid using them. Finding out about known invasive plants is far less challenging than predicting invasiveness, and there are numerous invasive plant resources available.

Suggested Replacements for Invasive Species

Common Names	Scientific Names	Suggested Replacements
Tree of Heaven	*Ailanthus altissima*	Florida Leucothoe (*Agarista populifolia*) Yaupon (*Ilex vomitoria*) Wax Myrtle (*Myrica cerifera*) Smooth Sumac (*Rhus glabra*)
Mimosa, Silktree	*Albizia julibrissin*	Redbud (*Cercis canadensis*)
Coral Ardisia	*Ardisia crenata*	American Holly (*Ilex americana*) Winterberry (*Ilex verticillata*) Chokeberry (*Photinia pyrifolia*) Elliott's Blueberry (*Vaccinium elliottii*)
Giant Reed	*Arundo donax*	Sugarcane Plumegrass (*Saccharum giganteum*)
Oriental Bittersweet	*Celastrus orbiculatus*	Crossvine (*Bignonia capreolata*) Carolina Jessamine (*Gelsemium sempervirens*) Coral Honeysuckle (*Lonicera sempervirens*) Virgin's Bower (*Clematis virginiana*) Woolly Dutchman's Pipe (*Aristolochia tomentosa*)
Russian Olive Silverthorn Autumn Olive	*Elaeagnus angustifolia* *Elaeagnus pungens* *Elaeagnus umbellata*	Winterberry (*Ilex verticillata*) Yaupon (*Ilex vomitoria*) Possumhaw Viburnum (*Viburnum nudum*) Blackhaw Viburnum (*Viburnum prunifolium*) Walter's Viburnum (*Viburnum obovatum*) Alabama Snow Wreath (*Neviusia alabamensis*)
Winged Burning Bush	*Euonymus alata*	Chokeberry (*Aronia arbutifolia*) Sweet Pepperbush (*Clethra alnifolia*) Spicebush (*Lindera benzoin*) Virginia Sweetspire (*Itea virginica*) Elliott's Blueberry (*Vaccinium elliottii*)
English Ivy	*Hedera helix*	Climbing Hydrangea (*Decumaria barbara*) Allegheny Spurge (*Pachysandra procumbens*) Yellowroot (*Xanthorhiza simplicissima*) Mapleleaf Viburnum (*Viburnum acerifolium*)
Lantana	*Lantana camara*	Shrubby St. John's–wort (*Hypericum prolificum*) Sterile *Lantana* Cultivars
Japanese Ligustrum Glossy Privet Privet, Chinese Ligustrum Common Privet	*Ligustrum japonicum* *Ligustrum lucidum* *Ligustrum sinense* *Ligustrum vulgare*	Wax Myrtle (*Myrica cerifera*) Meadowsweet (*Spiraea latifolia*)
Japanese Honeysuckle	*Lonicera japonica*	Crossvine (*Bignonia capreolata*) Carolina Jessamine (*Gelsemium sempervirens*) Coral Honeysuckle (*Lonicera sempervirens*) Virgin's Bower (*Clematis virginiana*) Woolly Dutchman's Pipe (*Aristolochia tomentosa*)

Common Names	Scientific Names	Suggested Replacements
Bell's Honeysuckle	*Lonicera ×bella*	Shrubby St. John's–wort (*Hypericum prolificum*)
Sweet-Breath-of-Spring	*Lonicera fragrantissima*	Ninebark (*Physocarpus opulifolius* 'nanus')
Amur Honeysuckle	*Lonicera maackii*	Arrowwood (*Viburnum dentatum*)
Morrow's Honeysuckle	*Lonicera morrowii*	Virginia Sweetspire (*Itea virginica*)
Standish's Honeysuckle	*Lonicera standishii*	Alabama Snow Wreath (*Neviusia alabamensis*)
Tatarian Honeysuckle	*Lonicera tatarica*	
Japanese Climbing Fern	*Lygodium japonicum*	Crossvine (*Bignonia capreolata*)
Old World Climbing Fern	*Lygodium microphyllum*	Carolina Jessamine (*Gelsemium sempervirens*)
		Coral Honeysuckle (*Lonicera sempervirens*)
		Virgin's Bower (*Clematis virginiana*)
		Woolly Dutchman's Pipe (*Aristolochia tomentosa*)
Purple Loosestrife	*Lythrum salicaria*	Blazing Stars (*Liatris* spp.)
		Butterflyweed (*Asclepias tuberosa*)
		Queen-of-the-Prairie (*Filipendula rubra*)
		Swamp Milkweed (*Asclepias incarnata*)
Cat's Claw Vine	*Macfadyena unguis-cati*	Crossvine (*Bignonia capreolata*)
		Carolina Jessamine (*Gelsemium sempervirens*)
		Coral Honeysuckle (*Lonicera sempervirens*)
		Virgin's Bower (*Clematis virginiana*)
Chinese Silvergrass	*Miscanthus sinensis*	Purple Muhly Grass (*Muhlenbergia capillaris*)
		Eastern Gamagrass (*Tripsacum dactyloides*)
		Split-Beard Bluestem (*Andropogon ternarius*)
		Switchgrass (*Panicum virgatum*)
		Sugarcane Plumegrass (*Saccharum giganteum*)
		Little Bluestem (*Schizachyrium scoparium*)
Nandina, Sacred Bamboo	*Nandina domestica*	Devil's Walking Stick (*Aralia spinosa*)
		Weeping Yaupon (*Ilex vomitoria* 'Pendula')
Princesstree, Paulownia	*Paulownia tomentosa*	Northern Catalpa (*Catalpa speciosa*)
		Southern Catalpa (*Catalpa bignonioides*)
Golden Bamboo	*Phyllostachys aurea*	Sugarcane Plumegrass (*Saccharum giganteum*)
Bradford Pear	*Pyrus calleryana*	Eastern Redbud (*Cercis canadensis*)
McCartney Rose	*Rosa bracteata*	Crossvine (*Bignonia capreolata*)
Cherokee Rose	*Rosa laevigata*	Carolina Jessamine (*Gelsemium sempervirens*)
Multiflora Rose	*Rosa multiflora*	Coral Honeysuckle (*Lonicera sempervirens*)
		Alabama Snow Wreath (*Neviusia alabamensis*)
		Ninebark (*Physocarpus opulifolius* 'nanus')
Popcorn Tree, Tallow tree	*Triadica sebifera* (=*Sapium sebiferum*)	Pond Cypress (*Taxodium ascendens*) Eastern Redbud (*Cercis canadensis*)
Japanese Wisteria	*Wisteria floribunda*	American Wisteria (*Wisteria frutescens*)
Chinese Wisteria	*Wisteria sinensis*	

The several invasive plant councils and native plant societies across the southeastern United States regularly monitor the invasive potential of selected species as well as conduct conferences and research to advance knowledge, produce lists of plants known to be invading natural areas, and conduct targeted eradication programs. The lists of invasive species are updated frequently as new information becomes available and are excellent resources for gardeners.

Statewide and regional exotic pest plant councils include lists on their Web sites, as do a number of native plant societies. The Web site of the Southeastern Exotic Pest Plant Council (http://www.se-eppc.org/) provides links to information about all of the southeastern invasive plant councils, including regional and statewide invasive plant lists, and the jointly sponsored Web site http://www.invasive.org/ includes a list of all known invasive species for thirteen southeastern states. The Web site of the Invasive Species Specialist Group of the World Conservation Union (http://www.issg.org/) includes a worldwide searchable database of known invasive species. The Web site of the South Carolina Native Plant Society includes an excellent list of recommended replacements for invasive species (http://www.scnps.org/) as well as a number of other resources related to invasive plants.

Botanical gardens and arboreta have also become active. The North Carolina Botanical Garden (NCBG), in particular, has been a leader in challenging other gardens to be mindful of invasive species. The NCBG Web site includes an excellent handbook for controlling invasive species (http://ncbg.unc.edu/), numerous articles about invasive plants and conservation, and a list of plants to avoid in the southeastern United States. The Brooklyn Botanic Garden's handbook *Native Alternatives to Invasive Plants*, written by Colston Burrell, details many recommendations appropriate for the southeast.

Native Replacements for Invasive Species

One challenge associated with removing or avoiding invasive species in the garden is finding native alternatives to replace them. The accompanying table lists thirty-seven of the southeast's worst invasive species, all of which were introduced to the United States primarily for ornamental horticulture. Each species is paired with one or more suggested native replacements selected to match as many of an offending plants' primary gardening characteristics as possible. With nearly five hundred recognized invasive species in the southeast, this "short list" was not easy to devise and is certainly not exhaustive. Admittedly, it leaves off a number of problematic horticultural introductions as well as some horribly invasive plants that found their ways into natural areas mostly by means other than gardening. It should be noted that the invasive species on this list are still likely to be seen for sale at retail garden centers and continue to be widely used in residential and commercial landscaping. They should be avoided or replaced whenever possible.

The Worst of the Worst: A Few Examples

Many horticulturally introduced invasive species are traditional landscape plants with long histories in southern gardens. Examples include the several species of wisteria and

Heavenly bamboo.

elaeagnus; nandina or heavenly bamboo; and the once popular mimosa and popcorn trees. Following are descriptions of these and other of the most infamous examples, including a little of their horticultural history and odious tendencies; gardeners new to the concept of invasive species might see many old friends in this discussion.

Nandina. My childhood home was lined along one end with a dense stand of nandina or heavenly bamboo (*Nandina domestica*), presumably as additional screening for the windows, but also as a backdrop for the successive tiers of lower shrubs, perennials, grasses, and liriope that fronted it. It fruited prolifically, putting on hundreds of bright red berries that were relished and spread by birds and other wildlife. I well remember hand pulling the numerous seedlings that had strayed from the planting as part of my weekly summer yard maintenance chores. Many similar plantings are the suspected origins of plants that today have become established in shady woodlands.

Wisteria. The showy, draping racemes of the non-native wisterias still grace many southern lawns, often trimmed as a stand-alone shrub but sometimes climbing and scrambling over adjacent hedges, trees, and shrubbery. Most old-timers refer to their plants as Chinese wisteria, but it may well be that Japanese wisteria is the more common species. The two are difficult to separate. Both were introduced into this county for horticulture in the 1800s and both are problematic in natural areas.

American wisteria (*W. frutescens*) is increasingly used as a good replacement species for the non-native wisterias. This is especially true for the cultivar 'Amethyst Falls,' which flowers first in spring, again in early summer, and one more time in the fall. The flowers of American wisteria are a little more deeply colored, borne in smaller racemes, and appear later in the spring than those of the non-natives, and the plant is far less aggressive. It occurs naturally in wet areas but adjusts to garden conditions. Once established, it is easy to care for.

Elaeagnus. Two species of *Elaeagnus* have been used extensively in southern landscaping. Both have been preferred hedge plants in large landscapes but have also been used in shelterbelt and roadside plantings due to their rapid growth, dense forms, at least partially silvery leaves, and attraction to wildlife. Silverthorn (*E. pungens*), the only evergreen *Elaeagnus* included here, is sometimes used as a foundation plant, but it produces long, arching branches that are a nuisance to tidy gardeners and require regular pruning to keep in check. The second species, autumn olive (*E. umbellata*), was first planted to improve wildlife habitats and reclaim abandoned strip mines. It has also naturalized in the southeast and become a troublesome weed but is less commonly used in landscaping than silverthorn. A third species, Russian olive (*E. angustifolia*), has invaded the southeast only in Tennessee and Virginia but is widely distributed in forty of the lower forty-eight states. It appeared in the southeast in the early 1900s and is likely to spread farther southward with time. Numerous native shrubs, both evergreen and deciduous, can be used to replace these species. Honeycups, or dusty zenobia (*Zenobia pulverulenta*), is a potential native replacement for silverthorn, depending upon use. Honeycups is deciduous rather than evergreen, but some forms, notably 'Woodlanders Blue,' are adorned with very attractive bluish gray foliage. Honeycups tolerates xeric conditions and produces showy racemes and axillary clusters of bell-shaped flowers followed by capsular fruit.

Popcorn tree.

Tallow Tree. Popcorn tree or tallow tree (*Triadica sebiferum*, =*Sapium sebiferum*) was introduced into South Carolina from China in the 1700s and first proliferated mostly in coastal areas but has since extended its range inland. It is an often-planted ornamental along the northern Gulf Coast, mostly due to its fast growth, colorful fall foliage, and interesting fruit, which turns whitish and resembles popcorn at maturity. It has the ability to reproduce vegetatively by root sprouts and is also a prolific seed producer with excellent dispersal and high germination. The three-parted capsule splits at maturity and forcibly expels the seeds, which birds eat and scatter widely. It is not unusual to see literally hundreds of seedlings below and near a single mature tree. Popcorn tree has become a major pest in both fresh and saltwater wetlands, including along riverbanks, pond and lake margins, and roadside ditches.

Mimosa or silktree.

Mimosa. The commonly planted mimosa, or silktree (*Albizia julibrissin*), was also introduced from Asia in the 1700s. It is seen mostly near roadsides and homesteads and invades natural areas much less commonly than the silverthorns. Its pink and white, puffball-like flowers and emerging multiparted leaves are sure signs that summer has arrived. It is a short-lived tree, usually not persisting more than about twenty years, and is known to harbor webworms. More recently, it has been afflicted with a fungus-caused wilt that kills trees within a year of infestation, a condition that has curtailed its use and stands to augment control efforts. Nevertheless, many mimosas have been planted in lower elevations of the Piedmont and in the coastal plains, some of which have invaded river and stream banks. Mimosa spreads readily by root sprouts and is a prolific seed producer, as evidenced by the numerous pods that hang on the tree in late summer and fall. The seeds remain viable for many years and are easily distributed by water and wildlife.

Vines. Most of the foregoing species are shrubs or trees. However, numerous invasive vines also have long histories in southern landscapes, many of which have become significant problems for the gardener as well as the environment.

Vines make their living by scrambling and climbing for light and are, by nature and adaptation, opportunistic. They often grow in shaded woodlands and have developed numerous adaptations for finding sunlight. Even native vines often grow aggressively, taking advantage of openings in the forest canopy and the increased sunlight of relatively open lawns and artificial clearings. This natural ecological tendency has contributed to the spread of numerous problematic non-native climbers that are particularly difficult to control. Large infestations are extremely challenging to remove by hand or machine and their tendency to twine around supporting trees and shrubs makes selective herbicide treatment nearly impossible. English ivy (*Hedera helix*), another plant long-favored in southern landscapes, as well as cat's claw (*Macfadyena unguis-cati*), Japanese honeysuckle (*Lonicera japonica*), and the two climbing ferns (*Lygodium japonicum* and *L. microphyllum*) have all become problems in southern landscapes.

Oriental bittersweet. Courtesy of James H. Miller, USDA Forest Service, Bugwood.org.

The speed with which an invasive species can colonize is aptly demonstrated by the history of oriental bittersweet (*Celastrus orbiculatus*), a high-climbing and scrambling vine that has become a serious pest plant in the Piedmont and mountains. In the middle 1970s, when woody plant expert Ron Lance was creating his first herbarium near Asheville, North Carolina, the plant was so scarce in the wild that he had difficulty finding a specimen to collect. Introduced for ornamental horticulture some years earlier at the nearby Biltmore House gardens, it had yet to escape cultivation to any significant degree. Today, the plant is rampant, and Lance worries that in the next decade or two, it may overcome and smother vegetation in the interior of rich Southern Appalachian forests as well as along disturbed roadsides. "In a recent survey of invasive species along the Blue Ridge Parkway," reports Lance, "seedling plants of bittersweet were recorded in every square meter plot measured." According to a fact sheet published by Indiana's Invasive Plant Species Assessment Working Group (IPSAWG), oriental bittersweet was brought to the United States in the middle of the nineteenth century and is now naturalized in twenty-one of the thirty-three states where it has been introduced. IPSAWG recommends planting virgin's bower (*Clematis virginiana*), coral honeysuckle (*Lonicera sempervirens*), and woolly dutchman's pipe (*Aristolochia tomentosa*) as alternatives to this deleterious vine.

Japanese climbing fern.

The climbing ferns, too, are excellent examples of how seemingly innocuous plants can quickly get out of hand. Japanese climbing fern was first reported as escaped from cultivation in the United States in the early 1900s near Thomasville, Georgia. In the middle 1930s, a Jacksonville, Florida, fern enthusiast found it in a swamp where it had escaped from her garden. In the seventy-five years since, it has spread across much of northern Florida, large portions of southern Georgia, Alabama, and Mississippi, and nearly throughout Louisiana. Although not yet considered a problem in the Carolinas and apparently not yet present in Virginia, its potential northern range is not fully known. Its aggressive nature is augmented by deep, tuberous roots that hold substantial food supplies and are extremely difficult to dig up and remove. Pulling vines from the top merely severs the aboveground stem from the rootstock, allowing the plant to return time and again. In addition, the spores are extremely long-lived—perhaps remaining vital for thirty years or more—travel widely by the wind, and readily germinate to produce new individuals in locations far distant from the parent plant.

Old World climbing fern (*Lygodium microphyllum*) is an even more ardent aggressor. It found its way into Florida only in the 1960s and was rarely seen even as late as 1976. By 1997—a span of only thirty years since its arrival—it had infested about 39,000 acres in southern Florida. It has now invaded more than 200,000 acres, and experts project that the infestation could reach 2,000,000 acres by 2014. It has steadily spread northward along the Florida peninsula and has reached at least the Orlando area in the interior of the peninsula and even farther north along the warmer east coast.

Like oriental bittersweet, these aggressive, high-climbing, vinelike ferns have spread rapidly into natural landscapes and have proven extremely difficult to eradicate. All provide evidence of how quickly invasive plants can colonize and how much damage they can do.

English ivy. Courtesy of James H. Miller, USDA Forest Service, Bugwood.org.

In contrast to these relatively recent introductions, English ivy was introduced during the earliest days of New World colonization and has a long and intimate history with eastern gardens. It is exceptionally shade tolerant and is often used as a groundcover, climbing vine, or to conceal and provide ornamentation to brick walls. It produces long trailing stems that root at the nodes and can easily get out of hand. Smart gardeners have learned to confine English ivy by surrounding it with regularly mowed lawns or other frequently manicured landscapes. Less careful gardeners have let it escape beyond their fence lines to encroach on adjacent property or into nearby parks and natural areas. It

Avoiding the Use of Invasive Species

The Invasive Plant Species Assessment Working Group, a multiagency initiative based in Indiana, recommends eight ways that gardeners and homeowners can help to reduce the spread of invasive species.

1. Ask for only noninvasive species when you acquire plants. Request that nurseries and garden centers sell only noninvasive plants.
2. Seek information on invasive plants. Sources include botanical gardens, horticulturists, conservationists, and government agencies.
3. Scout your property for invasive species and remove them before they become a problem. If plants can't be removed, at least prevent them from going to seed.
4. Clean your boots before and after visiting a natural area to prevent the spread of invasive plant seeds.
5. Don't release aquarium plants into the wild.
6. Volunteer at local parks and natural areas to assist ongoing efforts to diminish the threat of invasive plants.
7. Help educate your community through personal contacts and in such settings as garden clubs and civic groups.
8. Support public policies and programs to control invasive plants.

---

thrives in the low light of moist woodlands and can easily overwhelm and eliminate native vegetation. A dense ground infestation can be a foot or more deep and leaves no room for the growth of other plants.

Four native vines are most often recommended as replacements for these invasives: yellow jessamine (*Gelsemium sempervirens*), coral honeysuckle (*Lonicera sempervirens*), crossvine (*Bignonia capreolata*), and trumpet creeper (*Campsis radicans*). In addition, climbing hydrangea, or wood vamp (*Decumaria barbara*), a mostly coastal plains and Piedmont species that is increasingly available from mail order and retail nurseries, can be trained to the ground and makes an excellent substitute for English ivy. Allegheny spurge (*Pachysandra procumbens*), whose species name means "creeping forward and lying flat on the ground," is another excellent replacement, especially in the Piedmont and Upper Coastal Plain. All of these species are covered in greater detail later in this book.

Shrubs. Several species of invasive shrubs serve similar purposes in southern gardens. The showy non-native roses (*Rosa* spp.), bush honeysuckles (*Lonicera* spp.), winged burning bush (*Euonymus alata*), and heavenly bamboo (*Nandina domestica*) all grow rapidly, provide screening or foundation concealment, and display showy flowers, fruit, or foliage. All are known invaders and at least one even enjoys a modicum of legal protection. Cherokee rose (*Rosa laevigata*) is the state flower of Georgia, so designated in 1916 under the mistaken notion that it was indigenous to the state. It and several of the related climbing and shrub-forming roses are now listed as invasive species across all of the southeastern United States. Most are prolific bloomers that produce numerous attractive bright white flowers and glossy green foliage. They have the propensity to

Cherokee rose.

scramble and climb onto surrounding vegetation and are armed with sharp thorns that make both pruning and removal difficult.

Chinese silvergrass. Courtesy of Arthur E. Miller, USDA APHIS PPQ, Bugwood.org.

Grasses. Grasses are often ecologically adapted for quick growth and rapid colonization. Many non-native species have shallowly buried stolons or rhizomes, which lend to their establishment and expansion. Giant reed (*Arundo donax*) and golden bamboo

(*Phyllostachys aurea*) are large plants with culms often more than ten feet tall. Both have long been planted for ornamental purposes. Chinese silvergrass (*Miscanthus sinensis*) is a more recent introduction that has quickly become popular in the southeast. It is a large, clump-forming species that is regularly sold in nurseries and increasingly used in landscaping. It easily escapes to woodland margins and roadsides and can quickly become problematic.

In Summary

The message to be gleaned here is that gardeners have an important role in ensuring the health and well-being of native ecosystems and natural areas. Diligent, environmentally sensitive gardening not only benefits the gardener by reducing the work associated with aggressive plants that overrun our personal creations, but also augments the efforts of those who manage our public lands by reducing the number and spread of potentially deleterious weeds. While this book does not doggedly advocate a "natives only" approach to gardening, it does advocate that our interests should extend well beyond our individual domains, and that as gardeners we should view our individual plantings as integral parts of a much larger and increasingly imperiled landscape.

4

Re-creating Nature

Theme Gardening with Native Plants

Native plants offer a wide range of theme gardening opportunities, ranging from wildlife and habitat gardens to gardens that specialize in collections of a particular family, genus, or other groups of related species. Among the most popular specialty gardens are those designed to attract butterflies and birds or that attempt to create replicas of bogs or ponds, but the huge array of possible permutations is limited only by imagination and interest.

Wildlife Gardens

Since most native plants provide an assortment of ecological services to native wildlife, they are an excellent resource for attracting birds, butterflies, mammals, and a host of pollinating insects to the garden. Depending upon one's preferences, a wildlife garden can be large and expansive or small and compact, and it can be specifically designed to entice a small or large array of wildlife. Although almost any native plant garden will attract at least a few birds and butterflies, planning and forethought can significantly increase visitation and carrying capacity.

The fruiting and flowering cycles of native plant species are intimately synchronized with the needs of native wildlife, placing them among the better choices for wildlife gardening. Although birds, mammals, and insects are likely to visit all sorts of plants, cultivars and hybrids that have been selected for earlier or later flowering might be less useful than typical unadulterated species, and some non-native species might produce fruit or nectar at less optimal times. Hence, using locally adapted native species takes some of the guesswork out of plant selection.

In addition, some non-native species are prolific fruit producers. Their spread by birds and other garden visitors can enhance their motility in the garden and encourage unwanted distribution into nearby natural areas.

The best wildlife gardens provide food, cover, and water, and even though some animals prefer one type of cover over another, or are adapted to specific types of foods, there is tremendous overlap in what is suitable for birds, mammals, and insects. Food plants, in particular, have tremendous elasticity. Plants that produce fleshy or juicy fruit—hollies, blueberries, dogwoods, crabapples—are universally important, whereas

Birdsong Nature Center

A Study in Wildlife Gardening

In many ways, Birdsong Nature Center is a 565-acre wildlife garden. At least that's the way Kathleen Brady, the center's director, sees it. Purchased by Ed and Betty Komarek in 1938, Birdsong's property had been a typical southern crop farm for many decades, complete with open fields and depleted soil. The Komareks turned their acquisition first into a cattle ranch and later into an outdoor laboratory for the study of effective land management, with an emphasis on prescribed fire, ecosystem ethics, and a strong commitment to environmental stewardship.

The Komareks were friends with and inspired by the late Dr. Eugene Odum, one of the leading ecologists of the time and considered by many to be the "father of modern ecology." It was Odum's perceptions of holistic ecosystems and ecological succession that Betty modeled in the development of the six-acre garden that surrounded her circa 1860s farmhouse.

Prevailing ecological theories of the day detailed the stages through which an abandoned field passes in its return to a healthy, natural system, the final stage of which ecologists then called the climax community. There is probably no clearer nor succinct description of these successional stages than that of B. W. Wells in his classic 1932 *Natural Gardens of North Carolina*. Wells describes the regenerative powers of natural communities to heal themselves from even the most destructive wounds as one of life's most important aspects. "Naturally, years, instead of days, are involved," Wells wrote, "but immediately following the injury or destruction of any original native vegetation, the advance guard of certain species begins to reclaim the bare area and initiates a series of plant communities which follow one another until at last the original plants reenter and the green epidermis of the earth is fully restored."

Viewed in Wells's terms, gardens are essentially old fields whose ecological succession has been artificially arrested somewhere along the way by the activities of its gardener. For Betty Komarek, motivated to increase the number of plants and animals near her homestead, the idea of arrested ecological succession coupled with Odum's holistic approach to ecosystem management was an awakening. Together, the two principles became her paradigm for garden design.

Betty reasoned that each successional stage not only played an important role in the progress toward the ultimate rebuilding of the native landscape but also came equipped with a unique suite of wildlife specifically adapted to its particular environmental circumstances. Betty realized that the birds, insects, and other animals that inhabit grasslands differ demonstrably from those that make their living in shady, close-canopied forest, and different again from those of open, sunlit pinelands. To maximize the wildlife in her dooryard, Betty decided that her garden should represent as many stages on the ecological road map as possible. She determined to provide varying habitats attractive to a varying collection of wildlife. The small expanse of lawn became her early successional grassland, a patch of longleaf pines her conifer forest, and the relatively open pecan grove behind the house her oak–hickory woodland. The beech and magnolia trees that adorned the edges of the house assumed the role of climax forest.

continued

continued

Betty clearly understood that the artificial habitats surrounding her home were not eco-logical stages in the true sense, but she just as clearly understood that providing diversity in her garden ensured a larger array of wildlife for her and her children to enjoy. Her goal was not to replicate but to model, not to restore but to simulate. In short, she wanted a landscape that championed diversity.

A stroll through Betty's garden today reveals the success of her design. More than two hundred bird species have been recorded in her landscape, from the meadow-dwelling bluebirds, meadowlarks, and swallows to the warblers, sparrows, woodpeckers, and nut-hatches that crowd her forested feeding table. Even bobwhite quail sometimes visit the courtyard outside of her bird window. Foxes, white-tailed deer, and raccoons have been recorded near the house, and the gardens are typically alive with insects.

Gardeners today would do well to follow Betty's lead and to learn from her grand de-sign—regardless of the size of their available real estate. The oft-repeated requirements for effective wildlife gardens—cover, food, and water—should be supplemented with diversity. It is clear from Betty's experiments that a combination of open woodlands, tall trees, shrubby borders, dead snags, and grassy meadows, regardless of how small, add im-measurably to garden wildlife. Though it is not always possible to re-create entire natural communities in our own backyards, it is certainly possible to borrow from nature's design in making our gardens favorable to wild inhabitants.

Betty Komarek in her bird window garden. Courtesy of Donna Legare.

Betty Komarek's bird window.

the many members of the aster family, especially our native sunflowers, produce prodigious amounts of tiny achenes that are particularly attractive to seed-eating birds. Water can be provided in birdbaths; artificial ponds and water features; muddy, ground-level puddles; or through timer-controlled sprinklers and misters. Small and large trees and densely foliated shrubs can provide cover.

Gardening for Butterflies

Butterfly gardens, in particular, have become hugely popular accoutrements to residential landscapes. Approximately 750 species of butterflies occur naturally in North America, well over 200 of which are found in the southeastern United States. While not all of these can be expected to visit a particular garden, at least two dozen species can be easily attracted to most backyards, and well over 30 with an effective garden design. Many native plant nurseries, plant societies, and chapters of the North American Butterfly Association offer workshops and advice on designing butterfly gardens, including both design and plant recommendations.

Butterflies are part of the order Lepidoptera, or scale-wing insects, which also includes the night-flying moths. They are among the best-known representatives of a larger, more inclusive group—often called the holometabolous insects—that undergo complete metamorphosis, passing through four distinct life stages from egg to maturity. Others in this group include beetles, flies, bees, lacewings, fleas, and caddisflies. Although all holometabolous insects pass progressively from egg to larva, pupa, then adult, only the pupal stage of Lepidopterans results in the hardened, papery chrysalis that is so often associated with butterfly maturation and emergence.

Understanding the rudiments of the Lepidopteran life cycle is essential to design-

Butterfly garden featuring *Coreopsis*. Courtesy of Donna Legare.

Purple coneflower anchoring a butterfly garden. Courtesy of Donna Legare.

ing an effective butterfly garden. To have butterflies at all stages and throughout much of the year, each of the butterfly's life forms must be accommodated. For the egg stage it is important to provide the appropriate larval food plants, which are often called host plants. Adult female butterflies seek out one or only a very few species of the host plants upon which to deposit their eggs. Usually, the preferred plants are closely related to each

Butterfly garden at Callaway Gardens, Georgia. Courtesy of Donna Legare.

Terraced butterfly garden in Tallahassee, Florida. Courtesy of Donna Legare.

other—often belonging to a single genus or family—and are attractive to only one or a very small group of butterfly species. For example, monarch and queen butterflies feed on milkweeds, zebra swallowtail on pawpaws, Gulf fritillaries and zebra longwings on passion vines, and sulphurs on sicklepod and partridge pea. The more varied the array of host plants in the garden, the wider the variety of butterflies the garden will attract.

The Gulf fritillary is widespread across the southeast, especially the coastal plains.

Moreover, since female butterflies can detect their favored host plants from great distances, knowing which plants a particular species requires will increase the chances of having that species in your landscape.

In warm weather it takes only a few days—fewer than ten for most species—for the eggs to hatch and the caterpillars to begin feeding. Observant gardeners will spot the rounded, pinhead-sized eggs that adorn the leaves and stems of each butterfly species' preferred plant, as well as the newly hatched caterpillars that feed voraciously on the foliage. Like adult butterflies, the eggs and caterpillars of each species are unique in color, shape, and ornamentation and can be identified to species (or at least to genus) with only a little practice.

Newly hatched caterpillars often eat their eggshells first before turning their attention to their host. Most are gluttonous feeders that can nearly defoliate a plant as they munch their way to metamorphosis. Some caterpillars eat only at night or on dark days, rolling up in a leaf or hiding under foliage during daytime to avoid predation. Others seem to be less temporally limited. Even though tidy gardeners might think otherwise, the apparent foliar damage caterpillars inflict is slight and certainly not permanent. Given a caterpillar's very short life span—usually less than a month—most plants easily recover from their minor injuries just in time for the next batch of hungry interlopers.

Once a caterpillar reaches maturity, it stops eating and seeks a place away from the host plant to pupate. Pupation involves the caterpillar attaching itself to a twig or branch, covering itself with a bed of silken material, hardening into a papery chrysalis, transforming itself from caterpillar to butterfly, and emerging as a newly formed adult. How long this transformation takes varies with species, time of year, and weather. In summer the complete transition from caterpillar to butterfly might take as little as ten

Butterfly Larval Food Plants

Butterfly	Larval Food Plant
American painted lady	Asters, cudweed
Banded hairstreak	Oaks
Black swallowtail	Carrot family (Apiaceae)
Cloudless sulphur	Sennas
Common buckeye	Gerardia, plantains
Giant swallowtail	Wild lime, Hercules'-club, hoptree
Gray hairstreak	Legumes
Gulf fritillary	Passion flowers
Hackberry butterfly	Hackberries
Long-tailed skipper	Legumes
Monarch	Milkweeds
Mourning cloak	Elms, willows
Orange-barred sulphur	Sennas
Palamedes swallowtail	Red bay, sassafras
Pearl crescent	Asters
Pipevine swallowtail	Pipevines
Polydamas swallowtail	Pipevines
Queen	Milkweeds
Red-spotted purple	Black cherry, hawthorns, willows, tulip tree
Skippers	Native grasses
Sleepy orange	Sennas
Spicebush swallowtail	Sassafras, spicebush, red bay
Spring azure	Dogwood, viburnum
Tiger swallowtail	Sweetbay magnolia, cherry, ash, tulip poplar, native plums, other broad-leaved trees
Variegated fritillary	Passionflowers
Viceroy	Elms, willows
Zebra longwing	Passionflowers
Zebra swallowtail	Pawpaws

days. With the advent of cooler weather, adult emergence might be delayed a month or two, or even until the following spring. Since chrysalises are normally formed on woody plants, gardens that are augmented with an adequate and nearby selection of shrubs or small trees are likely to produce the most butterflies. Some woody plants can double as host or nectar plants—climbing aster and wafer ash are good examples—and as a source of permanent cover for sleeping, resting, and protection from wind and rain.

Proper siting is almost as important as plant selection in butterfly garden design. Most butterflies prefer plenty of sun with adequate access to food, cover, and water. Since they lack internal temperature control, they depend upon the sun for warmth and usually do not feed on cloudy days or when temperatures fall below about 60° F (or above about 108°, for that matter). Hence, shady gardens typically attract the fewest butterfly species.

Unlike caterpillars, most adult butterflies feed on nectar rather than foliage. Their long, often coiled, tonguelike proboscis is perfectly adapted for accessing the special nectary glands that lie inside and at the base of many flowers. In return for the flower's food services, butterflies often help effect cross-pollination by carrying pollen from one plant to another.

Also unlike caterpillars, adult butterflies are less selective in their choice of food plants, which gives the gardener more latitude in plant selection and allows for a relatively small array of plants to service a relatively wide array of butterflies. Colorful plants with crowded, easily accessible flowers; a flattened landing pad that allows butterflies to alight as they feed; and flowers that are more or less vertically oriented to allow feeding from the top, are all important. Species from the milkweed and aster (see Chapters 12 and 13) families are among the more popular.

Butterflies typically extract their drinking water from wet, muddy sands. It is not unusual to see a gaggle of Lepidopterans seemingly dancing around the edges of a muddy puddle or shallow, sandy pool of rainwater. To drink, they poke their strawlike proboscis into the mud and extract water in much the same way that they extract nectar from a flower. Providing water in your garden may mean burying a shallow pan or piece of pond liner, filling it with sand, saturating it with water, and keeping it continuously wet. Fountains and typical birdbaths are of little use as butterfly water sources.

Most successful butterfly gardeners first familiarize themselves with the butterflies likely to visit their locale, then design with these species in mind. No matter how well designed a garden might be, it will only be successful in attracting butterflies that are either resident in or migrate through your area. Mass plantings of dense concentrations of nectar plants should form the main attraction—especially if you want to enjoy the butterflies from a central vantage—but ancillary plantings in other parts of your landscape will offer diversity and ensure butterfly visitors in all parts of your yard. Tidy gardeners can keep their creations as neat and manicured as desired—as long as they don't snip off egg-laden or caterpillar-defoliated branches—whereas naturalistic gardeners can allow a few "weeds" to infiltrate their plantings. A few of these weeds, notably the cudweeds (*Gamochaeta* spp.) and shepherd's-needle (*Bidens* spp.), serve as host or nectar plants and are likely to increase your butterfly concentration.

Good butterfly gardens are also usually attractive to other insects, especially bees, as well as hummingbirds. The insects, in particular, provide additional pollination services for the garden. Providing a succession of flowering plants throughout the season ensures maximum visitation. Some of the better native species for attracting insects—including butterflies and skippers—include black-eyed Susan, goldenrods, purple coneflower, sunflowers, scarlet sage, Joe-Pye-weed, rosinweed, and New Jersey tea.

Gardening for Birds

I recall as a child making frequent visits to my grandmother's bird garden. Located just outside a small sunroom, the tiny patch of marginally manicured landscape was perfectly designed to attract a variety of dooryard birds, all easily viewed by indoor visitors. When they built the house, Granddad left a narrow strip of woodland along one edge of the yard that widened to about twenty-five feet as it neared the sunroom. The woods provided excellent cover for resting and nest building. Like most bird gardens, there

The best bird gardens provide food, water, and cover. Courtesy of Donna Legare.

Elaborate bird garden with groundwater and large boulder, Native Nurseries, Tallahassee, Florida. Courtesy of Donna Legare.

Simple bird garden. Courtesy of Donna Legare.

were at least two feeders as well as a water supply. Beyond the standard birdbath, a small mister provided a steady, foglike spray that served as a major attraction, and a sunny spot allowed for a small collection of flowering annuals and perennials.

Although Grandmom was a generalist, interested mostly in common neighborhood species, it is possible to tailor your garden to attract a wide range of birds. Humming-birds, in particular, are one of the more sought-after species and are much more common in the garden than often assumed. Many people use specialized hummingbird feeders filled with sugar water to attract them. However, native plants with brightly colored tubular flowers can do the same job without concern for constant maintenance or the potential for mold, fungus, bacteria, and disease problems that sometimes plague feeder maintenance. Coral honeysuckle, scarlet sage, trumpet creeper, red buckeye, two-winged silverbell, crossvine, scarlet hibiscus, cardinal flower, native azaleas, and the several beebalms are among the best. If feeders are used, they should be dismantled and thoroughly cleaned at least once a week—even more often during the hottest part of summer. Nearby vegetation should provide hummers with plenty of perching spots between feeding forays. Since many hummers prefer to perch ten feet or more above the ground, the availability of small trees or low branches near the feeding site is optimal.

Other birds with special needs include owls, woodpeckers, flycatchers, and bluebirds. All are cavity nesters that prefer natural holes in dead or decaying trees for resting, nesting, and rearing young. Leaving (or even artificially erecting) dead snags in the landscape can be important in attracting these species. So can well-placed nesting boxes. For birds that don't frequent feeders—like owls, flycatchers, and bluebirds—providing extra enticements may be the only way to lure them.

Other Wildlife

Numerous species of mammals visit gardens, even in relatively urban environments. And while not all gardeners welcome such species as gray squirrel and white-tailed deer, for others the enjoyment of having wildlife in the garden overshadows the damage some of these animals inflict on the plants. For the most part, a garden design that attracts birds and butterflies will also attract other animals, but a few additions can be helpful.

One of the best ways to ensure the presence of small terrestrial animals is to construct a brush pile. Animals such as rabbits, box turtles, opossums, raccoons, and a number of reptiles and amphibians are attracted to the cover a brush pile provides and will use it for resting and as protection from predators, such as neighborhood dogs and cats. The best brush piles are constructed by laying a crisscrossed ground-level cover of relatively large limbs covered by increasingly smaller branches. Dome-shaped piles are preferred, about as wide as they are tall. Using a mixture of large branches at ground level allows passageways for small animals while the more densely constructed upper layers will provide hiding places for birds.

A small pond with flowing or misting water also ensures the presence of wildlife. As Caroline Dorman admonishes in *Natives Preferred:* "By all means, have a pond." A ground-level water feature surrounded by adequate cover and nearby food plants can round out a backyard wildlife habitat. Using native species in pond plantings is probably more important than for any other backyard garden. Aquatic plants are often prolific—sometimes rampant—growers, reproducing vegetatively and by seed.

Nest Box Dimensions for Cavity-Nesting Birds

If natural cavities are not available in or near your garden, the following table, borrowed from a publication by the Florida Fish and Wildlife Conservation Commission, suggests dimensions for building nest boxes for several common backyard birds.

Species	Floor Size (inches)	Cavity Depth (inches)	Entrance Height (inches)	Entrance Diameter (inches)	Aboveground Height (feet)
Carolina Wren	4 × 4	8	1–6	1¼	6–10
Eastern Bluebird	5 × 5	8	6	1½	5–10
Great Crested Flycatcher	6 × 6	10	6	2	8–20
Purple Martin	6 × 6	6	1–2	2–2¼	10–20
Downy Woodpecker	4 × 4	10	8	1¼	6–20
Red-Bellied Woodpecker	6 × 6	15	9	2	8–20
Red-Headed Woodpecker	6 × 6	15	9	2	8–20
Northern Flicker	7 × 7	18	14	2½	8–20
Tufted Titmouse	4 × 4	8	6	1¼	5–15
Carolina Chickadee	4 × 4	8	6	1⅛	5–15
Eastern Screech-Owl	10 × 10	24	20	4 × 3	10–30
Barred Owl	12 × 12	28	12–16	7 × 7	10–30
Barn Owl	12 × 12	28	12–16	7 × 7	10–30

Source: Adapted from *Planting a Refuge for Wildlife*, by Donna Legare and Susan Cerulean (1986, Florida Fish and Wildlife Conservation Commission).

Brush piles can be artistic additions. Courtesy of Donna Legare.

This pond at the Hobbit Garden, near Raleigh, North Carolina, is also flanked by a bog garden.

Native pond at Native Nurseries, Tallahassee, Florida. Courtesy of Donna Legare.

Non-native species such as water hyacinth (*Eichhornia crassipes*) can easily clog back-yard pools, crowding out other plants and turning the pond into an environmental hazard and a chore to manage. Birds can easily transport seeds and plant fragments to surrounding natural ponds, lakes, and waterways, increasing the potential for these plants to escape the garden and invade natural areas. More than one infestation of aquatic weeds has gotten its start this way.

Botanical Collections

Many native plant enthusiasts are essentially collectors who have turned their attention to plants rather than stamps, coins, antiques, or vintage baseball cards. Like all collectors, their interests are directed toward a particular group of related objects, which in this case might include all native species from a single genus, family, or geographic region, or perhaps all of the dominant species of a particular habitat or natural vegetative assemblage.

The more popular groups of collectible woody plants include the magnolias, hollies, deciduous azaleas, and evergreen rhododendrons. Trilliums top the list of herbaceous species, especially in the Piedmont, but ferns, irises, and native orchids are also favorites, with many collectors showing interest in more than one group. Steve Yeatts, a collector in Athens, Georgia, for example, grows most of the southeastern native azaleas as well as at least thirty species of trilliums. His trillium collection includes virtually all trillium species native to the eastern United States as well as a few from Asia.

Gardeners in the Piedmont and lower elevations of the Appalachians can grow at least twelve of the fifteen deciduous azaleas that are native to the eastern United States as well as several of the native rhododendrons. Azalea enthusiasts often become interested in producing artificial hybrids and learn to hand pollinate the stigmas of one species with the pollen of another to produce plants with a fascinating variety of flower colors. Some of these crosses become registered as named cultivars and are offered for sale to the public in retail nurseries. Earl Sommerville, an avid and well-known azalea collector and breeder from Marietta, Georgia, maintains that native azaleas cross so readily that few pure species can be found in the wild in Georgia, a situation that has probably been encouraged by the increasing numbers of native aza-

Caroline Dean's native azalea garden, Opelika, Alabama.

leas in southern gardens. According to Sommerville, "The bees cross-pollinate these plants much more effectively than we can."

Private arboreta of native woody plants, especially trees, are also popular. Some enthusiasts restrict their collection only to species plants, whereas others also include as many named cultivars as possible. The several holly cultivars that vary in fruit color, size, and persistence are excellent examples, with many holly collectors showing increasing interest in the southeastern deciduous species.

Many woody plant collections are augmented with non-native species, especially for groups that lack a wide assortment of cultivars. Magnolias are a good example. This showy group of primitive flowering trees (see Chapter 8) enjoys a long history of worldwide popularity. But with only eight species native to the southeast—not all of which grow well in every locale—many magnolia enthusiasts have added a few of the showy Asian species to their assemblages. The Tobe Botanical Garden, a private collection near Quitman, Georgia, and Dick and Anita Figlar's private magnolia collection near Seneca, South Carolina, are examples.

Some collectors choose to specialize in difficult-to-cultivate plants, like the two native stewartias, the Georgia plume, or the Ben Franklin tree, all of which are included in Chapter 6. Jack Johnston, a gardener and grower near Clayton, Georgia, for example, has amassed extensive knowledge about growing our native stewartias and is motivated by learning to grow species that others have found difficult to keep alive.

Habitat and Regional Gardens

Habitat and regional gardens are specialized collections of native plants that attempt to replicate, or at least represent, a particular geographic region or native plant assemblage.

North Carolina Botanical Garden coastal plains habitat garden.

Although akin to ecological restoration, most regionally dependent or habitat-specific gardens are thought of more appropriately as celebrations of a region's flora rather than as re-creations of it. Many habitat gardens, for example, are not even situated in the floristic province in which their modeled habitat naturally occurs.

The North Carolina Botanical Garden (NCBG), located at Chapel Hill, is one of the southeast's best examples of regionally specific gardens. At its inception NCBG was designed to showcase the southeastern flora and today includes a large collection of native species divided into several habitats. Although located squarely in the Piedmont, its collections include an excellent coastal plains garden featuring species characteristic of sandhill, flatwoods, and bogs; a garden replica of the Appalachian Mountains; and two miles of nature trails that pass through eighty-eight acres of typical Piedmont forest. NCBG bills itself as a conservation garden whose mission is "to inspire understanding, appreciation, and conservation of plants in gardens and natural areas and to advance a sustainable relationship between people and nature." Indeed, turning one's yard into a replica of its floristic region is an exciting adventure that commemorates the indigenous landscape and reinforces one's sense of place.

Habitat gardens take on many forms. Some consist only of small, isolated collections with only a handful of representative species; others consume most of a yard or even several acres. Plantings representative of mountain coves, temperate hardwood forests, moist hammocks, longleaf pine sandhills, wetland bogs, and wildflower meadows are all possible. Establishing such gardens often means researching plant lists of specific habitats, matching the listed species to what is available for purchase from local and mail-order nurseries, then deciding which plants to try in your garden.

Longleaf pine–dominated uplands constitute one of the Southeastern Coastal Plains' more historically important and expansive natural communities, making it a community well suited for an adventure into habitat gardening. Majestic longleaf pinelands once dominated as many as ninety million acres of the coastal plains, stretching in a nearly continuous swath from southeastern Virginia to eastern Texas. As the name suggests, the community's overstory is composed primarily of longleaf pine that overtops a midstory of xeric oaks and a groundcover of numerous grasses and several hundred species of shrubs and perennial wildflowers. Wiregrass (*Aristida stricta*) is the dominant groundcover grass in the east—from Virginia to about Mississippi—and broomsedge (*Andropogon* spp.) in the west. This is a xeric community, adapted to dry conditions, intense sun, sandy soils, and frequent fire. The plants that grow here are generally tough, easy to grow, and require little maintenance once established. Many residential landscapes in the coastal plains now rest on what was formerly occupied by longleaf pine forests, making many yards especially adapted for the plants that once grew in them. Since the restoration of longleaf pinelands has become an increasingly important industry in the southeast, many of the most important of these plants are commercially available and easy to acquire, even from small retail nurseries.

As might be expected, one or more longleaf pines should form the anchor of a longleaf pineland garden. Longleaf pine (*Pinus palustris*) can be purchased in several forms, from grass-stage "tubelings" to potted saplings several feet tall. Longleaf is noted for its growth habit. Unlike most pines, longleaf seedlings appear as tufts of grass without a visible aboveground trunk. As an adaptation to frequent fire, the trunk enlarges below the ground, usually reaching 1–2 inches in girth before shooting up rapidly. Tubelings and seedlings are essentially grass-stage plants that are poised for rapid growth. Under optimal conditions, they may reach heights of twelve feet or more in only three growing seasons and are excellent for planting in the garden. Larger potted specimens are also often available from nurseries that specialize in trees or native plants. However, the tendency of many gardeners to purchase the tallest longleaf pine possible is often not rewarded with success. Since longleaf pines develop a deep vertical taproot that cannot develop sufficiently in a pot, potted specimens that are larger than about twelve inches tall often perform poorly when planted out. Their taproot just cannot keep pace with vertical trunk growth and, once in the ground, they may require long-term staking to keep them upright. Trees that have been in the ground even for several years are prone to fall over in strong winds. Moreover, the growth rate of tubelings and small potted plants often exceeds that of larger potted plants, resulting in healthier and even taller plants in as little as five years after planting.

Fire in the Garden

Modern ecologists often call longleaf pinelands "fire forests." During presettlement times the expansive longleaf uplands that once clothed over 90 million acres of the Southeastern Coastal Plains ignited naturally every 1–3 years, often burning great expanses of landscape. These fast-moving, cool-burning fires favored the continuation of a grassy and herbaceous groundcover over the intrusion of woody plants, leaving parklike stands of longleaf pines underlain by a richly diverse groundcover. Replicating this natural process through controlled burns and prescribed fire has become a major tool for managing the remainder of our natural longleaf pine forests as well as commercial timber plantations. Forest managers on both public and private lands have come to rely on the replication of natural fire as the single most important tool for ensuring healthy forests and a diverse ecosystem.

Managing a longleaf–sandhill habitat garden is not the same as managing an entire forest. Nevertheless, at least a few gardeners have learned to utilize fire as a gardening tool, and some even espouse annual burning to replicate natural processes. Nowhere is this truer than at the North Carolina Botanical Garden at Chapel Hill. Each February a team of garden professionals, fire-certified experts, students, and volunteers participate in an annual application of fire to NCBG's Coastal Plain Habitat Garden. This relatively small garden is about a half-acre in size and nearly encircled by wooden walkways. Fires are set along the edges of the walkways and burn inward, ensuring that they are naturally extinguished when they reach the center of the garden. "Regardless of how much you plan," says the garden's curator and fire boss Chris Liloia, "it always gets a little exciting once the fire starts to burn."

Burning the coastal plains habitat at the North Carolina Botanical Garden. Courtesy of North Carolina Botanical Garden.

Bog Gardens

Artificial bogs, especially those supporting carnivorous plants, are popular additions to many sunny southern gardens. Inground bogs can be large, expansive wetlands that cover many square feet; or small, easily managed gardens only 2–3 feet in diameter. Moveable, aboveground bogs can also be maintained in watertight containers of almost any size and relocated as desired. How large a bog becomes depends directly on the amount of water, space, and time available to maintain it.

There are about as many recipes for building a bog as there are people who build them. It seems that all active bog gardeners have at least one favorite formula; some have several. Veteran bog builders Caroline Dean and her son, the late Dan Dean, of Opelika, Alabama, whose habit of rescuing pitcher plants from the path of destruction led them to become prolific bog builders, have said that none of their eight bogs was constructed precisely alike. Interestingly enough, all of the Deans' bogs are successful, as are those of most other southeastern bog builders. In short, there is wide latitude in bog garden construction; as long as you follow most of the rules, your own bog should be a success.

There are at least five ingredients on which nearly all bog gardeners agree: peat, sand, plastic, water, and site selection. Quality, type, proportion, and quantity of these ingredients are another matter.

The Deans use Promix, a commercial mixture of Canadian sphagnum peat moss,

"Bog queen" Kathryn Gable tending a bog garden at Georgia Perimeter College Native Plant Garden in Atlanta.

One of the bog gardens at the Georgia Perimeter College Native Plant Garden in Atlanta.

perlite, vermiculite, and other minor disease-resistant ingredients, as their source of peat. Others prefer unblended Canadian sphagnum peat moss (not to be confused with sphagnum moss). In reality, sphagnum is the key here and just about any good commercially available sphagnum peat moss will work.

The preferred type of sand is also variable. Many agree that playground, sandbox, and beach sands are all too fine and should be avoided. However, Peter D'Amato, writing in *The Savage Garden*, recommends "washed 'play sand' meant for use in children's sand-

Bog plants can also be grown in containers.

boxes" because it is clean and likely contains no contaminating particles. River sand and builders' sand are mentioned most often by successful bog gardeners, either of which is satisfactory as long as it is well washed and free of impurities. Lee Norris, a Florida bog gardener, recommends pool filter sand because it is uniform in grain size, lacks impurities, is chemically inert, does not contain clay, and is readily accessible. Pool filter sand is somewhat expensive and thus probably best for container or smaller inground bogs. It can be obtained from swimming pool supply outlets and large hardware stores.

Proportion of peat to sand also varies. Most gardeners use a 50–50 mix but some recommend much higher proportions of peat. George Sanko of the Georgia Perimeter College Native Plant Garden in Atlanta, for example, recommends 75–80 percent peat, pointing out that the more peat in your mixture, the less quickly the bog will dry out in hot summers. Hal Massie, who has built numerous bogs in the Piedmont, recommends slightly more peat than sand—two parts peat to one part sand—to prevent the bog from appearing unnaturally sandy. A few bog gardeners, such as Darwin Thomas of Cullowhee, North Carolina, use only peat with no sand at all.

Garden pond liners, children's swimming pools, prefabricated backyard pond containers, or concrete-mixing tubs serve well as containers for inground bogs. If you are fortunate enough to have a constant natural water supply and poor drainage, you may not need a liner. Steve Yeatts built one of his Athens, Georgia, bogs at the base of a gentle slope by excavating, widening, and contouring the head of a small seepage stream. Likewise, heavy clay soil with extremely poor drainage may also obviate the need for a liner. For most situations, however, a water-holding barrier of some sort is essential.

Whether to provide extra drainage for your bog depends largely on soil type and bog depth. Some gardeners recommend cutting slits or punching holes in the bottom of the liner to allow for drainage. If your bog has a sloping bottom, these slits or holes can be located on the downhill end. Others recommend punching holes in the side of the container, nearer to the ground surface. Still others recommend no holes at all. Hal Massie, for example, who has built bogs in such watertight containers as old wheelbarrows, recommends using no additional drainage.

Whether or not to provide drainage may also depend upon the quality of your water. Heavily mineralized water may leave residues that build up in the soil with evaporation. Drainage can retard but probably not eliminate this buildup.

Shallow bogs tend to dry out rapidly, especially when situated in full sun, and may perform better if allowed to dry by evaporation rather than by drainage holes. This is especially true for small container gardens. Shadier bogs, on the other hand, may remain too soggy without extra drainage. Bogs built over clay or poorly drained soils may require more drainage punctures than those built over well-drained, porous soils.

Aboveground bogs can be fashioned from a variety of containers, ranging from old dishpans and plastic tubs to wheelbarrows, old washtubs, concrete-mixing tubs, and small, prefabricated pond liners. They should be carefully observed over time to determine how quickly they dry and whether additional drainage should be provided.

Water is a bog garden's life source. A natural seepage with a continuous flow of fresh groundwater is preferred but is not possible in most home landscapes. An artificial seepage with a timed flow of tap water is a potential solution, but it is often complicated, expensive, and requires careful adjustment to ensure consistency. In the absence of natural or artificial seepages and regular rain, most bog gardeners irrigate their bogs from above with stored rainwater or tap water, or with a soaker hose buried a few inches deep on the upslope end of the bog. During the heart of a hot, dry summer, small, shallow bogs may need to be replenished once per week or more, whereas deeper bogs may do well with only occasional backyard watering.

How deep an inground bog garden should be is an open question. Recommended depths of 18–24 inches are most common. However, Hal Massie, writing in the July 2006 issue of *BotSoc News*, suggests that a depth of 6–8 inches is adequate, noting that bog plants often "thrive in shallow soil," and Rob Sacilotto, in his article *Making a Bog Garden* (www.pitcherplant.com/bog_making.htm), recommends 12–14 inches. Although a depth of 24 inches is generally considered maximum, a few bog builders suggest depths to nearly three feet. Regardless of the depth you choose, the sides of your excavation should be straight or only slightly sloping.

Bogs 18–24 inches deep seem to perform best and require less watering. According to Kathryn Gable and Paula Reith, who manage the bogs at the Georgia Perimeter College (GPC) Native Plant Garden in Atlanta, bogs can be much drier than one might think. The GPC bogs are irrigated regularly, but only along with the garden's normal watering regimen, and they receive no special irrigation treatment. The key factor, according to Gable—the garden's undisputed "bog queen"—is the combination of depth and method of construction; she cautions against overwatering.

Gable prefers her inground bogs to be at least two feet deep. After excavation, she lines the hole with a layer of sand to prevent roots and other debris from puncturing the liner from below. The liner is installed above this initial layer and filled to a depth of about eight inches (one-third the depth of the hole) with pure sand. In some of her bogs, Gable cuts four-inch horizontal slits every three feet or so along the sides of the liner, just above the first layer of sand. This allows the sand to retain moisture while ensuring efficient drainage of excess rain or irrigation. The remaining sand and peat are mixed and watered thoroughly in a wheelbarrow, then spread one load at the time in 2–3-inch layers across the surface of the developing bog. Each layer is compacted tightly by repeated stomping. "You should stomp until the water oozes out the side," says Gable, "to ensure that the composition is mixed so thoroughly that the sand does not rise to the surface."

Site selection is critical. For bogs to perform best, they should receive plenty of sunlight and provide equally for water retention and adequate drainage. Best is a western exposure with full sun all day; 5–6 hours of full sun is probably a minimum. If shaded part of the day, afternoon shade is preferred.

Jennifer Ceska, working through the Endangered Plant Stewardship Network (EPSN) and Plant Conservation Alliance at the State Botanical Garden of Georgia in Athens, prefers building her bogs on a gentle slope with a gradient of less than one inch per every three feet. Her bogs, fashioned after those of the Atlanta Botanical Garden, use an underground soaker hose as a water source. The hose is buried along the bog's upper end and a 2-foot-deep well is constructed on the lower end to catch the runoff.

Plant selection is one of the bog gardener's more important and enjoyable tasks. Most bogs, especially those devoted to native plants, are created initially to support a carnivorous plant collection representative of the southeastern United States. A diverse assemblage of variously colored pitcher plants, butterworts, sundews, and thread dews is very attractive and immensely interesting, even when flowers are absent. However, as most bog gardeners quickly learn, numerous additional wetland plants also do well in a bog garden. Several species of spider lilies (*Hymenocallis*) and orchids, especially species of *Habenaria* and *Calopogon*, perform well, as do yellow-eyed grass (*Xyris*), colicroot (*Aletris*), and American cranberry (*Vaccinium macrocarpon*). Some plants take so well to artificial bogs that they multiply rapidly and can become weedy. Diligent attention to the early removal of such plants will save time and aggravation later.

Southeastern Pitcher Plants

The southeastern United States is the center of distribution for several species of pitcher plants, the majority of which are endemic to the region. Favorites among gardeners include yellow trumpets (*Sarracenia flava*), Gulf coast purple and purple pitcher plant (*S. rosea, S. purpurea*), parrot pitcher plant (*S. psittacina*), redflower pitcher plant (*S. rubra*), hooded pitcher plant (*S. minor*), and white-topped pitcher plant (*S. leucophylla*). All are available for purchase. None should ever be removed from the wild.

Pitcher plants and other carnivorous plants for sale at Biophilia Nature Center near Elberta, Alabama.

Yellow trumpets are among the most popular bog garden pitcher plants.

Bog gardens are not maintenance free. In addition to what might sometimes feel like a relentless demand for water, healthy bog gardens can easily become weedy. Numerous annuals and some perennials may seed into the bog over the winter. Learning to distinguish weeds from desirable plants in late winter and early spring is challenging but essential for early detection and removal. Without diligent weeding, bog gardens can easily become overrun.

Watering cycles are also important. Bog gardens do not have to remain soggy, and overwatering is possible. Shallow bogs and those equipped with artificial drainage will need more water than deeper bogs or those without drain holes. Most carnivorous plants do well in only moderately wet soil once established, and their nutrition comes mostly from captured insects.

Finally, bog gardens do not last forever and must occasionally be rejuvenated. Most bogs need to be rebuilt every 4–5 years to prevent nutrient buildup. Rebuilding the bog essentially means starting over by first removing the plants, then removing and replacing all of the sand and peat, and finally replanting.

Where to See Bogs, Savannas, Carnivorous Plants, and Bog Gardens

Apalachicola National Forest
SR 379 and SR 65
Liberty County, FL
Maps can be obtained at National Forests in Florida, 325 John Knox Road, Suite F-100, Tallahassee, FL 32303, (850) 523-8500
Savannas with pitcher plants and other bog and savanna plants

Atlanta Botanical Garden
1345 Piedmont Ave. NE
Atlanta, GA 30309
(404) 876-5859
Raised bog gardens

Chattahoochee Nature Center
9135 Willeo Rd.
Roswell, GA 30075
(770) 992-2055
Inground bog gardens

Daniel Boone Native Gardens
651 Horn in the West Dr. (off US 421/321)
Boone, NC 28607
(828) 264-6390
Bog garden

continued

continued

DeSoto National Forest
U.S. Forest Service
P.O. Box 248
654 West Frontage Rd.
Wiggins, MS 39577
(601) 528-6160
Savannas with pitcher plants and other bog and savanna plants

Georgia Perimeter College Native Plant Garden
Decatur Campus
3251 Panthersville Rd.
Decatur, GA 30034
(678) 891-2668
Inground bog gardens

Lake Ramsay Preserve
The Nature Conservancy
Penn Mill Rd. off U.S. Hwy. 190
Covington, LA
(985) 809-1414
Savanna with pitcher plants and other bog and savanna plants

Meadowview Biological Research Station
8390 Fredericksburg Tnpk.
Woodford, VA 22580
(804) 633-4336
Private research facility; Visitors welcome, but call for appointment

State Botanical Garden of Georgia
2450 South Milledge Ave.
Athens, GA 30605
(706) 542-1244
Inground bog garden

University of North Carolina Botanical Garden
Mason Farm Rd. (off US 15/501 Bypass)
Chapel Hill, NC
(919) 962-0522
Raised bog gardens

II

Favorite Groups of Native Plants

5

Old-Timey Natives

That the use of native plants is not new to southern gardening is borne out by the numerous native species with long horticultural histories. Several native shrubs and trees have become sought-after ornamentals and have enjoyed extensive use across much of the southeastern United States. Some, such as southern magnolia (*Magnolia grandiflora*) and several species of rhododendron and native azaleas, are discussed fully in succeeding chapters and are not included here. The history and use of others, including the dogwoods, redbud, oakleaf hydrangea, sweetshrub, fringe tree, New Jersey tea, and cardinal flower, are detailed below. Many of these old-timey natives have been used for so long in southern landscapes that the question of nativity has seemingly lost its significance.

Native Plants Used in Colonial American Gardens

Scientific Name	Common Name	Form
Before 1700		
Acer rubrum	Red Maple	Tree
Asclepias syriaca	Common Milkweed	Perennial
Campsis radicans	Trumpet Creeper	Vine
Celtis occidentalis	Hackberry	Tree
Cercis canadensis	Redbud	Tree
Cornus amomum	Silky Dogwood	Shrub/Tree
Cornus florida	Flowering Dogwood	Tree
Gelsemium sempervirens	Carolina Jessamine	Vine
Hamamelis virginiana	Witch-Hazel	Tree/Shrub
Lindera benzoin	Spicebush	Tree/Shrub
Liquidambar styraciflua	Sweet Gum	Tree
Liriodendron tulipifera	Tulip Poplar	Tree
Lobelia cardinalis	Cardinal Flower	Perennial
Lonicera sempervirens	Coral Honeysuckle	Vine
Lupinus perennis	Sundial Lupine	Perennial
Magnolia virginiana	Sweetbay Magnolia	Tree
Monarda fistulosa	Wild Bergamot	Perennial
Myrica cerifera	Southern Wax Myrtle	Shrub
Parthenocissus quinquefolia	Virginia Creeper	Vine

continued

Scientific Name	Common Name	Form
Philadelphus coronarius	Mock Orange	Shrub
Platanus occidentalis	American Sycamore	Tree
Prunus americana	American Plum	Tree
Prunus virginiana	Choke Cherry	Tree/Shrub
Quercus alba	White Oak	Tree
Sanguinaria canadensis	Bloodroot	Perennial
Sassafras albidum	Sassafras	Tree

1700–1776

Scientific Name	Common Name	Form
Acer negundo	Box Elder	Tree
Acer saccharum	Sugar Maple	Tree
Aesculus pavia	Red Buckeye	Tree/Shrub
Amelanchier canadensis	Serviceberry	Tree
Amelanchier stolonifera	Serviceberry	Shrub
Amorpha fruticosa	Indigo-Bush	Shrub
Aquilegia canadensis	Wild Columbine	Perennial
Aralia spinosa	Devil's Walking Stick	Shrub
Aronia arbutifolia	Red Chokeberry	Shrub
Asimina triloba	Common Pawpaw	Tree
Baccharis halimifolia	Groundsel Tree	Shrub
Betula lenta	Sweet Birch	Tree
Betula nigra	River Birch	Tree
Bignonia capreolata	Crossvine	Vine
Callicarpa americana	American Beautyberry	Shrub
Calycanthus floridus	Sweetshrub	Shrub
Carpinus caroliniana	Ironwood	Tree
Carya ovata	Shagbark Hickory	Tree
Ceanothus americanus	New Jersey Tea	Shrub
Celastrus scandens	American Bittersweet	Vine
Cephalanthus occidentalis	Buttonbush	Shrub
Chelone glabra	White Turtlehead	Perennial
Chelone obliqua	Red Turtlehead	Perennial
Chionanthus virginicus	Fringe Tree	Tree/Shrub
Clematis virginiana	Virgin's Bower	Vine
Clethra alnifolia	Sweet Pepperbush	Shrub
Coreopsis lanceolata	Lance-Leaf Coreopsis	Perennial
Crataegus crus-galli	Cockspur Haw	Tree
Crataegus phaenopyrum	Washington Thorn	Tree
Cyrilla racemiflora	Titi	Shrub/Tree
Diospyros virginiana	Persimmon	Tree
Dirca palustris	Leatherwood	Shrub
Euonymus atropurpureus	Hearts-a-Bustin'	Shrub
Fagus grandifolia	American Beech	Tree
Fothergilla gardenii	Fothergilla	Shrub
Franklinia alatamaha	Franklinia	Shrub/Tree
Fraxinus americana	American Ash	Tree

Scientific Name	Common Name	Form
Galax urceolata	Galax	Perennial
Gleditsia triacanthos	Honey Locust	Tree
Gymnocladus dioica	Kentucky Coffee Tree	Tree
Halesia carolina	Silverbell	Tree
Hibiscus moscheutos	Eastern Rosemallow	Perennial
Hydrangea arborescens	Wild Hydrangea	Shrub
Ilex decidua	Possumhaw Holly	Tree/Shrub
Ilex glabra	Gallberry	Shrub
Ilex verticillata	Winterberry Holly	Shrub
Ilex vomitoria	Yaupon	Shrub/Tree
Itea virginica	Sweetspire	Shrub
Juglans cinerea	Butternut	Large Tree
Kalmia latifolia	Mountain Laurel	Shrub
Leucothoe axillaris	Coastal Doghobble	Shrub
Leucothoe racemosa	Coastal Fetterbush	Shrub
Magnolia grandiflora	Southern Magnolia	Large Tree
Magnolia tripetala	Umbrella Magnolia	Tree
Malus angustifolia	Southern Crabapple	Tree
Mertensia virginica	Virginia Bluebells	Perennial
Monarda didyma	Beebalm	Perennial
Morus rubra	Red Mulberry	Tree
Nyssa sylvatica	Black Tupelo	Large Tree
Ostrya virginiana	Eastern Hophornbeam	Tree
Oxydendrum arboreum	Sourwood	Large Tree
Persea borbonia	Red Bay	Tree
Phlox carolina	Phlox	Perennial
Prunus caroliniana	Carolina Cherry Laurel	Tree
Ptelea trifoliata	Hoptree	Shrub/Tree
Quercus falcata	Southern Red Oak	Large Tree
Quercus marilandica	Blackjack Oak	Tree
Quercus montana	Chestnut Oak	Large Tree
Quercus nigra	Water Oak	Large Tree
Quercus phellos	Willow Oak	Large Tree
Quercus velutina	Black Oak	Large Tree
Quercus virginiana	Live Oak	Large Tree
Rhododendron calendulaceum	Flame Azalea	Shrub
Rhododendron maximum	Great Laurel	Shrub
Rhododendron viscosum	Swamp Azalea	Shrub
Rosa palustris	Swamp Rose	Perennial
Rudbeckia hirta	Black-Eyed Susan	Perennial
Sambucus canadensis	Elderberry	Shrub
Saururus cernuus	Lizard's Tail	Perennial
Stewartia malacodendron	Silky Camellia	Shrub/Tree
Stewartia ovata	Mountain Stewartia	Shrub/Tree
Stokesia laevis	Stokes' Aster	Perennial
Taxodium distichum	Baldcypress	Large Tree

continued

Scientific Name	Common Name	Form
Tiarella cordifolia	Foamflower	Perennial
Tilia americana	Basswood	Large Tree
Ulmus alata	Winged Elm	Large Tree
Ulmus americana	American Elm	Large Tree
Viburnum acerifolium	Mapleleaf Viburnum	Shrub
Viburnum dentatum	Arrowwood	Shrub

Source: Adapted from Rudy J. Favretti and Gordon P. DeWolf Jr. 1971. Colonial garden plants. Arnoldia 31(4): 172–249.

Redbud in spring.

Redbud

Springtime in many southern cities is demarcated by showy street sides bordered with exuberantly floriferous redbuds and dogwoods. When fully decorated with their complementary magenta and creamy white flowers, these two widely divergent species— one a bean, the other related to the tupelos—create an unparalleled demonstration that excites the senses and heralds winter's end.

Redbud flowers.

Redbud pods. Courtesy of Ron Lance.

The redbud (*Cercis canadensis*) is typically the first of these two species to flower, often putting on blossoms as early as February, well ahead of leaf emergence. Despite its name, the flowers of redbud are more nearly magenta or rose pink than red and in outline show a profile similar to many leguminous flowers. Close examination reveals a somewhat butterfly-like shape with an upright central petal inserted within two spreading, winglike petals, all of which are positioned above two lower petals that are often folded together to look like the bow of a boat. The showy petals vary in color intensity from tree to tree and flower to flower, as well as within the parts of a single bloom. Flowers are small, are borne in profusion on new and old wood, and transform bare branches into a breathtaking show of color that is only the first of two of this tree's charming developmental stages. Spring flowers give way in summer to conspicuous clusters of dangling, flattened, several-seeded pods that turn purplish red at maturity and remain on the plant well into the fall. Gentle fall breezes often rattle the pendent pods, giving heavily fruited specimens a shimmering countenance.

Redbud is also sometimes called Judas tree, a name that is historically more often associated with the Mediterranean relative *C. siliquastrum* than with its American counterpart. The name derives from a legend that redbud is the tree on which Judas Iscariot hanged himself after betraying Christ. According to the myth, the flowers were originally white but changed to red due to shame and to staining by the blood of the Lord. Although this name is sometimes seen in American literature, it is not in common use. The name *redbud* has been used in gardening parlance since at least colonial times, and the tree was referred to as such by both George Washington and Thomas Jefferson, each of whom maintained extensive gardens and arboreta that likely included redbud in their plantings. The redbud was probably first cultivated in the early 1600s, testimony to its long popularity.

Redbud's eastern distribution extends as far north as Wisconsin, Michigan, New York, and Massachusetts, but the species is more common and reaches its best form from about Pennsylvania southward to Louisiana and central Florida. Its popularity

Redbud 'Floating Clouds.'

with gardeners is underscored by more than a dozen selections and cultivars, including several white-flowered forms—'Alba,' 'Dwarf White,' and 'Royal White'—as well as the variegated 'Floating Clouds.'

Redbuds are not tall trees. The crown spread is often about as wide as the tree is high. Trees in excess of 35 feet are considered very tall for the species and although the Florida champion redbud, measured in the middle 1990s, was nearly 70 feet tall, the height of cultivated trees is typically less than 25 feet. The relatively short, straight trunk divides into branches low enough to produce a broad, rounded crown but high enough to walk under, making redbud perfect for lawns, roadsides, and sidewalks. Mature trees often develop gnarly trunks with attractive scaly bark.

Provenance is especially important in selecting redbuds for the garden. *Cercis canadensis* is widely available in the nursery trade and is sold in a variety of outlets ranging from small specialty nurseries to large garden centers and home stores. Trees grown in Florida or the Deep South are likely to succumb to zone 6 winters, and northern trees are not likely to tolerate the intense heat and humidity of southern climes. The origin of trees sold by large retailers who buy in bulk may not be well documented, and the plants may be inappropriate for some locations. For long-term success it is best to determine the geographic origin of a tree before purchasing it.

Dogwoods

Flowering dogwood (*Cornus florida*) typically puts on blossoms a little later than redbud, but the flowering periods of the two often overlap in early spring. Gardens, lawns, and neighborhood streets that feature these species in mixed plantings can be astonishing. *Cornus florida* has been extensively cultivated in the United States since at least the early 1700s.

Dogwoods are best known for their exquisite creamy white flowers that display a deceiving morphological structure. What are often taken for large white petals are actually leaflike bracts that subtend a compact rounded head of tiny yellow to yellowish green, tubular, 4-petaled flowers. It is more appropriate to refer to this species' flowers as white-bracted than white-petaled.

Flowering dogwood.

Flowers of
flowering dogwood.

In summer and fall the tightly packed flowering clusters give way to an attractive collection of conspicuous, glossy red, hairless drupes, each of which is the product of a single flower. The fruits are relished by songbirds and provide an excellent food source for a variety of mammals from squirrels, rabbits, and raccoons to chipmunks and white-tailed deer. They also provide excellent ornamentation to the fall garden.

Next year's blossoms overwinter as conspicuous rounded buds at the tips of the branches, tightly enclosed by the latent bracts that will be the basis of the next spring's show. These attractive buds protect the developing flowers, ensure winter interest for the gardener, and serve as a useful guide for winter identification.

Similar to the redbud, provenance is also very important when selecting flowering dogwoods for the garden. Although the species is generally rated for zones 5–9, 9–5, the performance of a particular individual is highly dependent upon the source of its seeds. Progeny of coastal plains and Deep South plants are much less hardy or cold adapted than those from farther north, and cold climate plants are often intolerant of the heat and humidity of USDA zones 8 and 9.

In stature, flowering dogwood is a relatively short understory tree of well-drained woods and is distributed naturally throughout most of the southeast from the coastal plains to the mountains. Typical individuals do not exceed 30 feet in height but can have a broad crown. None of the three national champions is over 36 feet tall, but their spreads range from 36 to 42 feet. Open-grown cultivated trees produce low, laterally spreading branches and broader crowns that make them very decorative. The attractive bark is divided into small, blocky, dark gray to nearly black plates that are first evident on relatively young trees but become even more striking with age. The leaves are yellowish green in summer, more or less broadly elliptic to egg-shaped in outline, with a tapering point and attractively arcing lateral veins whose tips follow the curvature of the leaf margin. The leaves are borne two at a node, opposite one another along the branch. Fall color is generally good with at least some leaves turning a pleasing purplish red with

Flowering dogwood fruit.

Flowering dogwood bud.

the change of season, especially in cooler climates. When laterally creased and torn in half, the internal veins of fresh leaves exude strands of stringy latex that are easily visible as the leaf halves are slowly pulled apart.

Flowering dogwood is a shallowly rooted tree that cannot tolerate much disturbance within the circumference of the crown's drip line. Trees should be positioned a little high in the planting hole to encourage drainage and rapid root spread and should be mulched heavily—without piling mulch against the trunk—to keep the roots cool. Deep mulch is especially important in sunny locations or where foot traffic encroaches on the root zone. Weeds that appear within the mulch should be hand pulled rather than treated with herbicide in order to prevent damage to surface roots. The planting site should allow for at least part sun to encourage dense foliage and better flowering. The combination of sunny crown and shaded roots is optimal.

Even with care, flowering dogwood is subject to several problems and is usually not long-lived. Trees in excess of 50 years are considered old, and young trees seem to die at rates that exceed those of other species. In a study of tree loss in Baltimore, Maryland, flowering dogwood had an annual mortality rate of over 13 percent and ranked high among native trees predisposed to early transience.

One problem in cooler climes is the disease dogwood anthracnose (*Discula destructiva*), a fungus that was first described about 1980. Infected trees show tan and purplish-

Flowers of flowering dogwood.

ringed leaf spots, may develop adventitious branches along the trunk, and often suffer dieback of major branches. Dead leaves that hang onto trees for an extended period are an indication of infection. The fungus can kill diseased trees in less than three years and has resulted in the loss of numerous plants in the wild, especially in the north. In the southeast, dieback has been limited mostly to mountain populations. Southern trees in dense understory, especially at higher, cooler elevations, are most affected. The cultivar 'Appalachian Spring,' which has slightly larger than normal leaves, is specifically selected for resistance to dogwood anthracnose and may be a suitable choice for zones 6B–7A. The fungus is apparently unable to survive the typical heat of coastal plains and lower Piedmont landscapes. Even in disease-prone areas, healthy, well-cared-for, open-grown trees that get plenty of sun and air movement typically avoid infection. Well-situated healthy trees are also less susceptible to the several borers that attack dogwood and are also better able to withstand the Deep South's increasingly warmer and drier climate.

Despite its short-lived nature and modest tendency for disease, flowering dogwood is the source of at least a hundred varieties and cultivars. Most selections accentuate differences in flower color and size, variations in leaf color and morphology, or increased hardiness. Production of pink or pinkish-tinged bracts is a special preference. Pink-flowered forms, many of which originated from the putative variety *rubra* (meaning "red"), are usually neither as hardy nor as heat tolerant as some of the white-flowered forms, and they are usually not as vigorous. Better pink-flowered selections include 'Cherokee Chief,' 'Cherokee Sunset,' 'Purple Glory,' 'Red Cloud,' and the shrubby 'Red Pygmy,' which flowers profusely even at very early ages. Of the white-flowered forms, 'Weaver's White,' which originated from seeds collected in northern Florida, is excellent for Deep South gardens. It is particularly floriferous and produces among the largest and showiest bracts of any of the currently available cultivars.

The dogwood family (Cornaceae)—within which some authorities also include the tupelo trees (*Nyssa* spp.)—is represented by at least seven species in the eight states within the geography of this book; nine if Maryland and West Virginia are included. Although none of these is as popular as *C. florida*, several have found their way into

Flowering dogwood 'Weaver's White.'

Flowering dogwood var. *rubra*.

mmon Name(s)	Latin Name	Eastern Range	Form	Hardiness Zones
goda Dogwood, Alternate-aved Dogwood	*Cornus alternifolia*	Newfoundland, MN; south to AL, FL, MS	Shrub, Small Tree	3–7
ky Dogwood, Swamp ogwood	*Cornus amomum*	NY, MA; west to IN; south to GA, MS	Large Shrub	4–8
stern Rough-Leaf ogwood	*Cornus asperifolia*	Se. NC; south to FL; west to s. AL	Shrub, Small Tree	4–9
nchberry	*Cornus canadensis*	Greenland; west to AK; south to NJ, VA, WV	Dwarf Shrub	2–6
ugh-Leaf Dogwood	*Cornus drummondii*	NY, Ontario, SD; south to e. TN, nw. GA, LA, TX	Shrub, Small Tree	5–8
wering Dogwood	*Cornus florida*	ME; west to MI; south to FL, ne. Mexico	Small Tree	5–9
vamp Dogwood, Stiff ogwood, Cornel	*Cornus foemina*	NJ; west to MO; south to e. TX, LA, n. FL	Small Tree, Shrub	6–9
ay Dogwood	*Cornus racemosa*	ME, s. Quebec; west to s. Manitoba; south to VA, n. NC, s. IL, MO	Shrub	3–8
und-Leaf Dogwood	*Cornus rugosa*	Quebec to Manitoba; south to NJ, PA, w. VA, OH, IN, IL	Shrub	4
d Osier	*Cornus sericea*	ME; west to MN; south to KY, VA	Shrub	2–7

horticulture and are regularly used across much of the region. None of our other eastern native dogwoods produces equivalently large bracts as those of flowering dogwood. Instead, their flowers are borne in showy flat-topped clusters of numerous tiny white flowers that give way to purplish, bluish, or blackish fruit at maturity, depending upon the species.

Silky dogwood (*C. amomum*) is a large, spreading deciduous shrub that commonly grows in wetlands along the edges of lakes and streams from about New York and Indiana south to Mississippi, Georgia, and the central portions of the Florida panhandle. It is best used in zones 5–8, 8–5. Typical plants grow to about ten feet tall and wide and can become somewhat scraggly, which has led some dogwood connoisseurs to question the use of this plant anywhere but in naturalistic plantings. Despite its informal habit, its numerous clusters of creamy white flowers can brighten a sunny shrub border or the edges of a pond, and full-grown plants serve well in summer hedges along partially sunny property lines.

Stiff cornel dogwood (*C. foemina*), also sometimes called swamp dogwood, is similar in habit and habitat to silky dogwood but has shinier leaves. Eastern rough-leaf dogwood (*C. asperifolia*) is also similar, but the upper surfaces of its leaves are rough to the

Silky dogwood.   Stiff cornel dogwood.

touch, like sandpaper, and it occurs in moist, well-drained uplands, often in association with limestone. All three of these latter species are variously available in the trade but may require persistence to obtain. Nearly Native Nursery, Mail Order Natives, Woodlanders, and several members of the Association of Florida Native Nurseries (accessible through the AFNN Web site) are among the more likely sources.

Pagoda or alternate-leaved dogwood (*C. alternifolia*) differs from all of our other dogwoods by bearing alternate rather than opposite leaves. This is a zone 3–8 plant that occurs naturally as far south as a few locations in the Florida panhandle, but it is much better known in the mountains and Piedmont and is more often available in the trade in the upper Midwest. Its foliage is similar in shape and appearance to that of flowering dogwood, but it produces flat-topped cymes of small, creamy white flowers, unlike the large-bracted flowers of *C. florida*. Nevertheless, it is an outstanding shrub with layered branches, multiple stems, and a spreading form. The rounded fruit changes from green to red to black during maturation and will hang on the tree into fall, but only if the birds don't find them. Retail and wholesale vendors of pagoda dogwood in the southeast are not easy to find. Meadowbrook Nursery offers this species online to retail customers, and Carolina Native Nursery in Burnsville, North Carolina, is a source for wholesale buyers.

Eastern rough-leaf dogwood.   Pagoda dogwood. Courtesy of Ron Lance.

Oakleaf Hydrangea

Oakleaf hydrangea (*Hygrangea quercifolia*) is a coarse deciduous shrub with four-season appeal. In late spring it puts on huge flowering panicles with numerous branches. Each branch bears along its axis several clusters of tiny, creamy white, fragrant fertile flowers and is terminated by a single, showy sterile flower. The sterile flowers are fitted with four much-enlarged sepals that spread laterally into a flattened cluster reminiscent of a 4-leaf clover. Flowers appear in late spring and persist into summer and early fall, with the exaggerated sepals turning from white to creamy, pinkish, burgundy, and finally golden brown as the season progresses.

New leaves are up to about eight inches long and are pale green at first but become darker with age. The leaf margins have 3–7 large, coarsely and handsomely toothed lobes. The veins on the upper leaf surfaces are deeply and conspicuously impressed and very attractive. Fall leaf color changes from green to burgundy or almost purple, and old leaves hang onto the branches for an extended period—often well into November or even December—before falling to expose the attractive form and scaly, flaking bark that characterize the naked winter stems.

Gardeners have planted oakleaf hydrangea since at least 1800, not long after William Bartram discovered the plant near Georgia's Ocmulgee River. In his wide-ranging 1791 chronicle of explorations, Bartram says of his discovery: "I observed here a very singular and beautiful shrub, which I suppose is a species of Hydrangea (*H. quercifolia*). It grows in coppices and clumps near or on the banks of rivers and creeks; many stems usually arise from a root, spreading itself greatly on all sides by suckers and offshoots."

Oakleaf hydrangea.

Oakleaf hydrangea flowers.

Of his chosen name, *quercifolia*, which means "with foliage like an oak," Bartram says: "the leaves which clothe the plants are very large, pinnatifid or palmated, and serrated or toothed, very much resembling the leaves of some of our Oaks; they sit opposite, supported by slender petioles, and are of a fine, full green colour."

In nature and the garden, oakleaf hydrangea performs best in shade or at least semi-shade. This is especially true for Deep South and coastal plains gardens, but it is also an important consideration for lower Piedmont gardens. Plants will survive and even flower well in sunny sites, but drought can leave the foliage chlorotic. Plants situated in dry, sunny sites typically require supplemental irrigation for best foliage and growth.

Oakleaf hydrangea adapts to a variety of soils. Natural occurrences in association with limestone suggest a preference for neutral to slightly basic soils, but it also grows well in rich, slightly acidic or even sandy soils, especially if amended with dolomitic

Oakleaf hydrangea.

Oakleaf hydrangea.

lime. It is rated for zones 5–9, 9–1, and is essentially a coastal plains and Piedmont species.

Some experts suggest that oakleaf hydrangea is too large and coarse for most residential landscapes, especially where space is restricted. While this may be true in extreme cases, I have seen it used very effectively along the edges or in the corners of ⅓–½-acre suburban lots. Well-tended plants often become large—up to eight feet tall and easily as wide—and can also spread by root suckers, both of which are eventualities that may require periodic pruning and control. Even though the dramatic year-round effect of this outstanding native shrub easily justifies the limited labor, those who prefer a smaller version may want to acquire the selection 'Pee Wee.' It is usually less than four feet high and wide, produces numerous sterile flowers, and is a good option for smaller spaces.

Many selections of oakleaf hydrangea are available in the trade, most of which favor larger or double-flowered inflorescences, more colorful sterile sepals, or richer fall leaf color. 'Snowflake' is particularly popular in the Piedmont and inner coastal plains. As its name suggests, it produces an increased number of bright white sterile flowers that are sometimes borne in such profusion and close proximity that the flowers appear to be doubled. The flowering panicles of 'Snowflake' and several other bright white selections are sometimes so large and heavy that their weight overpowers the subtending branches, causing fully flowered stems to droop and sag. Large branches sometimes bend all the way to ground level following heavy rains. Michael Dirr's selection 'Amethyst' is a smaller plant that also produces bright white sterile flowers, but with sepals that turn wine red at maturity. Dirr's selections 'Alice' and 'Alison' tout better fall color, as does Flowerwood Nursery's 'Dayspring.' All of these selections are readily available.

Smooth hydrangea (*H. arborescens*)—sometimes also called wild hydrangea—and the closely related ashy hydrangea (*H. cinerea*) are related to oakleaf hydrangea but are smaller in stature and generally more northerly in distribution. These species were

Oakleaf hydrangea 'Snowflake.'

Oakleaf hydrangea 'Snowflake.'

Oakleaf hydrangea 'Pee Wee.'   Oakleaf hydrangea 'Amethyst.'

once believed to be varieties of a single variable species and were both referred to as *H. arborescens*. Most experts today consider them to be distinct. Both are common in nature only at higher elevations and in cooler climes, smooth hydrangea from New York to Missouri and southward to Georgia and the Carolinas, and ashy hydrangea from

Smooth hydrangea.   Ashy hydrangea.

Ashy hydrangea.

Missouri and Indiana southward to South Carolina, Alabama, and Arkansas. Smooth hydrangea also occurs in the coastal plains, but its distribution there is rare and spotty and known mostly from two small populations in the Florida panhandle and westward to Alabama, Mississippi, and eastern Louisiana's Florida parishes. Smooth hydrangea, the more commonly seen garden species in our region, is more cold tolerant and less heat resistant than oakleaf hydrangea. Although it is generally recommended for zones 4–9, 9–1, the zone 9 suggestion may exceed optimal conditions and require that plants be sited in shaded gardens and mulched to keep the roots cool.

Most garden specimens of these species are less than 5 feet tall and broad. However, like other members of the genus, established plants produce numerous root suckers that allow a single individual to eventually colonize a large area. The flowers are similar in form to those of oakleaf hydrangea but have smaller (or sometimes nonexistent) sterile sepals and are borne in flat-topped compound cymes rather than pyramidal panicles. The leaves are dark green above, toothed, up to about eight inches long, and more or less heart- or egg-shaped in outline. The leaves of ashy hydrangea are grayish white beneath, hence the common name.

Smooth hydrangea is an excellent garden shrub for borders and naturalistic settings. Typical seed-grown plants produce relatively compact inflorescences composed mostly of the smaller, fertile flowers and have a look reminiscent of Queen Anne's lace. Hence, most cultivars have been selected for an increased quantity of sterile flowers, denser cymes, and a less delicate look. 'Annabelle', 'Grandiflora', and 'Bounty' are three of the best of the predominately sterile-flowered selections. At least the first two of these are commonly available in the trade. Hydrangea enthusiasts will want to visit the Web site of Wilkerson Mill Gardens (www.hydrangea.com) for these and other selections.

Sweetshrub

Sweetshrub, or Carolina allspice (*Calycanthus floridus*), was introduced to horticulture in 1726, even earlier than the flowering dogwood and oakleaf hydrangea, and has long been a favorite in southern gardens. It is widely planted across the south for its dull, brick red flowers, dark green foliage, and aromatic presence. The species ranges widely across the eastern United States, primarily from Virginia to Mississippi, but with a few locations reported as far north as New York and as far west as easternmost Louisiana. Its distribution is more often associated with the Piedmont and mountains than the coastal plains, but it is not uncommon in westernmost Florida and southern Alabama. There are two varieties. The twigs, leafstalks, and leaf undersurfaces are hairy in variety *floridus* but lack hairs in variety *glaucus*.

The primitive, complicated, and aromatic flowers top the list of sweetshrub's most important garden attributes. The genus *Calycanthus* is classified as part of the botanical order Laurales, a group of plants that may be only one evolutionary step removed from the even more primitive magnolias. Like the magnolias, sweetshrub flowers have undifferentiated petals and sepals, referred to by most botanists and horticulturists as tepals, and numerous stamens and pistils. (The Greek name *Calycanthus* means "sepalous flower" and derives from the close similarity of its showy but difficult-to-distinguish flower parts.) Unlike magnolias, sweetshrub tepals are strap-shaped and are produced at the tip of a cup-shaped floral tube that bears the stout stamens just inside of its inner rim.

Flowers appear in late spring and early summer and can be extremely fragrant with an enticing fruity bouquet that has been variously described as citrus- or banana-like. Not all plants are equally aromatic, and the flowers of some individuals, apparently including an especially large number of those grown from wild collected seed, give off no scent at all. Ensuring the fragrance of plants selected for the garden means either purchasing plants while they are flowering, or searching out cultivars of known aroma. 'Michael Lindsey,' 'Alease,' and 'Urbana' are among the more reliably scented selections.

Sweetshrub.

Sweetshrub.

Sweetshrub 'Athens.'

The tepals of typical sweetshrub flowers are brownish red or purplish red, but yellow-flowered forms are also available. 'Athens' (also sometimes labeled 'Katherine') is the more often cultivated and more commonly available of the yellow-flowered selections. It is also revered for its outstanding fragrance. Azalea expert Clarence Towe's selection 'Towe' also produces yellow flowers, but it lacks the intense 'Athens' fragrance. 'Athens' is generally recommended for zones 5–9, 9–1, but it may do less well in USDA zone 9's heat and humidity if not protected with shade. Both red- and yellow-flowered forms can be seen growing together at the State Botanical Garden of Georgia, just outside the city limits of Athens.

Sweetshrub typically grows as a large, colonizing shrub. Mature plants are usually 6–7 feet tall and less than nine feet wide but can produce numerous wide-ranging root suckers. Left unchecked, suckering plants can spread rapidly and cover an expansive area. One large colony along the hiking trails at Three Rivers State Park in the Florida panhandle began as only a handful of plants but now stretches along the trail for several hundred feet. Typical garden plants begin putting up new stems in as little as a year after planting, especially if properly sited, and can easily form a small, multistemmed colony in less than five years.

Crushed foliage gives off a pleasing spicy fragrance and can be used as a short-lived indoor potpourri. Flowering branches are also sometimes brought indoors for their fragrance. Once established in the garden, sweetshrub is virtually indestructible.

Fringe Tree

If uniqueness in common names correlates with long cultural association, then fringe tree (*Chionanthus virginicus*) must certainly be an old-timey native. Other common names include white fringe tree, old-man's-beard, granddaddy graybeard, and grancy gray-beard—highly descriptive monikers that could only have been bestowed by observant plant lovers. The species has been used in landscaping since at least the early 1700s, was probably grown by George Washington at Mount Vernon, and has long been a staple in southern lawns. It is recommended for zones 4–9, 9–1.

All of fringe tree's common names as well as its scientific name derive from its unique, creamy white flowers. Blossoms are individually small—the four strap-shaped petals average about ⅛ inch wide and one inch long—but are borne in conspicuous, loosely arranged clusters that dangle gracefully from last year's twigs. Flowers typically appear in mid to late spring as the new leaves emerge and can literally engulf the tree in blossoms. Common names reflect the grayish, bearded countenance of trees in full bloom, and the scientific name, which is Greek for "snow flower," underscores the flower's bright, delicate form. Fringe tree's pendulous, multiflowered panicles create a

Fringe tree with native azaleas.

Fringe tree flowers.

Fringe tree's olivelike fruit.

floral effect that demands attention and presents a beauty that is unparalleled among native southern trees.

This is a mostly monoecious species. Individual plants typically bear unisexual flowers that are either functionally male or functionally female, although some trees may also have a few bisexual, or perfect, flowers. Male flowers are typically larger and showier than female flowers but do not develop the female's attractive panicles of olivelike drupes. Given this species' small size and slow growth rate, there is probably room for at least one or two trees in most gardens.

In form, fringe tree is a large shrub or small deciduous tree that does not often exceed about twenty-five feet tall. It is rather nondescript for much of the year and often goes unnoticed in natural landscapes, even where it occurs in abundance. The leaves are elliptical, up to about eight inches long and four inches wide, and are borne in opposite pairs along the branch. The foliage changes in fall from medium green to an attractive dingy yellow but is usually not heralded for intense autumn color.

The combination of its rather commonplace form and annual springtime surprise makes fringe tree an excellent choice for shrub borders and sunny naturalistic woodlands. It blooms when very young—only 2–3 feet tall—and becomes densely foliaged when grown in a sunny opening. Although it is often set off as a specimen plant in an open setting, it may be at its best in combination with other plants. The abundance of spring flowers will light up a dreary edge of winter greenery and it is particularly stunning when mixed with spring-flowering native azaleas.

Fringe tree is not for impatient gardeners. It is slow to germinate from seed and grows slowly once in the ground. Young trees may take several years to reach a respectable six feet in height, but they are typically tough, trouble-free plants once established. They may require irrigation for the first year or two, especially if sited in open sun, but are surprisingly drought tolerant. Poorly tended street-side plantings in open sun underscore the species' successful adaptation.

Pygmy or dwarf fringe tree (*C. pygmaeus*) is a smaller cousin that occurs naturally in only a few counties along the central spine of peninsular Florida. It is listed as an endangered species by both the United States and Florida governments and is not common in nature or in the nursery trade. It has been successfully sold by both Woodlanders and The Natives. Although it is suggested for zones 6–9 by Woodlanders, its endangered status prevents its being sold across state lines and renders it difficult to purchase.

The non-native Chinese fringe tree (*C. retusus*) has found recent favor in many gardens and may be encountered in garden centers. Its flower petals are somewhat brighter than the native species, making flowering specimens very attractive. Chinese fringe tree tends to have darker foliage and a more ornamental shape than the American species; its increasing popularity in manicured landscapes is easy to understand.

Pygmy fringe tree.

Cardinal Flower

When Thomas Jefferson planted his 1807 oval bed of cardinal flower (*Lobelia cardinalis*), he surely must have known that the plant grew wild along the streams at the bottom of his beloved Monticello Mountain. Nevertheless, according to Peter Hatch, in *Thomas Jefferson's Flower Garden at Monticello*, Jefferson obtained the seeds for his new addition not from local sources but from Philadelphia's Bernard McMahon, the well-known colonial gardener and author in 1806 of *The American Gardener's Calendar*. McMahon was an early advocate of native wildflowers in manicured gardens and gently admonished his readers to search nearby fields and forests for "the various beautiful ornaments with which nature has so profusely decorated them." He also questioned whether plants should be rejected for the garden simply because they are indigenous. Jefferson's emphatic answer to McMahon's query was to adorn his personal garden with a variety of delightful natives that included not only cardinal flower but also such modern favorites as wild columbine, Virginia bluebell, Turk's-cap lily, mayapple, atamasco lily, and blue-eyed grass.

That cardinal flower was one of Jefferson's favored species should not be surprising. It is a short-lived native perennial that has become a sought-after and readily available ornamental. It takes its name from the tall upright terminal racemes that are decorated with showy, bright red flowers. In its southernmost locations, especially along spring runs and clear-water streams, plants can grow six feet tall with a thickened, fleshy stalk that can be at least one inch in diameter. The larger leaves (up to about seven inches long and two inches wide) are at the base of the plant, with smaller leaves farther up the stem and passing into the inflorescence. Individual flowers are up to about 1½ inches long, tubular at the base and flaring at the tip into showy, red, deeply divided lip petals. The two-parted upright petal is erect and smaller; the lower petal is deeply three parted, drooping, and extremely showy. The flower's crimson to vermilion color, which gives the plant its common name, is unparalleled among our native garden wildflowers and underscores cardinal flower's popularity.

Cardinal flower is a wetland species that is found in nature along wet stream banks as well as in soggy floodplains and bogs across much of the eastern and southwestern United States. It adapts to shady moist sites or wet sunny sites in the garden but cannot tolerate both dry and sunny. Performance is best in shadier sites. Garden-grown plants are

Cardinal flower.

shorter, more robust, and often appear healthier than ones that grow in nature. Plants overwinter as small, ground-hugging rosettes of basal leaves, undergo stem elongation in late spring, and put on flowers from summer to early fall. The leaves of well-situated plants are dark green whereas the foliage of less well-placed plants can become splotchy, lighter in color, and chlorotic, especially in drier, sunny locations. Cardinal flower cannot tolerate heavy mulching, especially while in the rosette stage, and plants should be cleared of debris periodically throughout the winter and early spring. Marking or otherwise remembering cardinal flower locations in your garden is probably a good idea.

It is also probably wise to follow Jefferson's lead and plant cardinal flower in groups rather than as individual plants. Grouped plantings are more attractive and help ensure a continuing presence in the garden. Cardinal flower can be somewhat short-lived, and gardeners often report its disappearance in 2–3 years following planting. This loss may be largely due to the moist rather than wet conditions of most gardens but can be remedied by annually harvesting and planting garden-produced seeds.

Veteran wildflower propagator Jan Midgley, writing in her *Native Plant Propagation* handbook, suggests that most species of *Lobelia* germinate easily and in relatively large percentages. Midgley recommends collecting the seeds in early fall when the capsules are tan and papery, storing them dry at 40°, and sowing them either in the greenhouse in January or February or outside in March. Since the seeds are very small and can be difficult to keep up with, Harry Phillips (*Growing and Propagating Wildflowers*) recommends snipping entire stalks of mature capsules, storing and drying them for a few days in a paper bag, then shaking the bag vigorously and collecting the loosened seeds that fall to the bottom.

New Jersey Tea

The list of Jefferson's native woody plants is even more impressive than that of his perennials. A number of today's important native shrubs graced Monticello's planted and natural landscapes. One of the more memorable is New Jersey tea (*Ceanothus ameri-*

New Jersey tea.

New Jersey tea.

canus), whose history is intimately entwined with Native American heritage as well as with the earliest days of American independence.

Like many early American garden plants, New Jersey tea was initially valued more for it practical utility and political overtones than its ornamental prowess. Beginning with the English-engineered tea embargo—King George's hard-nosed retaliation for the Boston Tea Party and Greenwich, New Jersey, Tea Burning—and continuing throughout the Revolutionary War, the leaves of New Jersey (and probably other easy-to-find indigenous species) were used as worthy substitutes for European-controlled East Indian brews. What started as a stern lesson to the presumably wayward colonists likely catapulted our native *Ceanothus americanus* into prominence at the same time it was fueling America's resolve.

By the time Jefferson introduced New Jersey tea to his Monticello garden in the early 1800s, its use as a tea substitute may have been mostly surpassed by its ornamental qualities. It has now become a time-tested garden staple with wide uses in manicured landscapes.

New Jersey tea is a low-growing, more or less rounded shrub with opposite leaves and showy clusters of tiny white flowers. Mature plants are 2–5 feet tall and wide with dense foliage. The leaves are about three inches long and two inches wide, more or less triangular with toothed margins, and with the conspicuous venation typical of the buckthorn (Rhamnaceae) family. The flowers appear in early to midsummer and are borne in numerous showy, rounded two-inch clusters at the tips of the branches. Well-situated plants often flower profusely.

Although its common name suggests otherwise, New Jersey tea has a wide-ranging distribution from Maine to Florida and west to Nebraska and Texas. It is drought tolerant and fire adapted and grows in a variety of natural habitats from sandhills and dry woodlands to rocky openings and woodland margins, and it is as equally adaptable in the garden as it is in nature. Although it performs well in partly shady garden soils, it is at its best in harsh, dry, sandy conditions in full sun and is especially appropriate for longleaf pine–sandhill habitat theme gardens. New Jersey tea is also an excellent addition to the butterfly garden and is a recognized larval food plant for dusky-wing and azure butterflies.

Like many xeric plants, New Jersey tea produces a mass of thick, twisted, deep-seated roots and is very difficult to transplant from the wild. It should never be dug from natural areas. Mature plants may not survive removal, even if transplanted as part of organized plant rescues, making it best propagated from seed or summer-collected cuttings.

6

Challenge Plants

Native plants are often touted as no-fuss ornamentals that are easy to establish, easy to grow, and require little continuing care. This is certainly true for some species, especially the more popular and widely marketed shrubs and perennials. Most, however, require at least an average amount of garden care, and several are so challenging to grow that they test the skills of even the most patient and accomplished gardener. Included in this list of challenge plants are three species of native camellias, the wetland-loving Georgia fever tree (*Pinckneya bracteata*), and the Peach State's infamous Georgia plume. Although this book focuses primarily on "good doers"—plants that perform well in the garden with only reasonable care—the outstanding ornamental value of these important southern specialties makes growing any of them a challenge worth mastering.

Native Camellias: *Stewartia* and *Franklinia*

Four species of native camellias occur in North America, all of which are restricted in distribution to the southeastern United States. All have showy flowers characteristic of the camellia family, but only the evergreen loblolly bay (*Gordonia lasianthus*) has proven relatively easy to grow. Our two species of native *Stewartia* and one species of *Franklinia* are somewhat finicky species that can be difficult to establish and maintain.

The camellia family (Theaceae) is probably best known in this country for the genus *Camellia*, a group of mostly Asian plants with long horticultural histories. The Asian camellias grown in North America are excellent garden plants, most valued for their wintergreen foliage, easy cultivation (at least for some selections), and attractive flowers. Like their Asian azalea counterparts, they are not invasive and do not stray beyond where they are planted. About 3,000 cultivars are available, including about 2,000 of the popular *C. japonica*, more than 300 of *C. sasanqua*, and numerous double-flowered selections of *C. reticulata*. Camellias produce flowers from early spring to late fall, depending upon species, but are probably more often cherished in southern landscapes for the touch of color that signals winter's end. All other factors aside, a camellia's flowers are by far its best-loved attribute.

Our two native stewartias are no exception. Both are stunning plants, considered by many to be among the most beautiful of our native flowering trees and shrubs. Both are deciduous species that in early spring put on soft, yellow-green foliage that expands laterally along slender horizontal branches. In May and June the spreading branches

Silky camellia.

Silky camellia.

Silky camellia.

Silky camellia.

are transformed into arresting sprays of pure white flowers, each of which has a central mass of dark purple to white or yellowish stamens surrounded by five pure white, crinkly edged petals. On mature plants in optimum conditions, seemingly every leaf node supports a flower.

Silky camellia (*Stewartia malacodendron*) is primarily a coastal plains species, distributed from Virginia to Texas and performing best in zones 7–9, 9–8. Its form is that of a small tree or shrub to about fifteen feet tall with spreading branches and toothed, ovate leaves. The flowers are about three inches wide when fully expanded, making

Mountain stewartia flower. Courtesy of Ron Lance.

them appear inordinately large against the 2–4-inch leaves. The blossoms are composed of five crinkled petals that start out pure white but change to creamy or yellowish white by maturity. A mass of deep purplish or burgundy-red stamens decorates the center of the blossom, lending a regal air to the flower.

Mountain stewartia (*Stewartia ovata*) is a plant of rich shady slopes of the Southern Appalachians and in our area ranges from northern Alabama to south-central Virginia. Mature trees are 10–15 feet tall and nearly as broad, especially when open-grown, and do best in part shade and well-drained soils. The leaves are ovate in outline, with fewer marginal teeth than those of silky camellia, and the flowers typically have white or transparent stamens, though stamen color in natural populations can also range from purple to blue. Some horticulturists recognize *S. ovata* var. *grandiflora* as a distinct variety based on its larger flowers and consistently purple stamens. Others consider it a seed-grown cultivar and prefer the name *S. ovata* 'Grandiflora.'

Unlike the several non-native Korean and Japanese stewartias that have become popular in southern landscaping, the native species are definitely not of the "plant and walk away" type. They require forethought and preparation in planting and careful attention at least until well established. Both grow naturally in the shady understory of rich woods but seem to prefer sunny edges in the garden, probably due to their need for proper drainage and rapid evaporation. Both are subject to root rot from the earliest stages—even the seeds will rot in wet soil—and neither will tolerate moisture-retentive conditions. Stewartia specialists suggest examining the roots of pot-grown plants to ensure that they are not spongy. For best results, plants should be placed in shallow holes in well-drained soils that have been liberally amended with coarse pine bark.

Tips for Growing *Stewartia*

Jack Johnston has specialized in observing and cultivating native *Stewartia* for more than fifteen years. Through trial and experimentation he has learned to propagate, grow, site, and maintain both of our native species and has become a recognized expert in *Stewartia* cultivation. His home near Clayton, Georgia, is perfectly situated for his *Stewartia* habit and has afforded him opportunities for extensive experimentation. His successes in growing these difficult plants from seeds and cuttings are extremely instructive.

Johnston recommends planting *Stewartia* in raised mounds or along the edges of a low, steep slope at the base of a terrace. This is especially important in clay-based soils or where drainage is poor. Mounds can be fashioned by digging a shallow 2–10-inch hole and filling it to about 10 inches above ground level with a mixture of soil and pine bark. The plant should be placed in the mulch so that the top of the root-ball is well above ground level—perhaps as much as ten inches—and additional soil and pine bark mulch should be built up around it to the top of the root-ball. Because the roots are at or above ground level, the planting will need regular irrigation but will drain rapidly. This essentially aboveground planting encourages the development of healthy roots by allowing them to find their own level and avoid saturation. Plants should be sited in moderate sun, as too much shade slows growth and retards flowering. Johnston maintains that sandy, well-drained soils amended with leaves, pine straw, pine bark, or rotting wood chips mimic *Stewartia*'s natural conditions and helps ensure good growth.

Silky camellia seedlings at Jack Johnston's nursery.

Ben Franklin Tree (*Franklinia*)

The Ben Franklin tree (*Franklinia alatamaha*), more commonly known simply as *Franklinia*, is a botanical enigma. It was first discovered in the fall of 1765 by John and William Bartram at a site along the Altamaha River at Fort Barrington, southwest of Savannah, Georgia. Neither of the Bartrams had encountered this species in their previous explorations, and the late fall season made it impossible for them to identify it or even to determine its botanical family. William visited the site again in 1773, this time in April, and included an account of the visit as well as a meticulously detailed description of the new species, including its exquisite flowers, in part 3, chapter 9 of his well-known *Travels*. Since this second visit was far too early in the season for flowers to be present, Bartram must have collected cuttings or seeds for his Philadelphia garden and based his description at least partly on cultivated specimens. The Bartrams named the new genus in honor of Benjamin Franklin, a close and longtime family friend and cofounder with John Bartram of the American Philosophical Society.

As far as is known, Bartram's 1773 visit was one of the last times *Franklinia alatamaha* was seen in the wild. The exact location of the original population has not been rediscovered, and no new wild populations have been found. Even though *Franklinia* is readily available in the nursery trade and is widely planted by collectors, it is known today only from cultivated specimens. All of the plants currently growing in arboreta, botanical gardens, and private landscapes are descended from Bartram's initial collection.

At first, Bartram thought his discovery was a new species of *Gordonia*—the two genera are closely related and similar in many ways—but later discerned enough differences between them to justify a more stringent botanical separation. The two are easy to tell apart. *Gordonia* is evergreen; *Franklinia*, deciduous. *Gordonia* fruit is an abruptly pointed capsule; the capsules of *Franklinia* are rounded. The leaves of *Gordonia* are el-

Loblolly bay.

Loblolly bay.

Loblolly bay.

Franklinia fruit.

liptic and leathery; those of *Franklinia* are widest toward the tip and membranous. Both have exquisite three-inch flowers with five white crinkly petals surrounding a conspicuous mass of numerous yellow stamens. *Gordonia* flowers usually appear in summer; *Franklinia*'s mostly August to October.

In his original description, Bartram described *Franklinia* as "a flowering tree of the first order for beauty and fragrance of blossoms. . . . ; the flowers are very large, expand themselves perfectly, are of a snow white colour, and ornamented with a crown or tassel of gold coloured refulgent staminae in their centre, the inferior petal or segment of the corolla is hollow, formed like a cap or helmet, and entirely includes the other four, until the moment of expansion." Bartram's description alone is enough to excite the interest of any self-respecting gardener.

Franklinia is a small tree or large, somewhat gangly shrub with spreading branches and an open crown. Mature plants are 10–20 feet tall and may have single or multiple trunks. Old plants are often sprawling or leaning and sometimes root from layered

Franklinia flower. Courtesy of Ron Lance.

Franklinia fall leaves.

branches. The oldest living specimens were planted in 1905 at Harvard University's Arnold Arboretum in Jamaica Plain, Massachusetts. The larger of these is about 21 feet tall, over 53 feet wide, and has eight vertical stems over five inches in diameter. The smaller plant is about 30 feet wide, with six stems. *Franklinia* leaves are technically alternate but are often borne in attractive superficial whorls at the branch tips. In fall the leaves change from medium green to various shades of yellow or intense red and are extremely attractive.

Despite the fact that it has survived in cultivation for more than two hundred years, *Franklinia* can be difficult to grow. It is rated for zones 5–8, 9–6, but at least a few USDA zone 9 gardeners have been successful with it, including at least one report from as far south as Gainesville, Florida. However, the leaves of even successfully grown zone 9 plants often look chlorotic and splotchy, unlike the evenly deep green leaves of more northern plants.

Franklinia requires acidic soils with pH 5–6 and, like the closely related native stewartias, demands good drainage, coarse soil, and adequate moisture. Jack Johnston's strategies for planting *Stewartia* work equally well for *Franklinia*. Some experts suggest that *Franklinia* performs best if planted on top of the ground, with coarse, bark-laden soil mounded up around the root ball. Several specimens planted in the parking lot medians at the North Carolina Arboretum near Asheville demonstrate this point. Such plants (with very good drainage) may require at least thirty minutes of direct irrigation nearly every day in summer and at least weekly during the winter for a year or two after planting, especially during hot, dry spells, but they may be sited in partial or full sun. Specimens of *Franklinia* that are planted at or below ground level or that are sited in areas where water stands for even short periods usually do not survive.

Recent work by breeders at the Mountain Horticultural Crops Research and Extension Center in Fletcher, North Carolina, has resulted in a successful cross between our native *Gordonia* and *Franklinia*. Researchers Tom Ranney and Paul Fantz named the new progeny ×*Gordlinia grandiflora* and are continuing to study it for possible introduction into the retail gardening market. The new plant is extremely fast-growing, can reach six feet or more in less than a year from a cutting, and preserves the best ornamental features of both species. It flowers profusely in the fall, is semievergreen, and can be nearly twelve feet tall after only two growing seasons.

×*Gordlinia grandiflora*.

Fevertree

At the same time and location that Bartram collected seeds of *Franklinia*, he also noted and collected another "new, singular, and beautiful shrub" that he had seen in only a few places in his wide-ranging explorations. He originally assigned the name *Bignonia bracteate* to his new discovery, presumably because the tubular flowers resemble those of the trumpet creeper or other members of the bignonia family. Today, his discovery is placed in the Rubiaceae, or madder family, and is known as Georgia fevertree, Georgia bark, or simply pinckneya (*Pinckneya bracteata*).

Fevertree at Dr. Charles Keith's private arboretum near Raleigh, North Carolina.

Fevertree flower.

The flowers of *Pinckneya* are tubular and surrounded by large sepals. Courtesy of Bill and Pam Anderson.

White-flowered form of *Pinckr* Courtesy of Bill and Pam Ande

The common names "fevertree" and "Georgia bark" come from pinckneya's purported but perhaps overstated medicinal value. The genus *Pinckneya*—of which Georgia fevertree is the only member—is in the same botanical family as *Cinchona*, a group of South American trees that once served as the world's leading source of quinine. Also known as Peruvian bark, *Cinchona* became highly valued in the treatment of malaria and was a diligently guarded resource in Columbia, Peru, and Ecuador, where attempts at illegal exportation were common practice. Peruvian bark was very difficult to obtain in the United States, especially in the 1800s, and its reputation led to an intense search for worthy substitutes. Pharmacologists with the Confederate army experimented with numerous indigenous plants, including dogwoods, willows, and tulip tree, but settled on a bitter, tealike concoction from the bark of Georgia fevertree as the most often recommended malarial treatment. It is unclear how well the therapy actually worked. Little modern research suggests a strong comparison between Peruvian and Georgia bark.

The madder family also includes buttonbush (*Cephalanthus occidentalis*), an easy-to-grow and popular native landscape plant that is included in Part III. It is ironic that two species so closely related and demonstrably similar in habit, habitat, and foliage could express such divergent horticultural utility. Buttonbush is easy to grow and relatively long-lived in moist garden soils; pinckneya is not.

Pinckneya is set apart in nature and in the garden by its interesting rosy pink to (less often) white flowers. The corolla is composed of five yellowish brown, fused petals that form a narrow flaring tube. Individual corollas are not particularly showy but are subtended by five brightly colored sepals, at least one of which is usually much enlarged to about the size of a small human hand. The large flaglike sepals are conspicuous even at some distance, making the tree extremely showy and attractive when in flower.

In nature fever tree is a plant of wet, boggy habitats along the edges of swamps, streams, and shallow pineland drainages. It is restricted in distribution to the coastal plains of South Carolina, Georgia, and northern Florida and is probably best suited for the warmer parts of zone 8 as well as zones 9–10. Pinckneya can tolerate below-freezing temperatures for short times, but it is not particularly cold hardy and is intolerant of drought. Lack of irrigation for as little as a week can kill it.

Pinckneya prefers acidic soils with adequate moisture, but not soils that are saturated. Seeds germinate quickly and the plant grows well in pots, but seedlings and saplings are finicky when planted out and very fussy about placement. Many skillful gardeners report difficulty with growing it, and firsthand accounts of short-lived specimens are common. Most successful plantings seem to be in locations where the roots have access to water but are never inundated. Successful plantings at Dr. Charles Keith's private arboretum near Raleigh, North Carolina, and at Callaway Gardens suggest that short, steep slopes at the edge of a pond are optimal. Such plantings allow the roots to seek an appropriate depth and find moisture on their own terms.

Georgia Plume

Georgia plume (*Elliottia racemosa*) is a large, deciduous, often multistemmed shrub or small tree of the heath family (Ericaceae). Wild-grown plants can reach heights of 30 feet or more—the Tattnall County, Georgia, champion is 43 feet tall and about half as wide, with a trunk circumference of 28 inches—but the few cultivated specimens

Georgia plume. Courtesy of Hew Joiner.

Georgia plume. Courtesy of Hew Joiner.

typically do not exceed heights of about 15 feet. Georgia plume is native mostly to dry, sandy ridges and evergreen oak hammocks of the coastal plain of eastern Georgia. It is the second largest and arguably showiest of our native heaths but is seldom seen in cultivation. Only the superficially similar sourwood (*Oxydendrum arboreum*), among the heaths, grows taller.

The common name "Georgia plume" derives from the foot-long racemes of bright white flowers that constitute the plant's chief horticultural attraction. Numerous plumes of long-stalked blossoms appear in great profusion in early summer, transforming fully attired plants into dazzling shows of whites and greens. The four or five strap-shaped petals are divided to the base and become conspicuously recurved with age. Mature flowers are strongly reminiscent of the American snowbell (*Styrax americanus*) and bear little resemblance to the typical urn-shaped corollas of most other heaths.

The Georgia plume and *Franklinia* share similar histories. Both were discovered by William Bartram along famous Georgia streams—*Franklinia* along the Altamaha in 1765 and Georgia plume along the Savannah in 1773—and both pose considerable cultivation challenges. Although wild colonies of Georgia plume still exist, the plant is considered threatened in Georgia, and most of the known populations are not expanding in size. In her 2007 review of the rare plants of Georgia, Linda Chafin reports Georgia plume from more than fifty wild populations in nineteen Georgia counties, only nine of which are located on protected lands. She also notes that Georgia plume was formerly known from adjacent sites in South Carolina that are now destroyed.

Georgia plume's troubles under cultivation closely mirror its problems in the wild. It manufactures very few viable seeds, produces few seedlings in the wild, and is difficult to grow from either transplants or cuttings. Although growers report that it is relatively easy to grow from seed (if seeds can be found), container-grown seedlings often don't survive transition from pot to ground. Martha Joiner, who helps keep track of this species for the Georgia Plant Conservation Alliance, including monitoring the plantings at the Georgia Southern Botanical Garden, reports that seed production is often not reliable from year to year, making seeds hard to come by, and that seed production in recent years may be hampered by drought. According to Joiner, time of seed collection is very important as the seeds fall quickly after the capsule opens.

Mature capsules weren't observed until 1903 (130 years after the plant's discovery), and ripe seeds weren't reported until Mary Henry's 1941 account in *National Horticultural Magazine*. Successful germination from seed wasn't effected until the early 1960s and then only a handful of plants were produced.

Even though wild plants sucker readily and form dense thickets from root sprouts, early attempts by botanical gardens to collect and grow the plant from cuttings generally failed. It wasn't until the turn of the twentieth century that cultivated transplants became even marginally widespread—Kew Gardens in England in 1903; Biltmore Forest in Asheville, North Carolina, in 1934; and the gardens at the Henry Foundation in Gladwyne, Pennsylvania, in 1936—and it wasn't until the 1960s that Alfred Fordham and other propagators at the Arnold Arboretum learned the secrets of propagating it from root cuttings.

Even with this newfound success, Georgia plume is still not widely grown. It continues to be only marginally available in the trade and is usually expensive to purchase. Its rarity, threatened status, and difficult cultivation mean that few retail or wholesale nurseries stock it, and few public gardens or arboreta display it in their collections. It is probably more difficult to grow than *Franklinia* and is certainly more difficult to obtain. One of the best places to see it in the wild is at the Big Hammock Natural Area along the Altamaha River where Georgia highways 121, 144, and 169 cross the river southwest of Glenville, southwest of Savannah. For garden-grown plants, the modest collection at the Georgia Southern University Botanical Garden (GSBG), located in Statesboro within the plant's natural range, is probably the best option. GSBG has a number of rescued plants, and researchers and students have used the collection to study the best way to grow these plants. At least one of GSBG's plants flowers annually.

Georgia plume. Courtesy of Ron Lance.

7

Native Azaleas, Mountain Laurel, Blueberries, and Other Heaths

Few families of flowering plants have contributed more to horticulture and regional biodiversity than the heath family (Ericaceae), and nowhere is this more obvious than in the southeastern United States. Heath species dominate much of the southern landscape, from the mountains to the coast, and are adapted to the full range of climatic zones. Mountain laurel, native azaleas, evergreen rhododendrons, fetterbushes, and the blueberries, huckleberries, sparkleberry, and mountain cranberry all belong to this expansive family, as do the numerous species and cultivars of evergreen Asian azaleas that continue to be among the south's most popular lawn and garden shrubs.

There are about 4,000 heath species worldwide, nearly 100 of which are native to the southeast. Most are evergreen or deciduous shrubs. Only one, the sourwood (*Oxydendrum arboreum*) that graces fall woodlands with its fiery leaves, becomes a relatively large tree. Only a handful are herbaceous—at least in the United States—and almost all are acid-loving plants that grow best in garden soils with pH ranging 4.5–6.5.

Native Azaleas

Native azalea enthusiasts make a distinction between deciduous and evergreen species. Although both types are classified in the genus *Rhododendron*, growers and gardeners typically call the deciduous species native azaleas and use the name "rhododendron" only for the evergreens, a preference that may be a holdover from older classification schemes. Some early southeastern botanists, notably John K. Small in the several editions of his southeastern flora, included all of the deciduous species within the genus *Azalea* and the evergreens in the genus *Rhododendron*. Other authorities, such as A. W. Chapman, whose work preceded Small's, segregated the evergreen and deciduous species into natural subgroups within the genus *Rhododendron*, distinguishing the azaleas by their two-lipped, funnel-shaped flowers and deciduous habit. Most modern taxonomists agree more closely with Chapman's approach and classify both the evergreen and deciduous species within one of several subgenera of the genus *Rhododendron*.

Eighteen species of deciduous native azaleas occur naturally in North America, including a single western species and seventeen eastern species. Fifteen of the eastern species are found within the southeastern United States, some of which are more common and widespread than others and more often seen in cultivation. The majority are

Azaleas and Rhododendrons for Southeastern Gardens

Common Name	Latin Name	USDA Hardiness Zones	AHS Heat Zones	Leaf Retention
Alabama Azalea	R. alabamense	6–9	9–7	Deciduous
Sweet Azalea	R. arborescens	5–9	9–4	Deciduous
Coastal Azalea	R. atlanticum	6–9		Deciduous
Florida Azalea	R. austrinum	6–9	9–6	Deciduous
Flame Azalea	R. calendulaceum	5–8	9–4	Deciduous
Piedmont Azalea	R. canescens	6–10	9–4	Deciduous
Carolina Rhododendron	R. caroliniana	5–8		Evergreen
Purple Rhododendron	R. catawbiense	4–8	8–1	Evergreen
Chapman Rhododendron	R. chapmanii	7–9		Evergreen
Red Hills Azalea	R. colemanii	7–9		Deciduous
Cumberland Azalea	R. cumberlandense	5–8		Deciduous
May-White Azalea	R. eastmanii	6–9		Deciduous
Oconee Azalea	R. flammeum	6–9	9–7	Deciduous
Rosebay Rhododendron	R. maximum	3–7	9–1	Evergreen
Dwarf Rhododendron	R. minus	5–8		Evergreen
Pinxterbloom Azalea	R. periclymenoides	4–8		Deciduous
Roseshell Azalea	R. prinophyllum	4–9		Deciduous
Plumleaf Azalea	R. prunifolium	7–9	8–6	Deciduous
Pinkshell Azalea	R. vaseyi	4–7		Deciduous
Swamp Azalea	R. viscosum	4–9	9–1	Deciduous

Flame azalea.

Smooth azalea.

excellent garden plants that are easy to grow, readily available, and unsurpassed for color and beauty in the spring garden.

The more widely used and successful species for coastal plains gardens include the Piedmont (*R. canescens*), Florida (*R. austrinum*), Oconee (*R. flammeum*), swamp (*R. viscosum*), Alabama (*R. alabamense*), plumleaf (*R. prunifolium*), and coastal (*R. atlanticum*) azaleas. All have a relatively large natural range or an otherwise proven adaptability to hot summers. The relatively recently described red hills azalea (*R. colemanii*), currently known from a narrow band mostly in southern Alabama, and similar in many respects to Alabama azalea, will also likely prove to be a worthy and widely used azalea for coastal plains gardens.

Gardeners in the Piedmont have more choices and can grow all of the coastal plains species as well as the flame (*R. calendulaceum*), pinxterbloom (*R. periclymenoides*), and smooth (*R. arborescens*) azaleas. The Cumberland (*R. cumberlandense*) and pinkshell (*R. vaseyi*) azaleas are best adapted for Southern Appalachian gardens, but many Piedmont collectors also grow it successfully.

Despite its common name, the Piedmont azalea, also sometimes called southern pinxterbloom, has an expansive range that includes both the Piedmont and the coastal plains. It grows naturally from Tennessee and southern North Carolina southward to central Florida, and west to eastern Texas. Piedmont azalea is an early-flowering species in the coastal plains, with flowers often appearing early to mid-March, typically well before the appearance of new leaves. Bloom time is somewhat later in the Piedmont and often is delayed until May. The flowers are pinkish white inside and darker pink outside, with the darkest portions near the base of the tube. This species occurs in nature along the wet edges of swamps, bogs, and pineland drainages, as well as along the drier lower slopes of woodland streams. Piedmont azalea is one of our most widely used native azaleas, performing well in zones 6–9, 9–4.

Azalea Flowers

All of our deciduous native azaleas are classified in the genus *Rhododendron*, subgenus *Pentanthera*. With one exception, all southeastern species have tubular, funnel-shaped flowers with five conspicuous anthers borne at the tip of usually very long stamens. The name *pentanthera* literally means "with five anthers," a name that could have as easily been *pentandrus*, "with five stamens." The single exception is the narrowly endemic pinkshell azalea, which has a short, stubby flower tube and seven anthers.

The flower petals of all southeastern native azaleas are fused at the base, forming a tube that flares at the apex into five distinct lobes. With the exception of pinkshell azalea, the flower tube is long, narrow, and often colorful. The shape of typical azalea flowers has led to the common name "wild honeysuckle" being used for many species.

The color of the filament (the part of the stamen that serves as the stalk on which the anther is situated) varies from species to species and can sometimes be helpful with identification. The red pistils and stamens of *R. arborescens*, for example, can help distinguish it from the somewhat similar swamp azalea, which has white stamens.

Flower color in native azaleas is extremely variable, even within a single species, a phenomenon that suggests the work of natural or artificial hybridization. Some species, notably the Alabama and Piedmont azaleas, hybridize regularly in adjacent natural populations, leading to intermediate plants that bear a mix of flower features and colors. The typical creamy white petal with a large yellow splotch of the Alabama azalea is becoming increasingly difficult to find in either nature or the garden. Earl Sommerville, an azalea grower and hybridizer who gardens north of Atlanta, speculates that most azaleas in Georgia may now well be of hybrid origin and that there are probably few genetically pure species left in the wild. Many native azalea species readily hybridize, and growers have experimented with all sorts of crosses in search of varying flower color, bloom time, leaf characters, and growth form. The results of many of these crosses are now available to gardeners as named cultivars.

Fragrance is not universal in native azaleas. For example, most white-flowered species, such as the Alabama, coastal, swamp, May-white, and sweet azaleas, have sweetly fragrant flowers, as does the yellow- to orange-flowered Florida azalea, whereas several of the more brightly colored red- and orange-flowered species, notably the Oconee, flame, plumleaf, and Cumberland azaleas, do not. Most of the pink-flowered species in our region are fragrant, again with the single exception of pinkshell azalea.

Piedmont azalea.

Florida flame azalea.

Florida flame azalea.

Florida flame azalea.

The Florida azalea is closely related to the Piedmont azalea but is much more restricted in natural range. Its center of distribution is the Florida panhandle, hence its common name, but it also occurs in southwestern Georgia, southern Alabama, and southeastern Mississippi. This narrow range notwithstanding, Florida azalea is one of the most-used native azaleas in the south, with proven adaptability throughout the region. Its popularity probably stems from the sweet fragrance and pale yellow to bright orange color of its flowers. In its natural range it usually flowers slightly later than Piedmont azalea, more commonly in April and May, but gardeners near Auburn, Alabama, often report it to be the first azalea to flower in their section of the lower Piedmont.

In coastal plains gardens, Florida azalea is followed in flower by the Oconee azalea, a species discovered in and almost restricted to the Georgia Piedmont. It, too, has brightly colored flowers that range in hue from yellow to orange or red. It is particularly heat tolerant, hence its successful use

Florida flame azalea.

in the coastal plains, but is not as readily available as either the Piedmont or Florida species. Lazy K Nursery, a wholesaler, and its retail outlet, Garden Delights Garden Center, located in Pine Mountain, Georgia, are two of the best sources for the Oconee azalea (as well as many other species of native azaleas and heaths). Both are owned by Ernest Koone, a longtime, extremely knowledgeable, and very successful grower of high-quality native azaleas.

The coastal, swamp, red hills, and Alabama azaleas are predominantly white-flowered species with varying flowering times. Coastal or dwarf azalea is a low-growing plant, less than five feet tall, with a restricted range. It is found in nature only in easternmost Virginia, North and South Carolina, and a small portion of eastern Georgia, normally

Oconee azalea.

Coastal azalea.

Coastal azalea.

Coastal azalea.

Swamp azalea.

within about two hundred miles of the coast. The flowers are white with a pinkish blush, larger than those of swamp azalea, and the leaves are somewhat stiff to the touch. This is a naturally clonal species that in nature forms small colonies by the spread of underground stems. Coastal azalea performs well in southern Georgia, seems to be at least somewhat drought tolerant, and should be more widely tested across the coastal plains.

As its name implies, swamp azalea is typically a wetland plant in nature. Its preferred habitat includes swamps, bogs, and wet pinelands, but like many wetland species, it adapts well to normal garden conditions. Large plants may take a year or two to become established, especially in dry years, and may even drop many of their leaves and appear to be poorly situated for their initial summer. Patience and water will usually get them

Alabama azalea, *left* and *above*.

through their first annual cycle. Once established they are tough and easy to care for. The scientific epithet *viscosum* means "viscous" or "sticky" and refers to the glandular hairs that give a somewhat sticky feel to the flowers. Swamp azalea flowers are sweetly fragrant and much smaller than those of most other native azaleas, with very narrow tubes that bear a resemblance to honeysuckle. They typically appear in mid to late summer, though some forms flower in early spring. Some plants in some years flower as late as August or early September. Swamp azalea performs well from Maine to Florida, zones 3–9, 9–1.

A form of swamp azalea is sometimes sold under the name *R. serrulatum*, with the common name "hammock-sweet azalea." Some growers and botanists argue that *R. viscosum* and *R. serrulatum* constitute distinct species and can be separated based on

Red hills azalea.

Red hills azalea.

the latter species' habit and much earlier flowering time. Other specialists lump them into a single species. Noted azalea expert Clarence Towe, in his book *American Azaleas*, suggests that the difference in flowering time and other characters warrants recognition at least as a variety and suggests the name *R. viscosum* var. *serrulatum*. Botanist Alan Weakley, whose online flora of Virginia, the Carolinas, and Georgia is fast becoming the standard botanical reference for the southeastern United States, also suggests that *R. serrulatum* deserves recognition.

The Alabama azalea is distinguished by having white stamens and a bright yellow spot at the base of the lip petal. Its natural range includes nearly all of Alabama as well as closely adjacent regions of Georgia, Florida, and Mississippi. Individuals of this species can grow to nearly sixteen feet tall, but statures of less than ten feet are more common. Alabama azalea has become a popular garden plant due to its attractive flowers. Some suggest that it is best suited for zones 6–8, 9–7, but it is regularly planted with success in the northernmost edges of Hardiness zone 9A and occurs sporadically in natural populations in extreme southern Georgia and the Florida panhandle. This species tends to hybridize regularly with Piedmont azalea, making pure forms increasingly difficult to find. Dodd and Dodd Native Nurseries, a wholesale grower based in Semmes, Alabama, specializes in native azaleas and is one of the best sources for unadulterated plants of *R. alabamense*. The two newly described species May white azalea (*R. eastmanii*), centered in South Carolina, and red hills azalea (*R. colemanii*), found mostly in southern Alabama, are similarly flowered and bloom mostly in May, after the leaves have fully expanded.

Sweet or smooth azalea (*R. arborescens*) puts on its yellow-blotched white flowers from late May to July, depending upon elevation. The red anthers and pistil of most individuals provide an attractive contrast to the white petals. It ranges from northern Alabama to about Pennsylvania and is typically associated with the Piedmont and mountains, but it is also known from the upper coastal plains of Alabama, Georgia, and the Carolinas. It performs best in zones 5–8, 9–4 but can also be grown in Hardiness zone 9A. It is recognized even without leaves by the smooth, shiny brown appearance of the new twigs, a character that also gives it one of its common names.

Several species of native azaleas are noted for flower colors that range from striking pinks to orange and red. The most popular pink-flowered species include pinxterbloom azalea (*R. periclymenoides*), formerly known as *R. nudiflorum*, and the cool climate pinkshell (*R. vaseyi*) and roseshell (*R. prinophyllum*) azaleas. Pinkshell azalea is narrowly endemic to a small region of the Southern Appalachians and is mostly, if not entirely, restricted in distribution to North Carolina, but it is grown successfully in cooler sections of the Piedmont. Roseshell azalea reaches the southern extreme of its generally more northern distribution in western Virginia and extreme northwestern North Carolina and is only marginally used in southern gardens. It does best in the cool climates of higher elevations.

The highly favored orange- or red-flowered species include the aptly named flame azalea, whose flowers range from yellow to orange or red, and the equally brightly colored Cumberland, Oconee, and plumleaf azaleas. The Cumberland and flame azaleas are similar high-elevation species that do best in hardiness zones 5–8. Plumleaf and Oconee are distributed naturally mostly in the Piedmont.

Pinkshell azalea.

xterbloom azalea.

Roseshell azalea. Courtesy of Ron Lance.

Cumberland azalea.
Courtesy of Ron Lance.

The Oconee is the coastal plains gardener's answer to flame azalea. Its brightly colored flowers run the gamut from pink to yellow, orange, or nearly red, rivaling the beauty of its mountain counterpart, and its heat tolerance makes it suitable for gardens well south of its natural distribution. Some experts suggest hardiness zones 7–8 for this species, but Fred Galle, the longtime horticulturist and azalea expert at Callaway Gar-

Plumleaf azalea.

Plumleaf azalea.

Plumleaf azalea.

dens, lists it as hardy for zones 6B–9A, and horticulturist and nurseryman Dan Miller grows it successfully in Tallahassee, Florida. It does best if planted in the fall and may need careful attention during its first summer (at least in hardiness zone 9), especially during hot, dry periods, but will perform well thereafter with moderate care.

Plumleaf azalea enjoys one of the narrowest ranges of any of our native species and is restricted mostly to several counties along the Georgia–Alabama border. Providence Canyon State Park, near Lumpkin, Georgia, is near the center of its distribution and is an excellent place to see this species in the wild. It was first collected in 1913 near Cuthbert, Georgia, by the legendary southeastern botanist and naturalist Roland Harper, and it was first described by John K. Small in the 1913 Appendix to his *Flora of the Southeastern United States*. This species served as Cason Callaway's inspiration for establishing and pouring his fortune into developing Callaway Gardens. Callaway saw his first plumleaf at one of his favorite woodland springs near Pine Mountain. After learning the plant's identity and of its rarity, he purchased the spring and about three thousand acres surrounding it and resolved to launch the gardens, primarily to protect the unique summer-flowering azalea. The image of plumleaf azalea now graces Callaway Garden's logo, and numerous specimens have been planted along the winding drive that courses through the garden's naturally wooded native flora area. Its mid- to late-summer flowering period has made it popular in the garden for extending the native azalea flowering season and has made Callaway Gardens a summer destination for azalea enthusiasts. Plumleaf should be given somewhat more shade than its coastal plains complements—especially in coastal plains gardens—and does best out of the reach of intense afternoon sun.

Those interested in adding native azaleas to their garden may well want to begin with some of the more easily obtained and popularly grown species. Recommendations include the Piedmont and Florida azaleas for coastal plains gardeners from New Orleans eastward, plus the Oconee, flame, plumleaf, and sweet azaleas for the Piedmont and mountains. With increasing experience and a willingness to fail, it is easy to become hooked on experimenting with species from other regions.

It is best to start with regionally grown species that are genetically adapted to local conditions, even for those species that grow in several regions. Hence, coastal plains

Collecting Native Azaleas

Collecting native azaleas is an avid avocation for numerous southern gardeners. This is especially true in the Piedmont, where the collecting spirit is high, almost any of our native species can be successfully grown, and a spring garden excursion can be an overwhelming sensory experience.

One of the best ways to visit private azalea collections is to become affiliated with one of the several active chapters of the American Rhododendron Society or Azalea Society of America. At least a dozen chapters serve the southeastern region, many with overlapping membership. Almost all sponsor private garden tours during the height of the blooming season. Both organizations also publish interesting journals and Web sites. Contact the American Rhododendron Society by directing correspondence to Executive Director, American Rhododendron Society, P.O. Box 525, Niagara Falls, NY 14304. The Web site address is http://www.rhododendron.org/. Learn more about the Azalea Society of America by visiting the society's Web site at http://www.azaleas.org/.

Dr. Bob Greenleaf's azalea garden, Auburn, Alabama.

gardeners should select coastal plains genotypes rather than plants with Piedmont provenance. Locally developed genetic strains tend to perform better and be more adequately adapted to nuances of soil, precipitation, and climate. For Louisiana azalea gardeners, Florida azaleas that originate from lower Mississippi to westernmost Florida should perform well if sited in high shade. Most mail-order houses and native azalea nurseries know the provenance of their plants, and it is important to ask about this before purchasing.

Typically, native azaleas are best planted in late fall, after they lose their leaves. This allows several months for plants to put all of their energy into root development rather than diverting it to leaf and flower production. If the winter and spring are dry, irrigation to the root ball is important, and it is best not to expect heavy flowering the first spring.

Proper installation requires a hole about twice as deep and wide as the root ball. Since the root balls of nursery-grown azaleas are often densely packed and pot bound, agitating and spreading the roots before planting will ensure proper contact with the soil and encourage good root growth. If the roots are matted against the container, it helps to make several shallow vertical slits in the root ball before planting. If planting in very acidic soil, some experts suggest partially filling the hole with a mixture of bark and soil and placing the top of the root ball at or only slightly above ground level. Other experts suggest that mixing bark into the soil is not needed and actually ties up nutrients as the bark decomposes. Neutral soils can be amended with acidic organic matter. Place the top of the root ball well above the soil and cover it with mounded mulch, being sure not to put the mulch against the trunk. Water in and mulch heavily, but do not pack the ground tightly. It is better to leave the soil somewhat loose to encourage drainage and root growth.

It is also important to keep newly planted azaleas well watered—moist but not soggy—for at least the first year. Native azaleas have shallow roots that dry out quickly and can suffer rapidly from dry periods, especially when newly planted. Conversely, excessive moisture encourages root rot, which is equally destructive. Depending upon rain patterns, the root balls of new plantings should be watered thoroughly at least once or twice a week, especially during the early and mid-spring periods of active growth. During hot, dry weather in the coastal plains, foliage may brown, and plants may sometimes lose some of their leaves during their first summer. With sufficient attention and careful watering, the plants will recover, become established, and be much healthier the second summer. The first year or two is critical for the successful establishment of most native azaleas. Afterward, they will thrive with much less care and normal rainfall.

Ensuring optimal light conditions is probably the single most important consideration for siting native azaleas. According to longtime native azalea grower Dan Miller, inadequate light is the most common mistake home gardeners make in placing new plants in their landscapes. Deciduous azaleas need several hours of direct sun per day, preferably late morning to midafternoon. If placed in a shady environment, high dappled shade with overhead sun gaps between trees is much better than low dense shade. Low shade will cause the plants to be weak and flower less and their growth to become distorted in the direction of dominant light. As wild azaleas age, attention should be given to the advancing growth of nearby shading trees. Pruning of lower branches of nearby trees could well ensure the long-term health and flowering of nearby native azaleas. Generally, the more sun, the more flowers, although late afternoon shade will keep flowers looking fresh longer.

Annual or periodic pruning of native azaleas is usually not necessary and is not as desirable as it is for some of the Asian azaleas. Allowing plants to assume their natural form ensures more profuse flowering, a more charming habit, and a more naturalistic garden. Nevertheless, some enthusiasts prefer to keep growth in check or provide a more manicured shape. And there may be times when particularly old azaleas can be rejuvenated by selective pruning. To ensure no loss of flowers for the following season, prune immediately after flowering. Next year's flower buds develop very early on native azaleas; late pruning risks removing them and reducing flower production the following year.

For periodic pruning to encourage branching, remove ½ to ¾ of the current year's growth, leaving at least six inches of branch above the previous year's branch node. For rejuvenating aging plants, entire branches can be removed from near the base of the plant.

Evergreen Rhododendrons

With two exceptions, the evergreen rhododendrons are cool-temperature plants that perform best from the central Piedmont northward. Five species occur in our region, including two that are suited for the coastal plains and Piedmont, and three for the upper Piedmont and mountains.

The two species appropriate for coastal plains and Piedmont gardens are low- to medium-height shrubs that are striking when flowering but largely nondescript when flowers are absent. The dwarf or Piedmont rhododendron (*R. minus*) is the more widespread and attractive of the two, with larger, flatter, more attractive leaves and typically better, more upright form than the closely related Chapman rhododendron (*R. chapmanii*).

Dwarf rhododendron is technically a Piedmont plant, distributed principally from North and South Carolina to south-central Alabama, and northward to eastern Tennessee and extreme southern Kentucky. Chapman rhododendron is a coastal plains endemic, restricted in distribution to the central panhandle of Florida. Both are similar in appearance and so closely related that some authorities consider them to be varieties

Chapman rhododendron.

Chapman rhododendron.

Dwarf azalea.

Catawba rhododendron.

Rosebay
rhododendron.

of a single species. These are slow-growing plants that bear showy clusters of short pink flowers with five crinkly petals. Dwarf rhododendron tends to have the better form, especially when grown in cooler climates, but neither is likely to be much noticed in the absence of flowers. The leaves of Chapman rhododendron often curl and discolor in dry weather, and the foliage is often sparse. Even in its natural habitat, it often appears stressed. Despite Chapman rhododendron's natural range, both species are at their best in the cooler parts of the Piedmont, where they are typically much more attractive.

Of the three Piedmont and mountain species, the Carolina (*R. carolinianum*) and rosebay (*R. maximum*) rhododendrons are the best choices. Both are large shrubs that are regularly used in low- and high-elevation gardens and commercial plantings. Both have white to lavender flowers that are usually blushed with pink. Carolina rhododendron has smaller leaves and a smaller stature and usually does not exceed about six feet tall and wide at maturity. Rosebay rhododendron, on the other hand, can become fifteen feet tall and wide and potentially requires a large space to accommodate its mature dimensions. The leaves of rosebay rhododendron are 4–8 inches long, dark green above, slightly rolled under along the margin, and very attractive.

The Catawba rhododendron (*R. catawbiense*) is also a large-leaved rhododendron, but with showy clusters of bright purple to nearly magenta flowers. It is potentially a large, spreading shrub with attractive dark green foliage and mature dimensions that are only slightly smaller than those of the rosebay. Although it is not available in many southeastern outlets, it is well-known in the southern Appalachians and is the main attraction at Roan Mountain's Rhododendron Gardens, especially during its late June flowering period. It does well in full sun to part shade in cool soils and at higher elevations, and it is an excellent hummingbird plant. Several dozen cultivars have been selected from this popular rhododendron, including at least one white-flowered form.

The Laurels

Several species of *Kalmia* grow in our region, the most popular of which is the well-known mountain laurel (*K. latifolia*). Various authorities recognize up to six species of *Kalmia* in the southeastern flora, sometimes also including the sand-myrtle (*K. buxifolia*), a species that is probably more widely recognized as *Leiophyllum buxifolium*.

Mountain laurel ranges across much of the eastern United States from Maine to southernmost Alabama and Mississippi and has a somewhat misleading name. There is no question that it is a mountain species, sometimes flowering as late as early August along the higher elevations of North Carolina's portion of the Blue Ridge Parkway. However, it also grows in the Piedmont and coastal plains and flowers in northern Florida and along the Gulf Coast as early as April. Given its expansive latitudinal and elevational extremes, provenance is extremely important. Most of the more vibrant cultivars, with deeply colored, striped, or otherwise heavily ornamented flowers, have been selected from northern plants. Hence, coastal plains and even Piedmont gardeners who attempt to purchase crosses made in Oregon from plants obtained in New England may experience poor results. The flowers of most southern forms are typically pink in bud but open white. Only a few southern forms with deeper pink flowers are available.

Kalmia latifolia is not difficult to grow and is subject to few diseases or disorders. It prefers acidic soils and can withstand some degree of drought once established. Like other plants of well-drained habitats, it will develop root rot in excessively wet or poorly drained sites and should be planted where the roots are not subjected to excessive soil moisture or puddling water. Ensuring good drainage often requires a large planting hole that is wider (but not deeper) than the root ball and amended with coarse organic material. This is especially true for clay-based and other impervious soils that tend to hold water at the base of the hole. Installing plants slightly above ground level also helps mitigate poor drainage. Plantings should be heavily mulched to reduce weeds, increase moisture retention, and protect the root zone.

Although mountain laurel grows in nature in the shady understory, it flowers best and becomes more densely foliated in sunnier locations. High shade that allows adequate sunlight is optimal and makes mountain laurel an excellent companion for native aza-

Mountain laurel.

Mountain laurel.

leas. Pruning, especially deadheading, also helps foliage and flower production. There is evidence that the developing fruit retards stem growth and flower bud development. Mountain laurel plants that are deadheaded annually immediately after flowering tend to produce more new shoots and to flower every year. Those that aren't deadheaded tend to grow more slowly and to flower best only once every two years.

Pruning frequency and severity depend upon the desired form and size of the plant. Old plants that have never been pruned can become openly branched and somewhat leggy. This is not a problem for background plantings or for plants growing in large naturalistic landscapes, but it can be problematic for foundation screening. Annual pruning, with cuts made above the branch forks, can increase foliage density and maintain size without making plants appear naked.

Southern gardeners, especially those in hardiness zones 6–7A, who are interested in trying some of the more northern cultivars of mountain laurel will probably have to make their purchases from more northern nurseries. Broken Arrow Nursery in Hamden, Connecticut, established by laurel expert Richard Jaynes, and Rarefind Nursery in Jackson, New Jersey, are two of the best sources in the east. Both are available online.

Of the several other species of *Kalmia* that occur in our region, hairy wicky (*K. hirsuta*) is the newest for garden use. This species is much smaller than mountain laurel and is restricted in natural range to the coastal plains from South Carolina to southern Alabama. It usually grows no larger than about eighteen inches tall and has very small leaves that are reminiscent of those of the shiny blueberry (*Vaccinium myrsinites*). The flowers are typical of the laurels—with a cup-shaped, pinkish corolla and ten curving stamens—but are much smaller. Typical flowers average about ½ inch wide. Some forms are densely foliaged and compact; others are more openly branched. Hairy wicky is not yet widely available but may well become an excellent small garden shrub. The best source of this species at present is through Dodd and Dodd Native Nurseries in Semmes, Alabama.

Hairy wicky.

Hairy wicky.

Most gardeners probably know the pollination mechanism of *Kalmia* flowers, but the story bears repeating. The cup-shaped flowers produce ten stamens that curve away from the center of the flower, bending backward so that the anthers that tip each stamen are lodged under tension in small pockets in the petals. The weight of the bee that lands on the center of the flower trips the spring-loaded stamens, catapulting pollen onto the bee's flanks and back to be transferred to another flower. Perhaps lesser known is that the leaves, nectar, and honey derived from mountain laurel contain toxic chemicals that can cause a suite of unpleasant symptoms if ingested. These andromedotoxins are glycosides or grayanotoxins and are also present in the rhododendrons and native azaleas. These monosaccharide-derived compounds are the cause of the so-called "honey poisoning" or "honey intoxication" that afflicts livestock that eat rhododendron or mountain laurel leaves or flowers. The toxins are also poisonous to humans and can cause dizziness, nausea, and vomiting. Some sources suggest that ingestion is potentially fatal. Others suggest that recovery generally occurs in less than twenty-four hours.

Native Blueberries

If the azaleas, rhododendrons, and laurels are the window dressings of the heath family, the blueberries, fetterbushes, wickies, and honeycups are its stalwarts. Few groups of native plants are more adaptable or offer more variety.

Several species of native blueberries are touted for garden use, some primarily for ornament, some for wildlife food, and others for human harvest. Like most members of the family, all require (or in one case prefer) acidic soil, but offer wide latitude in soil moisture requirements.

The blueberries (genus *Vaccinium*) compose a complicated group of deciduous and evergreen shrubs, a few of which become large enough to take on treelike proportions. About two dozen occur naturally in our area, leading University of North Carolina botanist Alan Weakley to conclude that the southeast has a greater diversity of blueberry species than any comparably sized region in the United States. Unfortunately, only a handful of these are regularly used in gardening and landscaping.

The blueberries are often divided into highbush and lowbush types based on size and habit. The true highbush blueberry (*V. corymbosum*) is a deciduous, extremely variable 8–15-foot shrub with widely variable leaf characters and growth form. In the broadest sense of this species, it is naturally distributed across the entire eastern United States from Nova Scotia to Florida. However, blueberry taxonomy and classification seem to be in continuous flux, with a variety of conflicting interpretations. As many as a dozen forms have been lumped under the highbush blueberry moniker, and numerous cultivars and hybrids have been produced. Some horticulturists and botanists think that the true *V. corymbosum* reaches our region only in the mountains of Virginia, the Carolinas, and northern Georgia, and that plants farther south differ, albeit in minor ways, and deserve other names. The details of this botanical controversy are well beyond the scope of this book but suggest the difficulties gardeners may face with putting accurate names on the plants they find in retail nurseries or grow in their gardens. This taxonomic melee notwithstanding, highbush blueberry is a superb landscape plant deserving of a favored spot in a shrubby border. Nearly all selections produce numerous urn-shaped flowers in

Rabbiteye blueberry.

spring; large, juicy, edible fruit in summer; and offer excellent three-season ornamental value.

Two of the highbush types that occur in the southeast are somewhat easily identified. These include *V. virgatum* (often seen under the name *V. ashei*) and *V. elliottii*. Both were formerly lumped into the *V. corymbosum* complex but can now be found for sale in retail nurseries under the common names "rabbiteye blueberry" and "Elliott's blueberry" (or "Mayberry"), respectively.

Rabbiteye blueberry is very similar to *V. corymbosum* and is often considered to be the southern variant of this species. Its leaves have a distinctly bluish cast, and the lower surfaces of the leaves have tiny, stalked, whitish glands that require at least a 10× magnifying glass to see clearly. Rabbiteye is best known for its large, sweet, edible

Elliott's blueberry fall color.

Elliott's blueberry fall color.

fruit and is grown for human consumption at least as much as for ornament. Numerous selections have been made from this species, some of which are early fruiting and some late. 'Premier', 'Brightblue', 'Bluebelle', and 'Climax' are some of the best for flavor. Cross-pollination is essential for the best fruit production, and most gardeners plant at least two selections—three is better—to ensure an adequate supply of berries. Zones 8–9, 9–2 provide the best conditions for rabbiteye blueberry.

Elliott's blueberry is the more easily recognizable of the highbush group. It has small, shiny, dark green leaves that are finely toothed along the margins, and young branches that are arching and conspicuously green. Well-situated plants flower heavily in early spring before the new leaves appear and are very attractive. The leaves often turn bright red in fall and can be very showy. Elliott's blueberry is suitable for hardiness zones 6–9.

Given the complex identification of the highbush blueberries and the confusion manifested in the nursery trade, it is difficult to assign precise hardiness zones to the names found at local nurseries. Depending upon provenance, nearly all can be successfully grown throughout our region, with some forms being hardy at least to USDA zone 4. It is probably better to purchase highbush blueberries locally, as local vendors typically stock selections and species that work best within their particular region.

The highbush blueberries perform best in moist, very acidic, well-drained soils with pH ranging 4.5–5.5. Amending typical garden soils with bark, peat, or other organic material will increase acidity and reduce the leaf yellowing that often occurs with higher pH soils. Low pH soils will also ensure larger, sweeter, and more abundant fruit. In nature these species are typically found mostly in wetlands, often along the edges of swamps and bogs, but also sometimes in upland woods. They respond well in the garden, even in somewhat dry, sandy soils, provided that the pH is low enough. All species benefit from heavy organic mulch and root protection. They sometimes require irrigation for the first summer but are generally drought tolerant once established and require little in the way of continuing care. Some growers feed plants with an acid fertilizer, such as those used for azaleas and camellias, but excessive fertilization can be damaging to the roots and lower trunk and is probably not necessary.

Two other large blueberries work well for the garden. The sparkleberry (*V. arboreum*), sometimes called farkleberry, potentially reaches tree stature with heights to at least thirty feet, but it is slow-growing and more often seen as a large, upright shrub. It flowers heavily, even at low stature, and can be very showy along sunny borders. Sparkleberry occurs in dry, sandy woods and is both heat and drought tolerant. The reddish to grayish bark is smooth, very attractive, and peels off in layers as plants mature, somewhat reminiscent of the non-native crape-myrtle (*Lagerstroemia indica*). The 1–2-inch leaves are dark green and shiny during spring and summer but can turn brilliant red in fall. The small white flowers are bell-shaped and borne on relatively long, pendulous stalks on last year's wood, even as this year's leaves develop. The fruit of the sparkleberry is firm, with little pulp and not much taste. Birds seem to like it, but it is not a species to grow for harvesting. It is one of the only members of the heath family that can tolerate basic or alkaline soils, but it does not require them. It often grows in sandy upland woods and is considered a xeric landscape plant. It can be planted in full sun to light shade in zones 7–10, 10–8.

The deerberry (*V. stamineum*) is somewhat smaller than the sparkleberry, usually not

Sparkleberry.

Sparkleberry.

Sparkleberry.

Sparkleberry fall leaves.

Deerberry. Courtesy of Ron Lance.

Shiny blueberry.

exceeding about ten feet tall. It grows faster and is becoming increasingly available in the nursery trade. Individual plants vary significantly, some displaying relatively small leaves and others with leaves closer in size to those of highbush blueberry. In general, the leaves are pale green to nearly bluish above and conspicuously grayish white to bluish white below—though the intensity on the lower leaf surfaces varies with the age of the leaf, location of the plant, and perhaps the genetic legacy of the individual. The tiny bell-shaped flowers are borne in abundance and at maturity extrude a mass of stamens and pistils that extends well beyond the petals. The fruit is a dangling, variously colored drupe that is sometimes baby blue and at other times more nearly reddish or purplish black. The fruit is usually somewhat sour to the taste (sweeter forms are sometimes encountered) but must be relished by wildlife as it is often stripped from the plant before reaching maturity. Birds and mammals use the fruit and leaves as forage, making it an excellent plant for the wildlife garden. Deerberry occurs naturally in dry, sandy pinelands and is one of our more drought-tolerant large blueberries. It sometimes spreads by underground stems and, like most heaths, requires acidic soil for best development. It does best in USDA zones 5–9.

Two species of lowbush blueberry are typically available in the nursery trade: shiny blueberry (*V. myrsinites*) and Darrow's blueberry (*V. darrowii*). Both are small, evergreen shrubs. Shiny blueberry is the smaller of the two, usually forming a densely foliated rounded shrub that can reportedly reach heights of six feet but is usually well under half this tall. The common name comes from the lustrous leaf surfaces, which give the plant a shiny appearance. The flowers are borne profusely and are typical of the blueberry genus in shape and size. Hummingbirds relish the nectar, sometimes flying

Shiny blueberry.

Darrow's blueberry. Courtesy of Ron Lance.

only inches above ground level to probe the tiny blossoms. The fruit is a tasty blue-black drupe that is appreciated by wildlife. Shiny blueberry is excellent as a border along walkways or shrub beds and a good replacement for the non-native Mexican heather (*Cuphea hyssopifolia*).

Darrow's blueberry is very similar to shiny blueberry; the two were once thought to be varieties of the same species. Darrow's averages somewhat larger in size and has more colorful leaves that range from pinkish or grayish to green, often with an attractive glaucous cast. The flowers and fruit are similar to those of the shiny blueberry in shape, size, and number. Both of these species grow naturally in wet to dry pinelands, but they can easily be overwatered in the garden; this can be especially problematic for Darrow's blueberry. At least one native nursery refrains from selling this species because its customers routinely kill the plant by installing it in rich garden soil and watering it regularly. When treated with neglect, Darrow's blueberry is a tough, attractive garden shrub. The lowbush blueberries are appropriate for USDA zones 7–10.

Darrow's blueberry.

Staggerbushes and Fetterbushes

The staggerbushes and fetterbushes constitute the genera *Leucothoe*, *Lyonia*, and *Agarista*. Together, these groups encompass about ten southeastern species. All have hard, capsular rather than fleshy fruit and are valued ornamentally primarily for their flowers and foliage. Despite the fact that most of these species are regularly recommended for use in native gardens, only two are readily available, widely used, and reliable.

The most popular species in the upper Piedmont and mountains is the evergreen drooping leucothoe or doghobble (*Leucothoe fontanesiana*). New foliage starts out pinkish to red, becomes dark green throughout the summer, and turns bronzy to nearly burgundy in the fall and winter. The leaves are much longer than wide with excellent texture, and most plants are loaded with dangling racemes of urn-shaped flowers in the spring. Drooping leucothoe can be somewhat fussy in the garden and is usually recommended for USDA zones 6–7—perhaps more appropriately only to 7A. However, a relatively recent variegated selection from Head Lee Nursery in Seneca, South Carolina,

Drooping leucothoe.

Drooping leucothoe 'Whitewater.'

Doghobble.

may prove to expand the use of this species slightly farther southward. Named 'Whitewater' for its attractive dark green foliage edged in ivory white, this selection has proven to be a little more heat tolerant in the Piedmont. It is recommended for USDA zones 7–9, but its ability to withstand the hot summer temperatures of the coastal plains has yet to be confirmed.

Coastal plains gardeners can use *Leucothoe axillaris* as a replacement for the more northern *L. fontanesiana*. One of the better selections is Jenkins' fetterbush, *L. axillaris* 'Margie Jenkins,' named for longtime native plant nurserywoman Margie Jenkins, owner of Jenkins Farm and Nursery in Amite, Louisiana. This evergreen shrub has shiny upper leaf surfaces and numerous clusters of small, bell-shaped flowers that dangle from the leaf nodes. The original plant came from Florida by way of nurseryman David Drylie, but it performed so well for Jenkins's Louisiana and Mississippi customers that she asked Drylie to name it and to let her introduce it to the market. It became so popular with other native plant vendors that it was dubbed 'Jenkins Form' by Dodd and Dodd Native Nurseries, a name that was later shortened to 'Jenkins' before finally becoming 'Margie Jenkins.' It blooms in late spring and forms a low, arching shrub that grows to about three feet by three feet. It occurs naturally in floodplains and prefers shade. It requires moist soils that are not allowed to dry out and has proven a good choice for shaded foundation plantings. 'Margie Jenkins' fetterbush is recommended for hardiness zones 7–10.

Leucothoe axillaris 'Dodd's Variegated' is a variegated selection made by Tom Dodd III that can be grown in the coastal plains from Virginia to Louisiana. Dodd recommends it for hardiness zones 7–10 as a coastal plains substitute for the 'Whitewater' and 'Rainbow' selections of *L. fontanesiana*.

The Florida leucothoe (*Agarista populifolia*), formerly placed in the genus *Leucothoe*, is an evergreen, vase-shaped shrub or small tree with arching branches and an excellent form. It is somewhat similar in leaf and flower to drooping leucothoe, but it can become a much larger plant. It is about as wide as tall and is perfect in a shady background or as a specimen shrub. Most garden plants top out at about twelve feet, but in good situations plants may reach heights of fifteen feet or more. Like drooping leucothoe, it is adorned in spring with tassels of white flowers and is very attractive. It is recommended for zones 7–9, 9–7 and typically prefers at least partial shade. Although it has been used successfully in northern Florida as a closely pruned, sunny hedge, it is probably better to give it shade for at least the latter half of the day.

Of the several species of *Lyonia*, fetterbush (*L. lucida*) is most often offered for sale.

Florida leucothoe.

Florida leucothoe.

Fetterbush. Courtesy of Ron Lance.

This is a wetland species of moist, extremely acidic flatwoods and is very common on the coastal plains from Virginia to Louisiana. It is very attractive in nature and is often recommended for use as a native landscape plant in hardiness zones 7–9. Some gardeners report having difficulty maintaining its charm in the garden, and at least one native nursery has discontinued offering it for sale. However, the foliage, flowers, and form are very attractive, and Margie Jenkins highly recommends the selection 'Round Lake', discovered in the central panhandle of Florida. Jenkins reports that 'Round Lake' does not need pruning, produces lots of pinkish white flowers, and performs well in eastern Louisiana gardens.

Climbing Wicky

Climbing or vine wicky (*Pieris phillyreifolia*) is closely related to the staggerbushes and fetterbushes but is more akin in habit to a climbing evergreen vine or running groundcover than a shrub. In natural situations its main stem winds its way under the bark of supporting trees—mostly cypress and Atlantic white cedar—periodically poking leafy

Climbing wicky.

branches through the bark and confounding observers with what appears to be broad-leaved foliage on a needle-leaf tree. In the garden it forms a small, upright shrub or runs along the ground as a groundcover. Its natural range is restricted to the coastal plains of Alabama, Georgia, South Carolina, and northern Florida, but Dodd and Dodd Native Nurseries, which sells both shrubby and vining forms, recommends it for hardiness zones 7–10 and considers it an excellent and promising garden plant. Plants of the species have attractive, dark green, two-inch leaves and flower profusely in very early spring with showy racemes of small, white, bell-shaped flowers that mature to a hard, capsular fruit. The closely related mountain pieris (*P. floribunda*) takes on a more shrublike stature and is also used in gardening, but mostly in hardiness zones 4–6, outside of our region. *P. phillyreifolia* often grows on tussocks in swamps but performs successfully in well-drained acidic soils in the garden.

Most southern gardeners probably know the genus *Pieris* best from the profusely flowering non-native evergreen Japanese pieris (*P. japonica*). Numerous selections of this very attractive Japanese import are available, none of which seems to be invasive or environmentally problematic. Many become large shrubs, and virtually all are showy during their March–April flowering period, with long, dangling, many-flowered racemes. Hybrids between Japanese and mountain pieris have been produced but are not widely available.

Honeycups

Zenobia pulverulenta is one of the heath family's most underutilized and undersold celebrities. It occurs in nature primarily in the Carolina coastal plain, with small populations spilling over into two counties in southeastern Virginia and one in Georgia. However, it performs well in the garden throughout much of the coastal plains and is not particularly fussy about conditions. It flowers profusely in late spring and should be tried in gardens well beyond its narrow natural range—Louisiana native plant nurserywoman Margie Jenkins, for example, considers it one of the top twenty shrubs for her region. On some plants the white, bell-like flowers dangle from the leaf axils in attractive clusters; on others they form along a showy

Honeycups.

elongated raceme. Most plants retain at least some leaves during the winter but also display a bit of autumn color, especially after the passage of early-season cold fronts.

Honeycups has two vegetative forms. In some individuals, the foliage is essentially dark or medium green whereas others have bluish green or glaucous foliage and silvery-white stems. Both forms are very attractive. The tongue-twisting scientific epithet *pulverulenta* means "powdered as with dust," an apt description of the foliage and branches. Some experts suggest that the green form is more typical of coastal populations and the glaucous form of more inland populations nearer the Fall Line, but both types often grow intermixed. Cultivars with bluish foliage are probably more commonly available in nurseries than the green form, with 'Woodlanders Blue' being a favored selection due to the attractive bluish cast of the leaves.

Because *Zenobia* occurs naturally along the edges of pocosins and wet pineland depressions, it is often assumed to be restricted to wet soils in the garden. This is not the case. Although it tolerates wetland conditions, it prefers drainage and adapts very well to drier sites, even to some clay-based soils. During the intense spring and summer drought of 2007, three large newly planted honeycups showed virtually no stress in a mixed heath bed in southwestern Georgia, just a few miles north of the Florida state line. The honeycups and several species of native azaleas, all of which were obtained from Ernest Koone III of Lazy K Nursery in Pine Mountain, Georgia, were planted in full sun in the fall of 2006, just in time for one of the driest springs and summers on record. The honeycups were pruned to ground level before planting, but grew to about

Honeycups.

Honeycups.

three feet by early summer, with attractive turgid foliage. Although all other plants installed at the same time showed signs of browning and burning—even with moderate irrigation—the honeycups remained attractive and healthy. Severely pruning these plants while still in the pot probably added measurably to their success and may be an important practice to emulate.

Tarflower

Tarflower (*Bejaria racemosa*) takes its common name from the sticky exudate that covers the upper branchlets and flowers, an adaptation that may have developed to thwart the theft of pollen by nonpollinating crawling insects. Ants, for example, are often seen glued to the twigs that subtend the inflorescence. Tarflower is restricted in distribution mostly to the Florida peninsula, eastern Georgia, and extreme southeastern South Carolina. It is a 3–7-foot-tall evergreen woody shrub with rubbery leaves and extraordinarily beautiful flowers. Tarflower blooms mostly in June and July but is attractive other times of the year. Like most members of the heath family, it prefers acidic soils and occurs in nature mostly in organic flatwoods in association with saw palmetto and other heath plants. Tarflower is available from several Florida-based native nurseries but should probably be tried along the coastal plains north of Florida.

Tarflower.

8

Magnolias and Their Relatives

Magnolias are the masterpieces of native trees, ancient relicts thousands of millennia in the making and little more advanced today than at the time of their origin. They have been called the aristocrats of the garden and are well-known for their strongly fragrant flowers, interesting fruiting "cones," and attractive—and in our species, often super-sized—leaves.

There are about 225 species of magnolias worldwide, not including the numerous selections, cultivars, and hybrids. Nearly all have been successfully introduced into horticulture. About two-thirds of the known species are native to Asia, ranging in geography from India to China, Korea, and Japan. The remaining species are centered in the West Indies, Mexico, and the Americas. Nine species are native to North America, one of which is found only in the cloud forests of Mexico. The other eight are spread from about New York to Florida and west to Texas, making the southeast the center of distribution for magnolias in the United States. All of the states included in this book can count at least five native species in their flora, and Alabama, Georgia, and

Tulip poplar.

Southern magnolia 'Kay Paris,' showing spiral arrangement of pistils and stamens.

Ashe magnolia flower after pollination, with fallen stamens and darkened stigmas.

South Carolina, with their broad latitudinal or longitudinal gradients, are each home to seven.

Magnolias are closely related to the tulip trees (genus *Liriodendron*), the only other genus in the magnolia family. Only two species of tulip trees are known, the Chinese species *L. chinense*, and our own *L. tulipifera*, a well-known and stately tree of eastern deciduous forests. Both species produce very large trees with squared leaves and interesting, tuliplike flowers. They are marginally used in residential landscaping and are better suited to large properties due to their potentially large size.

Magnolias are highly valued in the garden for their showy, complicated flowers that display a fascinating floral morphology indicative of their ancient lineage. Magnolia flowers first appear in the fossil record during the Cretaceous period (135–70 million years ago) and have changed little since, making the blossom in your garden an aromatic link to prehistoric times. Numerous stamens and pistils spiral around an erect central axis, subtended by a whorl of creamy white petallike structures that in many species are difficult to differentiate into typical sepals and petals. Although some authorities use the names *petals* and *sepals*, most use the collective term *tepals*, a botanical permutation that shows deference to structural similarity.

The pollination biology of native magnolias is as interesting as the plants themselves. The strongly fragrant blossoms that attract our attention also attracted the attention of their ancient pollinators. The flowers are diurnal and protogynous, meaning that they open during the day and close at night, and that the pistils, or female portions of the flower, are recep-

Fertilized flower.

Southern magnolia "cone" (follicetum). An empty follicetum.

tive to pollen only in the time period before the stamens reach maturity. In bud, the flower is covered by a fuzzy bract that encircles and protects the developing tepals. The pistils of some species become receptive just prior to the flowers opening and are visited at this stage by an array of beetles that force themselves between or chew their way through the thick, fleshy tissue. In the smaller-flowered species, the flowers open only partly during the first day, then close during the evening and reopen the second day to shed pollen and drop their stamens. Blossoms of the larger-flowered forms are too big to close again completely and remain at least partially open throughout the pollination process. Removing a mature stamen from a second-day flower and sprinkling its pollen into the narrow opening of an early-morning first-day flower enhances the chances of fertilization and seed production.

The magnolia fruit, colloquially referred to as a "cone," is as structurally primitive as the flowers. Technically called a "follicetum," it consists of an aggregate of numerous podlike follicles that split along one suture to release one or two seeds that are coated with a brightly colored red, orange-red, or pinkish aril—the fleshy covering that surrounds the seeds. The aril is a tasty food source and serves as an attractant to birds, which eat the fruit and aid in seed dispersal. Each follicle represents a single expanded ovary and each seed a potentially new magnolia. Magnolia propagators usually look for ripening seeds in late summer and early fall, collecting them just before the dangling red dainties are plucked off by hungry wildlife.

Six of the southeastern native magnolias are easy to grow and are regularly planted in residential landscapes. These include Ashe magnolia (*Magnolia ashei*), bigleaf magnolia (*M. macrophylla*), umbrella magnolia (*M. tripetala*), cucumber magnolia (*M. acuminata*), southern magnolia (*M. grandiflora*), and sweetbay magnolia (*M. virginiana*). Fraser magnolia (*M. fraseri*) and pyramid magnolia (*M. pyramidata*) are somewhat more challenging in the garden, difficult to find in nurseries, and are less often seen in cultivation. Of the six species treated here, the first four listed are deciduous and the latter two evergreen—or in the case of the sweetbay, mostly evergreen.

Deciduous Magnolias

It is somewhat ironic that the most narrowly endemic of the deciduous magnolias is also one of the more widely planted. Ashe magnolia (*M. ashei*) is found in nature only in the Florida panhandle, primarily from about Tallahassee westward nearly to Pensacola. As an example of its wide and successful use, the national champion is located in Mary Henry's collection at the Henry Botanic Garden in Gladwyne, Pennsylvania. This plant was grown from seed collected by Henry and in 2005 was 44 feet tall with a 44-foot spread and 62-inch circumference. Although this champion might seem out of place given its restricted natural range, Ashe magnolia is noted for its cold hardiness and is grown as far north as Chicago, Ontario, and Maine. It is normally rated for USDA zones 6–9, but according to a 1994 publication by Paul Cappiello and Lyle Littlefield, specimens planted in the Lyle E. Littlefield Ornamentals Trial Garden at the University of Maine, Orono—situated in zone 4A—survived winter temperatures of -30° F with little or no damage. Ashe magnolia is typically considered a relict species that was pushed southward by Pleistocene glaciers and left stranded as the climate warmed. Its hardiness today may well stem from a primordial genetic lineage.

Ashe magnolia.

Ashe magnolia.

Ashe magnolia.

Ashe magnolia.

Ashe magnolia fruit.

In nature, Ashe magnolia is an understory tree or shrub, occupying the heavily shaded deciduous forests of slopes, bluffs, and ravines. Normally it is a relatively short, gangly, shrublike tree, but it can reach heights in excess of thirty feet if given room and sufficient light. The leaves are very large, measuring up to about two feet long, and have a tropical appearance and silvery gray undersurface.

Ashe magnolia.

Bigleaf magnolia.　　　　　　　　　　Bigleaf magnolia.

The wide use of this naturally restricted native is probably due to its relatively small size, rapid maturity, attractive habit, and surprising drought tolerance. Young, vigorous trees frequently flower when only 2–3 years old and less than 3 feet tall, putting on a single 12-inch-wide blossom nestled in the uppermost whorl of leaves at the top of the stem. The tepals are creamy white and often bear a striking purplish blotch near the base. Older trees planted in good light put on numerous blossoms and are very attractive during their late spring flowering period, as well as again in the fall as their bright red fruits mature. If well cared for and appropriately situated, they can grow for many years, sometimes sending up new shoots from the root crown and seemingly being reborn time and again through the years. In the spring before his eighty-fifth birthday, Angus Gholson, a well-known plantsman and botanist in Chattahoochee, Florida, was still enjoying the Ashe magnolia planted by his father well over a half century earlier. Magnolia enthusiasts as far north as hardiness zone 4 easily keep this species healthy and vigorous, although late-season freezes sometimes cause damage.

Bigleaf magnolia.　　　　　Bigleaf magnolia.

Bigleaf magnolia.

Bigleaf magnolia.

Umbrella magnolia.

Bigleaf magnolia.

Umbrella magnolia.

Umbrella magnolia flower. Courtesy of Ron Lance.

The Ashe magnolia is sometimes considered to be a variety of bigleaf magnolia. The two plants are very similar in general appearance but do not overlap in range. Bigleaf is a much larger tree with slightly larger leaves and a more expansive range. It occurs naturally in all of the states represented in this book except Florida (although gardeners in the Florida panhandle successfully grow it there), and it also occurs in Arkansas, Kentucky, Ohio, and Tennessee. It can reach heights of 100 feet, but typically tops out at about 60 feet, and its leaves can be nearly 3 feet long and up to 1 foot wide. The potentially large size has led some experts to suggest that it is too bulky for urban landscapes. Magnolia enthusiasts typically disagree with this assessment, preferring instead to plant at least one specimen in hopes that it will grow large enough to produce the spreading canopy of soft green leaves that defines its character.

Our only other deciduous magnolia with oversized leaves is the umbrella magnolia, which is typically a little less than 50 feet tall with 1–2-foot leaves. The common name derives from its spreading, umbrella-like canopy with branches terminating in whorl-like leaf clusters. The flowers are only about 4 inches across when fully open and are often described as having a malodorous or fetid aroma, although some observers report being unable to sense this. The inner whorl of creamy white tepals is subtended by three greenish sepal-like tepals, which is the basis of the somewhat misleading epithet, *tripetala*. Umbrella magnolia is the only southeastern native magnolia that is pollinated primarily by flies rather than beetles, which at least partially explains the flower's less than pleasant fragrance.

Umbrella magnolia occurs in our region in all states except Louisiana, though in Florida it is very rare and currently known from only two small populations. It is very accommodating of garden situations and grows well in many landscapes from the coastal plains to the mountains. It and the bigleaf magnolia are the two magnolias most commonly found and transplanted as part of the Georgia Native Plant Society's (GNPS) very aggressive plant rescue program. Rescue volunteers report that both species do very well when removed as very young trees (usually less than six feet tall) and virtually all transplanted specimens survive. Given the continuing expansion of residential communities into Piedmont woodlands near Atlanta, GNPS rescuers have the opportunity to save numerous native magnolias from destruction. It should be emphasized that removal of the plants targeted by GNPS has been approved by the landowner and focuses only on plants that will soon be destroyed in the course of clearing and development. Magnolias and other native plants should otherwise never be removed from the wild.

Cucumber magnolia comes as close to having a naturally yellow flower as any magnolia known, particularly the variety commonly referred to as *M. acuminata* var. *subcordata*. This tree, too, has the potential to become large—to as much as ninety feet tall—but its leaves are the smallest of our deciduous species. They usually do not exceed about ten inches long—but are sometimes much shorter than this—and are more or less reverse-egg-shaped (obovate) or elliptical in outline. Unlike most of our deciduous magnolias, which typically have smooth, grayish bark, the bark of cucumber magnolia is brown, narrowly furrowed, and more reminiscent of an elm or basswood than a magnolia.

The cucumber magnolia is also the only one of our southeastern deciduous magnolias that has given rise to more than a handful of cultivars, selections, and hybrids,

Cucumber magnolia.

Cucumber magnolia bark.

Cucumber magnolia flower. Courtesy of Ron Lance.

Fraser magnolia.

most of which have resulted from attempts at accentuating the yellow flower color. At least forty cultivars are known, many of which are difficult to find in either wholesale or retail nurseries. The most successful introductions seem to be those that resulted from crossing cucumber magnolia with other species, most notably the Chinese species *M. liliiflora* and *M. denudata*, which are often used in the production of new hybrids. The

Fraser magnolia.

Fraser magnolia.

Fraser magnolia flower. Courtesy of Ron Lance.

best known and most widely planted of these crosses is called 'Butterflies,' a cultivar that extends the hardiness range for yellow-flowered forms northward to USDA zone 4.

These four deciduous magnolias are tough garden plants. All are easy to grow and require little care once established. Impatient gardeners interested in immediate flowering should probably select Ashe magnolia, as young plants purchased in a nursery will often flower in the first year or two after they are planted. The other species sometimes require ten years or more for the first blossoms.

The other two deciduous magnolias that occur in our region are the Fraser or mountain magnolia (*M. fraseri*) and pyramid magnolia (*M. pyramidata*). These species are closely related to one another and have similar attributes. Pyramid magnolia was for a long time considered to be only a variety Fraser magnolia and is still treated as such by some specialists. Both have earlike lobes at the base of the leaves, bright white tepals that narrow significantly at the base, and reddish or pinkish fruiting "cones." Fraser is a tree of the southern Appalachians and upper Piedmont. It grows in mountain coves and rich woods from West Virginia westward to Kentucky and south to northernmost Georgia. Pyramid magnolia is found only in the lower Piedmont and coastal plains from South Carolina southward to northern Florida and west to eastern Texas. The ranges of the two do not overlap. Both are somewhat difficult to grow, and neither is commonly available in the nursery trade, although Nearly Native Nursery,

Pyramid magnolia.

Pyramid magnolia.

Pyramid magnolia.

Woodlanders, and Meadowbrook/We-Du Natives normally offer at least one of the two species.

Deciduous magnolias are subject to root rot in either the pot or the ground. When selecting container plants from the nursery, it is usually better to select young plants with firm roots than to select older, larger plants that have had more time to develop root problems. However, some growers have successfully combated root rot by growing young plants in larger pots, which ensures that excess water retained near the bottom of the pot does not affect the root system. As a general rule, it is wise to remove potential purchases from their pots and examine the roots carefully, looking especially for signs of excessive moisture in the bottom inch or so of the root ball. Roots should be creamy in color. Blackish or dark brown roots are a sign of deterioration.

For one-gallon pots it is probably also best to select plants less than three feet tall to ensure that stem growth has not exceeded development of the supporting root system. Young plants of some species, particularly the umbrella magnolia, often have weak stems with a propensity to break when exposed to even moderately gusty winds. Injured plants will usually resprout from the root or lower stem, even if left unpruned, but will take longer to reach maturity. Routinely staking large-leaved species until the stem strength catches up with root and leaf growth is a good way to prevent breakage.

Plant deciduous species in well-drained soil. Dig a hole as deep as the root ball and about twice as wide. A hole no deeper than the root ball will prevent the plant from sinking deeper after planting and protect the roots from the danger of standing in excess water. At least ½ inch of water should drain through the soil in less than an hour to ensure adequate drainage. Amend moisture-retentive soils with a coarse organic additive or a mixture of bark and soil. Alternately, new plantings—especially those situated in heavy clay soils—can be only partially submerged in the hole, leaving the top of the root ball above the ground with mulch and soil mixture built up to cover the top of the root ball. Gently agitate the roots along the edges of the container ball before planting and fill the bottom and sides of the hole with the amendment. Magnolias have tender, brittle roots, but it helps to spread them a little to ensure good contact with the soil.

Deciduous magnolias have shallow root systems and benefit significantly from mulching. It is important not to overwater during the first year or two and then only during periods of active growth. As with native azaleas, it is also a good idea to avoid the use of herbicides in the root zone of these plants, especially with newly planted young trees. Adequate mulching and hand pulling are the best ways to keep weeds at bay.

Evergreen Magnolias

Two species of native evergreen magnolias occur in the southeastern United States. Even though both are used in gardening and landscaping, the southern magnolia or bullbay (*M. grandiflora*) is by far the more popular of the two. Native only to the coastal plains, it is planted widely across the southeast, except in the coldest areas, and has become one of the most popular garden magnolias in the world. Well over a hundred cultivars are available in commerce, accentuating the plant's every feature, including selections for leaf size, flower size, extended flowering times, compact and columnar habit, and hardiness. Many cultivars emphasize the reddish color of the lower leaf surfaces while others are selected for their dark green upper surfaces. Several selections also purport increased cold hardiness. According to Barry Yinger, writing in the journal of the Magnolia Society International, the most successful of these cold-hardy selections is probably 'Bracken's Brown Beauty.'

Part of the southern magnolia's success as a

Southern magnolia.

Southern magnolia.

Southern magnolia flower bud.

garden plant stems from its wide tolerance of varying soil types, soil moisture regimes, and climate. In presettlement times it was a dominant species in dune fields and coastal sands and is still present as a small, scrubby tree within sight of the Atlantic Ocean along the Florida east coast. Ironically, it is probably more characteristic and better known as a component of rich, moist woodland slopes where, with its counterpart American beech, it takes on huge proportions and adds an evergreen component to predominantly deciduous woodlands.

Its capacity to adapt to tough situations has resulted in the selection of numerous cultivars, some of which can be seen adorning parking lots, roadsides, and highway medians, as well as decorating parks, yards, and suburban lot lines. Some of the more popular selections for hardiness zone 7–9 include 'Little Gem' and 'Bracken's Brown Beauty,' both of which have smaller leaves with a dense, rusty-brown color beneath.

Southern magnolia 'Bracken's Brown Beauty.'

Southern magnolia 'DD Blanchard' first day flower.

Field-grown southern magnolia 'DD Blanchard.'

Southern magnolia 'DD Blanchard' fruit.

Field-grown southern magnolia 'Little Gem.'

Sweetbay magnolia.

Sweetbay magnolia.

Sweetbay magnolia.

Sweetbay magnolia.

The long-flowering 'Kay Paris' and cold-hardy 'Edith Bogue' are often used in the colder climates.

The southern magnolia's success in colonizing new situations has led some Piedmont gardeners and native plant enthusiasts to worry about its increasing prevalence, especially in areas where early spring wildflowers, many of which are rare and unusual, depend upon deciduous canopies to allow late winter sunlight to penetrate the forest floor. On some sites the overlapping, evergreen foliage of low, dense stands of southern magnolia saplings effectively shades the ground all year, potentially altering the normal ecological processes associated with early spring woodlands.

Sweetbay is the other southeastern evergreen native magnolia. The southern form (referred to as variety *australis*) is an evergreen wetland tree to about sixty feet tall and grows naturally in coastal depressions, swamps, wet flatwoods, boggy edges, floodplains, and bottomlands across the coastal plains and lower Piedmont. The northern form (referred to as variety *virginiana*) is more often a deciduous multistemmed shrub that does not normally exceed about twenty feet tall. The leaves of both are smaller and paler than those of southern magnolia and are silvery white beneath rather than rusty red. Despite sweetbay's natural wetland preference, it adapts well to gardens, has given rise to more than twenty cultivars, and is regularly planted in both naturalistic and manicured landscapes.

The flowers of sweetbay are much smaller than those of our other magnolias. Most are less than three inches wide when fully open, but they often occur in great abundance, making flowering specimens very attractive but not overpowering. The fruiting "cone" is also smaller and is medium green when young, maturing to purplish

Getting a magnolia to market at Taylor's Nursery.

or pinkish red. The seeds are bright red, comparatively few in number, and enjoyed by wildlife. Sweetbay is typically planted in sun to part shade but also flowers well in deeper shade.

Both of our evergreen magnolias, especially the sweetbay, do best in acidic soils and tolerate being potted to a larger size than most of the deciduous species. Nevertheless, it is probably better not to purchase oversized trees, unless they have been field grown, extracted, and burlapped just before purchase. Larger nurseries with sufficient acreage, such as the four-thousand-acre wholesale Taylor Nursery in Raleigh, North Carolina, cultivate trees in the ground and extract them upon receipt of an order.

Propagating Magnolias

Most of the native magnolias mentioned above, especially the evergreen species, are readily available in retail nurseries and garden centers, or they can be ordered from one of several online mail-order outlets. For most gardeners, it is easier and quicker to purchase them than to grow them. Nevertheless, home gardeners often wish to try their hand at propagation.

Traditionally, magnolias have been propagated by grafting a cutting (scion) from a favorite plant onto the stock of another plant, often of a different species. Grafting allows cloning of trees with desirable characteristics and is most often used for creating genetically identical cultivars. Grafted trees are common in large magnolia collections, especially those containing trees and cultivars from around the world. Grafting requires skill, space, and the availability of seedlings or rooted cuttings as stock, much of which is beyond the facilities of many home gardeners, and it offers little to native plant enthusiasts who want only to grow a few native magnolias on native stock.

Genetic clones may also be reproduced from rooted cuttings. This process involves severing several inches of new growth from a favorite plant in early summer, removing the lowermost leaves and the outer half of the 2–3 remaining leaves, wounding and dipping the bottom of the stem into a rooting hormone, then sticking the cutting into a rooting medium, usually composed of a mixture of peat and sand or perlite. Greater sterility and better success are achieved with the use of a misting system and greenhouse. Growing magnolias from rooted cuttings has become one of the preferred methods of commercial propagation, but it may well be replaced by propagation through tissue culture.

Many home-based magnolia enthusiasts lack the time and facilities for grafting or rooting and prefer growing native magnolias naturally from seeds. Fortunately, most species of magnolias in the wild produce large enough seed crops to allow collection, and enthusiasts who already have flowering specimens can use seeds collected from their own gardens. Growing magnolias from seed does not allow for genetic copies of selected plants, but it does increase genetic diversity in the garden and allows for sharing the fruits of one's labor with other gardeners and magnolia enthusiasts.

Nurseryman Dan Miller, owner of Trillium Gardens, a wholesale nursery in Tallahassee, Florida, has been propagating and growing native magnolias from seed for many years. Although he has not spent much time with the evergreen species, his recipe for reproducing deciduous magnolias has been very successful. Miller collects seeds in late summer, just as they become visible on the cone. Fallen cones are often quickly robbed of seed by wildlife; collecting them before they fall means a larger, higher-quality crop. Miller soaks the seeds in water for 2–3 days, until they become soft and begin to putrify, then scrapes them between squares of screen to loosen the outer coating (aril). The seed coats of many species of plants, including the magnolias, are impregnated with chemical germination inhibitors designed to prevent untimely natural germination. Removing the seed coat and the oily substances below it will help ensure successful germination. Once the coats are removed, Miller washes the seeds thoroughly—an admittedly labor-intensive and time-consuming process—then dries them on blotter paper or paper towels, deposits them in a sealable plastic bag, and stores them in a standard refrigerator.

Some experts suggest that the seeds should be wrapped in peat before refrigerating. Others treat seeds with a fungicide before storing it. Miller uses no additional medium, preferring to store the seeds loose to prevent fungus and mildew, both of which are common problems in the storage of magnolia seed. Since Miller's nursery is located in zone 9A, he sows his seeds in early December, in anticipation of a late-February germination. He keeps the germination containers in the greenhouse until the chance of frost has passed, then pots and moves the plants outside. The shortened time frame between germination and potting reduces the likelihood of root rot, a serious problem with magnolia seedlings.

Miller also recommends hand pollination as the best way to obtain the largest quantity of viable magnolia seeds. Extracting ripe stamens with sufficient pollen from open flowers and sprinkling the pollen over the stigmas of receptive (usually vase-shaped) flowers, then monitoring the development of these hand-pollinated cones, will likely produce a higher percentage of viable seeds than collecting seeds in the wild. In floatation tests where seeds are floated in water to check viability, as many as 90 percent of some batches of wild-collected seeds float, suggesting a lack of viability that has been confirmed in germination tests. In hand-pollinated seed, the percentage of floaters is much lower. Only the seeds that sink are planted.

Magnolia Relatives

Systematic botanists categorize plants into increasingly inclusive assemblages based on evolutionary lineages and phylogenetic relationships. Species are grouped into genera, genera into families, families into orders, orders into subclasses, and subclasses into classes, each higher level representing an increasingly larger group of related species. The subclass Magnoliidae, which contains all of the world's magnolias, includes the most primitive of the flowering plants, most of which evolved between 135 and 70 million years ago. The custard-apple (or pawpaw), laurel, and star-anise families also belong to this ancient subclass. All have interesting floral, fruit, and foliar features, and several are regularly used in native plant gardening.

Pawpaws

The members of the Annonaceae (custard-apple family) are more closely related to the magnolias than are any other group of flowering plants. The family contains about 128 genera worldwide—distributed mostly in the tropics—with only the pawpaws of the genus *Asimina* being widespread in the southeastern United States. Like the magnolias, pawpaw flowers are primitive and aromatic, with a central axis, numerous stamens and pistils, and floppy, fleshy petals that attract and provide food for pollinating beetles. Unlike the magnolias, the

Common pawpaw.

Small-fruited pawpaw.

Common pawpaw.

fruit, too, is fleshy and consists of a many-seeded aggregate of numerous fused berries that coalesce inside of a tough, bronzy skin. Some members of the family, probably including at least a few pawpaw species, exhibit floral thermogenesis, a process by which the flowers produce heat at night to encourage visiting beetles to continue their pollination work well into the evening.

The common pawpaw, or Indian-banana (*A. triloba*), is by far the most common and widely used garden species. It often grows into a small, forty-foot tree with spreading branches but is sometimes multistemmed and shrubby. Common pawpaw spreads easily by root suckers, and it is not uncommon to find large colonies in the wild, especially in the moist soils of shady woodlands along small creeks and streams. An excellent population occurs along the hiking trails on Roosevelt Island, a ninety-one-acre national park surrounded by the Potomac River, just south of Washington, D.C. The flowers develop before the new leaves emerge and hang below the branch on short stalks. They are dark purplish red to almost blackish red with a fetid aroma that attracts both beetles and flies as pollinators. The fruit is somewhat sweet to the taste and is a good wildlife food that is relished by raccoons and by people. Pawpaw connoisseur Steve Christman reports making delicious pies and puddings from the fruit, especially from cultivars bred for enhanced taste. This species is not self-fertile and will produce fruit only if two trees are present to ensure cross-pollination. Common pawpaw makes a nice small specimen tree but can also be planted in a small group along a partly sunny border. Mature leaves are up to twelve inches long and six inches wide, and their shape is reminiscent of the leaves of some of our smaller-leaved deciduous magnolias. Com-

Slimleaf pawpaw.

Bigflower pawpaw.

mon pawpaw is appropriate for zones 5–9A, 8–6, although it probably does best from USDA zone 8 northward.

Small-fruited pawpaw (*A. parviflora*) is a diminutive version of common pawpaw, with smaller leaves, fruit, and flowers. It is listed by some nurseries as dwarf pawpaw, which is unfortunate as the white-flowered *A. pygmaea* of extreme southeastern Georgia and the Florida peninsula is also known by this name. Small-fruited pawpaw often occurs in coastal hammocks and other nearly xeric locations as well as in relatively rich woods. As a result, it can tolerate much drier sites than its larger relative. The flowers are very similar to those of common pawpaw but are borne stalkless or nearly so, and the leaves are not quite as long. This is a common shrub in nature but is not yet widely available in the trade. It is sold by Woodlanders and a few native plant nurseries in Florida (see http://www.afnn.org). It performs well in the coastal plains and Piedmont, hardiness zones 7–9.

Several white-flowered pawpaws occur in our region, most of which are restricted largely to Florida and hardiness zones 9–10. Few are readily available in the trade. All have very interesting and attractive flowers and are good wildlife food plants. More attention should be given at least to the use of the low-growing and profusely flowering slimleaf pawpaw (*A. angustifolia*) in coastal plains gardens. Florida gardeners should seek out one of the several predominately Florida species, such as the very attractive flag (*A. incana*) and bigflower (*A. obovata*) pawpaws, both of which produce relatively large and showy, creamy white flowers. Although slow-growing, all of the white-flowered species should make excellent garden shrubs in dry, sandy soils.

The True Laurels

Three species circumscribe the garden laurels: sassafras, red bay, and spicebush, the last of which is included in Part III of this book. All are well-known trees with long histories in southern landscapes. All are also members of the true laurel family (Lauraceae), which should not be confused with the mountain laurel and its relatives, which are members of the heath family.

Most members of the Lauraceae are characterized by the presence of aromatic foliar oils. The most famous member of the family is the ancient *Laurus nobilis* of European origin, the source of the culinary bay leaves used to flavor foods. The foliage of at least three native species contains similar oils. The red bay, at least, was formerly planted near homesteads, and its leaves were used to flavor soups, broths, and stews.

Two species of red bay occur in our area, both of which are very similar in general appearance and only marginally used in gardening. Red bay (*Persea borbonia*) is an upland species that can become a very attractive, dark-barked tree to at least fifty feet tall. Swamp red bay (*P. palustris*), also called simply "swamp bay," is a smaller, wetland tree generally confined to swamps with standing water. These trees are readily available from a variety of Florida retail nurseries but are less widely available elsewhere. Woodlanders

---

Laurel Wilt

Unfortunately, the persistence of the laurels as garden plants and as a continued part of our native flora is in jeopardy. A recent and rapidly expanding fungal disease that first appeared in Port Wentworth near Savannah, Georgia, in May 2002 has now spread well southward of its point of origin. The fungus is introduced to trees by a non-native insect—appropriately called the red bay ambrosia beetle *(Xyleborus glabratus)*—that likely arrived in the United States inadvertently in solid wood packing material. The fungus travels in special pouches in the beetle's head near the base of its mandibles and is transferred to the tree as the beetle tunnels into the wood to lay its eggs. The fungus reproduces rapidly to provide a food source for beetle larvae, clogging the water-conducting tissues of infected trees and causing them to wilt and eventually die.

By 2007 the infestation had spread southward along the Atlantic seaboard to several counties in northeast Florida and a single county much farther south along the Florida coast. Although the rate of spread by beetles alone is only about twenty miles per year, expansion is accelerated by human transport of wood for firewood and other purposes and perhaps by plants in the garden trade.

The primary host for the fungus has been the red bay, but all members of the laurel family are susceptible, and individuals of sassafras (*Sassafras albidum*), pond spice (*Lindera benzoin*), and pondberry (*L. melissaefolia*) have all succumbed. No effective strategies have been isolated to prevent infection, and there is considerable concern that the laurels may well go the way of the American chestnut and American elm. The U.S. Forest Service has implemented a seed collection program in an attempt to save the family's genetic diversity in case all or most of its members are wiped out.

Red bay dying from laurel wilt. Courtesy of Albert (Bud) Mayfield, Florida Department of Agriculture and Consumer Services, United States.

Swamp and red bay are only occasionally used in native gardens.

Red bay.

and Mail Order Natives are online sources. Both species have aromatic leaves, grow in partial shade to full sun in hardiness zones 7–10, and are listed as larval food plants for palamedes and spicebush swallowtails. Red bay, in particular, develops best in full sun and can be open-grown as an attractive specimen tree. The leaves of these species are subject to the development of insect galls, which can disfigure the foliage for part of the year but do no apparent damage to the health of the plant.

Spicebush (*Lindera benzoin*) is a must-have shrub or small tree for butterfly enthusiasts who want to attract spicebush swallowtails to their gardens. Young plants are more or less shrubby and multistemmed, but some individuals develop a single trunk and take on the form of a small tree to about twenty feet tall. The leaves are very aromatic when crushed, and the attractive, bright yellow, sweetly fragrant flower clusters appear on naked branches in early spring, adding a colorful accent to the still-winter woods. In early fall, female trees produce showy, bright red, ellipsoid fruit that give off a pungent spicy aroma when crushed and are a favorite food of thrushes. The fall foliage is bright yellow and provides an attractive contrast to the scarlet fruit in the Piedmont and mountains, especially where plants are shaded, but is somewhat less colorful in the hotter portions of the coastal plains. Spicebush performs well in zones 4–9, 8–1.

Sassafras leaves are often mitten-shaped and colorful in fall.

Sassafras male flowers.

It tolerates mildly acidic to sweet soils and, according to Dick Birr, writing in *Growing and Propagating Showy Native Woody Plants*, it benefits from an annual dose of lime in very acidic soils. Spicebush grows naturally in the shade of understory woodlands but does best in at least partial sun in the garden. See Part III for more information about spicebush cultivation.

The sassafras (*Sassafras albidum*) is a familiar eastern native with a colorful cultural history. As early as about 1500, American Indians used bark from the tree's roots to treat fevers, and a century later New World explorers used the roots for decocting a medicinal tonic for the treatment of rheumatism, skin disease, and syphilis. Modern enthusiasts still enjoy the sweet taste of sassafras tea, and commercial producers once extracted the active ingredient safrole for pharmaceutical products and to flavor soft drinks, especially root beer, a practice that was banned in 1960 with the discovery that oral ingestion of the chemical caused liver cancer in rats. Filé, a powder produced by grinding dried leaves and used to flavor gumbo and other Cajun dishes, has apparently not been linked to negative health effects.

Sassafras is easily recognized by its mittenlike leaves—some with two fingerlike lobes, some with three, some with none. In fall they add bright yellow, reddish, and purple hues to the lower south's often drab autumn color. Flowers are produced in rounded clusters during March or April, typically well before the new leaves emerge, and resemble bright yellow ornaments at the branch tips. The fruit is a dark blue drupe with an attractive, bright red stalk. The drupes are relished by an array of songbirds from flycatchers to vireos, as well as by squirrels and rabbits. Trees are either male or female, which means that both genders must be present to produce fruit. The bark of old trees is very attractive, more or less orange-brown with deep furrows running vertically between broad ridges.

This is a common native tree that is underutilized as a garden and landscape plant. It is fast-growing; tolerates a variety of soil and moisture conditions; spans zones 4–9, 8–3; produces brilliant red, yellow, orange, or pinkish foliage in the fall; and is useful for wildlife. It is extremely easy to grow and spreads readily by root suckering. Two plants can turn into many over time, which can be an advantage for screening and naturalistic landscapes but problematic for the tidy gardener. The suckering habit makes the tree difficult to transplant from the wild or from within the garden. What appear to be seedlings are often nothing more than sprouts. When severed from the subtending root, they loose vigor and die. True seedlings and pot-grown plants can be transplanted easily. Removing suckers reduces competition for the main tree and ensures a single-stemmed, treelike stature. Aggressive pruning and allowing suckers to freely develop ensure a colony of smaller, more shrublike plants. Sassafras seed should be collected in early fall and can be planted immediately or cold stratified through the winter for early spring planting.

Anise

Some plants are extremely restricted in natural range but widely adapted to garden use. This is certainly true of the Ocala or yellow anise (*Illicium parviflorum*). Found naturally only in five counties in east-central Florida, its introduction into the landscape trade has been extraordinarily successful, and it is now widely valued as a fast-growing evergreen screening shrub throughout the Piedmont and coastal plains from Virginia to Louisiana

Ocala anise flowers.

Florida anise.

Florida anise.

(zones 7–10, 9–7). The flowers are less than ¼ inch long, more or less bell-shaped in outline, and not particularly showy, but this deficiency is more than offset by the plant's dense foliage, upright stature, and broad form. The leaves are yellow-green, narrowly elliptic in outline, more or less upright in orientation, and exude the scent of root beer when crushed. This species' natural habitat includes moist woods and swampy wetlands where it often grows as an open, somewhat scraggly shrub, usually in dense shade. However, it is very adaptable and achieves its best garden form in partial sun and moist soils, especially when used to screen backyard decks, decorate fencerows, or to add bulk to shrubby borders. Increased shade produces darker green leaves. Ocala anise has no pest problems, tolerates a wide range of soils, responds well to pruning, can be shaped into a dense hedge if desired, and is sometimes used commercially to soften the austerity of parking lots. It is sometimes recommended as a foundation plant, especially for larger homes, but such installations usually require regular pruning to maintain size. If left to their own devices, unpruned plants can become twenty feet tall and nearly as wide.

Florida anise (*I. floridanum*) is more widely distributed in nature than Ocala anise but is somewhat more particular about garden conditions. It, too, occurs naturally in wetland habitats, usually along streams and rivulets near the bottoms of slopes and ravines. Its natural range is mostly within about one hundred miles of the Gulf from northwest Florida to eastern Louisiana, although it has been recorded farther inland in both Alabama and Mississippi. Unlike Ocala anise, Florida anise is prized not only for its foliage, which smells like anise or licorice when crushed and is darker green than that of Ocala anise, but also for its numerous primitive flowers, each of which can have up to about 35 tepals, 40 stamens, and 15 pistils. The typical flower color is an attractive brick red, but individuals with pink and white flowers are occasionally discovered in the wild, and selections of both are available in the trade. *I. floridanum* 'Semmes' and a form sometimes referred to as *I. floridanum* var. *album* produce white flowers, and a recent introduction discovered by Tom Dodd III and named 'Shady Lady' has lavender-pink flowers. Florida anise should be planted in partial to full shade in moist, acidic soils. Too much sun and drought will cause the leaves to turn yellow and droop and the plant to loose vigor and die.

The name "star anise" is sometimes used for these species and derives from the star-shaped cluster of follicles that follow the flowers. Each follicle splits along its upper side at maturity, forcibly expelling the single seed some distance from the tree and leaving the darkening cluster of spent pods on the plant well into the fall.

There has been some confusion about the identity of these species in the trade and in guidebooks. The white-flowered form of Florida anise is sometimes depicted as Ocala anise and both of the native species have apparently been confused with the white-flowered Japanese anise (*I. anisatum*).

9

Maples, Buckeyes, Sumacs, and Wafer Ash

The maples, buckeyes, sumacs, and wafer ash constitute a seemingly diverse but closely related group of species in the botanical order Sapindales, a monophyletic assemblage of plants all descended from a common ancestor. In recent years, the Sapindales (and its constituent families, genera, and species) have undergone significant taxonomic upheaval. Maples and buckeyes were once classified in separate families—Aceraceae for the maples and Hippocastanaceae for the buckeyes—but more recently have been included with the soapberries in the family Sapindaceae (soapberry family). The sumacs represent the Anacardiaceae or cashew family, and the wafer ash is a citrus (Rutaceae). All members of the Sapindales are woody plants with leaves that vary from alternate to opposite and simple to compound. Apart from these technical taxonomic maneuverings, many members of the order—and especially the families treated here—contain excellent garden plants with long horticultural histories.

Maples

Few trees are better known or more closely entwined with American culture than the maples. Even before the arrival of European colonists, Native Americans tapped the trunks of the sugar maple for its sugary sap. As early as 1606 the French author and lawyer Marc Lescarbot described the collection and production of maple sugar by eastern Canada's Micmac Indians. Since then, the maple has continued as a treasured commodity with uses that range from the production of sugars, syrups, and candies to the manufacture of high-quality lumber, exquisite furniture, and decorative veneers. Maple trees were part of the earliest American gardens and arboreta and today are seen lining streets, decorating parks, and bringing color, texture, and form to residential neighborhoods. Their opposite, palmately lobed leaves are unmistakable identifiers, and each year their orange, scarlet, crimson, and yellow autumn foliage allure thousands of "leaf peepers" to the eastern mountains.

Maples are essentially dioecious plants, meaning that their flowers are functionally either male or female and borne on separate trees (a few species are polygamodioecious, with unisexual and bisexual flowers intermixed). Maple flowers are small and individually inconspicuous but—depending upon species—are usually borne in such quantities as to impart a colorful yellowish, greenish, or reddish cast to an otherwise naked late-winter crown. Female flowers have a two-parted stigma and two ovaries, each of which develops into a single seed at the base of a winged samara. The samaras of a single flower

Red maple winged keys.

Red maple male flowers.

are typically fused at the base to form the "maple key" that flutters and spirals in even the gentlest breeze and can be carried by stronger winds great distances from the parent tree.

There are more than one hundred species of maples worldwide. Nine or ten are native to the southeast—depending upon the authority used—and range across all geologic provinces and climatic zones from the highest elevations to the edge of the sea. Nearly all are used in southern gardening, some more extensively than others, and most are readily available from retail and wholesale nurseries.

Red maple (*Acer rubrum*) is the most widespread and commonly used of our native maples. Its expansive range extends from eastern Canada to the southernmost tip of the Florida peninsula and westward to Minnesota and eastern Texas (zones 3–9, 9–1), and its elevation from sea level to at least 5,500 feet. As might be expected with such diverse geography, variability among populations can be extensive and provenance is extremely important for garden success. For best results, plants should be selected from local sources.

Red maple is certainly true to its name. In late winter or early spring its tiny red flowers offer the first hint of spring and are followed in quick succession by bright red to pinkish red samaras that become even brighter as the leaves unfurl. Even the new twigs and leaf stalks have a reddish tinge that persists throughout the summer. In autumn, the leaves turn clear yellow or fiery red, essentially making the red maple a four-season tree. Acidic soils tend to produce redder leaves; foliage on trees in neutral soils tends to be pale greenish yellow (or even chlorotic) and smaller. According to some observers, red maples situated in hardiness zone 9 are more likely to have yellow fall foliage, whereas the autumn foliage of trees situated in hardiness zones 6–8 is more often red.

Because of its expansive natural distribution, red maple is a forgiving tree with wide adaptability. It occurs naturally in swamps, wet woodlands, and bottoms, but it does not require them and often grows in drier sites. Trees planted in upland landscapes do very well as long as they are planted in acidic soils and kept reasonably moist; a few of the newer selections and cultivars even demonstrate a degree of drought tolerance.

The natural variation in red maple has led to numerous selections and cultivars. At least seventy are listed in the trade, a few of which derive from crosses between the red

Red maple.

Red maple.

Red maple.

and silver maples. Such crosses are usually recognized in the trade as *A. ×freemanii* (the original cross was engineered by Oliver M. Freeman). One of these crosses, now known as Autumn Blaze®, has become a popular and successful plant for southern gardens. It has much redder fall foliage, tolerates drier sites, and is widely available. Mature specimens can reach heights exceeding sixty feet and can be quite broad, which has led some experts to suggest that Autumn Blaze® is too large for the average home landscape. However, numerous forms of red maple regularly exceed heights of sixty feet, many of which are seen in residential settings. Local nurseries specializing in native plants or trees are among the best sources of information about how to obtain locally grown plants and which selections perform best in particular regions.

In addition to the almost dizzying number of selections and cultivars, two recognized varieties of red maple and a second, closely related species complicate the picture. The leaves of variety *rubrum* typically have 5–9 lobes, and those of variety *trilobum* typically have 3–5. According to at least one set of botanical descriptions, the leaves of

Sugar maple.

Sugar maple samaras. Courtesy of Ron

Chalk maple. Courtesy of Ron Lance.

Florida maple. Courtesy of Ron Lance.

Black maple. Courtesy of Ron Lance.

Drummond's or swamp red maple (*A. drummondii*), which is still considered by some authorities to be better treated as a variety of *A. rubrum*, are densely felty-hairy beneath, and the samaras are 1–2 inches long. The leaves of the other varieties of red maple have fewer hairs on their lower surfaces, and the samaras are less than 1¼ inches long.

If red maple is the most widespread of our native maples, the several members of the sugar maple group are certainly the most historical. At one point most authorities considered the sugar maple (*A. saccharum*) to be an exceptionally variable species that included several varieties and subspecies. The chalk, Florida, and black maples, long considered to be part of this sugar maple complex, are now treated as distinct species by at least some experts. As a result, several scientific names are regularly encountered in the trade but are easily sorted out. Chalk maple (*A. leucoderme*) is still often sold as *A. saccharum* subsp. *leucoderme*; Florida maple (*A. floridanum*) as both *A. saccharum* subsp. *floridanum* and *A. barbatum*; and black maple (*A. nigrum*) as *A. saccharum* subsp. *nigrum*. Fortunately, this seeming confusion in Latin monikers has not been generally transferred to these trees' common names.

All species in the sugar maple complex have more or less squarish leaves with pointed lobes and large blunt teeth. Leaf shape alone easily distinguishes them from the other maples, but not so readily from one another. Leaves of the sugar and black maples are decidedly larger, measuring 3–6 inches wide; those of the Florida and chalk maples usually do not exceed widths of about 3½ inches. Of the larger-leaved species, the leaves of black maple usually droop at the tips of the lobes; those of sugar maple usually do not. The smaller-leaved species are most easily distinguished by the lower surfaces of the leaves: those of Florida maple are whitish; those of chalk maple, green. All display exceptional autumn color.

The sugar and black maples are northern trees that extend into our region in the mountains and upper Piedmont. Sugar maple, at least, is widely planted across the southeast, but both species are best suited for zones 4–8, 8–1 and are likely to struggle in the heat and humidity of coastal plains gardens. Southern sugar maple or Florida maple (*A. floridanum*), on the other hand, is an excellent southern tree widely distributed across the Piedmont and coastal plains from Virginia to Florida and west to Texas. Florida maple is a popular street and landscape tree that is easy to grow, moderately drought tolerant, and adjusts well to neutral or even calcareous soils. Chalk maple is similar in most respects to Florida maple, with perhaps slightly better fall color. Both species are appropriate for hardiness zones 5–9 and are particularly good trees for smaller landscapes.

Silver maple (*A. saccharinum*) is nearly as widespread as red maple, except that its range does not extend as far south in Florida; it is best suited for hardiness zones 4–8. It, too, is a wetland tree found mostly in floodplains and river bottoms, but it is not as universally present across the region as red maple. It is very attractive with scaly, grayish bark and deeply incised leaves that are pale green above and silvery beneath. The central lobe on most leaves is narrower at the base than at the apex, which provides an excellent field character for separating it from our other native maples.

Despite its patchy distribution and a somewhat bad reputation, silver maple is a commonly planted lawn and garden tree, probably due to its rapid growth, attractive two-toned leaves, and ability to adapt to virtually any situation. However, it can be messy

Silver maple. Courtesy of Ron Lance.

A row of silver maples.

due to its brittle branches, which tend to break off and clutter the ground in even the mildest winds. Tidy gardeners who choose to plant this tree will want to place it in the background where the continuous rain of disorderly litter doesn't disrupt a manicured setting. Less tidy gardeners will want to situate it to easily see its attractive trunk and low-hanging limbs.

Silver maple is somewhat short-lived, has less autumn color than some species, and suffers from a number of diseases and insect pests. Some trees do not live long in artificial landscapes, and even those in wild populations sometimes look like they struggle to stay alive. The surface roots are aggressive, large enough to break up concrete and make mowing difficult, and sometimes breach septic tanks and waterlines. Silver maple works very well in natural wetlands where little else will grow and the threat of surface root damage is minimal. Nevertheless, more than a dozen named cultivars have appeared in the trade, and the tree continues to be a favorite of residential and commercial landscapers as well as maple aficionados throughout the eastern United States.

Some people refer to the box elder (*A. negundo*) as "poison-ivy tree," a somewhat unfortunate designation. The typically three-parted leaves certainly resemble those of its toxic cousin but are borne opposite rather than alternate and are in no way poisonous to touch. Perhaps the misleading name derives from a shared habitat. Both box elder and poison ivy grow in swamps, floodplains, and bottomland woods, and box elder's

Box elder fruit.   Box elder.

leaning trunk and spreading branches sometimes provide purchase for poison ivy's high-climbing stems.

Box elder's pinnately compound leaves set it apart from all of our other maples. The leaves are typically and frequently trifoliolate (with only three leaflets), but leaves with five leaflets are also common, leading to its other common name, "ash-leaf maple." Terminal leaflets resemble the leaves of some forms of red maple, with two lateral lobes and a large, pointed central lobe. The twigs and branchlets are green or purple, which makes box elder easy to recognize in floodplain woodlands, even in winter when leaves are absent.

Box elder is somewhat weedy in manicured landscapes, spreads in the garden on its own accord, and may require diligent pruning and regular cleanup. Individual plants are typically short-lived, but root sprouts are common and can extend the life of a single tree indefinitely. Box elder is quite adaptable to both wet and dry sites but is probably best used in difficult sites that are blessed with few horticultural options.

Buckeyes

Buckeyes take their common names from their large brownish seeds that are said to resemble the eyes of the white-tailed deer. The fruit is a leathery, three-celled, pear-shaped or rounded capsule that splits in the fall to release 1–3 smooth, hard kernels. Each seed is marked at the base with a conspicuous light-colored, pupillike hilum. Seeds can be stored in the refrigerator over the winter (as long as they are not allowed to dry out) or collected and sown immediately, either in pots, seed beds, or directly into the landscape. Those that survive the inquisitive diggings of enterprising squirrels are likely to germinate over the winter or early the following spring, but some may take up to two years.

Yellow buckeye. Courtesy of Ron Lance.

Five buckeyes are native to the southeastern United States, all of which are available in the garden trade. The yellow (*Aesculus flava*) and Ohio (*A. glabra*) buckeyes are medium to large trees that are restricted in our region mostly to the Southern Appalachians and closely adjacent regions of the Upper Piedmont. Yellow buckeye, in particular, is one of the largest and most common trees of the southern mountains and is most easily recognized by its scaly bark, large opposite buds, and thickened twigs. It is an excellent tree for larger landscapes in hardiness zones 3–8, but it may be too overpowering for residential situations.

The two most popular buckeyes for home use include the bottlebrush (*A. parviflora*) and red (*A. pavia*) buckeyes. Both form small trees to about twenty-five feet tall in natural settings but are often smaller and shrubbier in the garden.

Bottlebrush buckeye.

Bottlebrush buckeye, *left* and *above*.

Bottlebrush buckeye has rapidly become one of the southeast's more popular native shrubs, especially in the Piedmont and inner coastal plains. Virtually no collection of southern native plants lacks at least one specimen. Because of its beauty it has come to rival the oak-leaf hydrangea for residential use. Well-situated garden plants average about ten feet tall, but can become nearly fifteen feet wide at maturity, an important consideration when siting these shrubs. Bottlebrush buckeye is excellent when massed as a background shrub but is as often used as an unobstructed stand-alone specimen plant where its form and texture can be duly enjoyed. In spring and early summer, it puts on hundreds of creamy white four-petaled flowers that are arranged in an abundance of upright foot-long, four-inch-wide racemes. At full anthesis, a showy inflorescence terminates nearly every branch. Bottlebrush buckeye's natural range is mostly in the coastal plain of central Alabama, but its horticultural use has extended far beyond, and it is often listed for zones 5–9, 9–4. It occurs naturally in moist, shaded woods of bluff and ravine slopes and sometimes struggles in the summer heat of AHS zone 9, or even 8B gardens, especially in full sun or during drought.

Red buckeye is noted for showy racemes of bright red flowers and is touted by backyard birding enthusiasts as an irresistible hummingbird magnet. Its early flowering period makes it an especially important nectar source. The erect to sometimes spreading panicles of tubular flowers are up to about ten inches long and six inches wide and are borne in early spring as the new leaves unfurl. Individual flowers are about one inch long, with 4–5 reddish petals that are fused below and flared at the apex. Up to seven red-tipped stamens protrude from the showy corolla and offer easy pollen access to visiting birds and insects.

Red buckeye.

Red buckeye fruit.

Red buckeye.

Red buckeye developing leaves.

Bottlebrush buckeye.

Red buckeye enjoys a more southerly distribution than bottlebrush buckeye and ranges mostly along the coastal plains from southeastern North Carolina to central Florida and west to eastern Texas, including nearly all of Alabama, Mississippi, and Louisiana. It is very tolerant of a wide range of soils and is generally recommended for zones 5–9, 9–5. According to Bill Fontenot, in the second edition of his *Native Gardening in the South*, red buckeye is "an absolute must for most landscapes." Fontenot cautions that for Louisiana, at least, it is important to harvest the seeds annually to prevent single trees from establishing expanding colonies in the garden.

All of our buckeyes have palmately 5–7-parted leaves that are borne oppositely along the branch, a foliar arrangement and texture that has added immensely to their landscape value. The leaves are soft or dark green, conspicuously veined, marginally toothed, and extremely attractive. New leaves appear in early spring, often as the flowers open, and emerge with folded leaflets that display a distinctly prayerlike countenance.

Sumacs

It is hard to imagine that a family revered for such tasty morsels as cashews, mangoes, and pistachios could also be the source of our three most dreaded dermatological nightmares: poison ivy, poison oak, and poison sumac. The family Anacardiaceae is well-known for its lopsided share of species with irritant internal fluids, some of which have been used for the production of resins, oils, and lacquers, and others for their edible fruits and nuts or outstanding ornamental value.

Three species of sumac occur naturally in the southeast, all of which are avail-

Smooth sumac.

Smooth sumac fall leaves.

Maples, Buckeyes, Sumacs, and Wafer Ash   169

Smooth sumac with fruit.

Winged sumac.

Staghorn sumac. Courtesy of Ron Lance.

Winged sumac.

able in the nursery trade but virtually none of which is widely used in landscaping. That popularity eludes them probably stems from their natural abundance in fields, forests, and roadsides, as well as the unfortunate association of their names with those of several of their poisonous cousins. All have pinnately divided leaves, large clusters of tiny, creamy white flowers, and showy panicles of reddish fruit. Winged sumac (*Rhus copallinum*) is the most widespread of the group, ranging across all of the southeastern floristic provinces. Smooth sumac (*R. glabra*) is primarily a Piedmont and mountain species that also extends onto the inner coastal plain. Staghorn sumac (*R. typhina*) is a Blue Ridge specialty that ranges to about 5,000 feet in elevation. All have pinnately compound leaves and can be dazzling in autumn, especially following a wet summer and early cold front. The tendency of at least the winged and smooth sumacs to quickly invade and occupy disturbed roadsides bears testimony to their easy cultivation.

Hoptree or Wafer Ash

Wafer ash (*Ptelea trifoliata*) is not an ash. It is in fact in the citrus family (Rutaceae), not the ash family. The common name probably stems from the combination of its compound ashlike leaves and rounded, waferlike samaras. The genus name *Ptelea* is the ancient Greek name for the elms and was apparently bestowed by Linnaeus due to the similarity of the fruit of this genus to the rounded winged samaras of the genus *Ulmus* (the true elms). *Trifoliata* refers to its three-parted leaves. According to Dan Austin, in *Florida Ethnobotany*, the fruits of the genus *Ptelea* were once used as substitutes for hops in the brewing of malt liquor.

Hoptree, another name for wafer ash, is a shrub or small tree that is adaptable to an array of soils and is moderately drought tolerant. It is relished by butterfly fanciers as an excellent host plant for the giant swallowtail, whose cryptically colored orange dog caterpillar is a sight to behold. Mature giant swallowtails are among the eastern United States' largest and showiest lepidopterans; even a single plant will increase your chances of having this fine butterfly pupate in your garden.

Tiny four-petaled flowers are borne in an upright panicle at the tip of new growth and are functionally either male or female. Both sexes are required to produce the pendent autumn clusters of flattened, one-inch wafers. Hoptree is available mostly from nurseries that specialize in native plants, including Mail Order Natives, Nearly Native Nursery, and Woodlanders.

Wafer ash flowers.

Wafer ash.

10

Hollies

Although hollies are the highlight of the winter garden, they are essentially four-season plants that provide attractive foliage for much of the year. They are enjoyed in all seasons but are probably best loved by gardeners for the decorative clusters of cold-weather fruit that offer a colorful contrast to what can otherwise be a drab December landscape. The thick, often glossy green leaves and bright red fruit of the evergreen species are widely used at Christmastime, and the showy fruiting spires of the deciduous species are a favored component of dried arrangements. All make an arresting statement in the landscape.

Like the magnolias, native hollies comprise a distinctly eastern genus. At least seventeen native species, two varieties, and one natural hybrid are distributed from New England to the southern tip of the Florida peninsula and west to Minnesota and Texas. The majority grow naturally from about Virginia to Louisiana. None is native to the western United States. Fifteen of the seventeen species occur naturally within the range of this book, six of which are evergreen and nine deciduous. At least seven take on the form of a small to medium tree, but only a few do so consistently. Most are large shrubs, varying from 3 to 15 feet tall.

The black-fruited Krug's or tawnyberry holly (*Ilex krugiana*), one of only two species not regularly used in the area covered by this book, is a mostly tropical plant that is restricted in the United States to the southernmost peninsular Florida. The other species largely outside of our range is catberry (*I. mucronata*), a boreal species distributed mostly across Ontario and the northernmost United States from about Maine and New Jersey westward to Minnesota and Illinois. Although catberry has been reported as growing naturally in Virginia, its presence there has not been confirmed.

The flowers of the hollies are individually inconspicuous but are very interesting in detail. They are small, creamy or greenish white, typically appear in mid to late spring, and are not particularly showy. Most are borne either along the stem or in clusters at the base of the leaves (never at the branch tip), are lightly fragrant, and attract an array of insect pollinators. Typical flowers of our native red-fruited hollies have 4–5 petals (winterberry may have up to 8); the two black-fruited gallberries can have up to 9.

Hollies are textbook examples of functionally dioecious plants, meaning that their flowers are either functionally male (staminate) or female (pistillate) and borne on separate, unisexual plants. The term *dioecious* is from the Greek words *dio*, "two," and *oikus*, "household." In reality, at least some plants of most holly species are more appropriately described as polygamodioecious, bearing a few bisexual flowers intermixed with either

Common Name(s)	Scientific Name	Form	Native Range	Hardiness Zones	Fruit Color	Leaf Retention
Sand Holly, Carolina Holly	*Ilex ambigua*	Shrub, Small Tree	NC, TN; south to central FL; west to e. TX	7–10	Bright red	Deciduous
Swamp Holly, Sarvis Holly	*Ilex amelanchier*	Shrub, Small Tree	NC to n. FL; west to e. LA	6–9	Dull red	Deciduous
Topal (Topel) Holly	*Ilex ×attenuata*	Small Tree	NC, SC, FL	6–9	Red	Evergreen
Dahoon	*Ilex cassine*	Small Tree Shrub	NC to FL; west to e. TX	7–9	Red, rarely yellow	Evergreen
Long-Stalked Holly	*Ilex collina*	Large Shrub	WV, VA, NC	5–6	Red	Deciduous
Large Gallberry	*Ilex coriacea*	Shrub	VA to FL; west to TX	7–9	Black	Evergreen
Suwannee River Holly	*Ilex curtissii*	Small Tree, Shrub	GA, FL	7–10	Red	Deciduous
Cuthbert Holly	*Ilex cuthbertii*	Shrub, Small Tree	GA, SC	—	Red	Deciduous
Possumhaw Holly	*Ilex decidua*	Shrub, Small Tree	MD; south to n. FL, west to e. TX	5–9	Red, rarely yellow	Deciduous
Inkberry, Gallberry	*Ilex glabra*	Shrub	ME; south to FL; west to TX	5–10	Black, white	Evergreen
Smooth Winterberry	*Ilex laevigata*	Shrub	ME; south to SC	4–7	Red	Deciduous
Georgia Holly	*Ilex longipes*	Shrub, Small Tree	NC; south to FL; west to e. TX	7–9	Bright red	Deciduous
Mountain Holly	*Ilex montana*	Tree, Large Shrub	WV, VA, NC, GA	5–7	Red	Deciduous
Myrtleleaf Holly	*Ilex myrtifolia*	Shrub, Small Tree	NC to FL; west to LA	7–10	Red, yellow	Evergreen
Scrub Holly	*Ilex opaca* var. *arenicola*	Small Tree	FL	8–10	Red	Evergreen
American Holly	*Ilex opaca* var. *opaca*	Large Tree	MA; south to FL; west to TX	5–9	Bright red, rarely yellow	Evergreen
Winterberry	*Ilex verticillata*	Shrub	VA to n. FL; west to MS	3–9	Bright red, rarely yellow	Deciduous
Yaupon	*Ilex vomitoria*	Shrub, Small Tree	NC to FL; west to e. TX	7–10	Bright red, rarely yellow	Evergreen

male or female flowers. For gardeners who want winter fruit on their hollies, this means ensuring that at least one male plant is planted for every five or six females. For the common woodland hollies or those used regularly in landscaping, such as the American holly and yaupon, male plants may well be present in nearby yards or forests. For

Female holly flower.　　　　Male holly flower.

Black-fruited hollies may have as
many as 9 petals.

less-common species or those whose natural habitats are not closely adjacent, planting at least one male plant is a necessity.

Determining whether a flower is male or female requires close observation, often with a 10× hand lens. Functionally female flowers have a short but conspicuous swollen ovary nestled atop the base of the petals. The ovary is tipped by an irregular disk-shaped stigma and surrounded by four or more underdeveloped stamens (each of which is called a staminode). The anthers of these staminodia are reduced in size, somewhat withered in appearance, and lack pollen. Male flowers display larger, conspicuous stamens tipped with functional pollen-bearing anthers that surround a short, underdeveloped ovary with no obvious stigma.

Once pollinated, female flowers produce a rounded, more or less fleshy fruit that is referred to variously as a berry, berrylike drupe, or drupe. The flesh in some species is

Ensuring Winter Fruit

Winter fruit production typically requires the presence of both male and female hollies of the same or similar species. At least one male should be planted for each five or six females and should be located within about a half mile of the plants it is intended to pollinate. Some experts suggest that bees, one of the principal holly pollinators, can travel up to two miles between male and female plants. However, practice has demonstrated that fruit production and quantity are greater when male and female plants are situated in close proximity to one another. The late Harold Hume, one of the twentieth century's more influential holly experts, even suggests planting male and female plants in the same hole and letting them grow together as one.

Hollies cross-pollinate best with plants of their own or closely related species, although having several species in the garden seems to result in higher overall pollination. The species accounts in this chapter suggest appropriate male pollinators for several species and selections.

Typical holly fruit.

not particularly pulpy and can be somewhat hard; other species can produce conspicuously juicy fruit. Each fruit encloses several hard stones, or pyrenes, that contain the seeds. Technically, both berries and drupes are indehiscent fleshy fruits with one or more seeds. In drupes, the seeds are enclosed within a hard, outer covering. In berries, they are not. Although the conventional definition of *drupe* once referred primarily to fruits with a single stone, the definition has been expanded over time to include fruits with multiple stones. Hence, the fruits of the hollies are more appropriately described as drupes than berries, albeit drupes possessing a somewhat specialized morphology. In reality, holly fruit does not fall neatly into either category.

When crushed, the fruit of a holly reveals several pyrenes that usually equal the petals in number. Each pyrene represents a single carpel (ovule-bearing unit of the flower) surrounding a tiny nutlet from which new plants can be started.

Evergreen Red-Fruited Hollies

Six evergreen red-fruited hollies are native to the southeastern United States, all of which are used to varying degrees in gardening and landscaping. The two best known include the widely planted and typically shrubby yaupon, and the tree-sized American holly.

Yaupon (*Ilex vomitoria*) is the native holly most often seen in cultivation, at least in the southeast. Its numerous forms, selections, and cultivars have become well-known favorites of growers, residential gardeners, and commercial landscapers. This is primarily a plant of the coastal plains from southeastern Virginia to Florida and west to Texas, but its natural range has been extended by its widespread use. It grows naturally in the Carolinas only along the coastal strand; becomes more common inland in Georgia, Florida, Alabama, and Mississippi; and is found in nearly every parish in Louisiana. The leaves are small and medium green, with bluntly toothed (crenate) margins. Those of cultivated plants are usually less than 1½ inches long and not more than about 1 inch wide, but leaf size is variable based on exposure and geography. Plants of the

Yaupon holly.

Yaupon holly.

Deep South that grow in xeric, sunny environments typically have the smallest leaves, whereas shade-grown plants and those of the Carolinas and Virginia often have larger leaves. Leaves of shade-grown plants are also generally darker green. Typical female plants produce numerous conspicuous bright red drupes in winter that are easily visible among the small leaves.

Yaupon's popularity as a landscape shrub stems from several factors. It is tough, adaptable, drought and salt tolerant, requires little maintenance, takes on numerous forms, and fits many landscape needs. Dwarf, densely foliaged, compact forms such as 'Schillings,' 'Nana,' and Bordeaux™ make excellent hedges and can be pruned to virtually any size up to about three feet tall. Most of the dwarf forms are similar in appearance and can be intermixed in a single hedge that includes both male and female plants. Bordeaux™ is a sport of 'Schillings' with burgundy winter foliage for added interest. Larger upright forms include 'Gray's Greenleaf,' 'Lynn Lowery,' 'Fencerow,' 'Will Fleming,' and the yellow-fruited 'Yawkey,' all of which can become twenty feet tall. Virtually all yaupon selections are appropriate for zones 7–10, 12–7.

Upright weeping forms such as 'Pendula' and 'Folsom's Weeping' (the latter introduced by Tom Dodd Jr.) have also become quite popular, especially to accent corners or tall facades, line driveways, or serve as a backdrop for hedges of lower-growing compact forms. Weeping forms are arguably the most attractive of all yaupon selections and have become increasingly popular and widely available in all types of garden centers. Most are narrow and upright, grow to about twenty feet tall, and have strongly drooping branches that are very attractive. Unfortunately, those used along urban sidewalks or in parking lots are often pruned to look like tall, unattractive toadstools, which distracts demonstrably from their graceful form.

The American holly (*I. opaca*) is probably the best known and most widely distributed of our native hollies, ranging continuously from Maine to the central peninsula

Bordeaux™ Yaupon.

American holly 'Fire Chief.'

American holly.

American holly
'Oak Grove.'

of Florida and west to Missouri and eastern Texas. It is common throughout the eight states covered in this book and grows naturally in a wide range of habitats from moist bottoms to xeric uplands. This was likely one of the first trees noted by the earliest British colonists in North America due to its similarity to the highly valued English holly (*I. aquifolium*). Although the colonists almost immediately put its decorative value to use, the New World version has never become as popular in the Old World as the English holly has in America.

American holly is typically a slow-growing tree with glossy, dark green, spiny leaves and attractive grayish bark. Mature, open-grown trees in natural habitats take on a pyramidal shape with an open crown and self-pruned lower branches that allow a view of the mottled trunk. Planted specimens are often more compact and densely branched, with branches sometimes extending almost to the ground. Southern trees—those from the Carolinas southward—may become fifty feet tall or a little more; the height of northern trees generally does not exceed about forty feet. Typical female trees produce conspicuous clusters of bright red fruit that contrast sharply with the dark green leaves and have long been popular in Christmas decorations, hence the often seen common name "Christmas holly." However, yellow-fruited forms are also available, including the cultivars 'Oak Grove' and 'Fire Chief.'

Ilex opaca is one of the slowest-growing native trees and is not a tree for impatient gardeners. It grows faster in sun than shade but may take twenty years or more to attain its most attractive form. Several faster-growing selections are available, including 'Angelica,' 'Carnival,' and 'Clarissa.' However, as with many American holly cultivars, the faster-growing forms have generally been selected for hardiness from more northern plants and may be less well suited for the heat and humidity of USDA zones 8–9. Several hundred named cultivars are known, few of which are from southern plants. Deep South gardeners will probably have the best success with locally adapted cultivars or plants grown from locally collected seeds or cuttings. The Ebersol Holly Garden at Sand Hills Community College at Pinehurst, North Carolina, the Bernheim Arboretum at Clermont, Kentucky, and the Elmore Holly Collection at the University of Tennessee Arboretum near Oak Ridge (http://forestry.tennessee.edu/) are official holly arboreta. All have display specimens of American holly that will perform well in the middle and upper south.

Florida gardeners should try the scrub holly (*I. opaca* var. *arenicola*), a smaller, often shrubbier variety of American holly that is especially suited for xeric sites. It has smaller leaves than variety *opaca*—usually less than three inches long—and the leaf margins are strongly rolled under instead of flat. Scrub holly grows naturally only in Florida and only on sandy inland dunes of the central peninsula, but it has been planted successfully at least as far north as the Florida panhandle and may have wider uses. It is not widely available in the trade but is usually carried by Environmental Equities, a wholesaler in Hudson, Florida.

The natural hybrid *I.* ×*attenuata*, or topal holly, is a good substitute for American holly in USDA zones 8–9. Most selections are similar to American holly but are typically faster-growing. The original *I.* ×*attenuata* arose as a natural hybrid whose parentage likely included the American and dahoon hollies (*I. cassine*), although the small-leaved myrtleleaf holly (*I. myrtifolia*) is also sometimes suspected as the second parent. (Human-made crosses between the American and both the dahoon and myrtleleaf hollies have been successful.)

The common name for this plant is somewhat confusing. It is sometimes seen spelled "topal" but is also sometimes spelled "topel." Fred Galle, in his extensive work on the hollies, used the name "topal," which is the name selected here. The Latin name *I. topeli* was reportedly an early name used for this hybrid, which likely explains the present common name. However, there is not complete agreement about whether this name actually applied to the same plant as what we know today as *I.* ×*attenuata*.

Topal holly 'East Palatka.'

Topal holly 'East Palatka.'

The selections of topal holly best for the Deep South include 'East Palatka,' 'Savannah,' and the Foster hybrids produced in Bessemer, Alabama, in the 1940s. 'East Palatka' was selected by the legendary holly expert H. Harold Hume in the 1920s from a tree near East Palatka, Florida. It produces abundant fruit, is readily available in the trade, prospers southward to at least USDA zone 10, and is hardy to about USDA zone 7. Mature plants are 30–45 feet tall with a 15-foot spread and symmetrical crown and are excellent as residential specimen trees. The uniformity in shape of 'East Palatka,' coupled with a positive response to pruning, also makes it useful in street side plantings where consistency of form and pattern is important.

'Savannah' is another natural hybrid and was found in the 1960s in Savannah, Georgia. It more closely resembles *I. opaca* than does 'East Palatka,' with dark green, lustrous, spiny-lobed leaves; a dense crown; and abundant bright red drupes. It grows faster than American holly and can become 45 feet tall with a 6–10-foot spread and symmetrical crown. It is best suited for zones 7–9, 9–4 and is an excellent residential specimen tree that is also useful in parking lots and along urban roadsides.

The Foster hybrids (sometimes seen listed as *Ilex ×attenuata* 'Fosteri') are chance seedlings of crosses of the dahoon and American hollies. There were originally as many as seven plants, of which the female 'Foster #2' and male 'Foster #4' were among the best. 'Foster #2' is a densely foliaged conical tree with glossy, spiny-lobed leaves that are reminiscent of American holly but are often longer than wide, like the dahoon holly. Typical trees are 15–25 feet tall, up to about 12 feet wide, and are useful where an upright, pyramidal, evergreen form is needed. This is an excellent screening tree on relatively large properties and can be used as a street or median tree, or to provide buffers in parking lots.

Holly hybrid 'Foster #2.'

Dahoon.

'Savannah' and the Foster hybrids are excellent choices for gardeners who would like an alternative to the slower-growing American holly. Their form and foliage are much more reminiscent of *Ilex opaca* than *I. cassine* and their hybrid origin ensures a more rapid growth rate.

The selection 'Greenleaf' is recognized by some experts as a cultivar of topal holly and by others as a form of American holly. Its actual parentage is uncertain. Greenleaf Nursery, a large wholesale nursery with locations in Texas, Oklahoma, and North Carolina, acquired a seedling of unknown parentage, probably in the 1970s, and later named it 'Greenleaf.' It is listed in Greenleaf Nursery's catalog merely as *Ilex* ×'Greenleaf.' It is

Dahoon, *left* and *below*.

Dahoon 'Perdido.'

Dahoon 'Tensaw.'

Dahoon 'Tensaw.'

similar to American holly with medium green, spiny-lobed leaves that are not as shiny as those of American holly, and it has become a popular selection for the southern United States. It is a female that grows to about twenty-five feet tall and is recommended for USDA zones 6–8.

The dahoon holly (*I. cassine*) is a strict coastal plains species, distributed in natural populations chiefly along the coast (but throughout Florida) from extreme southeastern North Carolina to Louisiana. It is primarily a wetland tree that occurs mostly in coastal swamps and depressions and along streams. It is faster-growing than American holly, adapts well to the garden despite its wetland tendencies, and will grow in partial shade or full sun. It is somewhat tender and is best suited to USDA zones 8–10. Nevertheless, some growers recommend it for zone 7. The 1–4-inch leaves are much longer than wide, medium green, somewhat glossy, and lack spiny lobes. Dahoon produces flowers and fruit at an early age, responds well to pruning, and bears numerous bright red drupes. Mature plants in their natural habitat can be 35 feet tall, but the height of garden plants often does not exceed about 20 feet.

The best dahoon selections include 'Perdido' and 'Tensaw,' both introduced by Tom Dodd III and distributed wholesale by Dodd and Dodd Native Nurseries in Semmes, Alabama. 'Perdido' is a small, very adaptable tree or large shrub with a pyramidal to rounded crown and a profusion of red winter fruit. 'Tensaw' is slightly smaller but is also a single-trunked tree or medium-sized shrub. 'Tensaw' has dense foliage with leaves that are shorter and more rounded than either 'Perdido' or species plants. Both selections are fast-growing, produce heavy fruit crops, and provide an excellent food source for wintering birds.

I. cassine has probably found its greatest horticultural utility as one of the parent plants for several of the popular topal holly hybrids. However, species plants also perform well and should be sought out by any coastal plains holly enthusiast. Woodlanders offers a yellow-fruited selection marketed as *I. cassine* forma *aureo-bractea*, which is ostensibly the same form as that referenced by Fred Galle in his voluminous and comprehensive summary of the genus. Species plants are available from numerous native plant retail outlets in Florida, including Environmental Equities in Hudson and The Natives in Davenport. Florida-based wholesale distributors include Chiappini Farm Native Nursery in Melrose and Panhandle Growers in Milton.

The closely related myrtleleaf holly is considered by some authorities to be a variety of dahoon but is treated here as a distinct species (*I. myrtifolia*). Intermediates between the two are rarely encountered and are better treated as hybrids. Myrtleleaf holly has the smallest leaves of any of our native evergreen hollies. They average ½–1 inch long and are only about ¼ inch wide, about the same length as those of typical yaupon but much narrower. The margins are usually smooth, rarely with a few tiny, sharp teeth. Myrtleleaf holly becomes a small tree to about fifteen feet with an open crown and a very attractive form. Acidic pineland depressions often support large colonies of myrtleleaf holly and are sometimes referred to as myrtleleaf holly ponds. Yellow-fruited forms of this species are not uncommon in nature and at least one yellow-fruited selection is offered by Woodlanders. Red-fruited forms are available retail from Environmental Equities in Hudson, Florida, and wholesale by Dodd and Dodd Native Nurseries.

Myrtleleaf holly.

Myrtleleaf holly.

Evergreen Black-Fruited Hollies

In addition to the red- and yellow-fruited evergreen hollies, two black-fruited species also occur in the southeast, both of which bear the common name "gallberry." The smaller *I. glabra*, sometimes called "inkberry" in the trade, is by far the more popular and widely available. It is primarily a wetland plant in nature, broadly distributed in the coastal plains from about Nova Scotia south to Florida and Texas. Inkberry's natural habitats include pine flatwoods, swamp margins, open savannas, and other wetland habitats, but it adapts well to garden soils, as long as they are at least moderately acidic. Mature plants can be up to about eight feet tall and wide but are usually smaller and can be pruned for a more compact form, making them excellent foundation plants. The main stem of inkberry grows somewhat slowly, but plants can spread fairly rapidly by vigorous, quick-growing underground runners, and mature plants of some selections can create a dense, pruned hedge.

There are at least two dozen inkberry cultivars, distinguished mostly on the basis of form, foliage, and fruit color. Compact forms are most popular, the best of which for southern gardens include 'Compacta,' 'Densa,' and 'Nigra.' 'Nigra' is a top choice for many gardeners and is widely available. Unlike other selections, 'Nigra' does not lose its lower leaves with age, which allows it to remain densely foliaged all the way to the ground. 'Leucocarpa' (sometimes referred to as forma *leucocarpa*) is a white-fruited form that originated near Marianna, Florida, and has been available since the 1950s.

The closely related large sweet gallberry (*I. coriacea*) grows taller than inkberry and has glossier, wider leaves. The two often grow in nature in close proximity. They are

Inkberry.   Large gallberry.

similar in appearance but can be easily distinguished by differences in their leaf margins. Those of inkberry have several blunt, notchlike teeth only near the tip of the blade. The marginal teeth of large sweet gallberry are spreading with sharp tips and, at least on some leaves, are borne well below the leaf's midpoint. Large sweet gallberry usually grows in wetter places than inkberry and sometimes takes on the form of a small, single-stemmed tree. It is not uncommon in the Southeastern Coastal Plains but is neither widely used nor readily available in the nursery trade.

Sources of Native Hollies

Company	Address	Phone	Web Site	Distribution
Dodd and Dodd Native Nurseries	P.O. Drawer 439 Semmes, AL 36575	(251) 645-2222	http://www. doddnatives.com/	Wholesale
East Fork Nursery	2769 Bethel Church Rd. Sevierville, TN 37876	(865) 453-6108		Retail
Environmental Equities, Inc.	Hudson, FL	(727) 992-8905		Retail, wholesale
McLean Nurseries	9000 Satyr Hill Rd. Baltimore, MD 21234	(410) 882-6714		Retail
Simpson's Nursery	1504 Wheatland Rd. PO Box 1216 Vincennes, IN 47591	(800) 781-0211 (812) 882-2441	http://www. simpsonnursery. com/	Wholesale
Sunlight Gardens	174 Golden Ln. Andersonville, TN 37705	(865) 494-8237	http://www. sunlightgardens. com/	Mail order
TNZ Nursery	1800 Wickham Way Louisville, KY	(502) 836-6908	http://www.tnz.us/	Retail, mail order, wholesale
Woodlanders	1128 Colleton Ave. Aiken, SC 29801	(803) 648-7522	http://www. woodlanders.net	Mail order

Deciduous Hollies

Deciduous hollies hold a special attraction. What they lack in winter foliage they more than make up for in fruit production. Unlike many deciduous species, which lose their charm after the leaves have fallen, deciduous hollies are at their best when their leafless branches are transformed into showy boughs of red or yellow. The fruiting period of many species extends well into winter, providing a long-lasting source of pleasure for people and wildlife. Crafty human artisans turn them into earthy home decor, and overwintering birds turn them into sustenance.

Winterberry in December.

Winterberry in December.

Winterberry.

Winterberry flowers.

Of the nine deciduous hollies that occur within the scope of this book, none are more popular than winterberry (*I. verticillata*). This species occurs naturally along streams and at the edges of bogs, pocosins, floodplains, and swampy woods across all of the eastern United States from Canada to northernmost Florida and west to Louisiana. It produces long branches of bright red drupes that color in the fall and last much of the winter. The leaves are deep green, up to about four inches long and two inches wide, and have an attractive quilted appearance. Species plants are difficult to find in the trade, but numerous cultivars are available. Simpson Nursery's Winter Red® is one of the best known for southern gardens and is widely available. It produces abundant ⅜-inch-diameter intensely red fruits that persist well into February. 'Southern Gentleman,' also selected by Simpson Nursery, is its best male pollinator, although new male pollinators for this and other selections are under development. Winter Red® is a large, rounded, slow-growing shrub that can reach 6–10 feet in both height and spread, but it may take nearly thirty years to reach its maximum size. It prefers moist to wet soils but adapts well to full sun and drier conditions. No southern garden should be without it. Other excellent selections for southern gardens include the red-fruited 'Red Sprite,' 'Sunset,' and 'Bright Horizon' (all of which have large fruit), as well as the yellow-fruited 'Winter Gold,' which was selected from a single branch of Winter Red®. 'Jim Dandy' is the recommended male pollinator for 'Red Sprite.'

Possumhaw holly (*I. decidua*) is another prolifically fruiting deciduous holly appropriate for zones 5–9, 9–1. This is a shrub or small understory tree of mostly organic soils. Mature plants in natural situations may reach heights of thirty feet or more and often have an attractive leaning or spreading form. 'Warren's Red,' an abundantly fruiting female selection introduced by Simpson Nursery in the 1950s, is a favorite possumhaw cultivar for southern gardens. Its leaves are darker green and somewhat wider than those of typical species plants. The leaves of 'Warren's Red' often persist into late fall and early winter and sometimes obscure the bright red fruit. Its overall habit is more or less multistemmed and arching and it is not easily trained to a single-trunked form. Nev-

Possumhaw
holly.

Possumhaw holly 'Sentry.'

Possumhaw holly 'Council Fire.'

ertheless, the long-lasting popularity of this cultivar has ensured its wide availability in the trade. Pollinator species include male possumhaw holly, such as 'Red Escort,' as well as American holly, although seedlings pollinated by the latter species may produce weak plants.

Other red-fruited female selections of *I. decidua*, at least some of which may be better than 'Warren's Red' for some applications, include 'Council Fire,' 'Sentry,' 'Red Cascade,' and 'Pocahontas.' 'Council Fire' and 'Pocahontas' are dainty 15–16-foot trees, usually with a single trunk, erect stature, and a rounded crown that is similar in form to some of the hawthorns. Both of these selections are northern forms that may perform better in our region in USDA zones 6–8. 'Red Cascade' is noted for its large fruit and 'Sentry' for its narrow, more or less columnar crown. 'Sentry' sometimes loses its leaves early in the season and retains its fruit throughout the winter and into spring. Yellow-fruited forms include 'Byers Golden,' introduced by Byers Nursery of Huntsville, Alabama, and 'Finch's Golden,' also discovered in Alabama and named for Mobile, Alabama, environmental writer and naturalist Bill Finch. 'Red Escort' is a male pollinator for most of the possumhaw types.

Suwannee River holly (*I. curtissii*) is also a possumhaw type that is believed by some experts to be a natural variety of *I. decidua*. It is distinguished from typical possumhaw by having shorter, narrower leaves that typically do not exceed 2 inches long and {5/8} inch wide. It also tends to grow in more nearly neutral conditions than true possumhaw, mostly in thin soils over limestone. It is available by mail order from Woodlanders and Mail Order Natives. Some gardeners report that it does not appear to pollinate true *I. decidua* in the garden, even when the two species are grown in close proximity to one another, underscoring its recognition as a distinct species. According to Ray Head, an avid holly enthusiast and expert near Rutherfordton, North Carolina, *I. curtissii* blooms later than *I. decidua* in his region, which reduces the possibility of pollination. Head's female Suwannee River holly produced fruit only after he included a male plant of the species in his landscape.

Of the seven remaining southeastern deciduous hollies, only four are available in the trade, all of which are only occasionally seen in southeastern landscapes and are grown mostly by collectors and avid holly enthusiasts. All should be more widely used.

Swamp or sarvis holly (*I. amelanchier*) is an upright shrub or very small tree that occurs mostly in standing water along slow-moving, tannin-stained streams as well as in pocosins and wet upland depressions. It is known in nature primarily from scattered populations in the coastal plains of the Carolinas, Georgia, and the Florida panhandle. Swamp holly is one of the few deciduous hollies with colorful fall foliage. It is excellent in the garden, even in relatively dry locations. The leaves turn soft yellow as the season progresses, forming an attractive contrast to the relatively large, ⅜-inch-wide, dull red fruit. Male and female plants are sometimes available by mail order from Woodlanders as well as Environmental Equities in Hudson, Florida.

Georgia or Chapman holly (*I. longipes*) is an uncommon upland holly found in scattered populations in the Piedmont of North Carolina, South Carolina, and Tennessee,

Swamp holly.

Georgia holly. Courtesy of Wayne Webb.

More Information about Hollies

There are several sources of additional information about the genus *Ilex* and the care and cultivation of hollies. The recent book by Christopher Bailes, *Hollies for Gardeners*, includes an excellent overview of the holly genus as well as chapters on garden uses, propagation, and diseases of hollies. Bailes's book is international in scope but includes the majority of species native to the southeastern United States, with the exception of those that have not yet become widely available in the retail trade.

Another reference, the late Fred Galle's *Hollies: The Genus* Ilex, is far more comprehensive than Bailes's book. Galle was for many years the horticulturist at Callaway Gardens in Pine Mountain, Georgia, with extensive experience in holly propagation and cultivation. This book, probably more appropriate for the avid holly enthusiast than the casual reader, offers great detail about all members of the genus. Early chapters include excellent information about landscaping with hollies. Galle's book was published in association with the Holly Society of America, Inc. and can be purchased through the society's Web site at http://www.hollysocam. org/.

Also available from the Holly Society are two short but very helpful handbooks for southern gardeners: *Hollies for the Landscape in the Southeast* (Alabama Cooperative Extension Service) and the Brooklyn Botanic Garden's *Hollies: A Gardener's Guide* (1993).

One of the earliest and now long out-of-print holly books was written by H. Harold Hume and entitled simply *Hollies*. Hume was the dean of the College of Agriculture at the University of Florida and a longtime holly enthusiast. As might be expected, his 1953 book includes information about species native to the southeastern United States as well as many Asian and European species. His detailed notes on holly pollination, propagation, cultivation, pruning, and uses are excellent.

Those interested in beginning a holly collection or just learning more about hollies may want to join the Holly Society of America, a small but enthusiastic group of holly fanciers, mostly from the United States. Several chapters serve the eastern United States, with the Harry Logan–Carolinas chapter being the most active in the southeast. The society publishes the *Holly Society Journal* and the *Holly Letter* several times a year and holds an annual meeting each fall. Contact the society through its Web site: http://www.hollysocam.org/.

---

often on dry, sandy gravel ridges in association with *I. ambigua*. It also occurs in the mountains in Georgia and in the coastal plains from Georgia and Florida west to Louisiana. The Latin epithet refers to the conspicuously long fruit stalk, which can exceed one inch in length. The exceptionally long pedicel helps distinguish this species from possumhaw holly, of which some authorities have considered it to be only a variety (*I. decidua* var. *longipes*).

Mountain winterberry. Courtesy of Ron Lance.

Carolina holly female flower.

Carolina holly.

Carolina holly. Courtesy of Wayne Webb.

Smooth winterberry (*I. laevigata*) is a mostly coastal plains species growing naturally in bogs, low woodlands, and acidic swamps. Its foliage is similar to common winterberry, but it produces fewer and more scattered fruit; the leaves often fade to a beautiful yellow in autumn. Mountain winterberry (*I. montana*) is another potentially tree-sized holly. As its name implies, it grows naturally only in the mountains and upper Piedmont of West Virginia, Virginia, the Carolinas, and north Georgia (although it has been reported without confirmation along the Chattahoochee River as far south as the Florida panhandle). Mature trees can reach forty feet tall. It is not uncommon.

With the increasing popularity of deciduous hollies and the successful introductions of native red-fruited forms, holly enthusiasts can expect future species and selections to enter the market. One likely candidate is the sand or Carolina holly (*I. ambigua*). This small tree or shrub is very attractive, grows predominantly in sandy uplands and dry forests, and has excellent potential for xeric gardening. It occurs naturally from North Carolina to central Florida and west to eastern Texas. As the epithet *ambigua* suggests, Carolina holly is quite variable, and botanists have divided it into numerous species and varieties through the years. Mature plants often assume the stature of a low shrub, but some individuals may grow to nearly twenty feet tall. The leaves usually have bluntly toothed margins but vary widely in size and shape. On some plants the leaves are consistently 1–2 inches long while on other plants most leaves may be 3 inches long or more. Leaves turn yellow in the fall and the fruit is about ⅜ inch in diameter and shiny red. The inherent variability in this species makes it an excellent subject for grower and breeder experimentation. Environmental Equities in Hudson, Florida, is one of the few commercial outlets that offer this species. Some growers suggest that it does not keep its fruit long enough into winter, which limits marketability. However, it begins coloring earlier than some other species, and the fruits are very juicy, making them an excellent food source for migrating and overwintering birds. Breeding work is currently under way to ensure a greater presence of this species in the retail trade.

John K. Small, in his expansive flora of the southeastern United States published in 1933, includes the species *I. beadlei* among our native hollies, a plant now considered by most botanists to be a form of *I. ambigua*. Keen-eyed holly enthusiasts recognize this form in natural areas, identifying it by the combination of its shrublike habit and very hairy leaves. Those who enjoy traipsing the Blue Ridge, Appalachian Plateau, and upper Piedmont will want to keep an eye out for this potentially distinct form.

Propagation and Cultivation

Propagating native hollies is not particularly difficult. Although some species are easier to propagate than others, growing hollies from either seeds or cuttings is certainly within the realm of most home-based propagators. Of the species mentioned above, the gallberries, yaupon, and some of the deciduous forms provide the best starting point. American holly is somewhat more finicky from cuttings and its seeds often require an extended period of stratification before they will germinate.

Species with quickly germinating seeds include *I. glabra*, *I. cassine*, *I. myrtifolia*, and *I. ambigua*, all of which will begin to germinate in 1–3 months and may continue for several months thereafter. Seeds of the deciduous *I. amelanchier* will also germinate quickly. Some reports suggest the latter species will germinate in only a few weeks if kept refrigerated through the winter and sown in early March, but seeds sown immediately upon collection in mid December also germinate quickly.

Seeds of most hollies should be collected in late fall or early winter after they ripen, immediately and thoroughly cleaned, and sown at once. Freshly collected fruit should be crushed or otherwise abraded and soaked in water for a few days to loosen the pulp surrounding the seeds. Once the pulp has been removed, viable seed will sink in water. Nonviable seeds will float and should be discarded. Viable seeds should be sown in a moist, commercially prepared seed-starting mix or in a moist mixture of peat and perlite. The seed can be sprinkled over the surface of the potting mix and lightly covered with a thin layer of vermiculite or potting mix before being gently wetted with a hand mister.

Growing hollies from seed has two potential limitations. Since hollies are insect pollinated and somewhat promiscuous, there is high potential for genetic mixing between species; seeds from favorite selections and cultivars rarely breed true to the parent plant. In addition, about half of seed-grown offspring will be male and half female. This will matter little to gardeners who are growing primarily for evergreen hedges or to increase the evergreen component in a residential landscape. However, those who value fruit production on deciduous species may have to wait for some time to be certain of the gender of the new progeny.

Propagating from cuttings eliminates gene mixing and ensures the production of a genetic duplicate of the plant being cloned. Cuttings should be taken from new growth, preferably from mid to late summer and into the fall. The most successful cuttings are 3–6 inches long and contain 3–5 leaves at the tip. Cuttings should be wounded near the base, dipped into a rooting hormone, and immediately stuck into a wet mixture of peat and perlite, or a commercially prepared seed-starting mix. Perlite can be added to the commercial mix to ensure good drainage. Cuttings should be kept in high humidity—preferably under mist with adequate air circulation—and not allowed to dry out. Commercial operations often invest in elaborate misting systems equipped with timers to provide continuous hydration, but home gardeners can set up a simple mist system using mister heads, a garden hose, and an inexpensive timer.

Some home-based growers, especially those without a greenhouse, shade house, or misting arrangement, report using a terrarium-type system. Humidity chambers can be fashioned from self-draining pots filled with moist potting mix and covered with a plastic bag or the top of a two-liter bottle, or Styrofoam coolers that have holes punched in the bottom. The bottom of the cooler can be filled with a moistened potting mix to a depth of about six inches. Once the cuttings have been inserted into the mix, the cooler can be covered with plastic wrap and kept in a shady, lighted place away from direct sun exposure. If kept indoors, these makeshift humidity chambers can be lighted with an inexpensive, two-bulb shop light fitted with a combination of cool and/or warm white fluorescent tubes. Plants should be adequately rooted in 45–90 days and can be transplanted to outdoor pots or to the garden once the threat of frost has passed. It should be noted that using humidity chambers can be problematic due to lack of air circulation. Cuttings should be inspected daily to ensure that the leaves are green and turgid, and that fungus has not become a problem.

11

Native Roses

The rose family (Rosaceae) is among the largest families of flowering plants. There are about 3,000 species and 85 genera worldwide, including more than 60 genera and nearly 900 species in the United States and Canada. Although a few of the North American representatives are naturalized from distant lands (several of which have become troublesome weeds), the vast majority are American natives.

The Rosaceae is an economically important family with numerous uses. It encompasses some of the world's best-known fruit crops, including apples, almonds, strawberries, cherries, apricots, pears, blackberries, raspberries, plums, prunes, and quince; and the fragrant essential oils of at least a few species have been used medicinally and in the manufacture of perfumes. Despite this pecuniary prowess, the family is probably best known for the showy aromatic blossoms that have long adorned southern gardens and perfumed Deep South parlors.

Although roses are most often associated with the boisterously colorful flowers of modern and old-time garden cultivars, the family also includes a large number of valuable natives, many of which have become important landscape plants and are readily available in the nursery trade. At least nine of the family's native genera contain garden-worthy species, ranging in habit from low-growing shrubs and vines to moderately sized trees.

Systematic botanists treat the Rosaceae as a monophyletic family, meaning that all of its species share a common ancestry and are assumed to be derived from a single interbreeding population. This is readily evidenced by a well-defined set of stable family features, not the least of which includes the form of the flowers and structural similarities in the leaves and fruit.

The flowers of all roses are best described as rotate, more or less circular and flattened with the sepals and petals spreading at right angles from the floral cup. In some genera the petals arise from the edges of the floral cup; in others they arise directly from the top of the ovary. The flowers of native roses typically have five sepals, five petals, and a central mass of numerous stamens. Some have a single pistil; others have several. Many are highly attractive to bees and other large pollinators, which use the disk of sturdy, spreading petals as a landing pad.

Typical rose flower.

Pome fruit of the crabapple.

Drupe fruit of Chickasaw plum.

Roses produce several distinctive types of fruit, of which the pome is among the best known and most often referenced. Pomes are fleshy fruits that contain an outer peeling, a thickened meaty flesh derived from the expanded floral tube, and a central seed compartment that is segregated from the flesh by a papery wall (the pericarp). A typical apple is the best example. Pomes are unique to the rose family and are common to several rosaceous genera, including the apples (*Malus*), shadbushes (*Amelanchier*), hawthorns (*Crataegus*), mountain ashes (*Sorbus*), and chokeberries (*Aronia*), all of which are represented in southern gardening. The fruits of the plums, cherries, and peach are drupes, each consisting of a juicy outer layer surrounding a hard stone (pyrene) that encloses and protects the seed.

Some rose genera produce an aggregate fruit composed of fused collections of achenes (small, dry, indehiscent fruit with a thin wall), drupelets (diminutive drupes), or follicles (dry pods that split along a single suture). The "hip" of the true roses (genus *Rosa*) is an aggregate of achenes, and the juicy "berry" of the blackberries (genus *Rubus*) is actually an aggregate of drupelets. Ninebark (*Physocarpus opulifolius*) is the only species among our native garden roses that produces an aggregate of follicles.

The leaves of the roses can be simple or compound (subdivided into several leaflets), but the blade margins are always at least minutely toothed. All members of the family produce stipules at the base of the leaf (small, leaflike structures that arise from the leafstalk or the subtending twig), at least when young. These tiny appendages fall quickly with age on some species—such as the plums and cherries—and are not at all evident on mature plants. In other species, such as the Carolina and swamp roses, the stipules are conspicuous, sheathlike, and envelop an extended portion of the leaf stalk.

True Roses

More than twenty species of true roses (genus *Rosa*) occur in the southeastern United States, only five of which are native. Several of the non-natives, most notably the Cherokee (*R. laevigata*), multiflora (*R. multiflora*), and McCartney (*R. bracteata*) roses, are known to be at least moderately aggressive and are listed by several states as invasive plants. All three have wicked prickles and are difficult to control, even in residential landscapes, often becoming invasive. Regardless of the fact that the Cherokee rose is the state flower of Georgia and is seen on fences throughout that state, these are certainly not plants to turn loose in a garden.

Carolina rose (*R. carolina*) and swamp rose (*R. palustris*) are by far the more commonly used and easily attainable native *Rosa* species. Both are widely distributed and bear striking 2–3-inch pinkish flowers with masses of yellowish stamens. Carolina rose is mostly an upland plant that grows in shady woods and roadside thickets. Swamp rose prefers wetland habitats (*palustris* means "marsh loving") and is most often found along the edges of lakes, swamps, streams, and roadside ditches. In fall these species produce reddish hips—a favorite wildlife food—and yellowish to reddish leaf color. Both have arching canes that are variously armed with straight or recurved, sharp-tipped prickles that can be piercing to the touch. When given free rein, either can form a nearly impenetrable thicket. They make excellent hedges or screens and are among our most attractive native flowering roses. Neither should be sited where they are likely to interfere with routine foot traffic, or where their thorny canes can creep out into a suburban lawn.

Carolina and swamp rose are very similar in general appearance but can be easily distinguished by their prickles, growth form, and size. Carolina rose has straight prickles, is usually scrambling and low-growing, and seldom exceeds three feet tall. Swamp rose

Swamp rose.

Carolina rose.

Prairie rose. Courtesy of Ron Lance.

has recurved or hooked prickles, forms an upright, arching shrub, and may be more than six feet tall. Both are appropriate for zones 5–9, 9–1. Although Carolina rose probably performs better than swamp rose in dry, sunny sites, both tolerate a wide range of soil conditions and are not particularly finicky in the garden. Regardless of its preferred native habitat, even swamp rose can withstand more or less dry conditions, as long as it receives at least occasional irrigation.

Two other pink-flowered roses are also used sparingly in southern landscapes but are not as readily available in the nursery trade. Prairie rose (*R. setigera*), also called Michigan rose, grows naturally from Michigan and New York southward to northern Louisiana, Alabama, Mississippi, and Georgia. It is also reported to be native as far south as Florida but performs best in the southeast in USDA zones 4–8A. The flowers of prairie rose start out pink but fade to white. Virginia rose (*R. virginiana*) occurs primarily from Newfoundland to Virginia. The flowers are up to about 2½ inches wide, fragrant, and bloom mostly in June. Virginia rose tolerates heavy clay soils and coastal environments and grows naturally along roadsides and salt marshes.

Hawthorns

The hawthorns (genus *Crataegus*) comprise a large and complicated group of small, showy trees, all of which produce attractive flowers and small, colorful, interesting pomes (similar to the fruit of the apple). The exact number of naturally occurring southern hawthorns is unclear. Woody plant expert and hawthorn specialist Ron Lance puts the number in the southeast at about 30, but other estimates range from as few as 20 to more than 400.

Cedar-Apple Rusts

Cedar-apple rusts are a group of fungal diseases that attack numerous species in the Maloideae, a subfamily of the roses that includes the apples, crabapples, hawthorns, serviceberries, chokeberries, and mountain-ash. The fungi that cause these diseases belong to the genus *Gymnosporangium* and spend one half of their life as a cedar gall and the other half as lesions on the leaves, fruit, and soft stem tissue of a rosaceous host. Common cedar hosts in our area include the native eastern and southern red cedars (genus *Juniperus*), as well as closely related non-native ornamental cedars. Infected cedars produce misshapen, {3/8}–1-inch, dark brown winter galls. The galls swell appreciably with spring rains and develop gelatinous, bright orange, hornlike tendrils that spread spores by wind to nearby rose-family hosts. Symptoms on the rosaceous host usually occur in late spring or early summer and include yellow leaf spots with dark centers. In midsummer, lesions on the lower leaf surface or fruit produce tubelike extensions that develop a second generation of spores that are transmitted by wind back to the cedar. Trees must be within about two miles of each other to transfer spores effectively, and cedar-apple rust fungus can only persist where both hosts are present and interacting. In mild cases, the fruits of the rose host are disfigured and stunted and the tree is plagued by early defoliation. Native cedar trees are usually not seriously affected by the fungus, and most rosaceous plants can withstand a single infestation. However, successive infestations over several years can result in the death of the rosaceous host. Suffice it to say that successful cultivation of the haws, crabapples, and other pome-fruited roses in residential landscapes may be dependent upon their adequate separation from potentially infecting cedars.

Cedar haw rust.
Courtesy of Ron Lance.

The exact number of North American species is equally undecided. Prior to 1900 some experts put the number at about 200. By 1930, due primarily to the tireless work of three American botanists—William Willard Ashe, Chauncey Beadle, and Charles Sprague Sargent—the number of purported species had risen to more than 1,000.

At least part of the hawthorn confusion derives from the extensive variation within and among species and the several reproductive strategies common to the genus. Hawthorns reproduce sexually through cross-pollination; they also hybridize readily and in ways that allow hybrid offspring to backcross with the parent plants. Many species are self-compatible, which depresses genetic diversity but gives rise to large colonies of slightly differing strains of "standard" forms. To confuse matters further, hawthorns are noted for their ability to reproduce through apomixis, an asexual reproductive strategy that allows unfertilized flowers to produce viable seed in the absence of pollen. Such seeds are essentially genetic clones of the parent and can give rise to several interbreeding colonies of identical plants that display slight but consistent variation with the species.

Needless to say, full treatment or resolution of this taxonomic problem is far beyond the scope of this book or its author. Except for a few cases, most of us will have to accept the confusion that exists with these delightful little trees and be satisfied with whatever species or forms we end up with in our gardens.

Several hawthorns are available in southern retail and wholesale nurseries. The best and easiest to identify—and hence most likely to be correctly labeled—include Washington thorn (*C. phaenopyrum*), mayhaw (*C. aestivalis*), green haw (*C. viridis*), and parsley haw (*C. marshallii*). All four are widespread across the southeast, easy to grow, and suitable for USDA zones 4–9. As with several other genera in the rose family, *Gymnosporangia* rust (in this case cedar-hawthorn rust) can be a problem for some plants. The leaves of affected plants develop yellow or orange spots with black centers, turn prematurely yellow, and drop in summer rather than fall.

Parsley haw has delicate, deeply cut foliage that resembles parsley and places it among the easier hawthorns to identify in the wild. It blooms profusely in early spring with numerous very attractive flowers of five white petals surrounding a cluster of attractive, bright red stamens. The mottled bark is scaly and very attractive, and like many of the haws its trunk is sometimes armed with sharp thorns. The bright red, hairless fruit is borne in late spring and early summer.

Mayhaw also blooms in early spring with white flowers. In nature it is typically found in large colonies along the edges of standing-water wetlands. The fruit matures in May,

Parsley hawthorn.

Mayhaw fruit. Courtesy of Ron Lance.

Mayhaw has shiny leaves and red fruit. Courtesy of Ron Lance.

Mayhaw flowers (*C. rufula* form).

Bark of a mature mayhaw.

hence the common name, and has long been used in the production of mayhaw jelly, a veritable delicacy that is considered by a few connoisseurs to be among the finest of wild-grown jellies. Mayhaw is distributed in the coastal plains from North Carolina to Mississippi but is most common in southern Georgia, northern Florida, and southeastern Alabama. The town of Colquitt, located in extreme southwestern Georgia near the center of the species' natural range, bills itself as the mayhaw capital of the world. The National Mayhaw Festival, held annually the third weekend of April in Colquitt, is testimony to the jelly's regional importance. Fruit is collected from the wild in May and boiled for the pinkish red juice that is used in the jelly making.

Native Roses 199

Washington thorn.

Washington thorn. Courtesy of Ron Lance.

Cockspur haw. Courtesy of Ron Lance.

Washington thorn enjoys the most expansive range of any of our region's haws—from the mountains to the coastal plains—and is also one of the more widely available and commonly used in landscaping. It is hardy to at least USDA zone 4 and typically grows as an upright tree to about thirty feet tall. It often produces several main stems that divide into a crown of numerous branches. The leaves are similar in shape and outline to those of the maples but are demonstrably smaller. The flowers are borne in June and are followed by bright red fruit. This is probably the most popular of the garden species and has given rise to several selections and cultivars. 'Vaughn,' which some say is a cross between Washington thorn and cockspur haw (*C. crus-galli*), and which others say is likely a hybrid of Washington thorn and green haw, is noted for particularly heavy fruiting.

As its name suggests, Washington thorn is densely vested with wicked thorns that are piercing and needlelike to touch. The selection Princeton Sentry™ is less thorny and is a good selection for high-traffic areas but is of northern origin and may do less well in Deep South heat and humidity.

Green haw flowers in the summer and develops fruit in early fall. The pomes are red, are about ¼ inch in diameter, and hang on the tree long after the leaves have fallen, rivaling some of the deciduous hollies for their midwinter show. Green haw occurs naturally

Green hawthorn.

Green hawthorn.

Green haw with winter ice. Courtesy of Ron Lance.

Green hawthorn. Courtesy of Ron Lance.

in floodplains and lowland woods but readily adapts to garden soils. Seeds collected and sown immediately in midwinter germinate quickly and are easy to grow and establish. 'Winter King' is a popular selection (probably a hybrid with Washington thorn) that seems somewhat less susceptible to rust, but it is probably more northern in provenance and likely to be at its best in USDA zones 7–8A.

Serviceberries

Like the haws, the serviceberries are a difficult-to-distinguish complex of closely related deciduous shrubs or small trees. At least seven species are native to the southeast, all of which are referred to by a suite of interchangeable common names that includes shadbush, shadblow, sarvis, sarvisberry, servicetree, and Juneberry. All are appropriate for zones 4–9, 9–4.

The etymology of the common names is somewhat obscure, but the names probably stem from natural and cultural events that are closely correlated with the serviceberry's time of flowering. One widely told but largely unfounded legend contends that the name serviceberry reflects the colonial custom of waiting until the spring thaw and softer ground to bury people who had died during the winter. Since serviceberry comes into flower at about the same time that winter loosens its icy grip, the appearance of service-berry blossoms became a convenient reminder of final remembrances. The word *sarvis*, the legend contends, is merely a colloquial corruption of the word *service*. The names *shadbush* and *shadblow* probably connect the serviceberry's flowering period with the time that the American shad (a tasty fish relished by early colonists) made its annual upriver spawning runs. *Juneberry* refers the serviceberry's sweet early summer fruit, once used to make Juneberry pie.

Serviceberries of the Southeastern United States

Common Name	Scientific Name	Form	Hardiness Zones	Fruit Color
Downy Serviceberry	*Amelanchier arborea*	Small Tree, Shrub	5–9A	Red
Eastern Serviceberry	*Amelanchier canadensis*	Small Tree, Shrub	4–7	Red, Purple
Smooth Serviceberry	*Amelanchier laevis*	Small Tree	5–8	Red
Nantucket Serviceberry	*Amelanchier nantucketensis*	Shrub	5–8	Red
Coastal Plain Serviceberry	*Amelanchier obovalis*	Shrub	3–8	Blue-Purple
Dwarf Serviceberry	*Amelanchier stolonifera*	Shrub	4–8	Red, Purple

Serviceberry.

Eastern serviceberry. Courtesy of Ron Lance.

Shrubby
serviceberry.

Amelanchier arborea, *A. laevis*, and *A. canadensis* are the three Latin names most often seen in retail nursery centers and plant catalogs. Whether potted specimens are always identified correctly is questionable, but this doesn't seem to matter. All are excellent landscape plants, festooned from February to March with showy clusters of pinkish to bright white flowers that form a particularly eye-catching display in late winter woodlands and gardens. The flowers have five narrow, ¾-inch petals that emerge erect but soon spread and become somewhat floppy and disheveled. Numerous yellow-tipped stamens arise from a lime green center, encircling five greenish styles that serve as the pollination source for a single pistil. The showiness of the flowers is accentuated by their tendency to arise at the same time as the new leaves, which causes them to stand out sharply in an otherwise mostly drab leafless landscape.

The early summer fruit is a rounded "berrylike pome," a description used by botanists to refer to fruit that resembles an apple but lacks a single papery wall at its core. Species of serviceberry contain up to ten leathery-coated seeds, each borne in a single locule (seed compartment). Not all of these tiny potential plants become viable. Those that do turn dark brown as they ripen.

The fruit of the serviceberries is an excellent wildlife food. Unlike the fruit of the haws—which is usually saved by avian predators until late in the year when winter food is scarce—birds relish serviceberry fruit and often strip trees clean at the earliest opportunity. Most serviceberries put on their reddish, purplish, or blackish fruit in early summer, a treat that is especially welcomed by voracious late-spring migrants. Serviceberry fruit is particularly preferred by robins, thrushes, waxwings, redstarts, blue jays, and catbirds.

A. arborea is also sometimes called "downy serviceberry" and *A. laevis* "smooth serviceberry." The stalks and undersides of newly unfolding leaves are densely woolly on downy serviceberry and hairless on smooth serviceberry. Downy serviceberry's fuzzy covering is an excellent field mark in early spring, but the hairs are quickly lost as the leaves mature. Mature serviceberry leaves are oval to somewhat egg-shaped in outline and up to about 3 inches long and 1½ inches wide with a soft appearance. The bases of the conspicuous lateral veins hug the central vein for up to 1/16 inch before diverging—a feature seen best with magnification and one that provides an excellent clue for field identification.

Serviceberries are easy to grow, tolerant of a wide range of soils, transplant easily from pots, and can be sited in full sun or filtered shade (sunny locations will produce more flowers). They do best in moist, well-drained soils and do not tolerate standing water or soggy conditions. Numerous retail nurseries and garden centers offer one or more species, and growing your own plants from wild-collected seed is relatively easy. Seeds can be collected and cleaned in summer and planted immediately either in the ground or in outdoor containers. Germination usually occurs the following spring but often in low percentages. Plant plenty of seeds to ensure success.

Serviceberry's small size, diminutive form, and relatively rapid growth (up to about a foot a year) make it appropriate for even the smallest residential landscape. All species work equally well in naturalistic edges, as open-grown specimen trees, as shady umbrellas overtopping perennial beds and low, shrubby borders, or off the beaten path in distant corners. Natural drainages and deciduous woodlands best accentuate their beauty, but they are sometimes also planted as street and median trees in association with dogwoods to ensure an extended flowering period.

A number serviceberry selections and cultivars are available in the nursery trade. Dirr's manual lists more than twenty. However, due to similarities between species and difficulties with serviceberry taxonomy, the precise parentage of many named selections is questionable. Although a large number are useful in a wide range of southern gardens, it is probably better to ask the advice of staff at local nurseries to determine which perform best in a particular region.

Southern Crabapple

No southern garden should be without at least one southern crabapple (*Malus angustifolia*). Despite its rather disturbing susceptibility to cedar-apple rust, southern crab is an iconic trademark of southern woodlands and one of our most attractive small trees. The laterally spreading branches and delightful fall fruit easily commend it for much of the year. When decked out in spring with showy masses of fragrant pink to whitish flowers, it displays a splendor that can make residents and tourists alike take to the road shoulder to determine its identity.

Southern crabapple is widespread in the southern United States (USDA zones 6–9), including the mountains and Piedmont, but is especially common in the coastal plains. It occurs naturally in dry, open woodlands and is especially common along fence lines and roadsides where in spring it becomes one of our most treasured small trees. It is not fussy in the garden and readily adapts to a variety of garden soils from acidic to

Southern crabapple.   Southern crabapple.

alkaline, as long as they aren't too wet. Selections and cultivars are now available that are resistant to rust and other common diseases; plants from wild-grown stock should never be planted closer than a mile or two to cedar trees.

The flowers are similar to many plants in the rose family, with five petals and a mass of stamens. Flower buds are often deep pink but normally fade to pale pink as the blossoms develop and may become closer to white at maturity. Mature blossoms are about one inch wide when fully open. The fruit is a yellowish green, one-inch-wide pome that begins developing in summer and reaches maturity in October or November. When split in half, the inside of the fruit looks like a miniature apple with a papery-walled seed cavity that contains numerous seeds, each with a black, leathery coat surrounding a creamy white cotyledon. As with apples and numerous other species in the rose family, crabapple seeds contain cyanogenic glycosides, which release cyanide as they break down and can be poisonous if ingested.

Crabapples are best sited in full sun or only light shade. Some gardening authorities recommend them mainly for the edges of naturalistic landscapes or to highlight out-of-the-way garden corners, primarily because of the heavy fruit crop that sometimes litters the ground below them. Indeed, crabs can be somewhat messy. Well-flowered trees produce abundant pomes, which usually hang on until mid-autumn, slowly changing from green to mushy yellowish brown before falling and eventually being consumed by birds, squirrels, or deer. If sited near driveways, patios, or along walking paths, the rotting fruit can be a not-so-mild nuisance for tidy homeowners. Nevertheless, fully flowered specimens situated in open settings easily rival the beauty of dogwoods and redbuds when in flower and certainly equal them in southern heritage.

This is not a tree for high-traffic or child-prone areas. Wild forms are notorious for producing numerous sharp-tipped spur shoots that readily develop into leafy thorns. Even casually brushing against well-armed woodland plants can be treacherous. Native plant purists who choose to use only native stock will likely have to accommodate this thorny inconvenience. Less-regimented gardeners can avoid the thorns by selecting their plants from among the numerous thornless cultivars.

Chokeberries

If scientific names are designed to enhance communication and provide universally agreed upon monikers, it appears that those who have assigned names to the chokeberries may have missed the point. Synonyms abound for these attractive shrubs or small trees, with old and new names disappearing and reappearing with regularity.

Three species of *Aronia* occur in our region, of which red chokeberry is the most popular for gardeners. In this book I choose to call this plant *Aronia arbutifolia*, the name by which I first learned it and the one followed by Alan Weakley in his revised flora of Virginia, Georgia, and the Carolinas. Linnaeus, the great Swedish taxonomist and undisputed father of modern botanical nomenclature, first named the species *Mespilus arbutifolia*, presumably assigning it to this genus based on the similarity between its fruit and that of medlar. The epithet *arbutifolia* means "having leaves like *Arbutus*," which is a genus in the heath family that is also well-known for its horticultural contributions.

Since Linnaeus's time, the red chokeberry has been assigned to at least four genera, including *Sorbus*, *Pyrus*, and *Photinia*, usually with Linnaeus's original epithet. It is often referred to today as *Photinia pyrifolia*, mostly by botanists, but is more commonly seen in the landscape trade as *Aronia arbutifolia*. Its common name should not be confused with that of chokecherry (*Prunus virginiana*), a widespread shrubby cherry that occurs only tangential to our region, mostly in the southern Appalachians.

Red chokeberry is a 6–10-foot-tall shrub or small tree with very attractive leaves that are characterized by interesting texture and finely toothed margins. It is widespread across the eastern United States and is generally rated for zones 5–9, 9–4. This is an essentially four-season shrub that in fall and winter is an excellent companion or substitute for the red-berried deciduous hollies. The flowers are borne in congested clusters in early to mid spring as the new leaves unfurl. The outer (or lower) surfaces of the petals are usually pink in bud, but both surfaces turn white as the blossoms expand. Fully open flowers are about ½ inch wide with five white petals and attractive pinkish red anthers.

Red chokeberry.

Red chokeberry.

The fruits develop slowly over the summer and come into their own in mid to late fall, often persisting into winter. In coastal plains woodlands the bright red, ⅝-inch, berry-like pomes are sometimes seen adorning naked branches as late as Christmastime, long after the leaves have fallen.

Red chokeberry is also excellent for autumn color, particularly in USDA zones 7–8. Early fall leaves change from splotchy green to orange-yellow or sometimes scarlet, revealing the fruit as they drop and leaving a skeleton-like stature on larger plants.

In natural areas red chokeberry is a plant of moist to wet woodlands and is at its best along the edges of bogs, wet flatwoods, pocosins, and narrow drainages through pinelands. It grows best in moist, acidic soils but adapts easily to the garden, even where relatively dry. In the landscape it is most appropriate for naturalistic woodlands or massed as a shrubby background. The plant is easy to grow and once established tends to increase in size by modestly aggressive underground runners. Plantings should be given room to expand or monitored to keep them in check. Red chokeberry tolerates filtered shade but flowers best in full sun. The cultivar 'Brilliantissima' is commonly available in retail nurseries and is certainly true to its name. Its foliage is darker green in summer and nearly scarlet in fall, and fruit production is reported to be heavier than that of wild plants.

Two other species of chokeberry occur in the southeast, neither of which is as widely used in southern gardening as the red chokeberry. Black chokeberry (*A. melanocarpa*) and purple chokeberry (*A. prunifolia*) are sometimes seen in the trade but are more widely available north of our region. Both are restricted in their southeastern distribution mostly to the mountains and upper Piedmont.

Blackberries and Raspberries

The blackberries and raspberries are members of the genus *Rubus*, a collection of plants probably best known for their sweet, juicy, early summer fruit and treacherously thorny canes. Only the flowering raspberry (*R. odoratus*) is used in southern landscaping and it only rarely. It is included here due to its showy flowers and thornless canes. It is a common thicket and roadside plant from Michigan and Nova Scotia southward to Virginia, North Carolina, and extreme northern Georgia and is restricted in our region mostly to the mountains. Mature plants can be nearly six feet tall and produce attractive two-inch flowers with five lavender, pink, or purplish petals. The leaves are large, dark green, maplelike, and very attractive. Flowering raspberry does best in moist, rich soils and is a good background plant for perennial beds or naturalistic gardens. It is not widely available in the nursery trade.

Flowering raspberry.

Queen-of-the-Prairie

Only two species of *Filipendula* occur naturally in the United States, queen-of-the-forest (*F. occidentalis*) of the Pacific Northwest and queen-of-the-prairie (*F. rubra*), confined mostly to the northeast from Maine southward to Virginia, North Carolina, and extreme northeastern Georgia. (Some authorities say that the northern limit of this species is actually along a line from Pennsylvania to Illinois and that occurrences farther north are probably the result of garden plants that have escaped cultivation.) Queen-of-the-prairie is nowhere common in our region but is an excellent showy garden herb for the mountains and upper Piedmont. Although the American Horticultural Society recommends this species for zones 3–9, 9–1, it is probably better to consider this a USDA zones 3–7 plant.

Queen-of-the-prairie.

Queen-of-the-prairie is a tall, herbaceous perennial topped with striking clusters of showy pink to pinkish red flowers. Average plants are 3–7 feet tall with large, 3–5-lobed leaves and are excellent as a tall, herbaceous background or as an emphatic statement to a mixed perennial bed. Plants do well in full sun as long as the soil is at least moderately moist. Butterflies and insects are attracted to the showy flowers, and milkweeds, Joe-Pye-weeds, bergamots, and purple coneflower are good companion plants.

Ninebark

Ninebark's (*Physocarpus opulifolius*) common name derives from its scaly and flaking bark, which strips off continuously to expose what proves to be only another in a seemingly endless series of fibrous, buff-colored layers (the word *nine* has long been used colloquially as a symbol of the infinite and extreme). Unfortunately, as Dick Birr points out in his excellent guide to propagating showy woody plants, this attractive feature is seldom seen due to ninebark's dense, shrublike stature and numerous arching, weeping, and often leggy, canelike branches.

This plant might well be classed with the old-time natives featured in Chapter 5. It was introduced into horticulture by at least the late seventeenth century, and the ornamental value of its attractive scaly bark was noted by Donald Wyman in *Arnoldia* as late as 1947. Its appeal for southern gardens seems to have dissipated in recent years, perhaps partly because it tends to outgrow small spaces and partly because of the drubbing given it by a handful of respected modern plantsmen. Michael Dirr, for example,

Ninebark, *left* and *above*.

in his *Manual of Woody Landscape Plants* opined that "about anything is better than a *Physocarpus*."

Whether this is true may well rest on a matter of taste. RareFind Nursery in Jackson, New Jersey, offers three selections and extols *P. opulifolius* Diabolo™ 'Monlo' as one of their best sellers. I have seen this species used in the middle of a naturalistic shrub bed in northern Florida with good effect, with the initially stiff, upright canes forming a delightful background and the flower-filled lateral canes arching out to the edge of the bed. Ninebark is also effective in shrub borders and hedges.

Diabolo™ 'Monlo,' Summer Wine™ 'Seward,' Summer Wine™ 'Duncan,' Copper-tina™ 'Mindia,' and 'Center Glow' are among the more commonly available selections, all of which are of northern origin—as are most cultivars of this species. Most selections are rated USDA zones 3–8 but are perhaps more successfully grown in zones 3–7, 7–1. The selection 'Nanus,' a dwarf form that usually does not exceed about six feet tall, is probably best for our region. Diabolo™ is touted for its dark purple foliage, which may turn purplish green during northern summers and dark green in hot, dry Deep South summers.

Ninebark's natural range extends from Maine to Florida and west to Colorado. It is typically a Piedmont and mountain plant of stream banks and river drainages. There are only a few occurrences in the coastal plains, including a few in Alabama, a single population in Florida, and none in Mississippi and Louisiana.

The flowers are small, five-petaled, creamy white, about ½ inch wide when fully expanded, and borne in numerous many-flowered compact clusters. The fruit is a tiny, tan-colored pod (technically a follicle) with 2–4 seeds. Flowers typically appear in May in the Carolinas, perhaps a little earlier in Florida, and literally cover the plant, rivaling the showiness of *Spiraea*. Ninebark does best in full sun or part shade and adapts to acidic or neutral soils. Plants can be controlled and rejuvenated by pruning to the ground in winter. Otherwise, they should be pruned immediately after flowering.

Alabama Snow-Wreath

Alabama snow-wreath (*Neviusia alabamensis*) is an enigma: rare and restricted in nature, successfully and widely planted in gardens. The plant was first discovered in 1857 near Tuscaloosa, Alabama, and was long thought to be restricted to the state. Although it was stumbled upon in 1955 at a single site in Missouri, and later at a handful of scattered locations in Arkansas, Georgia, and Tennessee, it is still considered rare in nature and is nowhere common or abundant.

Alabama snow-wreath's exceedingly narrow distribution once led to the assumption that it must have arisen as a new species in the vicinity of the Black Warrior River in central Alabama and never expanded its range. Such extreme endemism sometimes results when newly evolved species lack either the time or adaptive proclivity to radiate beyond their point of origin. Given today's better-known distribution, phytogeographers now regard it as a once-widespread but now ancient relict, pushed into its few remaining niches by the cataclysmic cooling and warming of the Pleistocene landscape. Its primary habitat today includes moist limestone woodlands in association with rich hardwood forests.

Unlike the other roses in this chapter, the flowers of Alabama snow-wreath have no petals—a condition often described by botanists as "petals lacking." Masses of numerous white stamens radiate 360° from the floral cup in mid spring, lending a showy, acacia-like aspect to the blossoms. Most plants produce numerous flowers simultaneously, all borne in 3–8-flowered terminal and axillary clusters after the new leaves have developed. The leaves are 1–3 inches long, about 1 inch wide, with conspicuous veins and sharply double-toothed margins.

This is a 2–5-foot deciduous shrub with arching, wandlike stems and a sometimes aggressive habit. It can form thickets—although somewhat slowly—in the garden and may require periodic maintenance to control its form and size. It will tolerate full sun with sufficient moisture and benefits from neutral or even slightly alkaline soils, but it does not prosper in excessively dry or extremely acidic sites. A mostly sunny planting at

Alabama snow-wreath.

Alabama snow-wreath.

the State Botanical Garden in Georgia in Athens has morphed into a respectable hedge several feet long and wide and suggests the plant's potential. Snow-wreath should be pruned immediately after flowering to maintain form and to ensure a more compact habit.

Cuttings root relatively easily, and older plants can be divided. New stems or root suckers arise from spreading underground stolons and can be severed from the parent plant and potted or immediately transplanted to other locations in the garden.

Mountain-Ash

The several plants of American mountain-ash (*Sorbus americana*) that adorn the grounds and parking lot of the Blue Ridge Parkway's Pisgah Inn are a magnetic attraction to October leaf peepers. The showy compound corymbs of bright red pomes that decorate the nearly naked branches draw cars into the parking lot about as well as the colorful vistas that spread out below the Peak of the Parkway overlook. For many who make the annual sojourn to the southern Appalachians, the arresting beauty of mountain-ash is the exclamation point of autumn color.

Many people who see this plant for the first time think it to be a sumac. The compound leaves—from which the appellation "mountain-ash" arises—are certainly reminiscent of several plants in the sumac genus. Few first-timers recognize the gnarly grayish trunk and twisted limbs as characteristic of the rose family.

It is probably unfair to put mountain-ash in this book. Its preference for high elevations—at least in the southeast—is unforgiving and its unwillingness to survive below 4,000 feet is legendary. Attempts to grow this species in the Piedmont, or even at lower elevations in the mountains, are usually predestined for failure. Although its natural range includes lower elevations in Maine, its range in the southeast extends only above about 5,000 feet in elevation along the spine of the Appalachians. The southernmost plants recorded are at Georgia's Brasstown Bald, at elevation 4,784 feet. It would be a wonderful plant to have in a residential landscape, but except for the few gardeners who have found their peace in the higher mountains, most southeasterners will have to opt for enjoying it only in the wild.

Mountain-ash.

12

Perennial Asters

The aster or composite family is one of the largest and most evolutionarily advanced groups of flowering plants. More than 1,530 genera and at least 23,000 species are known worldwide, including many of our showiest and best-loved native wildflowers. Such roadside beauties as the goldenrods, blanketflowers, blazing stars, sunflowers, black-eyed Susan, dog-fennels, coneflowers, and rosinweeds are among the more commonly recognized groups. The numerous species that have found their way into gardening and horticulture constitute only a handful of the possibilities.

The aster family has two botanical names: Asteraceae and Compositae. Asteraceae is the newer of the two and is composed of the genus name *Aster*—one of the family's most important genera—followed by the Latinized suffix *-aceae*. Since the early 1900s the rules of botanical nomenclature have required that the construction of all family names follow this pattern. However, for eight families the rules are relaxed to allow retention of older names, especially when such names have enjoyed long and widespread use. These "conserved" family names—of which the name Compositae is a well-known representative—are valid in every way, and their use in botanical and horticultural literature is considered completely acceptable, even if occasionally viewed as passé.

As it turns out, the name Compositae is far more descriptive and fitting of the aster family than the newer, Asteraceae. Most members of the family are characterized by a crowded, single-stalked composite flower head consisting of numerous individual

Composite flower head of lance-leaf coreopsis with both disc and ray flowers.

Composite flower head with only ray flowers.

Composite flower head wi[t] only disc flowers.

flowers of two types subtended—and sometimes completely surrounded—by a cup-like collection of bracts called an involucre. A classic composite flower head, like that of the black-eyed Susan, is composed of a tightly packed central cluster of disc flowers surrounded by few to numerous ray or ligulate flowers (ray and ligulate flowers are technically different from one another, but they appear very much alike and are referred to collectively here as rays). In species such as the aptly named rayless sunflower (*Helianthus radula*), only disc flowers are present. In others, notably the native but weedy false-dandelion (*Pyrrhopappus carolinianus*) and the non-native and very weedy true dandelion (*Taraxacum officinale*), the heads consist only of ray flowers.

Rays are often referred to colloquially as "petals," an appellation that is correct but misleading. Each ray in a composite flower is actually a fused strap-shaped corolla of a single flower or floret. Hence, the several showy "petals" of purple coneflower are actually a ring of eleven individual flowers surrounding numerous rusty-orange disc flowers. The typically tiny, five-petaled disc flowers are usually tubular in shape with a fused corolla that flares slightly at the apex.

The individual flowers of most composites are tiny and seem to lack some of a typical flower's requisite parts. The sepals—in the composites collectively called the pappus—are sometimes absent but more typically are reduced to a ring of bristles or featherlike hairs at the base of the disc flowers. Immediately below the pappus and seated in a swollen receptacle is a hard, dry achene composed of a close-fitting wall surrounding a single seed. Achenes typically darken with maturity and eventually loosen and fall. In species with lightweight achenes, such as the several thistles, the plumose pappus aids seed dispersal by giving buoyancy to the seeds and sometimes carrying them far from the parent plant. Heavier achenes fall directly to the ground. The seeds of many species propagate easily and quickly and are most easily collected just before they separate from the head, usually in summer or fall.

Stokes' Aster

Stokes' aster (*Stokesia laevis*) is among the most popular of our native perennials. Its blue or sometimes white frilly flowers, nearly evergreen basal leaf rosette, and wide adaptability have made it a sought-after plant. Gardeners who see it for the first time in a retail nursery invariably want it. It is distributed in the coastal plains from South Carolina and Georgia west to Louisiana, but it has become naturalized from plantings well beyond its natural range, including portions of the North Carolina Piedmont. Despite its increasing use in the garden, it is relatively uncommon in the wild and is considered to be a "species of special concern" in Georgia. It grows naturally along the edges of wet pitcher-plant savannas but is most often seen along perennially moist road shoulders, like those that traverse the DeSoto National Forest in southernmost Mississippi.

At least a dozen cultivars are available in the nursery trade, many of which are difficult to distinguish from the others but nearly all of which perform well in the garden. Typical flowers are blue to almost purple, but white-flowered forms are often encountered in natural populations, and lavender, white, creamy white, and even yellow cultivars are available in the trade. The selection 'Alba' is an example of the white-flowered forms.

Stokes' aster.

Blue-flowered Stokes' aster.

White-flowered Stokes' aster.

The flowers are exquisite and probably account for much of the plant's popularity. More than a dozen ray flowers radiate from a central mass of up to seventy tubular disc flowers. The four-inch-wide heads are borne at the ends of long leafy stalks and are subtended by spiny bracts. Mature plants are typically less than two feet wide and tall. Flowering stalks can be up to about eighteen inches long and vary in habit from erect to reclining. Typical plants flower in early to midsummer, but prompt removal of spent flower heads can prolong the blooming period. Stokes' aster does well in full sun and average garden soil and can tolerate relatively dry conditions. It is at its best in zones 5–9, 9–5.

Coneflowers

If the purple coneflower (*Echinacea purpurea*) does not exceed Stokes' aster in popularity, it certainly equals it. Perhaps no single native species in the aster family has been subject to more interest or has given rise to as many exceptional garden cultivars. It is excellent for butterfly gardens, tolerant of poor soils, flowers profusely in open sun, is nearly xeric in water requirements, and constitutes one of our more beautiful composites. Flower heads are composed of a mounded orange-red to rusty-orange disc surrounded by deep rosy rays that often droop sharply as if to accentuate the disc's conical profile. The leaves are large, dark green, and deeply veined and appear at the base of the plant well before the flowers are formed; they are very attractive. Flowering stems are

Purple coneflower, *above* and *right*.

Purple coneflower
'Kim's Knee High.'

mostly erect but sometimes flop over with age, especially on taller stalks or on plants grown in the shade. Purple coneflower is easy to grow, widely available, adjusts to most garden soils, and reseeds heavily (although only a small percentage of seedlings might actually make it to maturity).

Purple coneflower has only one aggravation: rabbits. Its young, thick, juicy leaves and flowering stems are considered delicacies by these long-eared herbivores. Cottontail bunnies will strip a plant clean if given an opportunity.

Numerous purple coneflower selections are available, including white-flowered forms like 'Alba' and 'White Swan,' dwarf forms like 'Kim's Knee High,' and large-flowered selections like 'Magnus.' There is even a double-flowering form with the fancy name 'Razzmatazz' in which the disc flowers also produce rays. Selections and cultivars have become so popular that the magazine *Horticulture* (August/September

Gray prairie coneflower.

2008) devoted an article to some of the numerous forms that have been introduced to the market.

Species plants and most selections begin blooming by at least May and will continue throughout the summer. Deadheaded plants will continue flowering sporadically well into early fall. Some authorities do not recommend purple coneflower south of zone 8, but the plant is heat tolerant and performs well in zones 3–9, 9–1. No southern perennial garden should be without this species. Kim Hawks, the former owner of Niche Gardens in Chapel Hill, North Carolina, is responsible for several selections of purple coneflower, and Niche Gardens remains one of the best retail and mail-order sources for this species.

Two other species of *Echinacea* are native to, or very near to, our region. Although less often used in gardening, pale coneflower (*E. pallida*) is available from a number of retail vendors, including online from Native Gardens. It has narrower, more softly colored ray flowers and a more delicate appearance than purple coneflower, and it is less heat tolerant. Like most species of *Echinacea*, it flowers best in full sun and well-drained soils and is most suited for USDA zones 4–8. The Tennessee coneflower (*E. tennesseensis*) differs by having laterally spreading or upright ray flowers. It is a federally endangered species that is available online from both Sunlight Gardens and Native Gardens, but it cannot be shipped beyond the state of Tennessee. Meadowbrook Nursery in Marion, North Carolina, offers a seed-grown hybrid between the Tennessee and purple coneflowers.

A second, yellow-rayed coneflower genus is also popular with southern gardeners. The upright prairie coneflower, or Mexican hat (*Ratibida columnifera*)—distributed naturally from Minnesota to Colorado, south to Mexico, and perhaps also native to northern and western Louisiana—is the best-known garden species of the group and is often planted in the east. The spectacular central disc is columnar (hence the scientific name) and is nearly two inches tall on some individuals. Mexican hat is showy, excellent for mixed butterfly gardens, and tends to reseed from year to year. The flowers are mostly yellow, but at least one subspecies has flowers with brownish purple rays.

Gray or pinnate prairie coneflower (*R. pinnata*) is also native to the central plains, but it extends farther eastward in range at least to Georgia and western Florida. It, too, has been widely planted in the southeast. The cone of gray coneflower is shorter than that of Mexican hat but is conspicuous and very attractive. Disc flowers start out with a gray cast, which explains the common name, but tend to darken with maturity. Both species of *Ratibida* produce robust clusters of basal leaves and tall flower stalks 3–4 feet high. They do very well in thin, dry or moist soils in full sun, in USDA zones 3–9.

Sunflowers and Sneezeweeds

At least thirty members of the sunflower genus *Helianthus* occur in the southeast, many of which have been co-opted by gardeners. Some are weedy species that have invaded the east from predominately midwestern ranges. Others are strict natives with essentially eastern distributions. Many—even the natives—can be aggressive in the garden, reseeding or spreading rapidly by root proliferation. Gardeners often report the need to cull or corral plants to curtail expansion. Suffice it to say that at least some of our native sunflowers demand annual attention to keep them in check.

One widely used control method for larger-growing sunflowers is to plant them in isolated rectangular or circular beds that are mowed along the edges to prevent them from escaping, while also allowing them to be viewed from a distant vantage. Such beds quickly develop into dense stands that produce hundreds of flower heads and always demand comment from neighbors and passersby. The plants in such beds can be cut to the ground at the end of the season and lightly mulched to allow formation of next year's basal leaves. Too much mulch may prevent some species from returning; others seemingly have the capacity to grow through concrete.

In addition to rapid growth, sunflowers are also known to hybridize freely, even in the garden, which explains why so many of the plants sold by retail nurseries evade precise identification. The narrow-leaved sunflower (*H. angustifolius*), one of the more popular and widely available species, is an excellent example. Hybrids and misidentifications of this species are common in nurseries; at least two species are sold under the same common name. Exceptionally tall plants with large flowers are probably hybrids with the much larger and later flowering muck sunflower (*H. simulans*), or they may

Purported narrowleaf sunflower.

Narrowleaf sunflower.

Muck sunflower.

actually be muck sunflowers that are incorrectly labeled. Both species have narrow leaves that are rough to the touch, and both produce numerous flowers. Narrow-leaved and muck sunflowers, along with the similar Florida sunflower (*H. floridanus*), are very closely related and are sometimes considered to be different forms of a single species.

True narrow-leaved sunflower has very narrow leaves, is usually less than six feet tall, and produces flowers in late summer and early fall. It is common in roadside ditches and wet pinelands across the southeast. Muck sunflower is much taller (to nine feet or more), with wider leaves, and produces flowers in October and November. It occurs mostly in southern Louisiana but has also been reported as either native or naturalized in the Florida panhandle. Some experts suggest that the muck sunflower is of hybrid origin and that its large size is indicative of hybrid vigor. The floriferous inflorescence is so crowded with blossoms that tall plants often fall over under their own weight. Plants usually put up stems in early summer and can grow rapidly. Pruning them to about three feet in June, again in mid-July, and once more no later than mid-August encourages branching, prevents toppling, and still preserves abundant flowering. Pruning them too late in the summer risks a flowerless fall.

Fortunately, gardeners who just want yellow fall sunflowers in their gardens do not have to bother with all of the taxonomic uncertainty when purchasing plants at their local garden center. Mixed sunflower beds are showy additions to any garden, and nearly all species produce large numbers of flowers, tolerate full sun and moist soil, reseed abundantly, and guarantee an unparalleled show for at least two seasons of the year.

The sneezeweeds of the genus *Helenium* are similar in many respects to the sunflowers. Most have flower heads that include a central, often buttonlike disc surrounded by numerous bright yellow rays. Of the nine species native to the southeast, only three are readily available in nurseries, all of which flower mostly in summer and fall. The most commonly seen garden species is the dogtooth daisy or autumn sneezeweed (*H. autumnale*), an upright 3–5-foot-tall perennial with attractive lance-shaped, coarsely toothed leaves. The popularity of this species has led to the selection of about a dozen named cultivars, varying mostly on flower color from coppery yellow to shades of red. Autumn sneezeweed prefers moist soil and full sun and does best in zones 4–9.

Purplehead sneezeweed (*H. flexuosum*) is similar to autumn sneezeweed, but the flower head has a dark central disc and the leaves are smaller and more conspicuously winged at the base. It is less available in the nursery trade than autumn sneezeweed but is similarly distributed in nature and equally effective in the garden.

Spanish daisy or bitterweed (*H. amarum*) is widespread across the southeast and is

Autumn sneezeweed.

Autumn sneezeweed.

Purplehead sneezeweed.

Spanish daisy.

generally considered to be a pasture weed. It colonizes disturbed fields and roadsides, especially in sandy soils, and can become problematic in agricultural areas. It works well in the garden but tends to seed readily and may spread beyond its bounds. Bitterweed takes its common name from the taste of its foliage, which is said to turn the milk bitter in cows that graze on it. Some experts consider bitterweed to be non-native to our region and to have been introduced from the west. Some strictly native plant nurseries decline to sell it.

Rudbeckias

Of the numerous rudbeckias (genus *Rudbeckia*) that are scattered across the southeast, the three best known to gardeners include the native black-eyed Susan (*R. hirta*) and the widely popular cultivars *R. fulgida* 'Goldsturm' and *R. nitida* 'Herbstsonne.'

Black-eyed Susan has been used so long in southern gardening that it could have easily been included in the discussion of old-timey natives in Chapter 5. The erect 2–3-foot stems bear hairy, rough-to-the-touch leaves and are topped by a 3–4-inch-wide flower head. Each head has a dark purple to nearly black central disc that provides an attractive contrast to the numerous showy yellow rays. This is an excellent and easy-to-grow wildflower for zones 6–9, 9–4 and is especially suited for the wildflower meadow. It is short-lived but readily reseeds in the garden and produces a random dispersal pattern after several years.

'Goldsturm,' a cultivar from *R. fulgida* var. *sullivantii*, is arguably one of the most often seen rudbeckias in human-designed landscapes. It is used to decorate mailboxes, mixed borders, parking lots, roadsides, and medians, as well as for many other purposes. It has orange-yellow ray flowers surrounding a dark brown disc, and mature plants maintain a rather uniform two feet in height. Its consistency in color and form likely accounts for much of its wide use in commercial applications. It has an extended flowering period (midsummer to fall), returns from year to year, and the spent flowering stems can be cut back to allow the basal leaves to serve as a late fall groundcover. It is relatively long-lived and nearly unparalleled for mass plantings. The Perennial Plant Association selected 'Goldsturm' as the 1999 Perennial Plant of the Year.

'Herbstsonne' is sold by some nurseries as *R. nitida* and by others as *R. laciniata*. Some experts suggest that it may actually be a hybrid of the two. True *R. nitida* is a rarity in nature found only in a few widely scattered locations in Florida, Georgia, and

Rudbeckia nitida 'Herbstsonne.'

Black-eyed Susan.

Rudbeckia fulgida 'Goldsturm,' *left* and *above*.

Rudbeckia nitida 'Herbstsonne.'

Rudbeckia nitida.

perhaps Alabama. Cutleaf coneflower (*R. laciniata*), on the other hand, is distributed widely throughout the Midwest and east. Both produce conspicuous clusters of large basal leaves and upright flower stalks that can be 3–6 feet tall. The cultivar 'Herbstsonne' is similar in form to both but seems to be intermediate between them, with cabbagelike basal leaves and numerous upright stems, each with numerous large flowering heads. Flowering stems can be up seven feet tall and are very attractive as vertical elements in the perennial garden, especially when cast against a taller background. It should be noted that both of the potential parents of this cultivar are wetland species that are normally found in moist to wet soils. Although 'Herbstsonne' does well in virtually any garden soil and can live for several years in average rainfall, extended droughts can challenge it.

Asters

The vagaries of botanical taxonomy and classification have essentially eliminated the genus name *Aster* from the native flora of the southeastern United States. In the January 2007 draft of his flora of the Carolinas, Georgia, and Virginia, Allan Weakley references this change without fanfare: "It is now abundantly clear that the traditional, broad circumscription of *Aster*, as a genus of some 250 species of North America and Eurasia, is untenable. All of our native asters have affinities elsewhere than with Old World Aster; most are now placed in *Symphyotrichum* and *Eurybia*, with fewer species in *Ampelaster*, *Doellingeria*, *Ionactis*, *Oclemena*, and *Sericocarpus*." These massive nomenclatural changes have caused confusion in botany and gardening circles alike, with many largely unrecognized scientific names now being used in association with well-known common names. To ease this transition the "asters" treated here are listed with both their new and old scientific names.

Climbing blue aster is among the more popular of the garden asters. Formerly called *Aster carolinianus* and now *Ampelaster carolinianus*, this species is often included in treatments of perennial plants but is actually more woody than herbaceous. It is found in nature in wetland habitats, often growing just above water level on decaying logs and acidic hummocks in the middle of springs, along shaded spring runs, and bordering clearwater streams. Its common name derives from the somewhat leggy branches that typically climb and twine over supporting vegetation. Garden plants do the same thing, which makes this species excellent for fences and trellises, or in situations where the base of the plant can be corralled or caged. Plants that are pruned heavily in winter (following the November flowering period) will eventually form a stand-alone shrub. The scrambling and climbing habit of this species makes it excellent for a naturalistic border around a low backyard deck. In sun it flowers profusely in mid to late fall when most

Climbing blue aster.

nessee aster.

White woods aster.
Courtesy of Ron Lance.

Bristly aster.

other flowering perennials are approaching winter dormancy, putting on numerous heads with pale blue to lavender rays around a central reddish or yellowish disc. It is readily available in the trade and performs well in USDA zones 7–9. It should be noted that this species has had two scientific name changes in the recent topsy-turvy nomenclatural realignments and may be found in some books and nurseries under the tongue-twisting name *Symphyotrichum carolinianum*. All three of its names refer to a single species.

A large number of native herbaceous asters are available throughout the south. The most popular in USDA zones 6–8 include the blue woods aster (*Symphyotrichum cordifolium*, =*Aster cordifolius*), white woods aster (*Eurybia divaricata*, =*A. divaricatus*), heath aster (*S. ericoides*, =*A. ericoides*), smooth aster (*S. laeve*, =*A. laevis*), New England aster (*S. novae-angliae*, =*A. novae-angliae*), aromatic aster (*S. oblongifolium*, =*A. oblongifolius*), Tennessee aster (*E. paludosa*, =*A. paludosus* var. *hemisphericus*), and the late purple aster (*S. patens*, =*A. patens*). All but the white woods aster produce blue to purple or pinkish flowers (although the flowers of the 'Snow Flurry' selection of the heath aster are also white) and cover the gamut of season, habit, and exposure. With a little research, it is possible to have one or another aster blooming for several months and in situations ranging from shade to full sun.

Most of the species in the above paragraph are best in USDA zone 8 and northward. Zone 9 gardeners might want to try bristly aster (*Ionactis linariifolius*, =*A. linariifolius*). This is another blue-flowered species that grows from Canada to Florida and west to Texas. It is upright with very narrow, spreading leaves and is very floriferous. It is distributed by Sunlight Nurseries but is not otherwise widely available.

Coreopsis

The tickseeds (genus *Coreopsis*) are excellent garden and roadside wildflowers, easily and quickly grown from seed and often included in mixed wildflower seed packages. About two dozen species occur naturally in the southeastern United States, several of which are widely available. Members of the genus have typical composite flower heads with a central disc surrounded by showy rays. In the tickseeds the leaflike bracts (phyllaries) that subtend the rays are borne in two overlapping series, each series of which is distinctly different from the other in size or shape. This character alone separates members of the genus from virtually all similarly flowered composites.

The lance-leaf coreopsis (*C. lanceolata*) is a tough roadside tickseed, tolerant of much abuse. It presently ranges throughout eastern North America and is usually considered native to our region. However, its original range may have been centered largely in the central United States, and it may be only adventive or escaped from cultivation in large

Leavenworth's tickseed.

Lance-leaf coreopsis.

Mixed coreopsis bed.

Threadleaf coreopsis.

Threadleaf coreopsis in a border.

parts of the southeast. Its preference for disturbed roadsides certainly underscores this possibility. Nevertheless, it has been widely planted as a native species and is considered as such by many experts. It is a short-lived perennial; individual plants last only 2–3 years in the garden but reseed prolifically, ensuring a continuing presence. Typical plants are about two feet tall. Lance-leaf coreopsis tolerates dry, well-drained soil, is very easy to grow, and has an extended springtime flowering period. Almost any location suits it. The flowers are 2–4 inches wide with orange-yellow, terminally toothed rays. It grows well in zones 4–9, 9–1. Leavenworth's tickseed (*C. leavenworthii*), with a smaller, daintier head, has also become a popular coreopsis for wildflower and butterfly gardens. It seeds in after establishment and pops up randomly, sometimes at distances from the original planting. The flower heads top a slender stem that tends to sway in even the slightest breeze.

Threadleaf coreopsis (*C. verticillata*) is arguably the best tickseed for perennial borders for much of the south. It is typically recommended for zones 4–9, 9–1 but is distributed naturally in the Piedmont and mountains and is not often used south of USDA zone 8. It is not native to southern Georgia or Florida, and natural occurrences in the coastal plains are limited primarily to North Carolina and Virginia. Threadleaf coreopsis is a small, low-growing herb (usually less than three feet tall) with finely divided foliage and a mounded form. It is often planted en masse along walkways and is very effective along shrubby borders. Flowering is prolific and occurs from May to July but can be extended into the fall by cutting plants back in late summer. Full sun produces the best show. Natural habitat includes dry, sandy, rocky, or clayey woodlands, making this one of the best tickseeds for xeric landscaping. Typical flowers are a bright rich yellow, but those of the popular selection 'Moonbeam' are softer in tint.

Tall tickseed (*C. tripteris*) also has divided leaves, but the segments are not as numerous or nearly so fine as those of threadleaf coreopsis. As the common name suggests, plants are also much taller, sometimes reaching ten feet. This species flowers in midsummer to fall with showy, two-inch flowers that are borne in open inflorescences

Tall tickseed.

Chipola River tickseed,
right and *above right*.

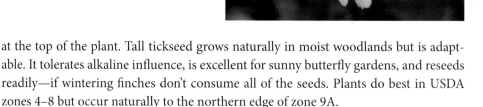

at the top of the plant. Tall tickseed grows naturally in moist woodlands but is adaptable. It tolerates alkaline influence, is excellent for sunny butterfly gardens, and reseeds readily—if wintering finches don't consume all of the seeds. Plants do best in USDA zones 4–8 but occur naturally to the northern edge of zone 9A.

Eared coreopsis (*C. auriculata*) is another low-growing species with bright yellow flowers. It takes its common and scientific names from the earlike lobes (auricles) at the base of its broad, three-inch leaves. The popular selection 'Nana' is a dwarf form that does not exceed one foot tall (species plants grow to about two feet) and forms a nice groundcover of dark green leaves. Flowers appear in late spring, but the leaves stay green well into the fall before eventually turning bronzy. This is a shade-loving coreopsis that should be planted in moist well-drained soils, out of the reach of afternoon sun. It is rare in nature but has become increasingly available at retail nurseries for zones 4–9, 9–1.

Chipola River tickseed (*C. integrifolia*) takes its common name from a spring-fed stream that courses through the central portions of the Florida panhandle. It is not common in nature and is listed as endangered in Florida and threatened in Georgia.

It enjoys a rather disconnected distribution with populations in Georgia, Florida, and South Carolina. Most natural populations are associated with riverbanks and floodplains, often where surface limestone is present, but garden plants perform well under average conditions. Chipola River tickseed has found its way into the garden trade but is not widely available. Plants can be thirty inches tall and typically flower from August to November. This is a coastal plains species that is best in USDA zones 7–9.

Rosinweed

More than a dozen species of rosinweed are native to the United States, many of which are used in gardening. Perhaps none is more popular, widespread, or successful in the southeast than the relatively recently introduced starry rosinweed (*Silphium asteriscus*). This is an upright species with erect, leafy, 3–4-foot stems. Plants flower profusely for several months beginning in early summer, and bloom time can be extended with regular deadheading. The leaves and the stem are hairy and rough to the touch, and the flowers are relished by bees and butterflies: gardens with several of these plants are alive with pollinators. A conspicuous cluster of basal leaves appears in spring and forms the base of the flowering stems. Starry rosinweed occurs naturally in well-drained sandy pinelands and adapts well to most garden situations in zones 8–10, 10–8.

Starry rosinweed.

The rosinweeds take their collective common name from the resin that exudes from broken stems. The gummy, sometimes aromatic exudates of some species were used as a breath-cleansing chewing gum in the 1800s, and a root tea concocted by American Indians was used for a variety of ailments, including diseases of the lungs, back, and chest. However, the chemical components of these extracts are not well studied. Suffice it to say that any purported medicinal value is better relegated to fanciful garden conversation than practical use.

Blanketflowers

Two southeastern native blanketflowers have found their way into regular garden use. Indian blanket (*Gaillardia pulchella*), often simply called gaillardia, is by far the more commonly seen. It is a short-lived perennial in USDA zones 9–10 but should be treated as an annual in the Piedmont and mountains. Plants sometimes return from seed in warmer climates, but self-sowing is variable and cannot be counted on for a continuing garden presence. Nevertheless, this is one of the southeast's toughest plants and is commonly used on sunny sandy roadsides and in other intensely disturbed landscapes. Indian blanket's natural habitat includes coastal environments, often in the deep sands

Lance-leaf blanketflower.

Indian blanket.

behind the first line of salty dunes. The flowers are an attractive whorl of overlapping reds, yellows, and maroons that mature to a rounded rusty-colored seed head. Numerous hybrids and southwestern species are available in the trade, many of which are very similar in foliage, form, and use. Indian blanket flowers from June to October and performs best in zones 8–11, 12–1.

Lance-leaf blanketflower (*G. aestivalis*) is less widely available in nurseries but no less attractive than Indian blanket. Its flowers have well-separated wholly yellow rays that are deeply three-cleft at the tip and encircle a dark, purplish brown disc. It occurs in sandy longleaf pine uplands from South Carolina south to Florida and Texas, USDA zones 7–9.

Both of our blanketflowers prefer well-drained soils in full sun. They are technically xeric species that do not withstand heavy soils or excessive moisture.

Ironweeds

Ironweeds (genus *Vernonia*) take their common name from the rusty color of the spent flowers. About a dozen species occur in the southeast, all of which are native. The flower heads consist of a congested cluster of lavender to purplish tubular disc flowers (white-flowered individuals are sometimes encountered). There are no ray flowers. The number of flowers in each head varies with species, with some bearing as few as ten and others as many as sixty-five. All of the ironweeds treated here are excellent butterfly plants and suitable for zones 5–9, 9–5.

Larger species include giant ironweed (*V. gigantea*) and New York ironweed (*V. noveboracensis*), both of which can easily exceed seven feet tall. Exceptionally tall plants often

Giant ironweed, *above* and *right*.

Narrow-leaved ironweed.

lean or topple at maturity and are best used in naturalistic gardens that offer nearby supporting vegetation and a distant vantage. Both prefer moist soils in nature but adapt readily to the garden. Flowering begins in midsummer and lasts into the fall, with New York ironweed the earliest to flower and giant ironweed the latest. Growing these species in conjunction with narrow-leaved sunflower, blue mistflower, and Joe-Pye-weed produces an excellent show. Height can be controlled by keeping these species moist and shady, but flower production will also be reduced.

Narrow-leaved ironweed (*V. angustifolia*) is a dry-site ironweed common in sandhills and dry pinelands. It is shorter in habit than those above, usually topping out at about three feet and remaining rigidly upright. Numerous narrowly linear leaves crowd the stem, imparting a finely divided form even when flowers are absent. Like the larger versions, the flower heads are purplish and very attractive. This is an excellent plant for the edges of dry naturalized woodlands and is particularly useful for residential landscapes that have been set into former longleaf pine–sandhill habitats. Full sun produces the most abundant flowering.

Blazing Stars

There are so many blazing stars (genus *Liatris*) native to the southeastern United States that is difficult to know where to begin. Nearly two dozen native species are reported, many of which have found their way into the garden. At least some species are also referred to as "gayfeathers"; both names are equally descriptive. Blazing stars come in a variety of heights and arise from corms that continue to produce upright stems for many years if protected by mulch in severe winters and uncovered in spring.

Tidy gardeners might want to start with some of the lower-growing species that remain mostly upright and turgid. Chapman's liatris (*L. chapmanii*), distributed by Mail Order Natives, is an excellent choice for sandy xeric spots in full sun. It is less than three feet tall, rigidly erect, and puts on congested spikes of overlapping purple flowers in late summer and fall. Tightly massed plantings of this species are particularly attractive and effective in butterfly gardens. This species is named for A. W. Chapman, one of the southern United States' most important botanists, and ranges from peninsular Florida to southern Georgia and Alabama. It is best suited for USDA zones 8–9.

Dwarf liatris (*L. microcephala*) is even shorter than Chapman's liatris. Heights rarely exceed two feet. This is an uncommon mountain and Piedmont plant, suitable for USDA zones 5–8. It occurs naturally in dry open woods and rocky glades and is an excellent rock garden plant. The leaves are linear, grasslike, and borne in dense clumps, and the flowers are produced in more or less loosely flowered spikes in late summer.

For taller species, the best choices are prairie blazing star (*L. pycnostachya*) and dense blazing star (*L. spicata*). The two species are similar in appearance but overlap in distribution in our region only in Louisiana and Mississippi. Prairie blazing star is a mid-

Chapman's liatris.

Dense blazing star.

western species and dense blazing star is eastern. Dense blazing star occurs mostly in moist, open meadows and prairie blazing star in dry prairies. Both species grow to six feet tall or more, especially in moist, southern locations, and have inflorescences that sometimes become heavy enough to topple the plants. Too much water will cause either species to grow too tall, but this is especially true for prairie blazing star. Both species produce densely flowered spikes with stalkless flower heads, and both work well in zones 4–9, 9–5. They should be planted in naturalistic settings or wildflower meadows, or at the back of large perennial gardens to allow for their floppy forms.

Joe-Pye and Ageratum

Joe Pye was an American Indian who reputedly cured typhus with a tea concocted from the roots or flowers of the genus *Eupatorium*. At least this is one of the several Joe Pye legends. Exactly who Joe Pye was, which species of *Eupatorium* was used, and whether or how the decoction worked is debatable. Nevertheless, at least five species now carry Joe Pye's name, four of which are large, showy herbs that have found wide use with gardeners.

The correct botanical genus name to apply to the Joe-Pye-weed complex is also difficult to determine. There is continuing debate about the group's affinities and all five species have been assigned to at least three genera, all of which are still in use by various experts and in various publications. I have elected to stick with *Eupatorium*, but the names *Eupatoriadelphus* and *Eutrochium* are also common. This is one of those cases

Hollow-stemmed Joe-Pye-weed, *left* and *below*.

where the common names may be more useful than the scientific ones. In spite of the nomenclatural controversy, retail nurseries usually get the common names correct.

As a group, the Joe-Pye-weeds are tall herbs with purplish lavender flowers. In form they are much like the ironweeds, with large, open inflorescences of strictly discoid flower heads (no ray flowers). Unlike the ironweeds, the Joe-Pyes have whorled leaves that are regularly spaced along the main stem and give the plants an attractive texture.

The hollow-stemmed Joe-Pye-weed (*E. fistulosum*), which is also called queen-of-the-meadow, is by far the tallest. Some individuals reach ten feet or more and tower above surrounding vegetation. They are best for the back of the garden or along fence

White snakeroot. Courtesy of Ron Lance.

Eupatorium dubium.

Blue mistflower, *above* and *right*.

lines where they can be enjoyed from some distance. Joe-Pye-weed (*E. purpureum*) and spotted Joe-Pye-weed (*E. maculatum*) are somewhat shorter but can still exceed seven feet tall. White-flowered selections of *fistulosum* and *purpureum* are available, as well as 'Gateway,' a dwarf hybrid of *maculatum* that only grows to about four feet tall.

The fourth species, *E. dubium*, is also shorter than the others (normally less than five feet) but is less often seen in the nursery trade. The selection 'Little Joe' is an attractive four-foot-tall version that will hopefully give this species a larger gardening presence.

All of these species but *E. purpureum*—which is found mostly in dry sites—are predominately wetland plants that occur in nature in bottomlands, along sunny drainages, and in moist, open woodlands. Acidic soils are generally preferred, but spotted Joe-Pye-weed is especially adapted to calcareous conditions. All will grow in zones 5–9, 9–1, although *E. dubium* is essentially a plant of the eastern seaboard from South Carolina northward and does not occur naturally south of USDA zone 8. Plant Delights Nursery near Raleigh, North Carolina, is an excellent source for many *Eupatorium* species, as are Niche Gardens, Sunlight Gardens, and Natural Gardens.

As a genus, *Eupatorium* is best known in nature for its numerous white-flowered species, many of which—called "thoroughworts"—add beauty and bounty to rural roadsides. The derivation of the common name has to do with the arrangement of the foliage in the species white boneset (*E. perfoliatum*). *Wort* comes from the Middle English word for plant, and *thorough* from the Middle English *thorow* or Old English *thuruh*, which mean *through*. The leaves of white boneset completely encircle the stem, giving the appearance that the stem passes *through* them.

Of the numerous white-flowered thoroughworts, only one has found wide use in the garden. White snakeroot (*Eupatorium rugosum*) is distributed naturally from eastern Canada south to the Florida panhandle and west to Texas. This is the species associated with milk sickness. The internal fluids contain a fatal poison that can be transmitted to humans through cow's milk. Hence, it should not be established near dairy farms. Like most plants in this genus, white snakeroot has more than one scientific name and may also be seen listed as *Ageratina altissima*.

White snakeroot grows to about five feet tall, produces several upright stems, and spreads rapidly by rhizomes. In the late 1990s the Mt. Cuba Center for the Study of the Piedmont Flora in Greenville, Delaware, introduced the cultivar 'Chocolate.' Its chocolate-tinted leaves and purplish stems contrast sharply with six-inch clusters of creamy white flowers. 'Chocolate' grows 2–4 feet tall, takes on the form of a small, rounded, densely foliaged shrub, and is very attractive. Plants flower in fall and do best in light shade in USDA zones 4–8.

The taxonomic realignments within the genus *Eupatorium* resulted in the removal of blue mistflower or hardy ageratum (formerly *Eupatorium coelestinum*) to the genus *Conoclinium* as *C. coelestinum*. It can be found in nurseries under either of these names. Blue mistflower is a popular and widespread blue-flowered species that occurs in a wide array of habitats from wet meadows, stream banks, and fields to roadsides and vacant city lots from New York south to Florida and west to Texas and Nebraska. It is easily established in the garden, spreads readily from rhizomes, and only takes a single season (with or without rain) to spread from a single small clump into a dense colony of several square feet. Left unchecked this species can crowd out other plants, such as several of the tickseeds and even purple coneflower, and can dominate the garden. A low-labor method for combating spread is to plant it in a bottomless pot, with the top edge of the pot slightly above ground level. More labor-intensive methods include pulling stray stems as they pop up or removing unwanted plants near the end of the season before they go to seed.

Blue mistflower's quilted leaves are opposite, stalked, and very attractive for much of the summer. Flowering begins in late summer and extends well into the fall, after which the plants begin to fall over and the heads transition into dirty brown. The colony can be cut to the ground after the first frost in anticipation of next year's crop, or it can be cropped just before the flowers go to seed to reduce the number of potential seedlings.

Ragworts

The genus *Packera*, often seen listed by the older genus name *Senecio*, includes at least ten species native to the southeast, some of which are widespread and often-seen road-side plants. A few are annuals, but most are perennials or biennials. Typical species have erect 1–2-foot stems topped with numerous showy yellow flower heads. Most members of the genus produce flowers in early spring and are among the early harbingers of the change of season. Their bright yellow flowers decorate many moist southeastern road shoulders and add a bounty of color to the emerging spring garden.

Butterweed (*P. glabella*)—also called "smooth ragwort" or "yellowtop"—is among the more popular annuals in the genus. It occurs in nature in wet to moist soils of bottoms, floodplains, and ditches and flowers best with wet feet and full sun. If allowed to go to seed, butterweed will return in the garden from year to year. Otherwise it may disappear.

Butterweed.

Roundleaf ragwort.

Golden ragwort (*P. aurea*) is a rhizomatous perennial and is more easily found in the nursery trade than butterweed; numerous vendors carry it. It too flowers in early spring and prefers moist soil. The delicately cut stem leaves are quite attractive and are distinctly different in form from its broadly rounded basal leaves. Golden ragwort seeds in easily and quickly and, since it is perennial, tends to increase from year to year, especially if the flowers are allowed to produce seed. Roundleaf ragwort (*P. obovata*) is also an excellent garden perennial. Although less available in the nursery trade than golden ragwort, it grows in nature in association with calcareous substrates and does well in neutral to slightly alkaline soil. Its name derives from its thick, rounded, shiny basal leaves. Virtually all of our native ragworts do well in zones 4–9.

Wild Quinine

Wild quinine (*Parthenium integrifolium*) is an excellent but underutilized native wildflower distributed in fields, prairies, and dry woodlands across much of the Piedmont and upper coastal plains. Its buttonlike clusters of tiny white flowers top an erect, leafy stem clothed with broadly lance-shaped, coarsely toothed leaves. Mature plants may reach nearly five feet tall, and large colonies of plants with their uniformly flat-topped inflorescences make quite a show. Depending upon region, wild quinine begins flowering in May, but it is at its best in June and July, making it a perfect follow-up to waning spring wildflowers. It is best suited for USDA zones 3–8.

Wild quinine.

13

Perennial Beans, Mints, and Milkweeds

The beans, mints, and milkweeds constitute widely divergent families with few close evolutionary relationships. They are included together here because of their well-known attractiveness to birds, butterflies, and an assortment of wildlife.

Beans

The beans—or legumes as they are often called—are third in number and breadth only to the asters and orchids: there are about 630 genera and 18,000 species worldwide. Like the asters (and for the same reason), the family has two Latin names, both of which refer to the characteristic podlike fruit of many members of the family. The meaning of the older traditional Latinized name, Leguminosae, is obvious. The newer name, Fabaceae, derives from the Latin *faba* for the broad bean or horsebean (*Vicia faba*). This European native is a garden escapee in North America and has become naturalized in the western and northeastern United States.

The legumes constitute one of the world's most economically important families, second only to the grasses (Poaceae) in food production. Such staples as beans, soya, lentils, peas, and chickpeas are representative of the family's highly nutritious foods.

At least part of the family's agricultural success derives from the ability of many species to convert atmospheric nitrogen to useful nitrogenous compounds, essentially allowing them to create their own sustenance. This nitrogen-fixing ability makes it possible for many beans to grow successfully in exceedingly poor soils and has made them important for agricultural crop rotation. When plowed into the ground, leguminous plants are called "green manure" and increase soil nitrogen levels for future plantings of nonleguminous crops.

In comparison to the family's large size, a relatively small number of beans have found a way into horticulture. Less than twenty genera are routinely used ornamentally, most of which are trees or shrubs and several of which—notably the silktree (*Albizia julibrissin*), whose history is described in Chapter 3—have become notorious weeds. The most-used native species in our region include the wild indigos, lupines, sensitive plants, coralbean, and Aaron's rod.

The fruit of the bean family is a podlike structure called a legume. Legumes are typically dry (as opposed to juicy), develop from a single ovary, and split (or dehisce) at maturity along two longitudinal seams (although the fruit of a few species do not split, instead falling to the ground intact and decaying to release their seeds). The number

Bean Flowers

The bean or pea family is usually divided into subfamilies based largely on flower form. Typical pea flowers (subfamily Papilionoideae) are bilaterally symmetrical (meaning that they can be divided into two equal parts along only a single plane) with a large upper petal (called the standard), two smaller lateral petals (wings), and two lower petals that are usually joined, appear fused, and constitute the keel. The flowers of the wild indigos and coralbean are good examples.

The second type of pea flower (subfamily Caesalpinioideae) is also bilaterally symmetrical, but the upper petal is typically smaller than or equal in size to the spreading, lateral petals, and the flower is not easily separated into standard, wings, and keel. The flowers of the partridge peas and redbud (see Chapter 6) are representative.

The third type of pea flower (Mimosoideae) is tiny, tubular, and typically borne in congested, many-flowered heads or spikes. Although the flowers are individually small, inflorescences of the Mimosoideae are often very showy. The rounded inflorescences of the sensitive plants are typical.

Typical flower of the Mimosoideae.

Typical flower of the Papilionoideae.

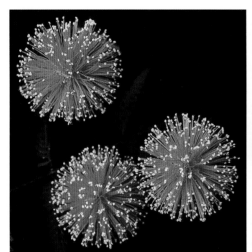

Typical flower of the Caesalpinioideae.

Coralbean pods.

of seeds in a single legume varies from one to many, and the seeds are often easy to germinate, with many species sprouting in only a few days and growing rapidly. Others sprout a little more slowly and are likely to germinate sporadically over several months. Collecting and sowing the seeds of common native beans is an efficient way to add native legumes to wildlife or habitat gardens. Seeds of perennial species that are not readily available in the trade can often be field collected in late summer or fall, sown in flats over the winter or in early spring, then potted or planted out before summer. Relatively little investment in labor and time often yields numerous plants to use and share.

Wild Indigos

The wild indigos (genus *Baptisia*) are herbaceous perennials that behave in the garden like small shrubs. Most are upright and profusely branched with a rounded form. Of the dozen or so species native to the southeast, about six are used regularly in gardening. As a group, the wild indigos are characterized by three-parted leaves; upright, spikelike inflorescences of blue, yellow, or creamy white flowers; and dangling, somewhat inflated legumes that darken with age. Most species develop slowly and may take up to three years to reach their full flowering potential. Indigo seeds develop and drop within the

Apalachicola wild indigo pods.

White wild indigo.

Wild blue indigo.

fruit well before the legume opens. The rattling sound of ripe fruit on a breezy day adds a pleasing dimension to the garden.

The white-flowered indigos include white indigo (*B. alba* and *B. albescens*), creamy wild indigo (*B. bracteata*), prairie false indigo (*B. leucantha*), and Apalachicola wild indigo (*B. megacarpa*), all of which are somewhat difficult to tell apart and are likely to be incorrectly labeled in the trade. To make matters worse, white indigo has masqueraded in both botanical and horticultural circles under several names, the most common of which include *B. pendula* and *B. lactea*, and is still considered by some experts to also include the species *B. leucantha*. Suffice it to say that there is significant confusion with both the names and identification.

Wild indigos range in size from 2 to 5 feet tall (or a little more) and equally as wide. All can be used in zones 6–9. White indigo is the more commonly sold of the white-flowered forms, growing naturally in dry, sandy woods and along roadsides across much of the Southeastern Coastal Plains. In spring white indigo is adorned with erect foot-long racemes of showy white flowers that offer an attractive contrast to the purplish gray of the stems and floral axes. Plants are tolerant of poor soils, full sun, and drought conditions once established. Like most *Baptisia*, well-established plants develop a large root mass and are difficult to transplant.

Prairie false indigo (also sometimes called *B. alba* var. *macrophylla*) is a mostly midwestern species that extends into the southeast in Louisiana and Mississippi. It is sometimes used in eastern gardens and is available from several southeastern native plant outlets. Its legumes are smaller and tougher than those of white wild indigo. Apalachicola wild indigo is a shade-tolerant species with large creamy white flowers and large pods. It is restricted in nature to northwest Florida and extreme southwestern Georgia and southeastern Alabama.

Wild blue indigo.

Yellow indigo.

False or wild blue indigo (*B. australis*) is the most popular of the blue-flowered indigos and is widely used in zones 3–8, 9–1. It, too, flowers in spring and assumes a 3–6-foot, shrublike habit. The flowers are lavender to strongly violet-blue, making it an attractive substitute for the native but often difficult-to-grow lupines. Similar to those of most members of the genus, the seedpods turn dark with age, and the leaves blacken as winter approaches. The dead stems of this and all of our native *Baptisia* can be cut back to one foot or less in late autumn, after the fruit has matured and the leaves have fallen. Wild blue indigo flowers best in full sun. It is less drought tolerant than white indigo but tolerates neutral to slightly alkaline soils with pH values of seven or slightly higher.

The natural hybrid 'Purple Smoke,' first discovered at the North Carolina Botanical Garden and jointly introduced to the market with Niche Gardens in 1996, also has blue flowers. It is a cross between *B. australis* and *B. alba*, with gray-green stems and foliage and purple-eyed flowers. Like many hybrids, it grows slightly taller than either of its parents and is a prodigious flower factory. This is a USDA zone 5–9 plant that thrives in well-drained soil in full sun.

The two yellow-flowered indigos most often encountered in the garden are yellow indigo (*B. sphaerocarpa*) and gopherweed (*B. lanceolata*). Yellow indigo is a mostly midwestern species that occurs naturally in our area only in Louisiana and Mississippi but has been widely and successfully planted in gardens throughout the southeast in USDA zones 5–9. It is drought tolerant, grows to about three feet tall and wide, and does well in average garden soils. The flower color ranges from pale, nearly creamy yellow to bright yellow. The selection 'Screaming Yellow' is one of the more brightly colored forms. The flowers of 'Carolina Moonlight,' a cross between the white and yellow indigos, are a softer, creamy yellow.

Gopherweed is not widely available in the trade but should be more adequately tested. It is endemic to the Southeastern Coastal Plains and is restricted in distribution to South Carolina, Georgia, Florida, and Alabama. It grows naturally in sandy pinelands, is a common component of acidic flatwoods along the Gulf Coast, and has the poten-

Gopherweed, *above* and *left*.

tial to become useful for xeriscaping. The flowers are similar to those of yellow indigo, and typical plants reach about three feet in height. Amy Webb of Mail Order Natives recommends it as both a garden and potted plant; her company is one of the few native plant suppliers to distribute it. It seems to be a little more finicky than some of other yellow-flowered species and should not be overwatered.

Tony Avent of Plant Delights Nursery in Raleigh, North Carolina, refers to the indigos as "redneck lupines," a not-so-veiled reference to the horticultural challenges inherent in growing the true lupines. The flowering racemes of the indigos are very similar to the lupines, and the two can be used similarly in the garden. Plant Delights, Sunlight Gardens, and Niche Gardens are excellent sources for an assortment of garden-ready indigos.

Lupines

Five species of true lupines are native to the southeast. Only the sundial lupine (*Lupinus perennis*) is found in the garden trade, and even it is not widely sold. This is purportedly one of the easier lupines to grow, especially if planted in sandy, well-drained soil in good sun, then left alone. It is the only perennial lupine native to the United States; the others are annual or biennial. Sundial lupine is a tough plant in nature, often seen thriving along harsh, sandy, sun-drenched roadsides where competition is restricted to xeric weeds. Nevertheless, gardeners often report difficulty keeping it alive. The American Horticultural Society recommends this species for zones 4–8, 9–1, but it occurs naturally in northern Florida and can be grown successfully in USDA zone 9. The common name derives from its palmately compound leaves, which are divided at the apex of the leafstalk into 7–9 narrow, attractive leaflets that fold up at night, similar to the leaflets of the sensitive plants and several other beans. It is easy to overwater this plant: too much

Sundial lupine.

Sundial lupine pods.

Sundial lupine.

irrigation may be detrimental. Like many xeric species, sundial lupine develops a large, deep taproot that makes digging them a challenge. They should never be removed from the wild and will likely die if transplanted.

Carolina Bush Pea

The Carolina bush pea (*Thermopsis villosa*)—or "Carolina false lupine" as it is often called—is an excellent companion for the indigo garden. This is a mountain plant by nature, endemic to the southern Appalachians of northern Georgia and western North Carolina and Virginia, but it readily adapts to Piedmont and coastal plains gardens. Its three-parted leaves, bushy habit, and tall spires of bright yellow flowers are reminiscent of yellow-flowered indigos, and its uses are similar. Unlike the indigos, the one-foot-tall inflorescence is shaped more like an elongated cone than a cylinder, and the seedpods are flattened rather than inflated. The base of the leafstalk is often subtended by a broad, conspicuous leaflike stipule that also distinguishes it from the wild indigos. Typical garden plants are 2–5 feet tall, about as wide, and do best in full sun and rich organic soil. Zone recommendations vary for this species. Some experts suggest USDA zones 4–8, others 4–9. Zone 7 may be the southern limit for ensuring long-lived plants. Plants situated in the coastal plains are often short-lived and usually require regular irrigation during dry summers.

Coralbean

No southern garden should be without coralbean (*Erythrina herbacea*). It is easy to establish, easy to grow, requires little care, and puts on a show in both spring and late summer.

Coralbean's scientific epithet is somewhat deceiving. From central peninsular Florida northward, typical plants are herbaceous, dying back soon after first frost to leave erect, leafless soda straws arising from the leaf litter. Farther south, at the southernmost tip of subtropical Florida, plants become soft-woody shrubs or even small trees to fifteen feet

Coralbean.

Coralbean leaves.

tall or more. Authorities once regarded the south Florida form as distinct and named it *E. arborea* in deference to its occasionally arborescent (treelike) habit. Most experts today concur with legume aficionado Duane Isely's assertion that the two forms are simply "manifestations of climatic adaptation."

Coralbean has papilionaceous flowers, as described above, although the typical morphology is not immediately obvious. The standard is elongated rather than upright and surrounds the much smaller and only marginally evident wing and keel petals. Flowers appear tubular in outline with long stamens that protrude only slightly from the tip of the corolla. The narrow shape and bright red color make coralbean an excellent addition to sunny butterfly and hummingbird gardens.

Coralbean is also sometimes called Cherokee bean or cardinal spear, all of which derive from the showy seeds that embellish the plant at the end of summer. As the fruits mature, the pods turn black and split open, revealing bright red fleshy arils that serve to protect the seed, retard early germination, and attract wildlife. Most parts of the plant, including the seeds, contain toxic alkaloids that if ingested can cause gastric upset and vomiting. This is not a plant to include in child-friendly landscapes.

The seeds can be collected from the open pods, soaked for a few days in water, and sown immediately, either in a protected outside location or in flats or pots. Most will germinate in a few days or weeks; others might require several months. It takes at least two years for seed-grown plants to reach maturity, but this is an easy and excellent way to increase coralbean's presence in the garden.

Coralbean prefers well-drained soils, does not tolerate overwatering, flowers in full sun or semishade, and is recommended by the American Horticultural Society for zones 8–10, 10–9. It is sometimes considered short-lived, but it volunteered and grew well in the middle of a semishady azalea garden on the cusp of USDA zones 8 and 9, where it flowered profusely for many years.

Mints

The mint family (Lamiaceae or Labiatae) encompasses about 252 genera and 6,800 species worldwide. Most are covered with tiny glandular hairs that contain scented ethereal oils and are often strongly aromatic when touched. Even brushing against some species can fill the air with a pungent fragrance. The family has long been valued for the production of perfumes and for its huge array of culinary herbs—spearmint, peppermint, and pennyroyal of the genus *Mentha* are examples. Most mints—at least the herbaceous ones—have a square stem that is easily discernable when the stem is rolled between the fingers. Garden mints are largely herbaceous plants, but the family also contains a variety of trees and shrubs.

American Beautyberry

Most people still don't think of the common American beautyberry (*Callicarpa americana*) as a mint. For many years it was aligned with the verbena family (Verbenaceae) and is still treated as such by some plant taxonomists. Its woody stems, shrublike stature, toothed leaves, and bright purple fruit certainly suggest a closer relationship with the verbenas than the Lamiaceae. The leaves are not particularly aromatic, and the main

American beautyberry.

American beautyberry.

stems are rounded in cross-section, becoming more or less square only near the tips of the newer branches. Nevertheless, recent phylogenetic studies suggest that *Callicarpa* as well as several other genera that have been traditionally included within the Verbenaceae might be better placed in the mint family.

American beautyberry is primarily a coastal plains and outer Piedmont plant, widely distributed throughout the southern United States from southern Delaware to eastern Texas and Arkansas. It is somewhat rare in rich, shady hardwood forests and mostly absent from the higher elevations of the Blue Ridge and southern Appalachians. But it can be abundant in sunny, low-elevation pinelands and sparsely vegetated semishady woodlands. It is reported for every parish in Louisiana and every county in Florida. The American Horticultural Society recommends it for zones 5–9, 9–1, though it may be shorter-lived in colder climates. It is drought tolerant, does not tolerate inundation or poor drainage, and flowers and fruits best in full sun or high, very light shade.

This is an excellent, easy-to-grow deciduous shrub with many garden uses, especially in warmer regions of the south. Mature plants can be up to six feet tall and wide but can be heavily pruned in spring to maintain size and density and to ensure abundant flowers and fruit. The flowers are small, pinkish, and somewhat inconspicuous. Although they appear in the leaf axils in late spring and summer when little else is happening, they can easily go unnoticed if you are not watching for them. The fruit, on the other hand, puts on a riotous performance, rivaling the winterberry hollies in showiness, if not in color. Tightly held clusters of small, greenish drupes begin developing shortly after the petals drop, enlarging slightly during maturation and changing to bright magenta or violet as the leaves fall. The resulting spires of purple to sometimes pinkish fruit are showy, long lasting, and extremely attractive. Massed plantings of this species are unparalleled in the fall garden.

White-fruited forms of American beautyberry are occasionally seen in the wild and are regularly available from a number of native plant vendors. Growing conditions are identical for both color forms. A mixed planting of white- and purple-fruited plants is an eye-catching combination that doubles as an excellent source for dried plant material. Nearly any dried arrangement benefits from the addition of one or two stems of beautyberry fruit.

White forms of beautyberry are distributed under several varietal and cultivar names, including varieties *alba* and *lactea* and the cultivars 'White' and 'Lactea.' All of these names probably refer to a single entity, and differently named plants are likely to be virtually indistinguishable in appearance and performance. Retail vendors for the white form include Garden Delights, Mail Order Natives, and Meadowbrook Nursery. Wholesale sources include Dodd and Dodd Native Nurseries, Chiappini Farm Native Nursery, Lazy K Nursery, Superior Trees, and Trillium Gardens.

Purple-fruited forms are extremely common in nature and often volunteer in yards, gardens, and vacant residential lots, especially where old sandhill pinelands once stood. In short, your own landscape may be your best source for new plants. American beautyberry is easily moved at almost any time of year and requires little care after relocation. Digging small plants is best, but even fairly large specimens survive transplantation, especially if moved in winter. If digging from your own land is not an option, nearly all native plant nurseries sell this species, at least a few of which offer several named selections.

Some experts recommend beautyberry as a wildlife food, noting its preference by deer, raccoons, thrushes, mockingbirds, thrashers, robins, catbirds, towhees, turkey, and bobwhite quail. The fruit is indeed edible and was used, at least marginally, by American Indians and early New World colonists, even though it is somewhat mealy and lacks flavor. The fact that it typically remains on the stem well into winter suggests that it is either slow to reach an edible stage or serves only as a winter food of last resort for most wildlife. Gardeners benefit by enjoying the colorful fruit well into late fall, at the same time providing sustenance to wintering birds when they need it most.

Horsemint, Beebalm, and Bergamot

Six species and several varieties of the genus *Monarda* are native to the southeast, at least four of which are regularly used in gardening. The genus is characterized by strongly aromatic leaves and flowers, an erect stature, and attractive headlike inflorescences of numerous tubular flowers. All species tend to spread in the garden, and several can become rampant under optimum conditions. Most species are also prone to powdery mildew, especially in shady locations, but are otherwise largely trouble free. All are excellent additions to butterfly and hummingbird gardens.

Two of our native species are called bergamot (*M. didyma, M. fistulosa*), a common name that likely comes from the orangelike aroma of their flowers, a fragrance reminiscent of the oils of bergamot orange (*Citrus ×aurantium* subsp. *bergamia*). Both plants were used by Native Americans to treat a variety of illnesses. Leaf teas treated coughs; flower teas treated colds and fevers; and boiled leaves applied to the skin and eyes were said to reduce pain and sooth skin irritations. The red-flowered *M. didyma* is also the plant from which the Oswego Indians and numerous other American tribes fashioned what is now known as Oswego tea, an aromatic brew that was passed on to New World colonists and later used as a substitute for English tea following the Boston Tea Party.

Oswego tea (*M. didyma*), which is also called beebalm, is a red-flowered species (though some plants produce white or pinkish flowers) with a large tuft of tubular, two-lipped flowers borne at the top of an erect 3–5 feet stem. Its natural range in our region is limited to the mountains and Piedmont, where it occurs mostly in seepage slopes,

Bergamot Orange

It is important not to get our native bergamot confused with the well-known and widely sold medicinal plant bergamot orange (*Citrus aurantium* subsp. *bergamia*, =*C. bergamia*). The latter is a small tree with yellow, rounded, orangelike fruit that has been cultivated in southern Italy and France for many centuries. As its name and fruit suggest, it is a member of the citrus family, and it probably originated in Asia and was imported to Europe. Its essential oils have long been used for a variety of medicinal and other purposes including as an antiseptic, insect repellant, aphrodisiac, and antidepressant. Extracts from the plant's fruit are sold as bergamot oil, a touted therapy for all sorts of debilitating medical and emotional conditions. It is beyond the scope of this book to comment on the authenticity of these values. Suffice it to say that it is always wise to investigate claims thoroughly before beginning use.

Oswego tea.

stream banks, bogs, and other moist places. It is present in Georgia only at the northern edge of the state and is absent from Florida, Alabama, Mississippi, and Louisiana. Nevertheless, it has been introduced to coastal plains gardeners as an excellent and easy-to-grow perennial and has been billed in garden centers as one of the better beebalms for the Deep South's hot, humid climate, a claim that is at least somewhat overstated. The American Horticultural Society has even recommended it for zones 4–10, 10–1. As much as I'd like to believe these recommendations, zones 4–8, 8–1 are far more reliable for successful plantings. Plants situated south of AHS Heat Zone 8 struggle mightily without sufficient water. They lack the typical dark green foliage and floriferous habit of more northern plants and may not return the second year. About two dozen cultivars of Oswego tea are available in the trade, varying mostly in flower color and resistance to powdery mildew.

The closely related wild bergamot (*M. fistulosa*) is similar in form to Oswego tea but shorter in stature. Mature plants rarely exceed three feet tall, and the flowers are more nearly lavender or purple than red. It also tolerates drier sites than its red-flowered sibling, and the southern limit of its natural range is much farther south, nearly reaching the Gulf Coast in southern Louisiana. It, too, is most appropriate for USDA zones 4–8.

The two Deep South species of beebalm include the widespread horsemint (*M. punctata*), which occurs widely across the eastern United States from New York and Minnesota south to New Mexico and Florida, and the Texas-centered lemon beebalm (*M. citriodora*), a highly valued garden species. Unlike the bergamots, the leaves of these species are much longer than wide, and the inflorescences are composed of several compact cymes—one below the other—rather than a single cyme at the top of the stem. Also unlike the bergamots, the stamens do not protrude from the corolla and the flowers are mostly overshadowed by colorful, showy floral bracts.

Wild bergamot.

Dotted horsemint.

Lemon beebalm is primarily a USDA zone 8–10 plant and is at once the least hardy and most heat tolerant of all of our native *Monarda* species. It is reported as native to the southeast only in parts of Louisiana, but it is widely established from plantings, especially in Alabama and Mississippi. The bilaterally symmetrical flowers are white or pale pink with purple spots and are subtended by two series of bracts, the outer ones small and spreading, the inner ones showy, purplish, about ⅝ inch long with a bristled tip, and curved upward to form a bowl under the flower. Several flower clusters are borne at varying levels near the top of a 1–3-foot upright stem, making this species an especially attractive addition to the perennial garden or wildflower meadow. Lemon beebalm is drought tolerant, pleasantly aromatic, easy to grow, and very attractive to butterflies, bees, and other nectaring insects. Native plant purists will likely consider this species non-native to the southeast and may want to avoid it. It reseeds easily and tends to form large colonies in nature and the garden. Removing spent heads at the end of the season will slow the spread, but well-situated garden plants can become aggressive if not monitored.

Dotted horsemint or spotted beebalm (*M. punctata*) takes its common names from the tiny dots that decorate the throats of its creamy yellow, two-lipped flowers, a feature that requires close observation to see clearly. Although the flowers are very attractive up close, the plant is most appreciated in nature and valued in the garden for the showy pinkish bracts that form the bulk of the inflorescence. The successive floral whorls are borne more closely together than those of lemon beebalm, giving them a more compact appearance. This 1–3-foot-tall, strongly aromatic perennial herb is largely a coastal plains species, with sporadic natural occurrences in the Piedmont and mountains. It occurs naturally in all of the southeastern states, including most of Florida, and is recommended for USDA zones 6–10A. It prefers neutral soils, is drought tolerant (but enjoys a little irrigation), and is easy to grow though it tends to be somewhat short-lived, especially north of USDA zone 9, yet reseeds aggressively. It is available from a wide assortment of Florida-based native nurseries.

Like many mints, our native species of *Monarda* will hybridize when grown in close proximity. Gardens that include large numbers of several species might end up with a variable range of form and flower color. Purists who worry about genetic separation should consider this when planting any of the herbaceous mints. Those less concerned with gene pool confusion can just enjoy seeing what comes up.

Salvias

The genus *Salvia*, collectively known as "sages," encompasses some of the world's most popular garden plants. There are about 800 species worldwide, a figure that is about 12 percent of the total number of species in the mint family. Many have achieved wide-ranging horticultural popularity. At least two dozen species are used in southeastern gardening, only seven of which are native to the United States. Some of the most popular non-native species include silver sage (*S. argentea*), pineapple sage (*S. elegans*), Mexican bush sage (*S. leucantha*), European sage (*S. sclarea*), bog sage (*S. uliginosa*), blue gentian sage (*S. patens*), and scarlet sage (*S. splendens*). No species of *Salvia* is currently listed as invasive in the continental United States, although our own scarlet sage (*S. coccinea*) is considered weedy in the Pacific Islands.

Of our seven natives, three occur mostly in Texas and four more broadly across the greater southeast. The most popular native species for our region include the blue-flowered blue (*S. azurea*) and lyreleaf (*S. lyrata*) sages, and the pink or red-flowered scarlet or red sage referenced above.

Salvias have handsome two-lipped flowers that are highly attractive to insects. The expanded lower lip serves as an excellent landing pad for bees and other relatively large pollinators and forms the basis of an ingenious pollination strategy. When bees land on the outstretched petal, the stamens bend outward, allowing the anthers to release their pollen onto the visitor's back. Large, fully flowered salvias can be alive with dozens of busily working bumblebees, sharing space and pollen with an assortment of smaller insects.

Lyreleaf sage is by far the most widespread of our native salvias and is among our better-known wildflowers. The somewhat modified adage that one person's garden treasure is another person's weed certainly applies here. In spring, roadsides and disturbed sites can be dominated with this relatively low-growing salvia that, for most of the year,

Lyreleaf sage.

Lyreleaf sage.

Blue sage.

is evidenced only by a flattened rosette of purplish green leaves. The erect flowering stems are typically less than two feet tall and are topped by a delicate 6–12-inch vertical inflorescence of tubular pale lavender flowers. The overall effect of a large colony in early spring is that of a bluish or purple haze resting just above ground level. Colonies flower for several weeks during March and April but die back fairly quickly, leaving tidy gardeners with little need to remove spent flower stalks. The natural abundance of this species has caused it to be largely regarded as a weed rather than a garden plant. Nevertheless, an increasing number of native plant nurseries now carry it. At least one cultivar, 'Purple Knockout,' which has very attractive purple leaves, is now available. Lyreleaf sage is a tough plant that requires little maintenance, tolerates sun or shade, grows in poor soil, withstands at least moderate foot traffic, and is relished by hummingbirds.

Two relatively tall blue-flowered native sages are used in southern gardening. Blue sage (*S. azurea*), which often has white instead of blue flowers, is probably the more commonly seen and readily available. Nettle-leaf sage (*S. urticifolia*) is similar but has larger leaves and a slightly shorter stature. Both are drought-tolerant species that do best in full sun and well-drained soils. Blue sage is a lower Piedmont and coastal plains plant that occurs naturally in our region from at least North Carolina to Louisiana. It grows 2–6 feet tall and has an extended flowering season that can last from late summer well into fall. Blue sage occurs naturally in a wide array of habitats and is adaptable to many soil types from moderately acidic to neutral. If allowed to grow unhindered, plants become sparsely stemmed and somewhat leggy and can flop over at maturity. Regular summer pruning produces smaller, more compact plants. This species is appropriate for zones 5–9, 9–1.

The red-flowered scarlet or tropical sage has become an extremely popular hummingbird plant for Deep South gardens. The tubular flowers are perfectly adapted to the hummingbird's needlelike bill, and its bright red color is an effective enticement. Plants are easy to care for, grow rapidly, and return from year to year, either from seed or from a perennial base. The natural range of this species is mostly along the coast from about South Carolina to Florida and west at least to Mississippi, but it is widely planted and has become established across much of the southeast. It does best in zones 8–10, 12–1. Flowers range from blood red to bicolored pink and white and are borne along an upright to sometimes leaning stem. Garden plants average 2–3 feet tall but can be slightly taller, especially if grown in partial shade. Deadheading the entire inflorescence immediately after the flowers fall encourages branching and extends the flowering period from midsummer into fall. Allowing at least a few flowering stems to reach maturity will encourage reseeding. This is a short-lived, drought-tolerant species that can be easily grown in well-drained soil.

Scarlet sage.

Skullcaps

Skullcaps take their collective common name from the persistent, saucerlike fruits that tend to remain on mature plants for an extended period. Whether these shallow structures resemble a skullcap is questionable. To me, they seem more akin to hubcaps, or the metal disklike seats that adorn old-timey farm tractors. The Latin name derives from *scutella*, a small dish or saucer, which should make the genus name easy to remember. Garden use of the skullcaps is similar to that of the salvias.

Of the twenty species of skullcaps that occur naturally in the southeast, only two are readily available in the trade, and even these are not offered by many vendors. Downy or hoary skullcap (*S. incana*) and helmet skullcap (*S. integrifolia*) are similar in appearance and are most easily distinguished by their leaves. The midstem leaves of downy skullcap are toothed whereas those of helmet skullcap are not (or only slightly so). Distinguishing them by habitat is less difficult. Downy skullcap is an upland species that grows in dry to moist shady woodlands and is distributed in our region from Virginia to Louisiana. The range of helmet skullcap is similar, but it prefers wetter habitats and typically occurs in moist to wet savannas, bottomlands, and seepages. Both species have tubular blue flowers and opposite leaves, grow 2–3 feet tall, and do best in USDA zones 3–9. Sources include Niche Gardens, Native Gardens, and Nearly Native Nursery. Sunlight Gardens also offers heartleaf skullcap (*S. ovata*), a relative newcomer to the market with several botanical varieties and a range that encompasses much of the eastern United States.

Helmet skullcap.

Downy skullcap.

Obedient plant.

Obedient Plants

Obedient plants (genus *Physostegia*) are erect, single-stemmed mints topped with a showy raceme of tubular pinkish to lavender flowers. At least four species are native to parts of the southeast, of which the fall obedient plant, or false dragonhead (*P. virginiana*), is most commonly used in gardening. *P. virginiana* is native mostly to the mountains and Piedmont with only a limited presence in the coastal plains of Virginia and the Carolinas. It is also considered native in Alabama, Mississippi, and Louisiana and is widespread in Florida, but it is not considered native there. It takes its odd common name from the stem. If bent, the stem remains obediently in the bent position—at least for a while. Fall obedient plant is an easy-to-grow perennial that is not without aggressive tendencies. It spreads in the garden by shallow underground runners. Errant plants can be easily pulled, if desired. Nevertheless, gardeners who wish to reduce their supervisory responsibilities might want to avoid this species. Fall obedient plant has been used in gardening for many years and several named cultivars are available. 'Summer Snow' and 'Miss Manners' produce white flowers. 'Vivid' is reportedly more brightly colored than the species. All of these selections flower from late summer nearly to the first frost and are recommended for zones 4–9, 9–1.

Calamints and Rosemarys

The calamints that occur in our region have masqueraded under several scientific names. Some experts include them in the genus *Clinopodium*, others classify them in the genus *Satureja*, and still others continue to hang onto the genus name *Calamintha*. The axiom that scientific names make communication easier does not apply here. The species included below are probably more likely to be found in nurseries under the genus name *Clinopodium*, but searching for them in the trade may require the use of multiple names. Our species are primarily woody plants but are included here alongside the other mints.

The calamints, also called "savories" or sometimes "basils," are typically low-growing shrubs with small leaves and showy flowers. One of the best species for southern gardens is Georgia savory (*Clinopodium georgianum*). This excellent eighteen-inch shrub is semievergreen with strongly aromatic foliage. It produces numerous lavender flowers in late summer and fall—to at least early November—and works equally well as a border, in a mixed shrub bed with other woody mints, or massed as a single species. The flow-

Georgia calamint.

Red basil.

Gray rosemary.

ers are typical of the mints, tubular with showy stamens and a spotted throat. Georgia savory should be planted in full sun to light shade, prefers well-drained soils, and is recommended for zones 7–9. It is available from several nurseries, including retail from Woodlanders and Nearly Native Nursery. It should be more widely used. The Indian grave mountain mint (*C. dissitiflorum*), a relatively recent discovery from Georgia, is similar.

Red basil, or scarlet calamint (*C. coccineum*), is a Deep South species (USDA zones 8–9) inhabiting deep sands along the coast from southwestern Georgia, central peninsular and panhandle Florida, and west to Mississippi. As its name suggests, the flowers are bright red. Mature plants do not exceed about three feet tall, have very small leaves less than one inch long, and produce numerous flowers in late summer and fall. Red basil is excellent in shrubby borders or as part of a mixed bed with rosemarys and other calamints. This is a xeric species that needs exceedingly well-drained soils; it cannot tolerate excessive irrigation. A yellow-flowered cultivar of red basil called 'Ohoopee Yellow,' selected from a plant in Tatnall County, Georgia, has become increasingly popular and is also available from Woodlanders and Nearly Native Nursery.

Several rosemarys (genus *Conradina*) also occur across the southeastern United States. These plants are not the same as the well-known Mediterranean rosemary (*Rosmarinus officinalis*) that is often sold in garden centers, traditionally used as a culinary herb, and widely planted in butterfly gardens. However, like their Mediterranean cousin, the native rosemarys are extremely aromatic and make excellent garden plants. Gray rosemary (*C. canescens*), Apalachicola rosemary (*C. glabra*), and Etonia rosemary (*C. etonia*) are the more commonly sold, with gray rosemary being both more widespread in distribution and easier to find in the trade. Gray and Apalachicola rosemarys are USDA zone 7–9 plants; Etonia rosemary is endemic to Florida and does best in USDA zones 8–9. All are low-growing, aromatic shrubs with bluish to pale lavender flowers that appear sporadically from spring to fall. These are xeric plants with a preference for full sun, dry, sandy soils, and excellent drainage.

Milkweeds and Bluestars

The milkweeds (genus *Asclepias*) and bluestars (genus *Amsonia*) are closely related genera that were once considered to be part of separate botanical families. More recently, the milkweed family—Asclepiadaceae—has been included with the bluestars in the Apocynaceae, or dogbane family. Most are characterized by the thick, sticky, milky sap that oozes from their stems, major veins, and fresh pods when crushed. With the milkweeds included, the Apocynaceae is represented worldwide by about 355 genera and 3,700 species. Oleander (*Nerium*), frangipani (*Plumeria*), confederate jasmine (*Trachelospermum*), periwinkle (*Vinca*), and wax plant (*Hoya*) are some of the family's best-known ornamental species, none of which is native to the United States.

Most members of the milkweed family are potentially toxic if ingested. The milky latex contains a variety of chemical compounds, including alkaloids and cardioactive glycosides that can cause a variety of debilitating effects if consumed in high doses. Although no human deaths have been reported from milkweed poisoning, livestock that ingest large quantities of milkweed develop weakness, staggering, and labored breathing and can die, depending upon the quantity consumed. In contrast, monarch butterfly caterpillars feed on milkweed with impunity and actually absorb these foul-tasting compounds into their systems. The toxicity is transferred to the adult butterflies, making them distasteful to birds and thus protecting them against predation.

Like many poisonous plants, milkweeds also have a long history of medicinal and culinary uses. American Indians ate the boiled leaves of some species and consumed the raw flowers and roots of others. Our native pleurisy root (*Asclepias tuberosa*) was named for its use in treating bronchial and pulmonary distress, and the genus name *Asclepias* was bestowed in honor of Asklepios, the Greek god of medicine and healing.

Milkweeds and bluestars produce paired podlike fruits that are technically referred to as follicles. Some are narrow and pencillike and others broad and bulky. Each follicle develops from a single carpel—the basic female reproductive organ of a flower—and splits along only one side at maturity. Milkweed pods (genus *Asclepias*), in particular, contain numerous tiny seeds, each outfitted at the apex with a mass of cottony hairs (technically called a coma) that aid in windborne seed dispersal. Dehiscing follicles are a conspicuous and interesting attraction in the wildflower garden and provide a demonstrable clue that the seeds are ready for collecting.

Milkweeds

More than two dozen milkweeds occur naturally in the southeastern United States, all of which have showy, complicated flowers and are especially attractive to butterflies. While a handful of species can be found in specialty nurseries, only three are widely sold, and even these are not universally available. This relative dearth of garden-ready species is especially striking given the rapid increase of butterfly enthusiasts and the increasing number of gardeners who desire butterflies in their landscapes. Numerous

Milkweed from Seed

Gardeners who desire a greater number of milkweeds in their gardens might want to try growing them from seed. Distribution of milkweed seed packets has been popularized by the increasing interest in butterfly conservation and butterfly gardening. The several online vendors included below currently offer seed in small quantities by mail order.

Butterfly Encounters
http://www.butterflyencounters.com/

Easyliving Native Perennial Wildflower
http://www.easywildflowers.com/

Milkweed Farm
http://www.milkweedfarm.com/

Prairie Moon Nursery
http://www.prairiemoon.com/

Butterflyweed.

native plant and butterfly gardening books tout the use of milkweeds as quintessential butterfly attractants, especially for the so-called milkweed butterflies. Unfortunately, most of the species these books mention are not available for purchase. The available plants are relatively large-leaved and have a coarse, shrubby appearance.

The most popular garden milkweed by far is butterflyweed, or pleurisy root (*A. tuberosa*). Unlike most species, this one is readily available in the trade and can be found at a wide array of retail nurseries and garden centers. Butterflyweed is a drought-tolerant and maintenance-free garden plant that returns annually despite minimum care. It is a common component of poor soils in well-drained sandy pinelands and is our only native milkweed that has clear instead of milky sap. The orange—varying to reddish or yellow—flowers are borne in great profusion in a compound inflorescence of numerous flat-topped, few-flowered umbels. Flowers appear throughout the summer and are followed by the development of single or paired follicles that reach six inches long at maturity. Butterflyweed is especially attractive to queen, monarch, and swallowtail butterflies and is also sometimes covered with tiny, attractive, reddish aphids. Mature plants develop a very large root mass and are difficult to transplant successfully, a feature that is intimately related to their tolerance of drought. Although plants in their natural habitat are often less than twenty inches tall, well-cared-for garden plants in good soil with a little irrigation are often more robust and can grow to three feet or more. Well-drained sites are essential for this species, as the elongated taproot is prone to rot in overly moist sites.

Some people consider the common milkweed (*A. syriaca*) to be an excellent garden plant. Others consider it a weed. Its large form and aggressive nature make it both beautiful and sometimes difficult to control. If planted in an isolated bed surrounded by a path or manicured lawn where its rhizomes cannot spread and errant plants are easily removed, it can easily be confined to a relatively small area. Nevertheless, its best use may be in a less formal wildflower meadow where it can be allowed to achieve its full expression. Mature plants can be up to seven feet tall and are festooned at flowering time with large, conspicuous clusters of purplish, rose, or greenish white flowers. The attractive, opposite leaves are thick, densely hairy below, and among the largest of our native milkweeds, varying 3–12 inches long and up to about 4 inches wide. Common milkweed is easy to establish, requires little care, and is particularly attractive to monarch butterflies. This species is less heat tolerant than butterflyweed and is best suited for USDA zones 3–7.

Milkweed Flowers

Milkweed flowers are complicated, exquisite structures that bear only scant resemblance to our grade-school concept of a typical flower. The five sepals and petals are often strongly reflexed (angled downward) and subtend a showy upright crown or corona, a unique accoutrement of specialized structures that is lacking in most flowers. The corona's outer whorl consists of tiny hoods that serve as nectar reservoirs adapted to bee, butterfly, and wasp pollinators. The hoods encircle and often enclose an inner whorl of parts called horns. In some species, such as *A. syriaca* and *A. incarnata*, the horns are conspicuous and exserted beyond the hoods. In others, like the butterflyweed (*A. tuberosa*), they are shorter than and concealed by the hood and may require close inspection to see clearly. The central part of the corona consists of five stamens, two styles, and a large, single stigma with five stigmatic chambers, all of which are fused into a conspicuous fleshy column referred to as a gynostegium. The pollen is borne in paired sacs called pollinia (similar in structure and function to those of orchid flowers) that are attached to each other by a tiny gland. Mature pollinia adhere to visiting pollinators, are torn away and carried as a unit to another plant, and become lodged in a stigmatic chamber to effect cross-pollination. The large number of pollen grains held in a single sac ensures that adequate pollen is available to fertilize the receiving flower.

This inimitable method of pollination places restrictions on cross-fertilization. Uniqueness in the size and structure of a species' stigmatic chamber means that its flowers can only be pollinated by matching pollinia, resulting in few natural or artificially induced milkweed hybrids. In addition, most milkweed species are not self-compatible. Hand pollination is possible but must involve at least two plants, adding to the challenge and adventure of producing home-grown seeds.

Milkweed flower.

Milkweed pod and seeds.

Swampforest milkweed.

Common milkweed., *above* and *below*.

Swamp milkweed (*A. incarnata*) also has rose-purple flowers, but its leaves are narrower than those of common milkweed and more or less lance-shaped in outline. Mature plants can be at least five feet tall, rivaling the height of the common milkweed, but are less bulky in appearance. As its name suggests, it performs well in wet, boggy conditions, but it does not require them. Average garden soil and moderate irrigation are suitable, and full sun is preferred. This species is sparsely distributed nearly throughout the eastern United States and is recommended by the American Horticultural Society for zones 3–8, 8–1, and by others for USDA zones 3–9. The confusion in zone recommendations likely results from the two named varieties. The range of the broad-leaved northern form (subspecies *pulchra*) does not extend farther south than about South Carolina. The narrow-leaved form (variety *incarnata*) occurs more widely, including along much of the Florida peninsula at least to the limits of USDA zone 9. Both prefer marshy, boggy habitats, hence the common name. This is another excellent food plant for monarch butterfly caterpillars. The selection 'Ice Ballet,' a white-flowered form, is the most popular of several horticultural selections.

The white-flowered *A. perennis*, also called swamp or swampforest milkweed, is occasionally encountered in the trade. Its leaves are narrow and lance-shaped and its flowers are smaller than those of 'Ice Ballet.' It is confined to swamp forests of the coastal plains but is adaptable in the garden.

Bluestars

The genus *Amsonia* includes fewer than twenty species worldwide, sixteen of which are native to the United States. Four species occur in the southeast, three of which are available from native plant nurseries.

Bluestars take their common name from their five-petaled flowers, which are tubular below but flare above into five distinct lobes. The inflorescence typically consists of a showy, crowded terminal panicle of numerous blooms. The petals are usually pale blue but may be slightly darker in some individuals. The fruit is a green, very slender, curving follicle with several seeds.

The midwestern narrow-leaf bluestar (*A. hubrichtii*), with a distribution centered mostly in Oklahoma and Arkansas, is often sold in our region and is well behaved in southeastern gardens. Plants become three feet tall and wide (or a little more) at maturity, with narrow leaves, a shrublike habit, and foliage that turns bright orange-yellow

Eastern bluestar.

in the fall. Narrow-leaf bluestar is an excellent—even if not strictly native—garden perennial that has proven to be a worthy addition to southeastern gardens in zones 5–9, 9–5.

Eastern bluestar (*A. tabernaemontana*) is by far the most commonly used of our truly native species. It has 2–5-inch leaves, grows to about 3 feet tall, and flowers heavily from about March to May. It occurs in nature in rich, deciduous forests and bottomland woods but does best in the garden in moist soil and full sun in zones 3–9, 9–1.

Threadleaf bluestar (*A. ciliata*) is a xeric species with very narrow needlelike leaves that are up to about 3 inches long but seldom exceed ⅛ inch wide. It is restricted largely to the coastal plains and is found mostly in sandhills and dry, sandy woodlands from North Carolina to Florida and Alabama; it does not occur in Mississippi or Louisiana.

Louisiana bluestar (*A. ludoviciana*) is a rare species, restricted in nature largely to Louisiana with outlying populations in Mississippi and Georgia. Several nurseries offer it, a few of which erroneously list it as also native to South Carolina.

Threadleaf bluestar.

Threadleaf bluestar.

14

Vines, Groundcovers, and Spring Ephemerals

Native vines are two-edged swords. Many are very attractive and worthy of garden use but often display weedy tendencies and can be difficult to control. Crossvine (*Bignonia capreolata*), trumpet creeper (*Campsis radicans*), Virginia creeper (*Parthenocissus quinquefolia*), and passionflower (*Passiflora incarnata*) are all good examples. Crossvine and trumpet creeper have abundant and beautiful brightly colored flowers; Virginia creeper can put on a startling show of fall color; and passionflower is a veritable magnet for butterflies. However, all four can be aggressive if not controlled or properly sited and can spread or climb rapidly, sometimes taking over once they are established.

Why vines are aggressive in the garden is evident from their place in nature. Many live naturally in the deep shade of rich hardwood forests or soggy floodplain woodlands where they compete for light and resources. Their natural climbing tendencies are generously rewarded with the abundant sunlight of the forest canopy, while their growth below is checked by the dim light of the forest interior. When released to the garden, they often respond with abandon, spreading and climbing in all directions, encouraged by the combination of sunlight, good soil, and an attentive gardener.

This is not to suggest that all native vines are problematic, or even that those that are should not be used. However, given many vines' naturally aggressive tendencies, including them in residential gardens is most successful when done with planning, forethought, and caution. If you are fortunate enough to live in a large, mostly natural landscape akin to a particular vine's natural habitat, you may be able to use the deeper parts of your woods to simulate its growing conditions and to plant certain species without fear of reprisal. For typical residential and commercial landscapes, it pays either to seek out native species that are not overly aggressive (examples of both aggressive and nonaggressive species are included below), plant only well-behaved cultivars, or to practice the dual strategies of isolation and containment.

Isolation involves situating plants in ways that prevent their spread and allow for greater control. Using an isolated tree or a strategically placed trellis or arbor are good alternatives. Just be sure that the crown of the selected tree does not intermingle in the canopy with those of other trees and that the trellis or arbor is located away from potentially supporting vegetation.

Containment means ensuring that the vine remains under your control and is not allowed to spread, either laterally or vertically. A deep, wide layer of mulch that allows for mowing or trimming completely around the base of a tree or trellis is an excellent strategy. Some vines, notably those like Virginia creeper, tend to run along the ground, putting down roots along the way and climbing on anything available. If keeping the mulched area clear of vegetation is desired, these runners will require periodic pruning or removal. If pruning is not a necessity, the vine can be allowed to scramble and puddle at the base of the supporting structure; but it may still need periodic monitoring. Either way, it is probably not wise to use the mulched area as a bed for other plants, as they will likely be quickly overtaken without continuous diligence.

Fences can also serve as isolating mechanisms, as long as they are not bordered by vegetation that encourages climbing or scrambling. Chain-link fences work particularly well and allow ample opportunity for twining vines. Plants are also more easily and less damagingly removed from chain-link rather than wood fences, should you change your mind.

Less-Aggressive Native Vines

Coral Honeysuckle

Of the several nonaggressive native vines that have found favor in the garden, none is more popular or showy than coral honeysuckle (*Lonicera sempervirens*). Unlike its invasive Japanese cousin mentioned in Chapter 3, this species is well behaved and very attractive.

In nature, coral honeysuckle occurs mostly in dry, well-drained uplands and open woods. It tends to take advantage of natural and artificial edges, including roadsides, fence lines, and firebreaks, but it sometimes also scrambles on scrubby oaks in xeric pinelands. The tubular, two-inch, nonfragrant flowers are bright orange-red outside, yellow-red inside, and borne in profusion from spring into early summer. Flowers are

Coral honeysuckle, *above* and *left*.

Coral honeysuckle.

Yellow honeysuckle. Courtesy of Ron Lance.

Yellow honeysuckle. Courtesy of Ron Lance.

followed in the fall by showy, bright red berries that provide food for birds and rabbits. The upper pair of leaves is typically perfoliate or connate, meaning that they are borne opposite one another on the stem and that their bases are fused so that the stem appears to pass through their center.

Coral honeysuckle does well on fences, trellises, arbors, arches, mailboxes, and trees, but it may require some initial staking and training to make it climb. It will also scramble on the ground if a supporting structure is not available and can make an attractive flowering groundcover or low shrub. Coral honeysuckle flowers best in full sun and should be planted where it is easily seen to enjoy the antics of hummingbirds that line up for its nectar. Numerous cultivars and selections are available, including the yellow-flowered forms 'Sulphurea' and 'John Clayton.' The latter of these was selected by the Virginia Native Plant Society and is offered by Woodlanders. 'Bonneau' is a long-flowering selection from Dodd and Dodd Native Nurseries that extends the flowering period into the fall and is touted as an important nectar source for migrating hummers. The yellow-flowered yellow honeysuckle (*L. flava*) is similar to 'Sulphurea' and is also sometimes used in gardens. Yellow honeysuckle ranges mostly in the southeast and does best in USDA zones 5–8. All selections do best in acidic to neutral soil in zones 4–9, 9–1. None are aggressive.

Carolina Jessamine

Carolina jessamine (*Gelsemium sempervirens*) has become an extremely popular screening vine that is increasingly used to decorate the chain-link fences that enclose parks, athletic fields, and residential landscapes. It is our earliest-flowering vine, sometimes putting on bright yellow tubular blossoms as early as January in the coastal plains, slightly later in the upper Piedmont and mountains. These bright splashes of yellow in

Carolina jessamine.

Swamp jessamine.

Carolina jessamine.

an otherwise drab, late-season landscape are a sure sign of winter's end. The leaves are opposite, lance-shaped, and somewhat reminiscent of the popular but aggressive non-native white-flowered jasmines. Unlike the jasmines, the stem sap of Carolina jessamine is clear and watery rather than white and sticky.

In addition to the typical form with single, bright yellow flowers, Woodlanders has traditionally offered a softer-yellow selection named 'Pale Yellow,' as well as a double-flowering form, 'Pride of Augusta.' Woodlanders was also the first to introduce swamp jessamine (*G. rankinii*), a closely related species that is not widely available in the trade. It is very similar to Carolina jessamine but produces flowers later in the spring—usually in March and April—and sometimes again in October and November. The two species are easy to tell apart by details of the flower but are otherwise very similar in general appearance, especially at a distance. Swamp jessamine requires wetter soils than Carolina jessamine and will probably need irrigation in dry or well-drained sites.

Both jessamines are high-climbing vines in nature, often reaching the canopy and producing flowers out of view of the ground. The first hint of their presence in natural woodlands usually comes from the fallen flowers that litter the forest floor. In the garden they can be trained to low trellises and arbors, where their flowers can be enjoyed. The jessamines usually flower most profusely when situated in full sun. Including both species in a single planting can ensure the presence of the yellow trumpets for several months.

Both species of *Gelsemium* were long included in the Loganiaceae, a family well-known for the poison strychnine and the extreme toxicity of some of its member species. Modern botanists now place this genus in its own family, Gelsemiaceae. This change in classification does not alter the fact that almost all parts of this plant, especially the nectar and roots, contain potent alkaloids and are extremely toxic if consumed. At least one native plant grower has reported extremely dangerous respiratory reactions just from smelling crushed roots.

Climbing Hydrangea

Climbing hydrangea (*Decumaria barbara*) may be one of our most versatile but underutilized native vines. It is common in nature but regularly overlooked. The 4–5-inch leaves are opposite, glossy, medium green above, more or less ovate or egg-shaped in outline, and very attractive. The stem attaches itself tightly to the trunks of wetland trees by short, hairlike adventitious roots that allow it to climb into the canopy. Under natural conditions the showy clusters of tiny, creamy white flowers are usually produced out of sight, high in the trees. However, planting it in full sun on a trellis, fence, or arbor allows the inflorescences to be enjoyed closer to ground level. It sometimes runs on the ground in moist hammocks and will do likewise in the garden. Although low-growing plants typically do not produce flowers, a mound or linear strand of this species makes an excellent groundcover and is useful for constructing a border along shady walkways or shrub beds. This species is probably more suited for shady sites, though some experts suggest that it can tolerate sun as long as its feet are kept moist. It is certainly true that full sun encourages more profuse flowering. Its preference seems to be for acidic organic soils, but it also occurs abundantly in moist hardwood ham-

Climbing hydrangea.

Climbing hydrangea.

mocks in thin soils over limestone, which suggests its adaptability to more neutral conditions. It is appropriate for zones 5–9, 9–6.

Passionflowers

Several species of passionflower (Passifloraceae) occur naturally in the southeast, especially when southern Florida is included. Almost all are sought-after plants by butterfly gardeners. Only two species occur widely in USDA zones 6–9: the somewhat diminutive and often unnoticed yellow or dwarf passionflower (*Passiflora lutea*) and the showy, even gaudy, maypop (*P. incarnata*). Corky-stemmed passionflower (*P. suberosa*) is valued for its attraction to the zebra longwing, Florida's state butterfly. Its garden use is restricted mostly to zone 9A and southward, and it is available from several central and southern Florida native nurseries, including The Natives, located in Davenport, southwest of Orlando.

Yellow passionflower is a weakly twining herb with an interesting three-lobed leaf and a gentle presence. The ones in Eleanor Dietrich's Tallahassee, Florida, garden climb

e complicated and ornate flowers of
low passion vine. Courtesy of Bill and Pam
derson.

Corky-stemmed passionflower.

ypop. Courtesy of Bill and Pam Anderson.

over low benches and garden ornaments and add a delicate touch to her shady perennial border. Dietrich's plants flower profusely throughout the summer, often only inches from the ground. The pale, greenish yellow flowers are small—less than ¾ inch wide—but have the typical complicated passionflower form that makes them one of her garden's more delightful annual discoveries. Yellow passionflower is a host plant for the Gulf fritillary and zebra longwing butterflies. It prefers shade and moist, well-drained soil in USDA zones 7–9 and is available by mail order from Sunlight Gardens and Mail Order Natives.

Maypop—or simply passionflower—is the most popular and best known of this group and is a host plant for several butterfly species. It has showy, complicated 2–3-inch flowers and attractive three-lobed leaves. The five blue to nearly white petals are surmounted by a frilly, fringelike corona that subtends an erect stalk topped by three pistils and five more or less spreading stamens. The common name "passionflower" refers to the Passion of Christ and was bestowed by Spanish missionaries who recognized the several parts of the flower as symbols of the crucifixion. The ten petals and sepals

Vines, Groundcovers, and Spring Ephemerals   267

represent the disciples, the fringelike corona the crown of thorns, the three pistils the three nails, and the five stamens the five wounds. The name "maypop" comes from the sound of the ripe fruit when it is stepped on.

Whether to group maypop with nonaggressive vines was not a clear-cut decision. This rapidly growing perennial herb can quickly fill an open space, easily covering several square yards with its lengthening herbaceous stem. It spreads rapidly by stolons, and new leaves often pop up through the mulch some distance from the parent plant, especially in sunny locations. Nevertheless, I have seen it used exceptionally well in mixed butterfly gardens. My preference is to corral it by putting it in its own bed and surrounding it with easily manicured terrain and that has a trellis in the center. Otherwise, it will clamber and twine over other garden plants. It tends to like disturbance and performs well in full sun and challenging conditions, including drought. It occurs naturally from northern Virginia southward to Florida and west to Texas and is appropriate for zones 6–9, 10–7. Gardeners who want to attract butterflies should definitely find a place for this vine in their landscape. Maypop is sometimes referenced as a woody vine but is more appropriately described as herbaceous in most of our area.

Wisteria

The several species of non-native wisterias were once so widely planted in the southeastern United States that they, along with the profusely flowering Asian azaleas, became part of a signature combination in southern gardens. Cherished for their showy clusters of pale blue to nearly white flowers, nearly every homestead, regardless of size, displayed

American wisteria.

American wisteria 'Amethyst Falls.'

one or more specimens as stand-alone shrubs, trellis decorations, or as ornamentation on the trunks of native pine trees. Two species were most popular, one from Japan and one from China, both of which are now included on the Southeastern Exotic Pest Plant Council's list of invasive species. They are extremely aggressive.

American wisteria (*Wisteria frutescens*) is a much less aggressive native vine that serves the same purpose as the Chinese and Japanese wisterias but without the need for constant control and maintenance. Wisterias are legumes that produce typical pea flowers and flattened pods. The native wisteria occurs naturally on the edges of swamps and wet thickets throughout the southeast and is recommended for zones 6–9, 9–6. It adapts readily to garden conditions and can tolerate considerable dryness, though it flowers best in full sun with its feet in moist, acidic soils. American wisteria is slow-growing but can reach thirty feet or more in length. It can be planted as a stand-alone shrub, trained to a trellis, or espaliered. The flower clusters are smaller than those of the Asian wisterias and the flowers are often more nearly purple than blue. American wisteria was probably first recommended for the garden in 1965 by Caroline Dormon and was later introduced and popularized with southern gardeners by Woodlanders. It has become an excellent substitute for the non-native wisterias and is now widely available in the trade. The selection 'Amethyst Falls' (USDA zones 5–9) is a compact, somewhat slow-growing form introduced by Head-Lee Nursery, Seneca, South Carolina. Its flowers are deeper in color, and plants flower at an earlier age than the species. It also has two flowering periods, first in April and May and again later in the summer. A white form, *W. frutescens* 'Alba,' is also available and is now under production by Monrovia Growers, which should ensure widespread availability.

Aggressive Native Vines

Trumpet Creeper and Crossvine

The flowers of trumpet creeper (*Campsis radicans*) and crossvine (*Bignonia capreolata*) are often confused. Both are tubular and reddish orange outside with flared petals that resemble the bell of a trumpet, making them excellent hummingbird plants. Trumpet creeper gets its name from the combination of its trumpet-shaped flowers and creeping growth habit, whereas crossvine's common name comes from its stem anatomy. When

Crossvine.

Trumpet creeper, *above* and *right*.

larger stems are cut in cross-section, four quadrants can be removed to leave a cross-shaped core.

The two species can be easily distinguished by their leaves. Those of trumpet creeper are divided like a feather with several toothed leaflets along either side of a central rib (rachis). Those of crossvine are divided into only two nontoothed leaflets. Both species are high-climbing vines that utilize distinctly different climbing methods. Trumpet creeper produces regular patches of aerial stem roots that fasten themselves to tree trunks and hold the entire vine tightly against the bark, a method that turns out to be a perfect adaptation for climbing wooden trellises. Crossvine, on the other hand, produces three-parted, elongated tendrils from the leaf nodes and climbs primarily by twining. The stem is usually free from the trunk, suiting the plant to clamber up metal trellises and chain-link fences. Crossvine is typically less aggressive than trumpet creeper and may be the better choice for most gardens, especially those situated in full sun.

Nevertheless, both of these vines can be aggressive and should be sited carefully. Both are native to a wide range of habitats and neither is particularly fussy about soil or moisture conditions. The stem of trumpet creeper, in particular, can grow four inches or more in diameter and can virtually smother small supporting trees. My first introduction to this plant was when I was about ten years old and was pressed into assisting my grandfather saw through the lower stem of a huge specimen that had completely encircled and climbed a large slash pine that Granddad thought was in danger of succumbing to the vine's relentless attack. The remains of that vine hung onto that tree for many years following the vine's demise.

Few selections of crossvine and trumpet creeper are available in garden centers. One of the least aggressive is Garden Debut's Madame Rosy®, a sterile hybrid produced by crossing our native *C. radicans* with the Chinese *C. grandiflora*. Madame Rosy® has larger, showier flowers than the native trumpet creeper and is much better behaved. The flowers are orange-red, slightly tinged with yellow in full sun, but a pleasing rosy red hue in the shade, hence the cultivar name. An old plant growing on a tree at Head-Lee Nursery has shown no invasive tendencies and continues to delight with dark green foliage and numerous large, trumpet-shaped flowers. *Campsis radicans* 'Flava' is a yellow-flowered trumpet creeper that otherwise has the features of the species, and 'Tangerine Beauty' is a selection of crossvine with bright orange flowers.

Campsis hybrid Madame Rosy®.

Virginia Creeper

Few vines have more spectacular fall color than Virginia creeper, *Parthenocissus quinquefolia*. The five-parted leaves turn varying shades of yellow, burgundy, and red at the first frost, giving the warmer parts of the coastal plains one of the few glimpses of fall color. The flowers are not conspicuous, but the black fruit is attractive and eaten by birds. Virginia creeper climbs by tendrils that produce flattened outgrowths and readily and persistently attach to the supporting substrate. These flattened dilations become so tightly fastened to painted surfaces that attempting to remove them either breaks them away from the stem, leaving the adhesive structures still attached to the wall, or worse, removes bits of both paint and wood. It is sometimes recommended as a groundcover due to its running habit. Virginia creeper is not widely available in the trade but is adventive and naturally present in many home landscapes.

Virginia creeper fall color. Courtesy of Ron Lance.

inia creeper.
rtesy of Ron Lance.

Virginia creeper.

Native Groundcovers and Spring Ephemerals

Native groundcovers range from low-growing, ground-hugging shrubs to upright perennials a foot or more in height. Some prefer moist, shady sites, while others are at their best in full sun. Some are deciduous in winter; others maintain a continuous foliar presence throughout the year. A few of the deciduous species are very early spring bloomers that show aboveground foliage for only a few months or weeks. In natural areas these so-called ephemerals take advantage of the warming temperature and filtered light that reaches the forest floor before the deciduous canopy puts on its summer leaves. Used effectively in the garden, these early-flowering delicacies can contribute to a subtly changing succession of flower and foliage during the transition from winter to summer.

Low-growing groundcovers often work best in relatively open sites where they are easily visible and where competition with other species is reduced. A few prefer shade. Others can withstand full sun and seemingly harsh conditions. Partridgeberry, green-and-gold, and dwarf smilax are among the better low-growing species for shady or partly shady sites. Blue-eyed grass, sunshine mimosa, and capeweed do best in full sun.

Shade-loving Groundcovers

Partridgeberry (*Mitchella repens*) is an evergreen, mat-forming groundcover of the madder family (Rubiaceae). Its hallmarks include paired dark green leaves, paired white flowers (it is sometimes called "twinflower"), and bright red, berrylike drupes that add an attractive aspect to the fall landscape. At a glance partridgeberry looks very much like an herbaceous vine but is technically classified as a shrub due to its woody stem and evergreen habit. Its use as a groundcover in shady or partly shady yards is unsurpassed. Only a few retail nurseries—Mail Order Natives and Niche Gardens are two—currently offer this plant. Fortunately, at least a few colonies may already be present in many residential yards. Encouraging and expanding these populations requires protection from excessive foot traffic, a shady or partly shady site, and the addition of fertilizer. Granular

Partridgeberry, *right* and *below*.

Green-and-gold.

Dwarf smilax. Courtesy of Ron Lance.

houseplant fertilizers (Peter's Special is excellent) diluted with water work particularly well. However, even without fertilizer partridgeberry spreads quickly. Caroline Dormon, writing in *Natives Preferred*, reported that a dam constructed to form her pond was carpeted with partridgeberry in only two years. Partridgeberry occurs throughout our region and does well in USDA zones 3–9. Its form is somewhat reminiscent of some of the creeping figs, except that the leaves are smaller and the plant is much less aggressive.

The hairy basal leaves of green-and-gold (*Chrysogonum virginianum*) can literally carpet a moist, semishady garden. This is probably not a plant to use in a mixture with other groundcovers as it tends to dominate the places where it is planted. However, I have seen a colony of this species covering a lawn in combination with golden ragwort (*Packera* sp.) that created a beautiful effect. Green-and-gold spreads by above- or belowground runners (depending upon variety), is easy to establish, and requires little maintenance. The species is usually recommended for zones 5–9, 9–2. Within these zones are two varieties and several cultivars. Variety *virginiana* may be best for USDA zones 6–8, and variety *australe* (which means "southern") for zones 8–9. The Don Jacobs selection 'Eco Lacquered Spider' has become a popular substitute for both varieties; it is somewhat more spreading than the species and has lustrous or "lacquered" leaves.

Mention *Smilax* to most southern gardeners and they instantly repel, with memories of the numerous species of thorny greenbriers that reappear every year to entangle shrubs, climb trees, and puncture the skin. The nonthorny dwarf smilax (*Smilax pumila*) is certainly an exception to this typical profile. This prostrate vine seldom climbs, is excellent for sandy, xeric sites, is a first-rate recommendation for the barren ground that dominates live oak woodlands, and is reminiscent in form to trailing arbutus (*Epigaea repens*). It prefers some shade, but doesn't demand water. Its natural habitat includes dry coastal hammocks, rich, moist woodlands, and scrubby pinelands. It is not as widely available in the garden trade as it should be but performs well in USDA zones 8–9.

Sun-loving Groundcovers

Blue-eyed grass (*Sisyrinchium angustifolium*) is a clump-forming member of the iris family that flowers profusely in early spring. The densely set leaves look more like a bunchgrass than a wildflower and are evergreen, making it a good border plant as well as a potential replacement for mass plantings of *Liriope*. Plants are heavy seed producers and have a tendency to spread around the garden, even popping up in places far distant from the original planting. If used as a perennial or walkway border, it will require at least periodic maintenance and will likely have to be dug, divided, and rejuvenated every 2–3 years. Otherwise, mature plants will die back in the middle, turn brown, and lose their charm. However, when planted en masse and adequately maintained, this species can form large patches that serve as an effective groundcover and can be mowed once a year, if desired. It is especially attractive when growing below some of the taller blue flag irises. Blue-eyed grass tolerates full sun, prefers some moisture, and performs best in zones 5–9, 8–5. It should be noted that several additional species of blue-eyed grass occur naturally in the southeast and a number of non-native species are offered in the gardening trade. Correct identification can be difficult.

The dwarf and crested irises (*Iris verna* and *I. cristata*) are also excellent groundcovers.

Blue-eyed grass.

Blue-eyed grass.

Dwarf iris.

Powderpuff.

274   Favorite Groups of Native Plants

Unlike the tall blue flag irises of marshes and wetlands, neither of these species exceeds about six inches tall. And unlike blue-eyed grass, these little dainties require shady sites with usually no more than about three hours of direct sun per day. Both have narrow, grasslike leaves and both reproduce by stolons or rhizomes that allow the colony to expand over time. Some gardeners report that it is possible to direct the stolons by gently removing and repositioning them along the desired tangent. Crested iris is slightly more northern in distribution, performing best in moist soils in USDA zones 3–8. Dwarf iris tolerates somewhat drier conditions as long as plants are shaded and the soil acidic.

Sunshine mimosa, or powderpuff (*Mimosa strigillosa*), is a prostrate vine that is similar in appearance to the closely related sensitive briar (*M. quadrivalvis*, =*Schrankia microphylla*) but is much more robust. It tolerates full sun, xeric conditions, and sandy soils and can spread rapidly. A single plant can cover several square yards in a year or less. This rapid colonization can be somewhat problematic, especially when this species is planted adjacent to close-cropped lawns. It quickly sends out runners, can easily overcome grassy groundcovers, and is sometimes recommended as a replacement for lawn turf. The leaves are featherlike, pale green, and borne on prostrate stems. The flowers are produced in rounded pink clusters at the tip of an erect 4–6-inch stalk. This plant requires little care, withstands mowing, can take much abuse, and is favored in Florida for decorating highway medians and road shoulders. It is a member of the bean family (Fabaceae) and is endemic to the Southeastern Coastal Plains from eastern Georgia to Texas. It performs best in USDA zones 8–10. Several Florida nurseries offer it for sale, as does Carol Lovell-Saas of Biophilia Nature Center near Elberta, Alabama. Lovell-Saas usually has a supply on hand and offers it retail or by mail order. This species is easily rooted from stem cuttings.

Powderpuff is one of a group of three southeastern beans known colloquially as "sensitive plants." They take their collective common name from their leaves. When touched, the leaflets immediately fold up flat against one another. How this happens is related to the plant's internal anatomy. Rapid loss of pressure in strategically situated cells apparently causes the leaves and leaflets to relax, droop, and fold. The ecological advantages of this behavior are somewhat speculative but may have to do with avoiding predation. Some observers suggest that herbivorous predators are less attracted to folded and drooping foliage, often passing by the apparently shriveled and dying leaves for those with a healthier appearance.

Biophilia is also probably the only native plant nursery that offers frogfruit, also called capeweed (*Phyla nodiflora*, =*Lippia nodiflora*). Lovell-Saas recommends it as a host plant for Phaeon crescent and buckeye caterpillars and because, in her words, "the more you walk on it, the better it looks." Capeweed is a mat-forming herb of the coastal strand that grows in xeric sands of beaches and coastal hammocks. It sends up small, attractive, tightly packed heads of purple and lavender-white flowers and can rapidly cover large areas. It is very tough and often considered weedy along roadsides and in other disturbed sites. With repeated foot or vehicular traffic, such as within walking paths or the ruts of unimproved driveways, it becomes densely matted and forms an attractive continuous carpet of flattened foliage. This species is restricted to the coastal plains from Virginia to Florida and west to California, does best in full sun, and is probably best suited in our region to USDA zones 8–9.

Mixed Perennials as Spring Groundcovers

Natural groundcovers in shady deciduous forests ordinarily include a varying palette of woodland herbs that provide subtly changing color, texture, and form throughout the spring. Re-creating such groundcovers in the garden requires mimicking this natural progression by including early spring ephemeral and deciduous species in association with evergreens, or with those that make their appearance in late spring or early summer. Evergreens provide the foundation that ensures at least some ground vegetation throughout the year, whereas the short-lived ephemerals provide interest, intrigue, and anticipation. Numerous species can be used in this mixture and more can be added every year. Some of the best companions include wild ginger, heartleaf, mayapple, Allegheny spurge, yellowroot, atamasco or rain lily, green-and-gold, Indian pink, fringed campion, bloodroot, foamflower, blue phlox, and the maidenhair ferns. All of these are described below.

Asarum canadense, *Hexastylis arifolia*, and *H. shuttleworthii*, are members of the birthwort or pipevine family (Aristolochiaceae). All are known by various common names ranging from "little brown jug" to "heartleaf" or "wild ginger." The two species of *Hexastylis* are evergreen, with stiff, heart-shaped leaves that are typically oriented

Shade-Loving Perennials for Southern Gardens[a]

Species	Family	Height	Flowers	Southeastern Distribution[b]	US Zo
Rue Anemone (*Anemonella thalictroides*)	Buttercup (Ranunculaceae)	4–8"	White to pink with 5 petallike sepals	AL, FL, GA, MS, NC, SC, VA	4–
Wild Columbine (*Aquilegia canadensis*)	Buttercup (Ranunculaceae)	2–4'	Red or orange-red and yellow; petals with elongated, nectar-bearing spurs	AL, FL, GA, MS, NC, SC, VA	3–
Jack-in-the-Pulpit (*Arisaema triphyllum*)	Arum (Araceae)	1–3'	Green; with an erect, flower-bearing spadix situated inside a hooded spathe	Throughout	4–
Canadian Ginger (*Asarum canadense*)	Pipevine (Aristolochiaceae)	6"	Brown; cup- or vase-shaped; borne at ground level	AL, GA, LA, MS, NC, SC, VA	3–
Tall Bellwort (*Campanula americana*)	Bellwort (Campanulaceae)	3–6'	Blue, bell-shaped, borne in terminal racemes	Throughout	4–
Pepper-Root (*Cardamine concatenata*)	Mustard (Brassicaceae)	8–15"	White, pink	Throughout	3–
Green-and-Gold (*Chrysogonum virginianum*)	Aster (Asteraceae)	12"	Yellow, with central disc surrounded by bright yellow rays	Throughout	5–
Spring Beauty (*Claytonia virginica*)	Purslane (Portulacaceae)		Lavender, plants producing colonies with hundreds of flowers	AL, GA, LA, MS, NC, SC, VA	3–
Yellow Trout Lily (*Erythronium americanum*)	Lily (Liliaceae)	6"	Yellow, nodding, turning upward as day progresses	AL, GA, LA, MS, NC, SC, VA	3–

cies	Family	Height	Flowers	Southeastern Distribution[b]	USDA Zones
ipled Trout Lily (*thronium umbilicatum*)	Lily (Liliaceae)	6"	Yellow, nodding, turning upward as day progresses	AL, FL, GA, NC, SC, VA	3–9A
otted Cranesbill (*ranium maculatum*)	Geranium (Geraniaceae)	1–2'	Rose-pink or lavender, with 5 petals above palmately divided leaves	AL, GA, LA, MS, NC, SC, VA	3–8
rp-Lobed Liverwort (*patica acutiloba [nemone acutiloba]*)	Buttercup (Ranunculaceae)	5"	Blue, pink, or white, with 6 petallike sepals and no true petals	AL, GA, LA, MS, NC, SC, VA	3–8
ind-Lobed erwort(*Hepatica ericana [=Anemone ericana]*)	Buttercup (Ranunculaceae)	5"	Blue, lavender, or white, with 6 petallike sepals and no true petals	AL, FL, GA, NC, SC, VA	3–9
erican Alumroot (*uchera americana*)	Saxifrage (Saxifragaceae)		Greenish yellow; most appreciated for leaf texture and color varying from purplish to suffused green and white	AL, GA, LA, MS, NC, SC, VA	3–8
ow-Leaf Ginger (*xastylis arifolia [sarum arifolium]*)	Pipevine (Aristolochiaceae)	6"	Brown, juglike, borne at ground level	Throughout	5–9A
ge-Flower Heartleaf (*xastylis shuttleworthii [sarum shuttleworthii]*)	Pipevine (Aristolochiaceae)	6"	Brown, juglike, borne at ground level	AL, GA, MS, NC, SC, VA	5–9A
Idenseal (*Hydrastis adensis*)	Buttercup (Ranunculaceae)	18"	White, with showy cluster of many stamens and no petals	AL, GA, MS, NC, VA	3–7
olina Lily (*ium michauxii*)	Lily (Liliaceae)	18"	Orange-red, nodding, with 6 spotted tepals	Throughout	5–9A
jinia Bluebell (*Mertensia jinica*)	Borage (Boraginaceae)	30"	Blue, tubular, nodding in showy clusters	AL, GA, MS, NC, SC, VA	3–8
egheny Spurge (*chysandra procumbens*)	Boxwood (Buxaceae)	12"	White, pinkish, borne in 4" spikes just above ground level; most valued for its ground-covering foliage	Throughout	
isewort (*Pedicularis adensis*)	Broomrape (Orobanchaceae)	12"	Yellow, reddish brown; reminiscent of snapdragons	Throughout	5–9
e Phlox (*Phlox aricata*)	Jacob's-ladder (Polemoniaceae)	18"	Blue, with 5 petals	Throughout	3–9A
yapple (*Podophyllum tatum*)	Barberry (Berberidaceae)	15"	Creamy white, nodding below leaves; only produced on 2-leaved plants	Throughout	3–9

(continued)

Species	Family	Height	Flowers	Southeastern Distribution[b]	USDE Zone
Solomon's Seal (*Polygonatum biflorum* var. *biflorum*)	Ruscus (Ruscaceae)	1–3'	Creamy white, borne in dangling pairs below the leaves	Throughout	3–9A
Solomon's Seal (*Polygonatum biflorum* var. *commutatum*)	Ruscus (Ruscaceae)	3–6'	Creamy white, borne in dangling pairs below the leaves	AL, GA, LA, MS, NC, SC, VA	3–8
Bloodroot (*Sanguinaria canadensis*)	Poppy (Papaveraceae)	8"	Bright white, very showy, with 8–16 petals and 24 stamens	Throughout	3–9A
Fringed Campion (*Silene polypetala*)	Pink (Caryophyllaceae)	18"	Pink, with 5 fringed petals	FL, GA	3–9A
Fire Pink (*Silene virginica*)	Pink (Caryophyllaceae)	18"	Bright red, with 5 petals and numerous flowers per plant	Throughout	3–8
Indian Pink (*Spigelia marilandica*)	Logania (Loganiaceae)	1–3'	Red outside, yellow inside and at apex; tubular and flaring at the tip	Throughout	3–9A
Foamflower (*Tiarella cordifolia*)	Saxifrage (Saxifragaceae)	15"	White, rosy pink, with yellow stamens, borne in an upright raceme	AL, GA, MS, NC, SC, VA	3–9A
Perfoliate Bellwort (*Uvularia perfoliata*)	Meadow Saffron (Colchicaceae)	20"	Yellow, nodding; bases of upper pair of leaves joined around the stem (perfoliate)	Throughout	3–9A
Bird's-Foot Violet (*Viola pedata*)	Violet (Violaceae)	15"	Blue, purple, about 1½" wide, with a white spot and orange stamens	AL, GA, LA, MS, NC, SC, VA	3–9
Yellowroot (*Xanthorhiza simplicissima*)	Buttercup (Ranunculaceae)	1–2'	Maroon, lavender, brownish; in loose, drooping panicle at top of plant	Throughout	3–9
Atamasco Lily (*Zephyranthes atamasca*)	Amaryllis (Amaryllidaceae)	12"	White, trumpet-shaped, arising directly from ground	Throughout	7–10

Notes: a. Most plants on this list require moist, well-drained soils, root protection in summer, and part to full shade.
b. Southeastern states in which the plant is native or naturalized.

parallel to the ground. The leaves of common wild ginger (*A. canadense*) are deciduous. The flowers of all three are brown, jug-shaped, and borne inconspicuously at ground level. The unique blossoms are unlikely to be noticed unless one knows to look for them, adding interest and surprise for the discerning gardeners who seek them out. Common wild ginger (*A. canadense*) has larger and more elevated leaves than the other two and occurs naturally mostly in neutral soils of the mountains, Piedmont, and the inner

Common wild
ginger.

Common wild ginger.

Little brown jug flowers.

Little brown jug leaves.

coastal plains of Virginia, North Carolina, and South Carolina. It prefers somewhat moister and richer soils, but has proven to adapt to drier sites, especially if shaded.

Little brown jug (*H. arifolia*) grows mostly in the Piedmont and coastal plains from Virginia to eastern Louisiana, and large-flower heartleaf (*H. shuttleworthii*) mostly in the Piedmont and mountains. Both of these species tolerate drier sites better than common wild ginger but do best in shaded, acidic soils. Where conditions allow, it is best to use *Asarum* and *Hexastylis* in combination. Neither species of *Hexastylis* creates the dense covering characteristic of common wild ginger, but both remain visible in the landscape for a larger part of the year.

Mayapple (*Podophyllum peltatum*) takes its common name from the yellowish, two-inch, edible fruits that appear mostly in May and are relished by turtles and other wild-life. The leaves are stalked in the middle like an umbrella—hence the name *peltatum* (from *peltate*)—and large colonies can form a low canopy of diminutive parasols over rich, shaded soils. The exquisite, nodding, creamy white flowers are borne on drooping stalks below the leaves and add additional spring interest to a plant that is already pretty

Mayapple, *above* and *right*.

spectacular. Some plants have only a single leaf, but flowers only occur on two-leaved plants. In good humus mayapple spreads easily to form large colonies. The seeds and vegetative portions of this species are poisonous but have also yielded numerous medicinal compounds, many of which were used by American Indians and early settlers to treat a variety of ailments. Alkaloids extracted from the underground stems are still used in the treatment of several cancers. Mayapple is widespread across the eastern United States. It is usually recommended for USDA zones 4–8 but grows naturally and in shady gardens in parts of the Florida panhandle.

Allegheny-spurge (*Pachysandra procumbens*) is an excellent companion to mayapple. It is slightly lower-growing, and the leaves are medium or dark green with light green mottling. It loses its leaves in winter in USDA zones 6–7A but is more nearly evergreen farther south. Allegheny-spurge grows naturally in rich and often calcareous soils, mostly in the Piedmont, with disjunct populations in Florida and Louisiana in USDA zone 8. The white to pinkish flowers are produced March–April in erect, elongated, 2–4-inch clusters. The non-native Japanese spurge (*P. terminalis*) has become popular in recent years. Japanese spurge tolerates somewhat drier conditions, spreads more rapidly, and forms a more dense cover than the native species. Both can be seen

Allegheny-spurge, *above* and *right*.

Indian pink.

Royal catchfly.

Indian pink.

in a naturalistic garden setting in and near the Dunson Native Flora Garden at the State Botanical Garden of Georgia at Athens. Although the Japanese species may be more tolerant of abuse, the native species is more attractive.

Indian pink (*Spigelia marilandica*) is the exclamation point of the shade garden and has fast become a very popular woodland garden herb across most of the southeast. Previously restricted in use by limited availability, it is now produced by many growers and is a regular offering in retail garden centers. It is relatively easy to establish and tends to spread by self-sown seed, making it a perfect addition to a mixed spring groundcover. Plants average 1–2 feet tall and bear cardinal red flowers that are tubular in shape, fringed with yellow, and borne in a multiflowered cluster above the uppermost leaves. Provenance may be an important consideration when purchasing plants of this species as it occurs naturally in all of our geographic regions from the mountains to the coastal plains and is recommended for zones 5–9, 9–2. Plants that originate from within a particular region might do better than those that originate outside of it. Young plants can be planted in acidic soils in the early spring, but they may not flower until the following year. Once established in the garden, plants pop up randomly from seed, lending an attractive, naturalistic aspect to the garden. Indian pink prefers acidic soils but often occurs in calcareous woodlands and adapts to more nearly neutral soils. It flowers profusely in shade.

At least two species of native campion are used in gardening in our region, both of which are short-lived perennials with bright red flowers. They are members of the Caryophyllaceae, or pink family, a name that comes from the notched or "pinking-sheared" petals. Royal catchfly (*Silene regia*) is the taller of the two, reaching three feet in optimum locations. It is primarily a midwestern plant confined to prairies and calcareous woodlands from Kansas and Oklahoma to Ohio, Kentucky, and Tennessee, and is generally considered rare in the southeast with only a few occurrences in Florida, Georgia, and Alabama. Fire pink (*S. virginica*) is shorter in stature but far more common. It is widespread across the southeast, mostly in the mountains, Piedmont, and upper coastal plain,

Fire pink.

but has been recorded at one location in the Florida panhandle, less than fifty miles from the coast. The bright red corolla is tubular below but expands at the apex into five narrow petals that give the flowers a star-shaped appearance. Numerous blossoms are borne in an open inflorescence at the top of the plant. Fire pink is a delightful garden addition that will definitely not go unnoticed. Full sun to light shade results in more flowers, but coastal plains gardeners will want to protect it from the hottest part of the day. The American Horticultural Society recommends this species for zones 4–8, 9–3.

Bloodroot (*Sanguinaria canadensis*) is a member of the poppy family (Papaveraceae) and gets its common name from the bright red sap that oozes from it roots when crushed. This widely available spring ephemeral is a "must have" plant for any spring shade garden. Plants situated in zones 8 or 9 often flower as early as late January, with or before the appearance of the new foliage. The leaves start out small and grow continuously in girth until well into June. Early leaves are typically less than four inches in breath; the width of older leaves may reach nearly twelve inches and can add an attractive presence to the garden well after the flowers and fruit are gone. The interestingly lobed leaves are unlike those of any other spring herb, with the possible exception of

Bloodroot, *above* and *right*.

Bloodroot.

the rare twinleaf (*Jeffersonia diphylla*). The upper leaf surface is dark bluish or yellowish green, and the lower surface is glaucous white. The two-inch flowers are borne on erect 4–6-inch stalks directly from the ground and are extremely attractive, especially given their early spring presence. Bloodroot is widespread across the entire eastern United States and grows naturally in rich, deciduous woodlands as far south as the Florida panhandle and southern Alabama and is suitable for zones 3–8, 8–1. The fruit is a slim, erect, ellipsoid capsule that opens at maturity to broadcast the seed. Seed can be collected as soon as the capsule begins to split, typically late spring, and can be sown in outside seedbeds. Alternately, the seeds can be allowed to drop in place as fodder for a naturally expanding colony.

One mark of a good groundcover is its ability to spread by runners or underground stems. Foamflower (*Tiarella cordifolia*) certainly exemplifies this character and is reported by many gardeners to creep around the garden, sending up new basal leaves

Foamflower dominating a shade garden.

Foamflower.

from underground rhizomes. This is one of the best spring-flowering groundcovers for mountain and Piedmont gardens. It is probably also suitable for the upper coastal plain, though it is known to occur naturally in the coastal plains only in Virginia. Some authorities have recognized two species, assigning the name *T. wherryi* (or *T. cordifolia* var. *collina*) to plants of the Piedmont and coastal plains and reserving *T. cordifolia* only for mountain plants. Some of these same authorities hold that only the mountain species is rhizomatous and hence likely to spread. The leaves are palmately divided into several segments and have the superficial appearance of maple leaves. Masses of tiny white flowers are attractively arranged on numerous upright racemes that stand well above the leaves. Foamflower's popularity is borne out by its numerous cultivars and selections, most of which accentuate leaf variation. Sunlight Gardens, alone, lists nine named cultivars on its Web site, and Allan Armitage, in his book on native perennials, reports having trialed over thirty in his Athens, Georgia, garden. Most online sources list at least two species, varieties, or cultivars. Foamflower is suited for zones 3–8, 7–1 and should be planted in organic soils that remain moist.

Ground-loving violets are the harbingers of spring, and none more so than the charming bird's-foot violet (*Viola pedata*) that appears in early April as the native azaleas begin to put on new blossoms. As a group, the blue-flowered spring violets can be difficult to identify; even expert botanists struggle over field recognition. Bird's-foot is an exception to this taxonomic ambivalence. The combination of distinctly palmate leaves, narrow leaf segments, conspicuous orange stamens, and preference for dry habitats is usually enough to set it apart. Well-drained, semisunny slopes and woodlands constitute the species' preferred natural habitat. Typical plants grow in little circular bunches with both flower and leaf stalks arising directly from a belowground stem. The showy little flowers are blue and about 1½ inches wide, with a distinct whitish spot at the

Bird's-foot violet.

Blue phlox.

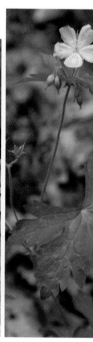
Wild geranium.

base of the lower petal. Fully decorated individuals may have as many as thirty flowers open at the same time. Bird's-foot violet is mostly a mountain and Piedmont plant in Virginia, the Carolinas, and Georgia but is also found in the coastal plains of Alabama, Mississippi, and Louisiana; it does not occur naturally in Florida. Some experts recommend it for zones 3–9, but plants situated in zone 9 may need protection from intense summer sun.

Blue or woodland phlox (*Phlox divaricata*) is one of the more widely available native wildflowers. Like foamflower, its popularity is borne out by the availability of an impressive array of cultivars. Typical plants have blue flowers, unlike the color of any of our other native phloxes, but selections with varying flower colors are available. Some, such as 'Louisiana' and 'Loddon Blue' (or 'London Blue') have deep blue to almost purple blossoms; those of 'May Breeze' and 'White Perfume' are mostly white; and the flowers of 'Clouds of Perfume' are lavender blue. The flowering stems of most selections are about eighteen inches tall and very showy. Plant Delights Nursery has introduced 'Blue Elf,' a dwarf form with a small, matlike cluster of leaves and 3–4-inch flower stalks topped with light blue blossoms.

Blue phlox is particularly attractive when grown in conjunction with spotted cranesbill (*Geranium maculatum*), the only one of our three native geraniums regularly used in gardening. This species' common name and scientific epithet derive from its leaves. *Maculatum* derives from Latin and means "marked with spots," which in this case is an excellent adjectival modifier. The one-inch-wide flowers are a delicate rosy pink, and the spotted leaves are deeply palmately divided, reminiscent of those of bird's-foot violet.

Southern maidenhair fern (*Adiantum capillus-veneris*) is a widespread, shade-loving, mostly evergreen fern that occurs nearly throughout the southern United States from Kentucky, Virginia, and Delaware, southward to Florida and westward to California. This delicate pteridophyte thrives in nature on limestone outcrops, often in association with the high humidity of spring runs, clear-water rivers, and other moist sites, and is adapted to the intense heat of the coastal plains at least as far south as the central peninsula of Florida, zones 7–10, 9–3. It requires shade but adjusts to typical garden soils if they are not too acidic and are kept moist. Low pH soils can be sweetened by

Wild geranium.

Maidenhair fern.

the addition of lime, or plants can be planted within small mounds of limestone gravel. Some gardeners construct limestone mounds that support an intermixture of southern maidenhair and wild columbine (*Aquilegia canadensis*). Piedmont gardeners are fortunate to be able to mix southern and northern maidenhair (*Adiantum pedatum*) ferns. The latter is an upright deciduous species (although the leaves are persistent throughout the winter in zone 9) about ten inches tall with interesting, laterally curving fronds. It is sometimes grown in shady coastal plains gardens but performs best in the Piedmont and mountains in zones 3–8, 8–1.

Southern maidenhair is particularly attractive when grown in association with atamasco lily (*Zephyranthes atamasca*) and dimpled trout lily (*Erythronium umbilicatum*). The former produces a white (often blushed with reddish pink), trumpet-shaped flower that appears to arise directly from the ground. Numerous plants often grow in close proximity in nature, the combined effect being reminiscent of a carpet of Easter lilies. Atamasco lily (also called rain lily or zephyr lily) grows from a deeply rooted bulb that produces a tuft of dark green, shiny, grasslike leaves at maturity. The leaves are conspicuous in the groundcover long before and well after the onset of flowering. Young plants put on a single, grasslike leaf that could easily be confused for some sort of weed for their first year or two. Tiny plants planted in spring will quickly lose this filiform foliage, spend the summer nursing the developing bulb, and return the following spring with a few new leaves. It may take several years for these baby plants to achieve their full potential, but mature plants are available in the trade. Although they are colloquially called "lilies," species of *Zephyranthes* are actually part of the amaryllis family (Amaryllidaceae) and are more closely related to daffodils than to true lilies.

Atamasco lily.

Dimpled trout lily.

Solomon's seal.

Dimpled trout lily is a true lily of the family Liliaceae. Three species occur in the southeast, including the rare, white-flowered blonde lilian (*E. albidum*) and two yellow-flowered species. Dimpled trout lily (*E. umbilicatum*) is the more southern of the yellow-flowered plants, distributed from Virginia and West Virginia southward to the Florida panhandle and west to eastern Alabama. Yellow trout lily (*E. americanum*), which is also sometimes planted in southern gardens, is more northern in distribution, ranging from southern Canada southward to North Carolina, Tennessee, and Arkansas. Very young plants of both species have narrow, grasslike leaves that increase in size from year to year but take several years to reach their mature 4–8-inch length. Juvenile leaves somewhat resemble the single leaf of first-year trilliums but are often somewhat paler with lighter mottling. Mature plants are unmistakable. Dimpled trout lily begins flowering as early as February in the warmer parts of its range, and large populations continue flowering into March. The nodding yellow flowers open slowly beginning early in the morning. By lunchtime they are often erect and may be bent upward to expose the stamens. This is a zone 5–8 plant that requires abundant shade and rich, moist soils. It would make an excellent groundcover were it not for the fact that it grows so slowly and that its leaves wither and completely disappear not long after the flowers are gone. Nevertheless, it is an excellent early spring ephemeral for rich shade gardens and a showpiece in deciduous woodlands.

For a taller spring-loving groundcover, few species surpass Solomon's seal (*Polygonatum biflorum*). The arching, frondlike stems are three feet tall and produce several alternate, more or less overlapping, leaves with conspicuous parallel veins and a pleasing form. Pairs of greenish or creamy white urn-shaped flowers dangle below the stem, nearly obscured by the foliage. Plants spread from underground rhizomes and have the potential to form large colonies when properly sited in rich shady woodlands. Solomon's seal ranges widely across the eastern United States from southern Canada south to northern Florida and west to Texas and is most effective in zones 3–9. Other species occur in our region, some larger than the present species. The more robust *P. commutatum* (recognized as a variety of *P. biflorum* by some experts) can grow to six feet tall.

Trilliums

Trilliums have become extremely popular shade-garden perennials, relished by a small but growing number of dedicated collectors and fanciers. These intriguing plants are among the best-known components of eastern North America's early spring flora, and their brief annual appearance is a delight to woodland wildflower watchers. Depending upon geography, some species put on new leaves and flowers as early as January, followed by the appearance of other species throughout April and into May. These are the ultimate spring ephemerals, serving as beacons to the vernal equinox and precursors to the floral year. It is little wonder that so many southern gardeners want them in their landscapes.

About 45 species of trilliums are native to North America. At least 35 occur naturally in the eastern United States, about 30 in the region covered by this book. All belong to the genus *Trillium*, a name that derives from these plants' typically three-parted morphology. For many years the trilliums were considered to be part of the lily family (Liliaceae) but more recently have been segregated by some authorities into the family *Trilliaceae*, of which *Trillium* is the largest genus, and by others into the death camas family (Melanthiaceae). Unlike true lilies, trilliums have net-veined leaves, solitary flowers, and flower parts that are conspicuously and easily separated into sepals and petals.

As a group, trilliums are easy to recognize. Mature plants have a single central stem (technically called a "scape") that is topped by a whorl of three leaflike bracts subtending a six-parted flower. In some species the flower is borne on a stalk and is said to be pedicellate—with a pedicel, or flower stalk. In other species the flowers are sessile—stalkless—and nestled in the center of the bracts. Flowers are typically composed of large, showy stamens surrounded by an inner whorl of three upright or spreading petals and an outer whorl of three spreading sepals.

Trillium Morphology

Trillium morphology is not straightforward. What appears to be a stem connecting roots to leaves is actually a scape (a fleshy flower stalk) that arises directly from the rhizomatous rootstock. What appear to be leaves are actually floral bracts; in precise botanical parlance, scapes cannot have leaves. Nevertheless, the terms *leaves* and *bracts* are used interchangeably in both popular and scientific literature with the colloquial *leaves* by far the more commonly seen. Here, I have also opted for *leaves*.

Despite their name, young trilliums produce only a single leaf for the first two years. Typical three-leaved plants are at least three years old, and it may take five years or more for a plant to produce its first flower. In addition, it is not uncommon in any large trillium colony to find individual plants with four, five, or six leaves. Plants with more than three leaves are probably genetically programmed to produce the same number of leaves each year.

Trilliums also lack a typical root system. The belowground part of the plant consists of a thickened stem or rhizome that elongates annually. Each spring the rhizome produces a few feeding roots that nourish the plant through the growing season and then wither as the leaves die back. Rhizomes can live for many years, and individual trillium plants can be very old.

The fleshy or mealy fruit contains several seeds that fall as the fruit wall decays or splits. The seeds, too heavy to be carried by the wind, are attractive to ants, which play a major role in dispersal and help account for the large trillium colonies that are often found in natural woodlands.

Least trillium.

Spotted wakerobin.

Pale yellow trillium in the garden.

Mixed bed of spring ephemerals, featuring yellow trillium.

Trilliums are shade-loving plants that typically occur in rich, deciduous woods in neutral to slightly acidic soils. Most are easily grown in the garden, especially in the Piedmont and mountains. Coastal plains gardeners will likely have to be satisfied with the four chiefly coastal plains species: Chattahoochee River wakerobin (*T. decipiens*), lanceleaf wakerobin (*T. lancifolium*), spotted wakerobin (*T. maculatum*), and longbract wakerobin (*T. underwoodii*). Piedmont gardeners can grow nearly all of the eastern forms, including all four from the coastal plains and many from the mountains. Fall planting of bare rhizomes works best, but spring plantings of leafed-out plants can also be successful. A complete guide to growing trilliums is beyond the scope of this book (or knowledge of its author). The accompanying table lists the species found in the eastern United States. Gardeners interested in growing trilliums will find complete descriptions and horticultural recommendations for all of our native species in *Trilliums*, by Frederick and Roberta Case.

Trilliums of the Southeastern United States

Scientific Name	Common Name	State Distribution	Conservation Status
Trillium catesbaei	Bashful Wakerobin	AL, GA, NC, SC, TN	
Trillium cernuum	Whip-Poor-Will Flower	CT, DE, IA, IL, IN, MA, MD, ME, MI, MN, ND, NH, NJ, NY, OH, PA, RI, SD, VA, VT, WI, WV	
Trillium cuneatum	Little Sweet Betsy	AL, GA, IL, KY, MD, MS, NC, PA, SC, TN, VA	
Trillium decipiens	Chattahoochee River Wakerobin	AL, FL, GA	
Trillium decumbens	Trailing Wakerobin	AL, GA, TN	
Trillium discolor	Mottled Wakerobin	GA, NC, SC	State Threatened (NC)
Trillium erectum	Red Trillium	AL, CT, DE, GA, IL, IN, KY, MA, MD, ME, MI, NC, NH, NJ, NY, OH, PA, RI, SC, TN, VA, VT, WV	
Trillium flexipes	Nodding Wakerobin	AL, AR, GA, IA, IL, IN, KY, MD, MI, MN, MO, MS, NC, NY, OH, PA, SD, TN, VA, WI, WV	
Trillium foetidissimum	Mississippi River Wakerobin	LA, MS	
Trillium gracile	Sabine River Wakerobin	LA, TX	
Trillium grandiflorum	White Trillium	AL, CT, DC, DE, GA, IL, IN, KY, MA, MD, ME, MI, MN, NC, NH, NJ, NY, OH, PA, SC, TN, VA, VT, WI, WV	

Scientific Name	Common Name	State Distribution	Conservation Status
Trillium lancifolium	Lanceleaf Wakerobin	AL, FL, GA, MS, SC, TN	State Endangered (FL)
Trillium ludovicianum	Louisiana Wakerobin	AL, LA, MS	
Trillium luteum	Yellow Wakerobin	AL, DC, GA, KY, MD, MI, NC, SC, TN, VA	
Trillium maculatum	Spotted Wakerobin	AL, FL, GA, SC	
Trillium nivale	Snow Trillium	IA, IL, IN, KY, MD, MI, MN, MO, NE, OH, PA, SD, VA, WI, WV	
Trillium persistens	Persistent Wakerobin	GA, SC	Federal Endangered; State Endangered (GA)
Trillium pusillum	Dwarf Wakerobin	AL, AR, GA, KY, MD, MO, MS, NC, OK, SC, TN, VA, WV	State Endangered (NC)
Trillium recurvatum	Bloody Butcher	AL, AR, IA, IL, IN, KY, LA, MI, MO, MS, NC, OH, OK, PA, TN, TX, WI	
Trillium reliquum	Confederate Wakerobin	AL, GA, SC	Federal Endangered; State Endangered (GA)
Trillium rugelii	Illscented Wakerobin	AL, GA, NC, SC, TN	
Trillium sessile	Toadshade	AL, AR, DC, IL, IN, KS, KY, MD, MI, MO, NC, NY, OH, OK, PA, TN, VA, WV	
Trillium simile	Jeweled Wakerobin	GA, NC, SC, TN	
Trillium stamineum	Blue Ridge Wakerobin	AL, MS, TN	
Trillium sulcatum	Furrowed Wakerobin	AL, GA, KY, NC, TN, VA, WV	
Trillium texanum	Texas Wakerobin	LA, TX	
Trillium underwoodii	Longbract Wakerobin	AL, FL, GA	
Trillium undulatum	Painted Trillium	CT, GA, KY, MA, MD, ME, MI, NC, NH, NJ, NY, OH, PA, RI, SC, TN, VA, VT, WV	
Trillium vaseyi	Sweet Wakerobin	AL, GA, NC, SC, TN, VA	

Source: Adapted from USDA Plants Database, Natural Resources Conservation Service, United States Department of Agriculture.

III

Catalog of 100 Good Doers

The following catalog of "good doers" highlights some of the best, most readily available, and most easily grown native plants for the eight southeastern states from Virginia to Louisiana. The species have been selected with the help of several regional authorities and experts, as well as from numerous visits to gardens and nurseries throughout the region. All are available from one or more of the nurseries listed in the Appendix.

Red Maple

Acer rubrum Linnaeus

Family: Sapindaceae (Soapberry)
Native Range and Habitat: Coastal plains, Piedmont, and mountains; sea level to nearly 5,000 feet. Upland and lowland forests, wet woods, moist slopes. Throughout the east, west to Minnesota, Oklahoma, and Texas.
Zones: 3–10, 11–1.
Form and Size: Erect, deciduous, single-trunked tree with a pyramidal crown and smooth grayish trunk (becoming roughened with age); potentially reaching 70 feet tall and 40 feet wide in garden settings (often smaller); larger in native habitat.
Characteristics: Leaves opposite, 3–5 lobed and maplelike in shape, 2–6 inches long, 3–4 inches wide, with reddish stalks and marginal teeth; fall color typically clear yellow varying to red or orange. Flowers red, appearing in late winter to very early spring, unisexual, male and female on

Red maple.

separate trees; small and individually inconspicuous but imparting a decidedly reddish cast to entire tree. Fruit a bright red to pinkish two-winged samara ("key"); appearing in mid spring and very attractive. Moderate- to fast-growing.
Culture: Wetland tree, but adapts to drier, sunny sites; plants sited in drier sites may require minimum to moderate irrigation until established.
Typical Use: Specimen tree in residential and commercial landscapes and parks; effectively used in medians and along roadsides.
Best Features: Erect pyramidal form, colorful fall foliage, red flowers and fruit. Excellent when set off as a specimen tree in residential yards, but also effective when planted in groups of three to several in larger landscapes, including parks and roadsides.
Companion Plants: Climbing aster, dahoon holly, loblolly bay, river birch, sweetbay magnolia, swamp azalea, Virginia sweetspire.
Similar and Related Species: Several maples occur in the southeast; red maple is closest in natural habitat to silver maple and box elder. More than 60 registered cultivars and varieties are known. Plants from regional stock fair better in the garden. Detail about all of our native maples is included in Chapter 9.

Sugar Maple

Acer saccharum Linnaeus

Family: Sapindaceae (Soapberry)
Native Range and Habitat: Piedmont and mountains; to more than 5,000 feet in elevation in the southern Appalachians. Rich, moist to more or less dry woods and cove forests,

often in association with calcareous soils. Widespread and present in all eastern states except Florida; west to the Dakotas, Kansas, and Oklahoma.

Zones: 4–8, 8–1.

Form and Size: Erect, deciduous, pyramidal tree with smooth grayish bark; to about 75 feet tall in the garden, potentially taller in natural areas.

Characteristics: Leaves 3–6 inches long and wide, more or less squarish in outline, lacking fine marginal teeth; fall color red, orange, or yellowish, sometimes splotched with green, very attractive; a favored tree for fall color in the southern Appalachians. Flowers individually inconspicuous; greenish yellow and lacking petals. Fruit a 1–2-inch, two-winged samara ("key"); green at first turning pinkish brown; maturing late summer to fall.

Culture: Prefers moist, well-drained, slightly acidic soils and a cool root zone. Performs best and is most attractive in open settings but very shade tolerant.

Typical Use: Specimen or shade tree, especially in large lawns, in parks, and along highways.

Sugar maple.

Best Features: Shade, fall color, and attractive form are sugar maple's more important attributes.

Companion Plants: Basswood, Christmas fern, flowering dogwood, Indian pink, mountain laurel, redbud, white oak, wild hydrangea.

Similar and Related Species: Numerous selections of sugar maple are available, varying mostly in growth rate, crown habit, and fall color. Coastal plains gardeners should use the very similar southern sugar maple (*A. floridanum*), also called Florida maple, instead of sugar maple. Southern sugar maple ranges across the coastal plains from Illinois, Kentucky, and Virginia southward to Florida and west to Texas and tolerates a warm root zone, summer heat, and high humidity. It is smaller in stature than sugar maple (mostly less than 50 feet tall), occurs naturally as an understory tree, and is tolerant of neutral to basic soils. Fall color is less vibrant than for sugar maple, with leaves turning from yellow to brown fairly quickly.

Bottlebrush Buckeye

Aesculus parviflora Walter

Family: Hippocastanaceae (Buckeye)

Native Range and Habitat: Coastal plains and lower Piedmont. Moist, rich soils of bluff and ravine forests. Restricted and uncommon in nature, occurring only in South Carolina, Georgia, and Alabama; widely used in landscaping throughout the Piedmont and as far south as northern Florida, and west at least to Louisiana.

Zones: 5–9, 9–4.

Form and Size: Large, deciduous, mound-forming shrub averaging 10 feet tall and 10 feet

Bottlebrush buckeye, *left* and *above*.

wide at maturity; potentially larger in well-sited plants. Upright in habit with dense foliage. Will spread by root proliferation.

Characteristics: Leaves opposite, long stalked, palmately divided into 5–7 leaflets each 3–8 inches long, with conspicuous and attractive venation. Flowers creamy white, tubular, with exceptionally long and very attractive protruding stamens; individual flowers borne in numerous congested, relatively long racemes at the tips of the branches, making this one of our showiest native shrubs. Fruit a 1–3-inch, pear-shaped capsule with a greenish brown to bronzy husk; ripening and splitting along three sutures in the fall to expose lustrous brown seeds; fruit development on any given plant is typically sparse.

Culture: Thrives in fertile, neutral to slightly basic soils; prefers several hours of sun each day as long as soil is moist and the root zone is relatively cool; moisture and mulch to keep roots cool are especially important for plants sited in USDA zone 9.

Typical Use: Excellent as a stand-alone specimen shrub or massed in large yards. Effective as a shrub layer under large shade trees. Also excellent for obscuring fence corners and as a background for other plantings.

Best Features: The profuse flowering, showy racemes, large rounded habit, and attractive foliage are this species' favored attributes. Attracts hummingbirds.

Companion Plants: Cucumber magnolia, maiden ferns (*Thelypteris* spp.), oakleaf hydrangea, sweetshrub, winged elm.

Similar and Related Species: One of five buckeyes native to the southeast and the only one with a strictly shrublike habit. The closely related and red-flowered red buckeye is the other widely used ornamental species. See Chapter 9 for additional information.

Red Buckeye

Aesculus pavia Linnaeus

Family: Hippocastanaceae (Buckeye)

Native Range and Habitat: Coastal plains, Piedmont, marginally in the mountains of Georgia. Moist woodlands and hammocks, ravine slopes, bottoms, drier parts of floodplains along large streams. Illinois and West Virginia south to Florida and west to Texas.

Red buckeye, *left* and *above*.

Zones: 5–9, 9–5.

Form and Size: Shrub or small tree, usually not exceeding 30 feet tall and often much shorter and shrubby in the garden.

Characteristics: Leaves opposite, long stalked, palmately divided into five 6-inch leaflets. Flowers tubular, red, borne in conspicuous, very attractive, 8–10-inch, conical panicles at the tips of the branches; appearing in early spring. Fruit a brownish bronze capsule, splitting into three parts to release several reddish brown seeds; seeds poisonous if ingested.

Culture: Flowers best in full sun, especially with sufficient irrigation; adaptable to a wide variety of soils from mildly acidic to mildly alkaline.

Typical Use: Mixed shrub beds, wildlife gardens, or as a specimen plant; works well in shady understory but flowers less profusely in such conditions; excellent in hummingbird and butterfly gardens.

Best Features: Spring flowers are unsurpassed; also highly valued for its 5-parted, highly textured, very interesting leaves, and for its overall attractive form.

Companion Plants: American beautyberry, American hornbeam, Christmas fern, coralbean, lady fern, needle palm, oakleaf hydrangea, parsley haw, Shumard oak.

Similar and Related Species: One of five buckeyes native to the southeast and arguably one of the two most popular for gardening and landscaping use. The closely related bottlebrush buckeye, the other widely used ornamental species, has creamy white flowers. See Chapter 9 for additional information.

Serviceberry

Amelanchier arborea (Michaux f.) Fernald

Family: Rosaceae (Rose)

Native Range and Habitat: Coastal plains, Piedmont, mountains. Moist to well-drained woodlands of various overstory compositions. Widespread in the east from Maine to northern Florida, west to Minnesota, Nebraska, Kansas, and Oklahoma.

Serviceberry.

Zones: 4–9, 9–4.

Form and Size: Deciduous shrub or small, often multistemmed tree; typically flowering when of shrubby stature; potentially to 30 feet tall but usually much shorter.

Characteristics: Leaves alternate, oval to egg-shaped in outline, 1–3 inches long, 1–1½ inches wide, with finely toothed margins and attractive laterally spreading veins; turning yellow or red in autumn. Flowers creamy white with five narrow, ¾-inch petals subtending a mass of up to 20 attractive stamens; petals sometimes suffused with pink; appearing in early spring. Fruit a reddish or reddish purple, applelike, ¼-inch pome.

Culture: Relatively easy to grow in moderately moist to dry acidic soils; varies in exposure requirements from full sun to full shade.

Typical Use: Specimen shrub or as part of a mixed, naturalistic woodland or shrubby border; also effective as an understory tree in mixed pine and deciduous woods.

Best Features: Early spring flowers are abundant and attractive; fruit eaten by birds and small mammals; flowers attractive to butterflies.

Companion Plants: Flowering dogwood, fringe tree, heartleaf, little brown jug, native azaleas, redbud, wild columbine, wild ginger.

Similar and Related Species: At least seven species of serviceberries occur in our region, all of which are difficult to distinguish from one another; scientific and common names are often confused in the trade. Select proven plants from local nurseries to ensure success in the garden. See Chapter 11 for additional information.

Climbing Blue Aster

Ampelaster carolinianus (Walter) Nesom

Family: Asteraceae (Aster)

Native Range and Habitat: Coastal plains. Swamps, spring runs, marsh edges, wet stream banks. Restricted in natural range largely to Florida, with a few occurrences in Georgia, South Carolina, and North Carolina; widely used in the coastal plains and Piedmont and available from numerous native plant nurseries.

Zones: 7–10, 11–7.

Form and Size: A woody or semiwoody shrub with slender, arching branches that are often scrambling and vinelike. Forms a low shrub with annual pruning.

Characteristics: Leaves alternate, grayish, 1–4 inches long, up to about 1¼ inches wide, more or less oval or lance-shaped in outline with a clasping base. Flowers borne in clustered heads along or at the tips of branches; heads very attractive, about 1 ½ inches wide with a yellow disc surrounded by 40–60 lavender rays; appearing in fall, typically October–November. Fruit inconspicuous nutlets (achenes) produced at the base of the disc flowers.

Climbing aster.

Culture: Occurs naturally in wetlands but adapts to garden conditions and can withstand moderate drought (especially if mulched). Flowers best in full sun. Benefits from annual pruning to keep leggy branches in check and to encourage a more compact form.

Typical Use: Best in naturalistic landscapes and butterfly gardens but also serves well along foundations, in mixed shrub borders, and to conceal the base of backyard decks and raised patios.

Best Features: Showy flower heads, late fall blooming period, attractive to butterflies.

Companion Plants: Dahoon holly, irises, possumhaw holly, purple coneflower, red maple, Stokes' aster, swamp rose.

Similar and Related Species: Climbing aster (also sometimes, and inappropriately, called Carolina aster) is the only species assigned to its genus. It has been the subject of significant taxonomic realignments and is also found in the trade under the alternate names *Aster carolinianus* and *Symphyotrichum carolinianum*. It is best to use all three names when searching online vendors or inquiring at garden centers. There are many relatives in the aster family (see Chapter 12), a number of which have similarly colored and similarly constructed flowers.

Wild Columbine

Aquilegia canadensis Linnaeus

Family: Ranunculaceae (Buttercup)

Native Range and Habitat: Coastal plains, Piedmont, mountains. Rock outcrops, limestone ledges, sunny edges of rich woodlands, often in association with calcareous soils. Throughout the east, west to the Dakotas and Texas (apparently absent in the east only from Louisiana).

Zones: 3–9, 9–1.

Form and Size: Herbaceous perennial with an upright, delicate, openly branched stature, medium-green attractively divided leaves, and showy flowers; to about 4 feet tall and 2 feet wide.

Characteristics: Leaves medium green above, paler and whitish below, delicately divided into 3 or more leaflets and very attractive. Flowers nodding, predominately reddish with suffusions of creamy yellow, composed of 5 short sepals and petals surrounding a mass of dangling, exerted stamens; petals with an elongated, upright, clublike spur that extends well above the flower's point of attachment to the stalk; appearing in early spring but flowering sporadically into summer. Fruit is a greenish papery follicle containing numerous shiny black seeds.

Wild columbine.

Culture: Prefers neutral to basic well-drained soils (do not overwater); benefits from the addition of lime to average garden soils. Prefers light shade but flowers in full sun and moderately dense shade; plants grown in USDA zone 9 may suffer in full sun. Will reseed.

Typical Use: Mixed perennial beds, limestone mounds and rocky garden edges, hummingbird gardens; especially attractive when planted in large masses but also very effective in small groups or as individual plants within a perennial border or bed.

Best Features: The arresting flowers, early spring flowering time, and attractiveness to hummingbirds are this species' favored attributes.

Companion Plants: Allegheny-spurge, atamasco lily, bird's-foot violet, bloodroot, Christmas fern, dimpled trout lily, flowering dogwood, green-and-gold, partridgeberry, redbud, southern maidenhair fern, sweetshrub, trilliums.

Similar and Related Species: Wild columbine is the only native member of its genus in the east (several others occur in the west, some of which are grown in eastern gardens). The buttercups are among the more primitive families of herbaceous flowering plants, rivaling the magnolias in antiquity. Numerous members of the family are considered to be "early spring ephemerals," occurring in rich deciduous forests and taking advantage of the filtered light that reaches the forest floor prior to the reappearance of leaves in the forest canopy.

Red Chokeberry

Aronia arbutifolia (Linnaeus) Persoon

Family: Rosaceae (Rose)

Native Range and Habitat: Coastal plains, Piedmont, mountains. Wet pine flatwoods, bog and swamp edges, wet savannas. Maine southward through Kentucky and the Carolinas to Florida and west to Texas, including all eight of the southeastern states.

Zones: 5–9, 9–4.

Form and Size: Deciduous, thicket-forming shrub to about 6 feet tall, occasionally reaching 10 feet or more in height and assuming an arborescent stature; sometimes spreading and colonizing beyond an original planting.

Characteristics: Leaves elliptical, 2–4 inches long, ½–2 inches wide, finely toothed along the margins. Flowers white, about ½ inch wide, with 5 spreading petals subtending an attractive mass of up to 20 stamens with reddish to lavender-pink anthers; appearing in spring. Fruit a bright red, ⅜-inch pome that persists on the plant well into winter, long after the leaves have fallen and then reminiscent of the hawthorns.

Culture: Occurs naturally in wet sites; prefers moist soils but is somewhat adaptable. Full sun and wet soils are best for prolific flower production.

Typical Use: Best in a naturalistic woodland border, especially when situated near wetland edges.

Best Features: Flowers are often borne in great profusion and are very attractive; bright red fruit persists well into winter; good fall color.

Companion Plants: Buttonbush, cinnamon fern, green haw, mayhaw, parsley haw, pepperbush, possumhaw holly, royal fern, scarlet rosemallow.

Similar and Related Species: The cultivar 'Brilliantissima' has lustrous leaves and fruit. Fruiting plants are similar to a number of the hawthorns. This species has been subject to several taxonomic realignments that have resulted in at least three additional names, including *Photinia arbutifolia*, *Pyrus arbutifolia*, and *Sorbus arbutifolia*, all of which may be used in the trade. See Chapter 11 for more on this and other native roses.

Red chokeberry.

Butterflyweed

Asclepias tuberosa Linnaeus

Family: Apocynaceae (Dogbane)

Native Range and Habitat: Coastal plains, Piedmont, mountains. Sandy roadsides, longleaf pinelands, dry woods, woodland edges. Throughout the east.

Zones: 4–10, 9–2.

Form and Size: Clump-forming tap-rooted perennial with coarse, lance-shaped leaves that exude nonmilky sap when broken; potentially 2–3 feet tall and wide.

Characteristics: Leaves alternate, 2–4 inches long, varying in outline from linear to elliptic. Flowers bright orange to yellow or reddish, borne in showy clusters at the top of the plant, above the uppermost leaves; appearing in summer. Individual flowers consist of a collection of 5 downturned petals subtending a collection of 5 upright hoods and horns surrounding a thickened column. Fruit an elongated 6-inch follicle, splitting at maturity to release cottony seeds that disperse in the wind.

Culture: Drought-tolerant herb performing best in full sun and dry, well-drained, sandy soils. Not easy to transplant from wild locations due to the large taproot; plants will likely not live if the taproot is cut. Seed-grown plants are easy to establish and grow, are relatively long-

Butterflyweed.

lived, and reseed in the garden. Some gardeners report that this species flowers in early June, a few weeks earlier than it does in natural settings.

Typical Use: A favored species for butterfly gardens, especially for attracting the so-called milkweed butterflies. Also popular in xeric gardens and mixed perennial beds and as a specimen plant.

Best Features: Bright orange to yellow flowers; drought tolerance; attractiveness to butterflies; potentially shrubby habit; interesting fruit; long life.

Companion Plants: American beautyberry, blazing stars, Carolina jessamine, coral honeysuckle, starry rosinweed, Stokes' aster, tickseeds, Walter viburnum, white wild indigo.

Similar and Related Species: This is one of more than two dozen native southern milkweeds, many of which are recommended for gardening but only a few of which are commercially available. See Chapter 13 for more on this genus.

White Wild Indigo

Baptisia alba (Linnaeus) Ventenat

Family: Fabaceae (Bean)

Native Range and Habitat: Coastal plains, Piedmont. Dry roadsides, longleaf pinelands, dry woods. Widespread in the east from Virginia and Minnesota south to Florida and west to Texas, including all eight southeastern states.

Zones: 4–9, 9–4.

Form and Size: Upright shrublike perennial to about 4 feet tall, with ascending branches and conspicuous, erect racemes of showy flowers.

Characteristics: Leaves alternate, 3-parted with 3-inch leaflets; upper surfaces of leaflets green with a whitish glaze. Flowers creamy white with an upright petal called a standard, 2 lateral or wing petals, and 2 fused lower petals often referred to singly as the keel petal; borne abundantly in numerous upright racemes. Fruit an inflated, 1–2-inch legume that becomes blackened with age; seeds typically fall and remain contained with the fruit, resulting in the pod producing a rattling sound at the slightest breeze.

Culture: Prefers well-drained xeric soil in full sun.

Wild white indigo, *left* and *above*.

Typical Use: Mixed perennial beds; massed or planted in clumps of 2–3 plants; naturalistic landscapes.

Best Features: The greenish to grayish white foliage is attractive; most highly valued for the abundance of showy late spring and early summer flowers.

Companion Plants: American beautyberry, blazing stars, butterflyweed, Carolina jessamine, coral honeysuckle, starry rosinweed, Stokes' aster, tickseeds, Walter viburnum, wild blue indigo.

Similar and Related Species: Several *Baptisia* are regularly used in gardening, including species with yellow and blue flowers. See Chapter 13 for more information about this and several other *Baptisia* species, especially the wild blue indigo (*B. australis*).

River Birch

Betula nigra Linnaeus

Family: Betulaceae (Birch)

Native Range and Habitat: Coastal plains, Piedmont, mountains. Floodplains, riverbanks, sandbars in larger rivers. Widespread in the east from New Hampshire to Florida, west to Minnesota and Texas.

Zones: 4–9, 9–1.

Form and Size: A fast-growing, single-trunked or more often multiple-trunked deciduous tree with a leaning stature and attractive, multihued flaking bark that peels off in thin, curly plates; leaves borne on thin branches and quiver attractively in the breeze.

Characteristics: Leaves yellowish green, nearly triangular in outline, 1–4 inches long, to about 1½ inches wide; margins doubly toothed, with several small teeth intervening between larger ones. Female flowers individually tiny, borne in short erect catkins in the leaf

River birch, *right* and *above*.

axils. Male flowers borne in long, drooping catkins from the branch tips. Both male and female flowers appear before or as the new leaves emerge. Fruit a small, flattened nutlet, borne in an erect "woody" catkin that bears a superficial resemblance to a miniature pinecone.

Culture: Occurs naturally in wet soils in floodplains and along rivers but adapts to most garden situations. Largely drought tolerant once established. Cannot be overwatered; roots may be inundated for several months at a time. Does best in full sun but tolerates moderate shade.

Typical Use: An excellent specimen plant. Commonly used as an accent tree to soften corners of residential and commercial buildings; also used to decorate the margins of retention ponds and drainage ditches.

Best Features: Has become a very popular landscape tree due to its moderate size, fast growth, multiple trunks, and attractive peeling bark.

Companion Plants: American hornbeam, baldcypress, Florida leucothoe, swamp chestnut oak, sweetbay magnolia, topal holly, weeping yaupon.

Similar and Related Species: At least six native birches occur in the southeastern United States, the more common of which are essentially mountain species. Only river birch has found wide popularity in southern landscaping. A handful of cultivars are offered in the trade, but most plantings are of species trees.

American Beautyberry

Callicarpa americana Linnaeus

Family: Lamiaceae (Mint)

Native Range and Habitat: Coastal plains, Piedmont, mountains; much more common in the coastal plains, rare in the mountains. Found mostly in disturbed sites, sandy woods, roadsides, and coastal forests. Eastern Virginia and Missouri south to and throughout Florida, west to eastern Texas.

Zones: 5–9, 9–1.

Form and Size: Large deciduous shrub with arching branches, to about 6 feet tall and wide.

American beautyberry, *right* and *above*.

Characteristics: Leaves opposite, pale green, more or less egg-shaped in outline, 3–6 inches long, 1–4 inches wide. Flowers small, pink, borne in delicate, attractive clusters in the leaf axils. Fruit of most plants a magenta, pinkish, or lavender drupe; rarely creamy white.

Culture: Tolerates varying conditions from dry, sandy soils to rich garden soils. So easy to grow that some consider it a weed. Often volunteers in established beds.

Typical Use: Large, old plants are excellent as specimens, especially the white-fruited forms. Also useful as part of shrub beds or in naturalistic landscapes. Perhaps best when magenta-, pink-, or white-fruited forms are massed under tall pines and mulched with pine straw.

Best Features: Most valued for its abundant fall fruit.

Companion Plants: Flowering dogwood, Georgia mint, honeycups, lowbush blueberries, native azaleas, saw palmetto, sparkleberry, sweetshrub.

Similar and Related Species: Most similar in form and habit to the non-native lantanas (*Lantana* spp.) and a good native replacement for them. See Chapter 13 for more on this species. At least two non-native beautyberries are also used in southeastern gardening.

Sweetshrub

Calycanthus floridus Linnaeus

Family: Calycanthaceae (Sweetshrub)

Native Range and Habitat: Coastal plains, Piedmont, mountains. Rich slopes, stream banks, forested uplands; somewhat uncommon in nature but widely used in gardening. Widespread in the east from New York south to northern Florida, west to Louisiana.

Zones: 4–9, 9–1.

Form and Size: Deciduous, upright, multistemmed colonizing shrub that spreads readily by underground runners; to nearly 10 feet tall.

Characteristics: Leaves opposite, dark green, oval in outline, 2–6 inches long. Flowers dull red (yellow in some selections), with numerous straplike tepals (undifferentiated petals and sepals); about 2 inches wide and often sweetly fragrant; appearing in mid spring. Fruit a nutlet enclosed within a fleshy receptacle.

Sweetshrub 'Athens.'   Sweetshrub, *right* and *above*.

Culture: Occurs naturally in deep shade and moist soils; readily adapts to drier sites and to neutral or slightly basic soils. Flowers more prolifically in at least partial sun. Not difficult to maintain once established. Will spread by underground stems.

Typical Use: Often planted near patios, decks, and outdoor recreation areas so the fragrant flowers can be enjoyed. Also excellent for naturalistic shrub beds, for shrubby borders, and as a ground-layer shrub under deciduous trees.

Best Features: Most valued for its fragrant flowers; some plants are much more aromatic than others. Spreads easily from underground runners.

Companion Plants: American beautyberry, Ashe magnolia, bottlebrush buckeye, flowering dogwood, mountain laurel, native azaleas, red buckeye, redbud, two-winged silverbell, witch-hazel.

Similar and Related Species: Several selections are available, including some with dependable floral fragrances. The selection 'Athens' has yellow flowers. See Chapter 5 for more information.

American Hornbeam

Carpinus caroliniana Walter

American hornbeam. Courtesy of Ron Lan[...]

Family: Betulaceae (Birch)

Native Range and Habitat: Coastal plains, Piedmont, mountains. Floodplains, riverbanks, lower slopes near wetlands, bottomland woods. Throughout the east from Maine to Minnesota, south to central Florida, west to Texas.

Zones: 3–9, 9–1.

Form and Size: Deciduous slow-growing, single-trunked, finely branched tree with smooth, grayish, fluted bark that displays a sinewy, muscular appearance; to about 30 feet tall.

Characteristics: Leaves alternate, birchlike, with doubly toothed margins (smaller teeth intervening between larger ones), borne in a spray-like arrangement on opposing sides of the branches; 1–2½ inches long, averaging 1 inch wide. Female flowers borne in inconspicuous catkins near the branch tips. Male flowers borne in 1–2-inch, slender, dangling catkins from points along the branch. Fruit a tiny nutlet concealed within a conspicuous and interesting drooping catkin with conspicuous leaflike bracts.

Culture: Does best in moist, rich soils but adapts to drier sites. Tolerant of variable pH from acidic to slightly basic.

Typical Use: Used as a specimen or as a component of shady understory woodlands. A preferred wildlife food; also a larval food plant for the tiger swallowtail and red-spotted purple butterflies.

Best Features: Shade tolerance, interesting fruit, very attractive bark, valuable as a wildlife and butterfly food plant.

Companion Plants: American beautyberry, blackgum, flowering dogwood, needle palm, redbud, sweetbay magnolia, sweetshrub, Virginia sweetspire.

Similar and Related Species: Closely related and similar to hophornbeam, differing in characters of the bark and preferred natural habitat. Bark similar to that of American beech.

Buttonbush

Cephalanthus occidentalis Linnaeus

Buttonbush.

Family: Rubiaceae (Madder)
Native Range and Habitat: Coastal plains, Piedmont, mountains. Swamps, pond and marsh margins, wetland depressions, stream banks. Throughout the east from Maine to Nebraska, south to Florida, west to Texas.
Zones: 5–11, 12–3.
Form and Size: Deciduous multistemmed shrub to about 10 feet tall; occasionally assuming a more or less arborescent habit.
Characteristics: Leaves opposite or whorled, yellowish green, elliptic in outline, 3–6 inches long, 1–4 inches wide. Flowers tiny, creamy white, tubular with long, conspicuous pistils; borne in congested, long-stalked, ball-like, 1–1½-inch heads. Fruit narrow, capsulelike, borne densely crowded in a brown ball-like head; splitting at maturity to reveal 2–4 nutlets.
Culture: Occurs naturally in wet, often inundated soils. Tolerant of long periods of standing water. Will adapt to somewhat drier sites but generally requires moderate and consistent moisture. Flowers well in full sun or partial shade.
Typical Use: Best for naturalistic wetland edges, or to provide height in moist lawns or gardens. Attracts beneficial insects.
Best Features: Whorled leaves; tolerance of wet conditions and standing water; showy ball-like head of creamy flowers.
Companion Plants: Baldcypress, cinnamon fern, dahoon holly, Florida anise, Ocala anise, red maple, royal fern, spicebush, Virginia sweetspire.
Similar and Related Species: Fevertree is closely related and vegetatively very similar, but the flowers of the two species differ significantly. See Chapter 6 for more information on both of these species.

Redbud

Cercis canadensis Linnaeus

Family: Fabaceae (Bean)
Native Range and Habitat: Coastal plains, Piedmont, mountains. Moist to dry woodlands, rich forests, thin soils over limestone. Throughout much of the east from New York and Nebraska south to central Florida and Texas.
Zones: 6–9, 9–3.
Form and Size: Small, fast-growing, delicate deciduous tree with smooth brown bark and

a rounded crown; potentially to 40 feet tall, often shorter in the garden.

Characteristics: Leaves alternate, mostly heart-shaped, palmately veined with an elongated tip; 3–5 inches long, about as wide. Flowers magenta, about ½ inch long, very attractive; similar to a typical pea flower but having the upright standard petal inserted within the wing petals (subfamily Caesalpinioideae); appearing in early to mid spring. Fruit a flattened, several-seeded pod, 2–4 inches long, turning brown and persisting on the tree well into winter.

Culture: Adapted to acidic or basic soils; tolerant of dry conditions once established. Easy to grow but relatively short-lived.

Typical Use: Highly valued as a flowering specimen tree, especially in conjunction with flowering dogwood. Adds color to suburban lawns, street sides, and understory woodlands.

Redbud.

Best Features: The mass display of showy magenta flowers is an anticipated spring event. Valued for its relatively small size, making it suitable for modest to small suburban landscapes.

Companion Plants: Bluestem palmetto, flowering dogwood, hophornbeam, needle palm, oakleaf hydrangea, serviceberry, two-winged silverbell, witch-hazel.

Similar and Related Species: No other native tree can be confused with or replace this species in residential or commercial landscapes. Several non-native cherries are confused with redbud in early spring. See Chapter 5 for more information about redbud.

Fringe Tree, Old-Man's-Beard, Grancy Gray-Beard

Chionanthus virginicus Linnaeus

Family: Oleaceae (Olive)

Native Range and Habitat: Coastal plains, Piedmont, mountains. Dry to wet woodlands, swamp edges, coastal sandy ridges, granite outcrops. Throughout much of the east from New York south to central Florida and west to Missouri and Texas.

Zones: 4–9, 9–1.

Form and Size: Small to medium-sized, slow-growing, and graceful deciduous tree to about 30 feet tall; bark grayish; sometimes produces multiple trunks.

Characteristics: Leaves opposite, simple, long-elliptic to oval in outline, to about 8 inches long and 4 inches wide but often smaller. Flowers borne in abundance in spring prior to new leaf growth; produced in showy, pendent clusters; individual flowers with 4 creamy white, narrow, strap-shaped 1-inch petals; male and female flowers typically borne on separate trees; appearing in mid to late spring. Fruit an olivelike, ½–⅝-inch drupe borne in dangling clusters; green at first, turning dark purple at maturity; late summer to early fall.

Culture: Often found in wet areas in nature but adaptable to a wide range of soil moisture conditions, including quite dry sites. Reportedly difficult to transplant. Flowers best in full sun.

Typical Use: Excellent as a specimen tree for its showy flowers. Also works well as an accent tree in combination with native azaleas. Increasingly planted along streets and highways.

Best Features: Showy flowering period, graceful form, olivelike fruit on female trees.

Companion Plants: American beautyberry, American hornbeam, flowering dogwood, hophornbeam, native azaleas, needle palm, red buckeye, redbud, Shumard oak, winged elm.

Fringe tree.

Similar and Related Species: Pigmy fringe tree (*C. pyg-maeus*) is endemic to sandy scrub in the central part of the Florida peninsula and is listed as a federally endangered species. It is sold by several Florida native nurseries as well as Woodlanders. Devilwood or wild olive (*Osmanthus americana*) is also in the olive family and is available from a few nurseries. It has the potential to become a medium-sized evergreen tree but is slow-growing and typically remains relatively small in the garden; zones 7–10, 10–7.

American Yellowwood

Cladrastis kentukea (Dumont de Courset) Rudd

Family: Fabaceae (Bean)

Native Range and Habitat: Piedmont (where probably not native), mountains. Coves, rich hardwood forests, rocky calcareous bluffs. Spottily distributed across the east from about

American yellowwood, *right* and *below*.

New York west to Missouri and Oklahoma, south to Louisiana and northern Georgia; apparently absent from Virginia and West Virginia. Becoming rare in nature but increasingly popular for gardening and landscaping.

Zones: 4–8, 8–1.

Form and Size: A medium-sized, slow-growing deciduous tree with a slender trunk, smooth grayish bark, and a finely branched crown. Open-grown trees produce an attractive rounded crown and may produce low branches.

Characteristics: Leaves are alternate and compound; typical leaves are 8–10 inches long, 7–11-parted, with 4-inch leaflets that are arranged alternately along the leaf axis. Flowers are white and pealike, reminiscent of those of the black locust; flowers appear in late spring and are borne in abundance on numerous dangling inflorescences. Fruit is a small, dry, 2–4-inch pod with several brown, flattened seeds; the pods ripen over summer and remain on the tree into winter; similar in habit to redbud.

Culture: An understory tree in nature but performs well in the garden in full to partial sun, especially where allowed to express its spreading form. Adapts to acidic or basic soils as long as they are well drained.

Typical Use: Primarily used as a specimen tree or as part of a naturalistic edge or understory, and for summer shade.

Best Features: The showy flowers, attractive form, and interesting compound leaves that turn clear yellow to nearly golden in fall are this species' chief attributes.

Companion Plants: Bird's-foot violet, Christmas fern, hophornbeam, Indian pink, mountain laurel, serviceberry, silverbell, trilliums, tulip poplar.

Similar and Related Species: The pea family is a large and important family of flowering plants. The related redbud has undivided leaves and magenta flowers; the black locust is similar in flower form and color, but its leaves are divided into numerous leaflets that are much smaller than those of American yellowwood. The cultivar 'Rosea' is a popular pink-flowered form of American yellowwood.

Sweet Pepperbush, Summersweet

Clethra alnifolia Linnaeus

Family: Clethraceae (Clethra)

Native Range and Habitat: Coastal plains, Piedmont. Swamps, pocosins, edges of low pinewoods depressions. Mostly along the eastern seaboard from Maine to Florida and west to Texas.

Zones: 3–9, 9–1.

Form and Size: Erect, medium-sized deciduous shrub with dense foliage and compact branching. Potentially to 10 feet tall and 5 feet wide but usually about half this size.

Characteristics: Leaves are alternate, 2–4 inches long, dark lustrous green above with finely toothed margins and conspicuous, attractive venation. Flowers are fragrant, white, small, and borne in conspicu-

Sweet pepperbush.

ous, abundantly flowered, upright racemes at the branch tips; appearing profusely in late spring and early summer. Fruit is a tiny, hard, brown capsule that remains on the plant for an extended period.

Culture: Prefers moist, acidic soils but will adapt to drier sites, especially if irrigated for the first year or two. Plants in full sun produce more flowers.

Typical Use: In naturalistic hedges, as a specimen shrub, within a mixed shrub bed, or as a screen around the bases of backyard decks.

Best Features: Showy white to pinkish, sweetly fragrant flowers. Erect stature. Attractive to butterflies, bees, and other insects. Colorful fall foliage.

Companion Plants: Blueberries, buttonbush, cinnamon fern, inkberry, loblolly bay, native azaleas, red maple, royal fern, sweetbay magnolia, Virginia sweetspire, yaupon holly.

Similar and Related Species: Several cultivars are available, many of which accentuate the pinkish flowers. The profusely flowering 'Sixteen Candles' produces an abundance of fragrant, 6-inch-long racemes, is compact in form, and is one of the more commonly used cultivars. Sweet pepperbush is sometimes confused with the somewhat similar Virginia sweetspire.

Georgia Calamint

Clinopodium georgianum Harper

Family: Lamiaceae (Mint)

Native Range and Habitat: Coastal plains, Piedmont. Longleaf pine–sandhill forests, dry edges, sandy woodlands. Southeastern United States from North Carolina south to northernmost Florida, west to extreme southeastern Louisiana.

Zones: 7–9, 9–7.

Form and Size: Low-growing, evergreen woody shrub to about 2 feet tall and 2 feet wide.

Characteristics: Leaves are 1 inch long, dark green, lance-shaped, and give off a mintlike aroma when crushed or bruised. Flowers are bluish outside, whitish inside, with a drooping, attractively spotted, 3-parted lower lip; produced in late summer and early fall in attractive, 3-flowered clusters along an upright stem. Fruit is a tiny, inconspicuous, brown nutlet.

Culture: Performs best in well-drained, sunny sites; drought tolerant.

Typical Use: Excellent for shrubby borders, massed in single species plantings, or in combination with other shrubby mints.

Best Features: The low-growing, rounded form, attractive flowers, aromatic foliage, evergreen to semievergreen habit, and drought tolerance make this an excellent plant for coastal plains gardens.

Companion Plants: American beautyberry, lance-leaf coreopsis, red basil, rosemary, sundial lupine, threadleaf bluestar, white wild indigo, wild blue indigo.

Similar and Related Species: Georgia calamint is one of several shrubby mints (see Chapter 13). It is an excellent, easy-to-care-for native shrub that should be more widely planted in southern gardens.

Georgia calamint.

Flowering Dogwood

Cornus florida Linnaeus

Family: Cornaceae (Dogwood)

Native Range and Habitat: Coastal plains, Piedmont, mountains. Dry to moist woods, mountain slopes, pinelands, and several other habitats. Widespread across the east from Maine to Michigan and Kansas, south to peninsular Florida and eastern Texas.

Zones: 5–9, 9–5.

Form and Size: Small to medium-sized deciduous tree with blocky grayish bark and a spreading symmetrical crown; well-known as one of the eastern United States' more beautiful trees during its spring flowering period.

Characteristics: Leaves opposite, about 6 inches long, oval, with distinctive lateral veins that curve upward along the leaf margins. Flowers tiny, yellowish green, borne in a small, dense cluster that is subtended by 4 large, attractive, creamy white bracts that take on the appearance of showy petals at maturity. Fruit a glossy, bright red or sometimes pinkish drupe; borne in dense clusters near the branch tips; ripening in fall and early winter.

Culture: An understory tree that does best in the garden in more or less open settings. Pre-

fers partial to nearly full sun and heavy mulch. Shallow roots grow close to the surface and are susceptible to high soil temperatures. Provenance is important for both hardiness and heat tolerance in this species; select plants adapted to local conditions.

Typical Use: Specimen tree, roadsides, woodsy borders, understory tree in deciduous woodlands.

Best Features: Best loved for its creamy white bracts and prolific flowering in mid spring. Also

Flowering dogwood, *above* and *below.*

valued for its attractive form, bright red fruit, and interesting winter buds. Fruit is eaten by birds.

Companion Plants: American beautyberry, American holly, Ashe magnolia, bottlebrush buckeye, fringe tree, mountain laurel, native azaleas, redbud, serviceberry, weeping yaupon, winterberry, witch-hazel, yaupon.

Similar and Related Species: Several dogwood species are used in southern gardening. At least 100 cultivars and varieties are known. See Chapter 5 for more on this and other native dogwoods.

Washington Thorn

Crataegus phaenopyrum (Linnaeus f.) Medikus

Family: Rosaceae (Rose)

Native Range and Habitat: Coastal plains, Piedmont, mountains. Floodplain forests, upland woods, disturbed sites. Widespread in the east from Pennsylvania west to Missouri, south to northern Florida and Mississippi (where rare).

Zones: 4–8, 8–4.

Form and Size: Small deciduous tree usually not exceeding about 25 feet in height and spread; trees in natural situations may be somewhat taller. Trunk is grayish and scaly, and the twigs and branches are armed with sharp, purplish, 1–2-inch thorns that are piercing to the touch.

Characteristics: Leaves are 1–3 inches long, more or less triangular in outline with toothed and lobed margins; at least some leaves on any tree may be reminiscent in shape, size, and red autumn color to those of red maple. Flowers are about ½ inch wide with creamy white petals, a greenish yellow center, numerous stamens, and yellow anthers; borne in compact, many-flowered clusters and typically appearing in late spring after the new leaves have emerged. Fruit is a shiny, red, ¼-inch pome; borne in showy clusters at the tips of the branches, ripening in mid fall and persisting into winter; attractive to wildlife.

Washington thorn. Courtesy of Ron Lance.   Washington thorn.

Culture: Sometimes a wetland tree in nature but very adaptable and widely planted. Flowers best in full sun to part shade; drought tolerant. Probably prefers rich soil but reportedly tolerates acidic to alkaline conditions as well as clay and sand. Reaches its natural southern limit in the Florida panhandle but performs best in more northern sites.

Typical Use: Specimen in residential landscapes; also valuable for decorating parking lots, walkways, and street sides.

Best Features: Attractive foliage, showy flowers and fruit, attraction to birds, delicate habit, winter form. The sharp thorns can be problematic in high-traffic areas.

Companion Plants: Flowering dogwood, Indian pink, mountain laurel, native azaleas, needle palm, parsley haw, redbud, southern crabapple, winterberry.

Similar and Related Species: The haws constitute a very large and botanically complicated genus (see Chapter 11). Several cultivars are available for the present species, including the upright and columnar 'Fastigiata,' and 'Vaughn,' a superior fruiting form that may actually be a hybrid with green haw.

Green Hawthorn

Crataegus viridis Linnaeus

Family: Rosaceae (Rose)

Native Range and Habitat: Coastal plains, Piedmont, mountains. Swamps, bottomland woods, wet pinelands, alluvial floodplains along large rivers. Southeastern United States from Pennsylvania south to northern Florida, west to Kansas and eastern Texas.

Zones: 4–9, 9–4.

Form and Size: Small deciduous tree to about 35 feet tall with thin, grayish, scaling bark; trunk often with a buttressed or fluted base. Branches with piercing 1-inch thorns.

Characteristics: Leaves 1–3 inches long and elliptical in outline; margins toothed and sometimes shallowly lobed. Flowers white with a pinkish blush, about ½ inch wide, with yellow or red anthers; borne in conspicuous clusters in mid to late spring. Fruit a rounded, orange-red pome ⅜-inch in diameter; often persists throughout the winter and into spring, making this one of the latest fruiting hawthorns.

Green hawthorn.

Green hawthorn 'Winter King.'

Culture: Occurs naturally in wetlands but is adaptable to garden conditions; will flower in shade or full sun. Adapts to acidic and alkaline soils. Seeds collected in midwinter germinate quickly and are easy to grow. Perhaps somewhat less susceptible to hawthorn rust than some other species.

Typical Use: Specimen in suburban landscapes, naturalistic understories, sunny woodland borders.

Best Features: Showy flowers, attractive persistent fruit, dense rounded crown, attractive winter form. The piercing thorns can be problematic in high-traffic areas.

Companion Plants: American hornbeam, American yellowwood, black locust, needle palm, parsley haw, southern crabapple, Washington thorn, winterberry.

Similar and Related Species: The hawthorns constitute a large and botanically complicated genus (see Chapter 11). The cultivar 'Winter King' (pictured in fruit), selected from Indiana stock, is one of the best selections of green haw but performs best from about USDA zone 8A northward. The immensely attractive parsley haw—with delicately incised leaves, clusters of small white flowers, red anthers, and very attractive mottled bark—is also an excellent garden hawthorn (see Chapter 11).

Titi, Cyrilla

Cyrilla racemiflora Linnaeus

Titi.

Family: Cyrillaceae (Titi)

Native Range and Habitat: Coastal plains, lower Piedmont. Restricted primarily to the coastal plains from extreme southeastern Virginia southward to central Florida and west to extreme eastern Texas.

Zones: 6–9, 9–4.

Form and Size: Densely foliaged evergreen shrub or small tree with attractive crooked branches, gray to reddish bark, and leaves that vary in size from tree to tree. Often not exceeding about 10 feet tall in the garden; old plants in natural habitats can reach twice this height. Clonal, potentially forming extensive thickets by the formation of root suckers, especially in natural swamps and wetlands.

Characteristics: Leaves evergreen, 1–4 inches long, more or less narrowly elliptical in outline. Flowers tiny, white, borne in conspicuous, elongated, cylindrical, 3–6-inch racemes; highly attractive to bees and other pollinators. Fruit a hard, tiny capsule that remains on the tree well after the seeds have fallen, perhaps even into the next flowering season.

Culture: A wetland tree of acidic woods but tolerant of dry conditions and a variety of soils. Flowers best in full sun but performs well in shade. May require irrigation the first year or two, after which it adapts to drier conditions.

Typical Use: Shrubby borders, naturalistic woodlands, evergreen screening hedge, specimen shrub. Has been used effectively in roadside plantings and to decorate the lawns of interstate highway rest areas.

Best Features: Titi (pronounced "tie-tie") is valued for its prolific flowering, dense habit, attraction to bees, and rounded form.

Companion Plants: Black titi, cinnamon fern, dahoon holly, loblolly bay, netted chain fern, red maple, royal fern, saw palmetto, swamp azalea, sweetbay magnolia, sweet pepperbush, Virginia chain fern.

Similar and Related Species: Closely related to and often found in nature with black titi (*Cliftonia monophylla*). Two related species—not accepted as distinct species by all authorities—include scrub titi (*C. arida*) and littleleaf titi (*C. parvifolia*). Scrub titi is a species of xeric sands in the central part of the Florida peninsula but has been grown successfully at least northward to zone 7. Littleleaf titi is restricted largely to the Florida panhandle. It has very small leaves not exceeding about 1½ inches long and ⅜ inch wide.

Climbing Hydrangea, Woodvamp

Decumaria barbara Linnaeus

Family: Hydrangeaceae (Hydrangea)

Native Range and Habitat: Coastal plains, Piedmont, mountains. Wet woods, swamp and bottomland forests. Distributed largely in the coastal plains and lower Piedmont from extreme southeastern Virginia south to central peninsular Florida and west to Louisiana, including all of the states represented in this book. Also reported for Long Island, New York.

Zones: 6–9, 9–6.

Form and Size: High-climbing, deciduous woody vine; climbing by the presence of numerous stem roots. Also runs on the ground and may be trained as a groundcover in the garden.

Characteristics: Leaves opposite, thick, and leathery; stalked, shiny above, 3–5 inches long and up to about 3 inches wide. Flowers with numerous creamy white petals and sepals; borne in a terminal inflorescence at the tip of new stem growth. Fruit a prominently ribbed capsule resembling a miniature crown.

Culture: Wetland species that adapts well to shady gardens. Flowers best when new stem

Climbing hydrangea, *right* and *above*.

growth occurs near top of the plant in full sun. Prefers acidic, organic soil; does not tolerate drought.

Typical Use: Climbing vine on trellises, fences, walls, and trees. Can also be trained as a groundcover and is especially useful for lining garden pathways, but it must be pruned regularly to prevent it from spreading laterally into the garden or over the path.

Best Features: Climbing habit, attractive opposite leaves, attractive inflorescence.

Companion Plants: American hornbeam, cinnamon fern, netted and Virginia chain ferns, needle palm, possumhaw holly, royal fern, Shumard oak, swamp chestnut oak.

Similar and Related Species: Related but not similar to oakleaf hydrangea and mock orange. See Chapter 14 for more about this species and other vines and groundcovers.

Purple Coneflower

Echinacea purpurea (Linnaeus) Moench

Purple coneflower.

Family: Asteraceae (Aster)

Native Range and Habitat: Coastal plains, Piedmont, mountains. Dry woods and roadsides. Distributed from New York south to a single county in the Florida panhandle, west to Wisconsin and Louisiana. A rare species across much of its range, especially in the coastal plains. Widely used in gardening; probably escaped from cultivation and not technically native to some areas in which it has now become established.

Zones: 3–9, 9–1.

Form and Size: A perennial herb, 2–3 feet tall and nearly as broad with a dense rosette of overlapping basal leaves.

Characteristics: Basally disposed leaves thick, dark green, with distinctive, depressed venation; up to about 10 inches long and 4 inches wide. Stem leaves similar but shorter and narrower. Flowers exquisite, with a large, orange-tinted central disc surrounded by numerous deep magenta to pinkish rays; appearing in late spring and continuing periodically throughout the summer, especially with the efficient removal of spent heads. Fruit a tiny, brown, rectangular achene.

Culture: Tolerant of alkaline soils but adapts to typical garden conditions. Drought tolerant. Flowers best in full sun. Deadheading extends flowering, but allowing a few flower heads to reach maturity will ensure a seed source for the garden. Plants seed in freely; some plants may not survive beyond the first pair of leaves.

Typical Use: Used in mixed perennial and wildflower beds, in masses with rudbeckia and other members of the aster family, to decorate mailboxes, and in perennial borders. Sought after by butterfly gardeners.

Best Features: The large, brightly colored flower heads and extended flowering time are this species' most valued attributes.

Companion Plants: Blazing stars, rudbeckias, starry rosinweed, tickseeds, yellow coneflower.

Similar and Related Species: Several species of *Echinacea* occur in the southeast, a number of which are available in nurseries and garden centers. The aster family encompasses a large and diverse assemblage of herbaceous species. See Chapter 12 for more information about this and other species and genera within the aster family.

Coralbean, Cherokee Bean, Cardinal-Spear

Erythrina herbacea Linnaeus

Family: Fabaceae (Bean)

Native Range and Habitat: Coastal plains. Sandy woods and longleaf pine–dominated uplands. A coastal plains species distributed from extreme southeastern North Carolina south to and throughout Florida, west to extreme eastern Texas.

Zones: 8–10, 10–9.

Form and Size: An erect semiwoody shrub to about 4 feet tall across much of its range, potentially becoming woody and reaching arborescent stature in southern Florida, where it is sometimes called *E. arborea*.

Characteristics: Leaves to about 10 inches long, 3-parted; leaflets arrowhead-shaped, to about 4 inches long, with a narrowly tapering tip and triangular lateral lobes. Flowers bright red, appearing tubular but actually beanlike with standard, petals, and keel; arranged in a showy, erect inflorescence; attractive to hummingbirds and butterflies; appearing in late spring and summer. Fruit a blackish, multiseeded pod that splits in the fall to expose several bright red poisonous seeds.

Culture: An easy-to-grow perennial that tolerates a wide range of soil types but generally does best in coarse sands and xeric conditions. Flowers best in full sun. Drought tolerant.

Typical Use: Mixed wildflower beds, woodland borders, naturalistic woodlands, pine-dominated forests. Also planted as a specimen plant.

Best Features: The bright red flowers and bright red fruit are this species' outstanding features. The 3-parted leaves with triangular leaflets are unique. Seeds collected in fall and sown over winter germinate readily and are easy to grow to maturity.

Coralbean, *left* and *above*.

Companion Plants: American beautyberry, blue wild indigo, Carolina jessamine, coral honeysuckle, Georgia calamint, purple coneflower, starry rosinweed, sundial lupine, white wild indigo.

Similar and Related Species: The bean family encompasses a large and diverse assemblage of horticultural specialties, none of which are particularly reminiscent of coralbean. See Chapter 13 for more information about the bean family.

Coastal Witch-Alder

Fothergilla gardenii Linnaeus

Family: Hamamelidaceae (Witch-Hazel)

Native Range and Habitat: Coastal plains. Wet savannas and margins of pineland depressions. North Carolina south to the western Florida panhandle, west to Alabama. Not common.

Zones: 4–9, 9–1.

Form and Size: A 3-foot-tall deciduous shrub, equally as broad, with zigzag branches and a rounded form. Clonal, forming colonies in nature and perhaps also in the garden.

Characteristics: Leaves very similar in appearance to witch-hazel, 1–3 inches long, nearly two-thirds as wide, leathery, with distinctive parallel veins that curve upward near the leaf margin; margins scalloped. Distinguished from the leaves of witch-hazel by the lowermost lateral veins being joined with the margin at the base of the leaf. The leaves of witch-alder provide excellent red, yellow, and orange fall color. Flowers fragrant, creamy white, lacking petals but borne in an attractive and very showy, upright, more or less ellipsoid 2-inch inflorescence; appearing mostly in mid to late spring, April–May. Fruit a brownish capsule.

Culture: Performs best in acidic, well-drained soils. Not tolerant of alkaline soils. Flowers

Coastal witch-alder, *right* and *above*.

best in full sun but tolerates some shade. Virtually carefree.

Typical Use: Used as a specimen or foundation plant, or to obscure unsightly borders of backyard decks. Excellent in mass plantings or as a component of a mixed shrub bed or shrub border.

Best Features: The showy and unique inflorescences, outstanding fall color, interesting summer foliage, and trouble-free care make this an excellent garden plant that should be more widely used.

Companion Plants: Bottlebrush buckeye, flowering dogwood, fringe tree, highbush blueberries, honeycups, mountain laurel, native azaleas, two-winged silverbell.

Similar and Related Species: This species and the large witch-alder are very similar but inhabit disparate regions and habitats. The foliage of both witch-alders is similar to that of the closely related witch-hazel, which becomes a small tree. Numerous superior selections are available in the trade. 'Blue Mist' (pictured) has become popular for its interesting bluish foliage.

Large Witch-Alder

Fothergilla major (Sims) Loddiges

Family: Hamamelidaceae (Witch-Hazel)

Native Range and Habitat: Piedmont, mountains. Dry ridges at middle elevations of the southern Appalachians. Eastern North Carolina, western Tennessee, northern Georgia and Alabama. Not common.

Zones: 4–8, 9–2.

Form and Size: An upright, multistemmed, rounded deciduous shrub; potentially to about 10 feet tall and nearly as wide, but usually about half this size.

Large witch-alder, *left* and *above*.

Characteristics: Leaves broadly oval to nearly round, 2–4 inches long, leathery, with scalloped or coarsely toothed margins; dark green above, bluish gray beneath, turning various shades of yellow, red, and orange in mid to late fall. Flowers similar to those of coastal witch-alder, borne in a showy, upright, 2-inch spike; lacking petals. Fruit a hard capsule.

Culture: Relatively carefree in well-drained, acidic soils.

Typical Use: Used mostly as a specimen or foundation plant, or to obscure the unsightly borders of backyard decks. Excellent in mass plantings or as a component of a mixed shrub bed or shrub border.

Best Features: The showy and unique inflorescences, outstanding fall color, interesting summer foliage, and trouble-free care make this an excellent garden plant that should be more widely used.

Companion Plants: Flowering dogwood, mountain laurel, native azaleas and rhododendrons, umbrella magnolia, wild hydrangea.

Similar and Related Species: This species and the coastal witch-alder are very similar but inhabit disparate regions and habitats. The foliage of both witch-alders is similar to that of the closely related witch-hazel, which becomes a small tree. Several selections are available. 'Mt. Airy' (pictured in fall foliage), selected by Michael Dirr from the Mt. Airy Arboretum in Cincinnati, Ohio, is among the more popular for its strong fall color, abundant flowers, upright habit, and vigorous growth. Some experts suggest that 'Mt. Airy' is a hybrid between the two native witch-alders.

Carolina Buckthorn

Frangula caroliniana (Walter) A. Gray

Family: Rhamnaceae (Buckthorn)
Native Range and Habitat: Coastal plains, Piedmont, mountains. Dry woodlands and forests, often in association with limestone outcrops in the coastal plains. Eastern and southeastern United States from Virginia to Missouri, south to Texas and central Florida.
Zones: 5–9, 9–4.
Form and Size: A small deciduous tree to about 30 feet tall with a smooth gray trunk

Carolina buckthorn.

and a spreading crown of fine, slender branches; often not more than about 15 feet tall in the garden.

Characteristics: Leaves alternate, oblong to elliptic in outline, 2–5 inches long, shiny green and very attractive above, decorated with 10–12 pairs of deeply impressed, regularly spaced, and uniformly spreading lateral veins; turning yellow to orange in autumn. Flowers small, cuplike, borne in clusters at the leaf axils; appearing mostly in spring. Fruit a rounded drupe, reddish at first, juicy and black at maturity; attractive to birds and other wildlife; appearing mostly in late summer and fall.

Culture: Tolerates full sun to part shade. Prefers well-drained soils but is tolerant of sand and clay as well as acidic or alkaline conditions.

Typical Use: An excellent specimen tree; also effective as one component of a naturalistic woodland.

Best Features: Valued partially for its fruit, which are attractive to wildlife, but mostly for its very attractive foliage and pleasing form.

Companion Plants: American hornbeam, hophornbeam, New Jersey tea, southern crabapple, winged elm, witch-hazel.

Similar and Related Species: Several species of buckthorn are used in landscaping, especially the somewhat weedy European buckthorn (*F. cathartica*).

Carolina Jessamine

Gelsemium sempervirens St. Hilaire

Family: Gelsemiaceae (Jessamine)

Native Range and Habitat: Coastal plains, Piedmont, mountains. Dry upland forests, rich, moist woods, ephemeral wetlands. Virginia south to Florida, west to Texas.

Zones: 7–9, 9–1.

Form and Size: An evergreen, high-climbing to trailing and twining vine with a thin, stiff, brownish, wirelike stem; often climbing well into the forest canopy. All parts of this plant are extremely poisonous if ingested. Some reports suggest that inhaling the aroma of broken roots and stems can precipitate respiratory distress and anaphylactic shock. Suffice it to say that exposing mucous membranes to fumes from this species should be avoided.

Characteristics: Leaves opposite, mostly lance-shaped, 2–4 inches long, about ½ inch wide. Flowers yellow, trumpet-shaped, appearing from midwinter to very early spring; fragrant. Fruit a ¾–1-inch capsule.

Culture: Easy to grow; adapts well to most garden soils. Easily transplanted within the garden. Typically occurs in moist, acidic soils but adapts to alkaline soils. Prefers and flowers best in full sun, but it is tolerant of and also flowers well in shady sites.

Typical Use: Excellent when allowed to climb on low native trees. Easily trained

Carolina jessamine, *left* and *above*.

to trellises and fences. Used in commercial and residential landscapes to obscure the harshness of chain-link fences.

Best Features: Yellow, trumpet-shaped flowers. Climbing and twining form. Evergreen habit. Winter flowering period.

Companion Plants: American beautyberry, coral honeysuckle, dahoon holly, gallberry, highbush blueberries, native azaleas, yaupon.

Similar and Related Species: The closely related swamp jessamine (*G. rankinii*) is similar, differing in its later bloom time, nonfragrant flowers, and minute differences in the form of its sepals. A few selections are available but are not particularly distinguishable from species plants. See Chapter 14 for more information of these and other climbing vines.

Two-Winged Silverbell

Halesia diptera Ellis

Family: Styracaceae (Storax)

Native Range and Habitat: Coastal plains. Bottomland and floodplain forests. Extreme southeastern South Carolina, south to the Florida panhandle, west to extreme eastern Texas.

Zones: 3–9, 9–4.

Form and Size: Small deciduous tree with a rounded crown; to about 30 feet tall at maturity but flowering and fruiting when of a shrublike stature.

Characteristics: Leaves mostly oval in outline, 3–7 inches long, to about 4 inches wide. Flowers white, borne in early spring in dangling clusters from the leaf axils, making this a very attractive small tree; differing from little silverbell by the petals being united only at the base and spreading at the apex of the flower. Fruit 1–2 inches long, laterally flattened, with two large conspicuous wings and two very small inconspicuous wings; appearing in late summer and fall.

Culture: Occurs naturally in wet soils but adapts to moist, well-drained soils. Flowers best in partial sun.

Typical Use: This species is excellent as a specimen, as one component of a woodland understory, or as part of a naturalistic landscape. A worthy addition to shrubby borders.

Two-winged silverbell, *left* and *above*.

Best Features: Prolific flowering in early spring; autumn color; delicate form; interesting, essentially two-winged fruit.

Companion Plants: American hornbeam, arrowwood, Ashe magnolia, climbing hydrangea, common pawpaw, flowering dogwood, green haw, needle palm, parsley haw, redbud, Virginia sweetspire.

Similar and Related Species: Two varieties are recognized for this species. The flowers of variety *diptera* are ⅜–⅝ inch long; those of variety *magniflora* are ¾–1¼ inches long. Variety *magniflora* is restricted in nature to northwest Florida and southwestern Georgia, but it adapts to a wider geographic range in the garden. Little silverbell, described below, is more widespread than the present species.

Mountain Silverbell

Halesia tetraptera Ellis

Family: Styracaceae (Storax)

Native Range and Habitat: Coastal plains, Piedmont, mountains. Cove forests, bottomland forests, moist slopes, moist to dry uplands. Most common in western North Carolina, northern Georgia, and northerm Alabama, but see comments below regarding similar and related species.

Zones: 5–9, 9–4.

Form and Size: Deciduous tree to about 75 feet tall, especially in higher elevations.

Characteristics: Leaves elliptical in outline, to 8 inches long or longer; usually about twice as long as wide; long-tapering at the apex. Flowers white, bell-shaped, ½–1¼ inches long; petals united nearly to the

Mountain silverbell, *right* and *below*. Courtesy Ron Lance.

apex; appearing in spring. Fruit a pear-shaped, ¾–1½-inch, 4-winged capsule; appearing in late summer and early fall.

Culture: Performs best in moist, acidic, well-drained organic soils; intolerant of alkaline soils; full sun to partial shade for optimum flowering.

Typical Use: Excellent as a specimen tree, or as one component in a naturalistic landscape.

Best Features: Bell-shaped flowers, medium-sized form, yellow fall foliage.

Companion Plants: Bigleaf magnolia, flowering dogwood, mountain laurel, native azaleas and rhododendrons, redbud, Virginia sweetspire, wild hydrangea.

Similar and Related Species: The taxonomy of this species is somewhat confusing. Plants sold in the trade as *Halesia carolina* and *H. tetraptera* are often representative of the same species, and some experts continue to treat these names as synonyms for a single, although variable plant. Others reserve the name *H. carolina* (little silverbell) for smaller, multi-stemmed plants of sandy soils with flowers less than ⅜ inch long. It is probably wise to question the provenance of plants found in retail nurseries.

Witch-Hazel

Hamamelis virginiana Linnaeus

Family: Hamamelidaceae (Witch-Hazel)

Native Range and Habitat: Coastal plains, Piedmont, mountains. Moist woodlands and dry forests. Widespread across the entire eastern United States, west to Minnesota and Texas, south to central peninsular Florida.

Zones: 3–9, 9–1.

Form and Size: A small, typically arching or vase-shaped tree, or sometimes multistemmed shrub, with smooth, grayish bark and an open crown; potentially to about 35 feet tall but often much shorter in the garden. Witch-hazel has naked buds, meaning that the new leaf buds are not protected by overlapping scales, which can be a good identification character when plants are leafless.

Characteristics: Leaves alternate, elliptic to more or less reverse-egg-shaped in outline, with scalloped margins, and borne in a single lateral plane along the stem (two-ranked); green in summer, turning a very attractive yellow in autumn. Flowers yellow (sometimes reddish), with 4 very narrow, ⅜–⅝-inch, straplike petals subtended by 4 small, triangular

Witch-hazel , *right* and *above*.

Witch-hazel.

sepals; fragrant; appearing in late fall, with or after leaf drop (sometimes later than this in warmer climes). Fruit a hard, egg-shaped capsule.

Culture: Typically occurs in moist, well-drained, slightly acidic soils. Tolerates shade but flowers best in part sun (full sun from zone 8 northward). Tolerates drier sites once well established.

Typical Use: Used mostly as a specimen in residential landscapes; also effective in naturalized landscapes, shrubby borders, at the corners of buildings, and in commercial installations where a large, winter-flowering shrub is preferred.

Best Features: The arching form, fall flowering period, and interesting foliage are this species' chief attributes; the arching, irregular branches are particularly attractive in winter.

Companion Plants: American hornbeam, arrowwood, Ashe magnolia, Carolina jessamine, mountain laurel, native azaleas and rhododendrons, oakleaf hydrangea, Shumard oak, swamp chestnut oak, sweetshrub, two-winged silverbell, umbrella magnolia, wild hydrangea.

Similar and Related Species: Other species of witch-hazel occur in the southeast. Springtime witch-hazel (*H. vernalis*) is mostly a midwestern plant that is also used in southern gardening. Its flowers tend more toward red and typically open in early spring. The non-native Chinese witch-hazel (*H. mollis*) and to a lesser extent the Japanese witch-hazel (*H. japonica*), which usually flower in late winter between the two native species, are also used in southern landscaping.

Scarlet Rosemallow

Hibiscus coccineus Walter

Family: Malvaceae (Mallow)

Native Range and Habitat: Coastal plains, Piedmont. Marshes, swamps, coastal wetlands. Southeastern United States, from Virginia southward to Florida, west to Louisiana. Perhaps truly native only to Alabama, Florida, and Georgia; introduced elsewhere due primarily to garden use.

Zones: 6–11, 11–1.

Form and Size: A tall herbaceous perennial with several upright stems that sometimes arch or sag under the weight of the flowers and fruiting capsules; potentially reaching 9 feet tall in the garden.

Characteristics: Leaves alternate, long stalked, deeply divided into 3–5 narrow lobes and superficially similar in appearance to the leaves of marijuana plants; leaf segments dark green, toothed, lance-shaped, up to about 10 inches long. Flowers with 5 large, 4-inch-long, showy scarlet pet-

Scarlet rosemallow.

als; borne in the leaf axils along the upper third of the stem and appearing throughout the summer. Fruit a 2–4-inch, brown, papery, egg-shaped capsule containing numerous brownish seeds that germinate quickly and are easy to grow. Seeds can be collected from the garden as the capsules turn brown.

Culture: Occurs naturally in sunny conditions in moist, acidic soils. Adapts well to the garden in full or part sun but should be kept moist for best performance. Should be cut back in fall to within a few inches of the ground.

Typical Use: Excellent as a background in a mixed perennial bed, especially against a fence or large shrubs; works well along walkways in larger landscapes. Should be given a space 6–8 feet wide to allow for its arching and drooping stems.

Best Features: Elizabeth Lawrence, in her classic *A Southern Garden*, dubs this plant "our most spectacular native." The showy red flowers, prolific flower production, extended flowering period, and interesting foliage rank this species at the top of our few showy native hibiscuses.

Companion Plants: Blue-eyed grass, buttonbush, cardinal flower, iris, purple coneflower, purple muhly grass.

Similar and Related Species: Several species of hibiscus are native to the southeast. Swamp rosemallow (*H. grandiflorus*) has large, showy pink flowers and woolly leaves. Halberd-leaf rosemallow (*H. laevis*) has large, white to pink flowers with a darker center and well-separated petals; its leaves are reminiscent in shape to the head of a medieval battle-ax (halberd). Rosemallow (*H. moscheutos*) has beautiful white flowers with crinkly petals and a dark red center; the leaves are grayish and broadly lance-shaped. All are mostly wetland species that adapt to the garden, are similar in cultivation to scarlet rosemallow, and grow well in USDA zones 5–9.

Wild Hydrangea, Smooth Hydrangea

Hydrangea arborescens Linnaeus

Family: Hydrangeaceae (Hydrangea)
Native Range and Habitat: Coastal plains, Piedmont, mountains. Upland forests and rocky woodlands. Widespread across the eastern United States from New York and Massachusetts south to the Florida panhandle, west to Louisiana. Most widely distributed in the mountains; rare in the coastal plains and known in Florida from only two counties.

Zones: 4–9, 9–1.

Form and Size: A relatively low-growing, rounded shrub to about 6 feet tall and nearly as wide; forming colonies and spreading easily and broadly from root sprouts.

Characteristics: Leaves opposite, egg-shaped to broadly elliptical in outline; to about 8 inches long and 5 inches wide; margins toothed.

Wild hydrangea.

Flowers white to grayish white, borne in showy, terminal, 6-inch-wide cymes above the leaves; appearing in late spring and summer and very attractive when plants are grown in a mass; in this species, the petaloid sepals that typically characterize sterile hydrangea flowers are irregularly spaced and fewer in number than in other hydrangeas. Fruit a brown, ribbed capsule.

Culture: Grows naturally in shade but adapts and flowers well in full sun if kept moist. Prefers rich, moist, acidic soils and will expand in coverage under optimum conditions. Will tolerate neutral soils.

Typical Use: Best as part of a naturalized shrub bed or shady shrub border. Also serves well as a background in a perennial bed. Should be pruned to the ground in winter.

Best Features: Fast growth and showy flowers make this species useful in the garden.

Companion Plants: Arrowwood, bottlebrush buckeye, bushy St. John's–wort, drooping leucothoe, flowering dogwood, oakleaf hydrangea, smooth sumac, two-winged silverbell, Virginia sweetspire, winterberry, witch-hazel.

Similar and Related Species: Several cultivars of wild hydrangea are available, of which 'Annabelle' has the largest inflorescences and may be the more popular. Four species of hydrangea are native to the southeast. Only the present species and oakleaf hydrangea are regularly used in southern gardening. See Chapter 5 for more information about our native hydrangeas.

Oakleaf Hydrangea

Hydrangea quercifolia Bartram

Family: Hydrangeaceae (Hydrangea)
Native Range and Habitat: Coastal plains, Piedmont, mountains. Rich forests and limestone bluffs. Endemic to the southeast, distributed from North Carolina (where probably not native) south to northern Florida, west to Louisiana.
Zones: 5–9, 9–1.
Form and Size: Large, coarse, deciduous multistemmed shrub with attractively exfoliating bark; can exceed 10 feet tall and at least as wide; spreads by underground runners and can form large colonies in favorable situations.
Characteristics: Leaves large, deeply lobed and toothed along the margins; up to about 12 inches long on 4–6-inch stalks; turning an attractive burgundy in autumn. Flowers borne in a large, conspicuous, showy, pyramidal panicle; sterile flowers with 4 large, white, petaloid sepals that persist on the plant well past flowering and change to an attractive bronzy pinkish color as the season progresses; fertile flowers also white but with smaller parts; appearing in late spring. Fruit a ribbed capsule.
Culture: Prefers moist, rich soil, but occurs naturally in association with limestone and is tolerant of neutral soils. Performs well in shade or sun. Plants in full sun should be heavily mulched to ensure cool roots and optimal foliage. Mulching and part shade are important for plants situated in AHS Heat Zone 9.
Typical Use: Large specimen shrub; massed in corners or in isolated beds in larger landscapes; an excellent addition to naturalistic woodlands. Should be a featured component of every southern garden.
Best Features: This is a four-season plant valued equally for its large, showy inflorescence,

Oakleaf hydrangea. , *right* and *above*.

outstanding summer foliage, pleasing fall color, and attractive winter form.

Companion Plants: Arrowwood, Ashe magnolia, atamasco lily, coastal witch-alder, flowering dogwood, mountain laurel, native azaleas and rhododendrons, needle palm, redbud, sweetshrub, Virginia sweetspire, yellowroot.

Similar and Related Species: One of four species of *Hydrangea* native to the southeast. Numerous cultivars are available, of which 'Snowflake', with oversized inflorescences and bright white sepals, is one of the most often seen; the panicles of 'Snowflake' are so large that they often droop nearly to the ground, especially after a heavy rain. See Chapter 5 for more about this species and some of its cultivars.

Bushy St. John's–wort

Hypericum densiflorum Pursh

Family: Hypericaceae (St. John's–Wort)

Native Range and Habitat: Coastal plains, Piedmont, mountains. Bogs, savannas, dry and moist forests. New York south to Georgia, west to Louisiana.

Zones: 5–8, 9–5.

Form and Size: A rounded, compact, densely foliaged, 4–6-foot deciduous shrub with smooth, shiny, brown bark that peels and flakes with age.

Characteristics: Leaves long, narrowly linear, usually not exceeding about ¼ inch wide. Flowers yellow, about 1 inch wide, with 5 spreading petals surrounding a mass of yellow stamens; borne abundantly in a crowded inflorescence; appearing from May to early summer. Fruit a brown, conical capsule with numerous tiny seeds.

Culture: Adapted to sun or shade and dry or moist soils.

Typical Use: Probably best in massed plantings with other St. John's–worts. Can also be used in mixed shrub beds or as a specimen.

Best Features: Rounded form and abundance of small, showy, yellow flowers.

Companion Plants: American beautyberry, blueberries, honeycups, native azaleas, other St. John's–worts, purple coneflower, virtually any species of *Coreopsis*, yaupon.

Bushy St. John's–wort. Courtesy Ron Lance.

Similar and Related Species: The selection 'Creel's Gold Star,' found by Mike Creel, has been introduced by Dodd and Dodd Native Nurseries. Numerous species of St. John's–worts occur in the southeastern United States, a few of which have found their way into gardening circles. Nearly all produce attractive yellow flowers, some with four petals and some with 5. Many more have promising garden uses. Flowering times vary across the genus. An observant coastal plains gardener who planned carefully could likely have one or another species of St. John's–wort flowering in the garden at least nine months of the year.

Golden St. John's–wort

Hypericum frondosum Michaux

Golden St. John's–wort.

Family: Hypericaceae (St. John's–Wort)
Native Range and Habitat: Coastal plains, Piedmont, mountains. Rich, often rocky woods. Spottily distributed and uncommon across the southeast from Virginia south to two counties in the northernmost part of the Florida panhandle, west to extreme eastern Texas. Regularly used in gardening.
Zones: 5–8, 9–5.
Form and Size: A rounded woody shrub with brown flaking and curling bark; to about 4 feet tall, nearly as wide in the garden; potentially approaching 9 feet tall.
Characteristics: Leaves 1–2½ inches long, less than ¾ inch wide. Flowers yellow, about 1½ inches across when fully open, with 5 yellow petals, 5 conspicuous sepals, and a mass of yellow stamens; appearing throughout the summer. Fruit a brown, conical, ⅜-inch capsule.
Culture: Performs well in mildly acidic to slightly alkaline soils. Often occurs in nature in association with limestone.
Typical Use: Probably best in mass plantings with other St. John's–worts. Can also be used in mixed shrub beds or as a specimen. Also useful as a background shrub for perennial beds.
Best Features: Rounded form, upright stature, and abundance of comparatively large, showy, yellow flowers.
Companion Plants: American beautyberry, Elliott's blueberry, native azaleas, other St.

John's–worts, purple coneflower, sweetshrub, virtually any species of *Coreopsis*, yaupon. Similar and Related Species: Approximately 40 species of St. John's–worts occur in the southeastern United States, with several potentially new garden selections currently under study. Although a few have found their way into gardening circles, many others have ornamental potential. Golden St. John's–wort is among the species with the largest and showiest flowers and is particularly suitable for wider garden use.

Possumhaw Holly

Ilex decidua Walter

Family: Aquifoliaceae (Holly)
Native Range and Habitat: Coastal plains, Piedmont, mountains. Floodplains, moist slopes, moist woodlands. Virginia to Kansas, south to peninsular Florida and eastern Texas.
Zones: 5–9, 9–1.
Form and Size: An upright, arching deciduous tree or multistemmed shrub with ascending branches, thin grayish bark, and a spreading crown; to about 30 feet tall in nature, usually shorter in the garden.

Possumhaw holly.

Characteristics: Leaves 1–3 inches long and 1½ inches wide; usually widest toward the tip with bluntly toothed margins. Flowers small; functionally male or female—some have a swollen ovary and reduced anthers, others have mature anthers and a diminutive ovary—with 5 white to greenish petals; typically appearing in spring either singly or in small clusters at the leaf axils. Fruit a red (yellow in some selections), rounded, multiseeded drupe about ¼ inch in diameter; borne in abundance in fall and very showy.
Culture: Occurs in wetlands in nature but adapts well to the garden in moist to somewhat dry conditions, especially when well established. Produces flowers and fruits in shade or sun, though more prolifically in at least partial sun.
Typical Use: Used in naturalistic woodland gardens, as a background to mixed shrub beds, along the taller sides of houses, to soften the corners of houses and commercial structures, within a mixed holly collection, or as an isolated specimen plant.
Best Features: The skeletal arching form is very attractive in winter; most valued for its prolific fruiting with fruit that lasts well into the winter and provides late-season forage for wintering birds.
Companion Plants: American beautyberry (white form), American holly, American hornbeam, bottlebrush buckeye, Elliott's blueberry, hophornbeam, red buckeye, serviceberry, swamp azalea, winterberry, witch-hazel.
Similar and Related Species: Several cultivars are available. 'Warrens Red' is one of the more popular red-fruited forms; 'Byers Golden' tops the list of yellow-fruited forms. Georgia holly (*I. longipes*) is similar in form and habit but has very long fruit stalks. Carolina holly (*I. ambigua*) is an upland species that is (or should be) becoming increasingly available in the market. Sarvis holly (*I. amelanchier*) is also an attractive deciduous small tree that is underrepresented in gardening. See Chapter 10 for more information about all of our southeastern native hollies.

Inkberry, Gallberry

Ilex glabra (Linnaeus) A. Gray

Inkberry.

Family: Aquifoliaceae (Holly)
Native Range and Habitat: Coastal plains, Piedmont. Pine flatwoods, margins of pineland depressions, swamps, savannas, drier longleaf pinelands. Essentially a coastal plains species, distributed largely in coastal states from New York south to Florida and west to Louisiana.
Zones: 5–9, 9–1.
Form and Size: A typically low-growing evergreen shrub; occasionally reaching 9 feet tall but usually not more than about half this height. Cultivars with dense foliage have been selected and are among the better choices for hedges and foundation plantings.
Characteristics: Leaves dark green, alternate, 1–2 inches long, less than half as wide, with small, blunt teeth near the apex. Flowers functionally male or female; small, with 5–8 white petals; borne in spring either singly or in branched clusters at the leaf axils. Fruit black (white on some selections), about ⅜ inch in diameter; borne in abundance in late summer and fall and persisting throughout the winter.
Culture: Prefers acidic soils and full sun. Occurs in nature in swamps and wetlands; performs best when mulched to ensure moist roots. Should be irrigated until established.
Typical Use: Among the best native species for foundations and hedges. Also excellent for use in mixed holly beds, shrub borders, or as a backdrop for perennial beds. An excellent native replacement for the black-fruited Japanese holly (*I. crenata*).
Best Features: Evergreen habit, dense form, extended fruiting period, abundant black fruit.
Companion Plants: Carolina jessamine, deerberry, highbush and lowbush blueberries, honeycups, native azaleas, sparkleberry, swamp azalea.
Similar and Related Species: Michael Dirr and John Alexander, writing in a 1991 issue of *Arnoldia*, suggest the cultivar 'Nigra' as among the best for maintaining a compact form. White-fruited forms include 'Alba' and forma *leucocarpa*. See Chapter 10 for more information about native hollies.

American Holly

Ilex opaca Aiton

Family: Aquifoliaceae (Holly)
Native Range and Habitat: Coastal plains, Piedmont, mountains. Widely distributed across many habitats from low, moist woodlands to dry ridges. Widespread across the eastern United States from New York and Massachusetts west to Missouri and south to eastern Texas and central Florida.
Zones: 5–9, 9–5.
Form and Size: Slow-growing, very attractive tree with laterally spreading branches, an

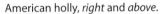
American holly, *right* and *above*.

open crown, straight trunk, and smooth, grayish bark. Among the more beautiful of our native trees.

Characteristics: Leaves dark green, shiny above, with spiny margins that can be piercing to the touch; 1–4 inches long, to about 2½ inches wide. Flowers functionally male or female; creamy white, 4-petaled, borne in spring either singly or in small clusters. Fruit a shiny, red, oval or rounded drupe about ⅜ inch in diameter; appearing in fall and persisting into winter.

Culture: Performs best in partial sun and mildly acidic soils. Tolerates brief flooding in nature but prefers well-drained soils in the garden.

Typical Use: Specimen tree. Be sure that male trees are situated nearby to ensure fruit production on female plants.

Best Features: The very attractive form, spiny evergreen foliage, attractive bark, and bright red (yellow on some selections) winter fruit commend this species to the garden.

Companion Plants: American beech, Ashe magnolia, atamasco lily, bigleaf magnolia, blue phlox, hophornbeam, sourwood, southern magnolia, sweetbay magnolia, sweetshrub, tulip poplar.

Similar and Related Species: Variety *arenicola*, with duller green and less spiny leaves, occurs in the sandy scrub of central peninsular Florida and is a popular holly for dry, sandy sites in USDA zone 9. Many cultivars of American holly have been named, but few are regularly available in the trade. The topal hollies (*I. ×attenuata*) constitute a collection of natural crosses between the American and dahoon (or myrtleleaf) hollies. They grow faster than American holly but retain some of its form and have become extremely popular for residential and roadside ornamentation. See Chapter 10 for more information about these and other native hollies.

Winterberry

Ilex verticillata (Linnaeus) A. Gray

Family: Aquifoliaceae (Holly)
Native Range and Habitat: Coastal plains, Piedmont, mountains. Bogs, floodplains, swamp

Winterberry Winter Red®.

Winterberry, *right* and *above*.

margins. Widespread across the entire eastern United States from Maine to Minnesota, south to several counties in the Florida panhandle, west to Louisiana and a single county in extreme eastern Texas. More common in the Piedmont and mountains.

Zones: 4–9, 9–1.

Form and Size: A large deciduous shrub; in the garden reaching at least 10 feet tall and equally as wide; reported to be potentially much taller in nature.

Characteristics: Leaves 1–4 inches long, to about 2½ inches wide, toothed, the veins on the upper surface with a distinctive and very attractive quilted appearance. Flowers functionally male or female with 5–7 white petals; appearing in spring. Fruit a round red drupe, about ¼ inch in diameter; borne in abundance and persisting well into winter; well-fruited plants are extremely attractive.

Culture: The combination of moist, well-drained, acidic soils in full sun produces the best fruiting response; does not tolerate alkaline soils. Will flower and fruit in relatively dense shade.

Typical Use: This is by far the most popular of our deciduous hollies, providing excellent winter ornamentation in massed plantings in large landscapes, along wetland edges, in naturalistic woodlands, as part of shrub borders, or as isolated specimens within open lawns.

Best Features: Most valued for its abundant fall and winter fruit.

Companion Plants: American hornbeam, bluestem palmetto, coastal and mountain witch-alder, needle palm, possumhaw holly, red buckeye, serviceberry, witch-hazel.

Similar and Related Species: Many cultivars and hybrids are available. Winter Red® and 'Red Sprite,' the former of which is particularly well suited for AHS zone 9, are among the more popular and easy to find in the trade. See Chapter 10 for more information about deciduous red-fruited native hollies.

Yaupon

Ilex vomitoria Aiton

Yaupon.

Family: Aquifoliaceae (Holly)

Native Range and Habitat: Coastal plains, Piedmont. Coastal forests, back dunes, sandy woods, moist hammocks. Essentially a coastal plains species distributed from extreme southeastern Virginia to south-central Florida and west to eastern Texas; perhaps escaped from gardens and not technically native to Virginia and North Carolina.

Zones: 7–11, 11–7.

Form and Size: In nature forming a sprawling upright shrub or small tree with spreading, drooping, and ascending branches; bark smooth, grayish, and attractive. The numerous forms and cultivars vary from low, compact, densely foliaged plants to upright weeping forms.

Yaupon.

Characteristics: Leaves stiff, leathery, oval in outline, with bluntly toothed or scalloped margins; typically not exceeding about 1 inch long and ½ inch wide, but some individuals, particularly those growing in shade, may produce somewhat larger leaves. Flowers functionally male or female with 4 creamy white petals; small; borne in spring on stalked clusters in the leaf axils. Fruit a lustrous, bright red, ⅛–¼-inch drupe, the outer covering often appearing translucent; appearing in fall and persisting throughout the winter.

Culture: Tolerant of widely divergent soil and exposure conditions from wet to xeric, acidic to alkaline, and full sun to shade. Our most adaptable native holly and among the most adaptable native plants.

Typical Use: Low, compact forms are excellent as low hedges, woodland borders, or to define paths and walkways; species plants with a more upright and freely branched form work well as naturalistic screens and unmanicured hedges; weeping forms are unsurpassed as specimen plants but can also be paired or grouped to decorate tall walls, accent building corners, or soften sharp angles.

Best Features: Dense foliage; availability of varying forms to suit virtually any situation; bright red winter fruit; adaptability; tolerance of widely divergent soil, drainage, and exposure regimens.

Companion Plants: American beautyberry, green haw, highbush and lowbush blueberries, needle palm, southern magnolia, sparkleberry, topal holly, wax myrtle.

Similar and Related Species: Yaupon is one of most highly successful native plants for landscaping and gardening and is regularly used for commercial and residential applications. Numerous low, compact, hedge-forming cultivars are available, as well as tall weeping forms and freely branching forms characteristic of the species. See Chapter 10 for more information about this and other evergreen native hollies.

Florida Anise, Florida Star-Anise

Illicium floridanum Ellis

Family: Illiciaceae (Star-Anise)

Native Range and Habitat: Coastal plains. Wet ravines, floodplain swamps. Extreme southwestern Georgia and the western Florida panhandle, west to southeastern Louisiana.

Zones: 7–9, 9–4.

Form and Size: Typically an irregularly branched evergreen shrub not exceeding about 10 feet tall in the garden; potentially achieving the proportions of a small 25-foot tree in its natural habitat. Plants that are pruned heavily when young can be trained to maintain a dense, shrublike stature.

Characteristics: Leaves dark green and leathery, without conspicuous venation; alternate, elliptic in outline, 2–6 inches long, about half as wide; giving off a conspicuous pungent aroma when crushed. Flowers red (occasionally lacking pigment and then white), primitive, with up to about 30 straplike and undifferentiated petals and sepals (tepals), 30–40 stamens, and about 15 pistils; appearing in late spring. Fruit a star-shaped collection of single-seeded follicles that split open forcibly at maturity to expel the seeds.

Florida anise.

Ocala anise.

Florida anise.

Ocala anise.

Culture: Prefers moist to wet organic, acidic soils. Occurs in nature at the edge of standing-water wetlands, usually where soil moisture is high. Will accommodate full sun if the roots are kept wet, but shade-grown plants have more attractive foliage with a deeper green color. Not drought tolerant.

Typical Use: Excellent for naturalistic landscapes, for shrub borders, to obscure building corners, or as a specimen for its interesting flowers and fruit.

Best Features: Primitive, red, many-parted flowers; evergreen habit. An excellent collector's item.

Companion Plants: Ashe magnolia, bigleaf magnolia, Elliott's blueberry, Florida leucothoe, inkberry, native azaleas, Ocala anise, red buckeye, Virginia sweetspire, Walter viburnum.

Similar and Related Species: About a dozen cultivars are available, including the white-flowered 'Alba' and 'Semmes' and the lavender-pink-flowered 'Shady Lady,' the latter two of which are available from Dodd and Dodd Native Nurseries. The closely related and similar Ocala anise (*I. parviflorum*), a rare species in nature that is restricted to only a few counties near Ocala, Florida, has become a widely used and much-favored landscape shrub; it may be even more popular than Florida anise. Such large wholesale growers as Monrovia sell Ocala anise, and it has found use well beyond its restricted range, normally being recommended for zones 7–9, 9–7. Typical plants have a densely foliaged form with medium green, ascending leaves. Although its small, greenish yellow flowers (pictured) are not showy, Ocala anise is excellent for hedges (pictured), foundation plantings, or as a background shrub, and it has proved to be one of the more successful native landscape plants. See Chapter 8 for more about both of our native anises.

Virginia Sweetspire, Virginia Willow

Itea virginica Linnaeus

Family: Iteaceae (Sweetspire)

Native Range and Habitat: Coastal plains, Piedmont, mountains. Swamps, streamside wetlands, moist woods. Eastern United States from Pennsylvania west to Missouri, south to south-central Florida, west to eastern Texas.

Zones: 6–9, 10–7.

Form and Size: Slender, open-branched deciduous shrub in its natural habitat, often with a denser form in the garden, depending upon cultivar; 3–6 feet tall, about as wide.

Characteristics: Leaves alternate, more or less oval in outline, 2–4 inches long, 1–1½ inches wide, with finely toothed margins. Flowers white, borne on crowded, elongated, curving racemes; produced in abundance in late spring and early summer, making the plant very attractive. Fruit a tiny brown capsule.

Culture: Prefers moist, acidic soils but is very adaptable. Flowers best in full sun but tolerates shade.

Typical Use: An excellent addition to

Virginia sweetspire.

shrub borders and naturalistic woodlands. Effective when used as part of a mixed shrub bed as well as along the margins of streams and wetlands.

Best Features: The long racemes of creamy white flowers are very attractive; several cultivars are valued for their striking fall foliage.

Companion Plants: Buttonbush, climbing aster, dahoon holly, Florida leucothoe, inkberry, red maple, swamp dogwood, titi.

Similar and Related Species: Often confused with the similar sweet pepperbush; most easily distinguished by the leaf margins being toothed from tip to base rather than just along the upper two-thirds of the leaf. Several cultivars are available, the more popular of which include 'Henry's Garnet,' with burgundy to purplish fall foliage, and 'Little Henry,' with similarly attractive fall foliage but with a smaller stature and somewhat shorter flower racemes.

Mountain Laurel

Kalmia latifolia Linnaeus

Family: Ericaceae (Heath)

Native Range and Habitat: Coastal plains, Piedmont, mountains. Bluffs, ravines, moist forests, bogs, sandhill streams; from nearly sea level to at least 5,000 feet. Eastern United States, Maine south to northern Florida, west to Indiana and Louisiana.

Zones: 5–9, 9–5.

Form and Size: An evergreen, openly branched shrub ordinarily to about 10 feet tall; old plants can be taller, potentially to 30 feet in nature; trunks of older plants often crooked, contorted, and very attractive.

Characteristics: Leaves alternate, leathery, elliptic in outline, without evident venation; 2–5 inches long,

Mountain laurel.

to about 2 inches wide. Flowers cup-shaped, white to reddish pink, borne in densely flowered inflorescences and very attractive; with 10 stamens lodged in pockets in the petals, poised to spring forward forcibly, catapulting pollen onto the backs of visiting bees; typically appearing from about April to June but as late as August at high elevations. Fruit a brown capsule.

Culture: Adaptable; performs best in moist, acidic, well-drained soils; often found in shade in nature but flowers best in sun in the garden; prompt removal of spent flowers ensures abundant flower production every year.

Typical Use: Shrub borders, naturalistic landscapes, specimen.

Best Features: Evergreen habit; interesting, very attractive, abundantly produced flowers.

Companion Plants: Ashe magnolia, atamasco lily, bigleaf magnolia, coastal and mountain witch-alders, drooping leucothoe, flowering dogwood, Indian pink, native azaleas, red buckeye, redbud, sweetshrub, witch-hazel.

Similar and Related Species: Six species of *Kalmia* occur in the southeast, of which mountain laurel is the more widely used in gardening. Cultivars accentuating variability in flower color are available, many of which are of northern provenance and do not perform well in the Deep South. See Chapter 7 for more about mountain laurel and related species.

Drooping Leucothoe, Mountain Doghobble

Leucothoe fontanesiana (Steudel) Sleumer

Family: Ericaceae (Heath)
Native Range and Habitat: Piedmont and mountains. Ravines, moist slopes, stream edges. Virginia and Kentucky south to northern Georgia and northwestern South Carolina; essentially endemic to the southern Appalachians and upper Piedmont. Not suitable for use in the coastal plains.
Zones: 5–8, 8–5.
Form and Size: A spreading and arching evergreen shrub to about 6 feet tall and wide.
Characteristics: Leaves alternate, lance-shaped or long-elliptic, 2–5 inches long, about half as wide; green in spring and summer, turning a purplish bronzy color in late fall and winter. Flowers white, small, urn-shaped; borne abundantly in congested, elongated, 2–4-inch racemes from the leaf axils; appearing April–May. Fruit a brown capsule, maturing in early fall.
Culture: Can be difficult to grow; prefers wet to moist well-drained soils in shady, high-humidity situations; not drought tolerant.
Typical Use: Shrub borders, naturalistic landscapes, foundations, massed in single- or multiple-species shrub beds.
Best Features: Graceful stature, attractive leaf color, abundant flowering.
Companion Plants: American hornbeam, bigleaf magnolia, blueberries, mountain laurel, native azaleas, red buckeye.

Similar and Related Species: Several species of *Leucothoe* and *Agarista* have similar foliage. Coastal plains gardeners can use doghobble (*L. axillaris*) as a replacement for drooping leucothoe. The drooping leucothoe cultivar 'Whitewater' is an interesting variegated form with attractive dark green leaves with ivory white margins. See Chapter 7 for more information about these and other members of the heath family.

Drooping leucothoe.

Spicebush

Lindera benzoin (Linnaeus) Blume

Family: Lauraceae (Laurel)
Native Range and Habitat: Coastal plains, Piedmont, mountains. Bottomlands, swamps, floodplains, rich woods. Widespread across the east from Maine south to central peninsular Florida, west to Kansas, Oklahoma, and Texas.

Spicebush, *left* and *above*.

Zones: 4–9, 8–1.

Form and Size: A delicate deciduous shrub or small understory tree; usually less than 12 feet tall in the garden, potentially a little taller in nature; twigs, leaves, and fruit pleasantly aromatic when crushed.

Characteristics: Leaves alternate, medium green, oval or reverse-egg-shaped in outline; 2–5 inches long, 1–2 inches wide. Flowers yellow, individually small; male and female flowers borne in separate clusters in early spring (typically March–April), well before the new leaves emerge. Fruit a bright red, ⅜-inch drupe, maturing in early fall, August–September.

Culture: Performs best in moist, neutral to slightly alkaline soils (use lime to sweeten very acidic soils), and at least partial shade; plants in cool climates can be given more sun; plants situated in full sun in warmer climes perform best when adequately mulched and regularly irrigated to ensure a cooler root zone.

Typical Use: As a specimen, in mixed shrub beds, as an accent plant for shrubby borders, or to decorate and provide color to shady corners.

Best Features: The early flowers, bright red fruit, and delicate form are the chief attributes.

Companion Plants: American hornbeam, atamasco lily, blue phlox, flowering dogwood, Indian pink, mayapple, mountain laurel, redbud, silverbell, swamp chestnut oak, trilliums, Walter's violet, white oak, wild columbine.

Similar and Related Species: Several species of the laurel family have similar leaves. This is the only garden species with bright red fruit. This and other species are under attack by an alien Japanese ambrosia beetle that infects trees in the laurel family with a fungus that completely kills infected plants. The disease, laurel wilt, was first noted in 2002 near Savannah, Georgia, but has rapidly spread north and south along the coast as well as inland. Unless a control mechanism can be found, it is reasonable to believe that the disease can devastate and perhaps eliminate much of the laurel family in the eastern United States. See Chapter 8 for more information about this disease and other members of the laurel family.

Cardinal Flower

Lobelia cardinalis Linnaeus

Family: Campanulaceae (Bellflower)

Native Range and Habitat: Coastal plains, Piedmont, mountains. Marshes, edges of clear-water streams, swamp forests. Widespread across the entire eastern United States, west to California.

Zones: 2–9, 9–1.

Form and Size: An upright, dark green herbaceous perennial; 18–24 inches tall in the garden, potentially to about 6 feet tall in nature, especially in the southern parts of its range.

Characteristics: Leaves elliptic to lance-shaped, to about 7 inches long and 2 inches wide; leaves at base much larger than those above. Flowers scarlet or crimson red (white- to pink-flowered forms are known), borne abundantly along an erect raceme; two-lipped, the uppermost lip with two divisions, the one below with three; appearing in summer and fall, July–October. Fruit a conspicuous, brown, $\frac{3}{8}$-inch capsule.

Culture: Performs best in partial shade and moist soil; not drought tolerant; typically short-lived, perhaps less than three years; forms a basal leaf cluster during winter that should be only lightly covered by mulch or not mulched at all.

Cardinal flower.

Typical Use: Showy wildflower for moist gardens; excellent as a single specimen or massed in a single- or multiple-species perennial bed.

Best Features: The bright red flowers are very showy and attract hummingbirds.

Companion Plants: Arrowwood, blue mistflower, cinnamon fern, coontie, coreopsis, dahoon holly, purple coneflower, red buckeye, red maple, royal fern, sweetbay magnolia.

Similar and Related Species: Several species of *Lobelia* occur in the southeast, some of which are used in gardening. Cardinal flower is the only one with red flowers, but Sunlight Gardens offers several interesting color variations. Giant blue lobelia (*L. siphilitica*) is the most popular and readily available blue-flowered species. See Chapter 5 for more information about cardinal flower.

Coral Honeysuckle

Lonicera sempervirens Linnaeus

Family: Caprifoliaceae (Honeysuckle)

Native Range and Habitat: Coastal plains, Piedmont, mountains. Dry woods, sandhills, maritime forests. Widespread in the east, from Maine to Iowa south to peninsular Florida and eastern Texas.

Zones: 4–10, 10–1.

Form and Size: Woody, climbing, nearly evergreen or late-deciduous vine to about 15 feet long; climbs and scrambles over vegetation, trees, and trellises; occasionally forms a weakly erect shrub.

Characteristics: Leaves opposite; mature leaves elliptic, 1–3 inches long, up to 2 inches wide; new leaves often

Coral honeysuckle.

very narrow and uncharacteristic of older leaves; terminal pair usually perfoliate (with bases of opposing leaves fused around the stem). Flowers tubular and trumpet-shaped, red to orange (rarely yellow), to about 2 inches long and borne in showy, terminal clusters; typically appearing March–July. Fruit a red ¼-inch berry; borne in clusters and showy; appearing July–September.

Culture: Performs best as a climber on trellises, trees, or other structures in full sun; moist acidic to neutral soils are best, but it is surprisingly drought tolerant and not uncommon in xeric turkey-oak woodlands; will flower in shade, but less profusely.

Typical Use: Most often used as a climbing vine on trellises, fences, and low-branched trees.

Best Features: The showy flowers and fruit and nonaggressive climbing habit are the chief attributes; an excellent hummingbird plant.

Companion Plants: American beautyberry, Carolina jessamine, coralbean, haws, yaupon.

Similar and Related Species: Numerous selections and cultivars are available, including the yellow-flowered 'Sulphurea,' which is probably not appropriate south of AHS Heat Zone 9. See Chapter 14 for more information about this and other native climbing vines.

Ashe Magnolia

Magnolia ashei Weatherby

Family: Magnoliaceae (Magnolia)
Native Range and Habitat: Coastal plains. Slopes, bluffs, rich woods. Rare in nature; endemic and restricted in distribution only to the Florida panhandle, but widely used in landscaping across the eastern United States, mostly in the Piedmont and coastal plains.
Zones: 6–9, 9–6 (potentially farther north).
Form and Size: Small deciduous tree or some- what gangling shrub with an erect trunk, thick, spreading branches, grayish bark, large winter buds, and an attractive form. Mature

Ashe magnolia.

plants in nature may reach 40 feet, but 25 feet is more common. Cultivated plants are often shorter, and even very young plants only 2–3 feet tall will produce flowers.

Characteristics: Leaves very large with a tropical aspect; up to about 18 inches long and about 10 inches wide, with an eared (auricled) base; green above, silvery white below. Flowers very large, up to about 1 foot wide when fully open, typically with 9 creamy white, fleshy tepals (undifferentiated petals and sepals), at least a few of which often bear a purplish blotch at the base; typically appearing April–May. Fruit a conelike aggregation of individual follicles, each follicle splitting in fall to expose a red-coated seed.

Culture: Occurs as an understory tree, but performs well and flowers best in sun. Prefers acidic soil and good drainage; will develop root rot and suffer if soil remains wet. Becomes more densely foliaged in full sun.

Typical Use: Often seen as a specimen plant or in mixed, naturalistic woodlands. An excellent and unique tree for residential landscapes that is sure to attract the attention of visiting gardeners and passersby.

Best Features: The large leaves and flowers are very attractive, and the winter form is excellent. Interesting fruit.

Companion Plants: Atamasco lily, blue phlox, flowering dogwood, fringe tree, Indian pink, mountain laurel, native azaleas, redbud, trilliums, wild columbine, wild hydrangea.

Similar and Related Species: Some authorities consider Ashe magnolia to be a subspecies of the more widespread bigleaf magnolia. The flowers and leaves of the two are very similar, but bigleaf magnolia becomes larger and takes longer to reach flowering age. See Chapter 8 for more information about growing all of our native deciduous magnolias.

Southern Magnolia

Magnolia grandiflora Linnaeus

Family: Magnoliaceae (Magnolia)
Native Range and Habitat: Coastal plains, Piedmont (where originally rare in nature). Maritime forests, rich, moist woodlands, hammocks. Largely restricted to the coastal plains from Virginia south to peninsular Florida, west to easternmost Texas. Widely used in gardening and landscaping and now naturalized in many parts of the Piedmont, where it commonly invades and becomes weedy in rich, shady woodlands, potentially to the detriment of early spring ephemeral wildflowers.

Zones: 6–9, 9–6 (depending upon selection).

Form and Size: A large evergreen tree to at least 100 feet tall at maturity with smooth, grayish bark, large branches, and a large, spreading crown; numerous selections are available, several of which mature to a smaller, more compact size. May lose many of its leaves in winter in cold climates.

Southern magnolia.

Characteristics: Leaves leathery, stiff, elliptical, 4–8 inches long (or a little longer), to about 4 inches wide; often with downwardly rolled margins; dark green above and rusty, brownish, or pale green below, depending upon cultivar. Flowers large with several creamy white tepals, opening as the pistils mature; typically appearing in late spring and early summer but sometimes continuing throughout summer. Fruit a conelike aggregate of follicles; follicles maturing in fall (usually October) and splitting to expose attractive, red-coated, and often dangling seeds.

Culture: Tolerant of varying conditions from dry, xeric sites to rich, acidic woodlands. Performs well and flowers best in full sun but is tolerant of heavy shade. Surface roots should be mulched heavily for moisture retention and protection.

Typical Use: Species trees can be used as specimens in large landscapes. Smaller, more compact cultivars are often used as part of a tall screening hedge, as specimens, or to decorate nooks and corners. An excellent, highly valued, and long-used native tree.

Best Features: Evergreen habit; dark green leaves with attractive undersurfaces; large white flowers and extended flowering period; availability of numerous cultivars and selections of varying forms and sizes.

Companion Plants: American ash, American beech, hophornbeam, Shumard oak, swamp chestnut oak, willow oak. Not conducive to underplanting.

Similar and Related Species: More than 100 cultivars are available, of which 'Bracken's Brown Beauty,' 'Edith Bogue,' 'Kay Paris,' and 'Little Gem' are among the more popular. See Chapter 8 for more information about some of these cultivars and about growing all of our native magnolias.

Sweetbay Magnolia

Magnolia virginiana Linnaeus

Family: Magnoliaceae (Magnolia)

Native Range and Habitat: Coastal plains, Piedmont, mountains. Swamps, wetlands, marshy edges, coastal swamps and depressions. Long Island, New York, south to southernmost Florida, west to extreme eastern Texas. More common in the coastal plains than elsewhere.

Zones: 6–10, 10–6.

Form and Size: Two varieties are recognized. Variety *australis*, the southern form, is a mostly evergreen (deciduous in zones 6–7) single-trunked tree to about 100 feet tall. Variety *virginiana*, the northern form, often expresses itself as a large, multistemmed deciduous shrub to about 30 feet tall. Both have grayish bark and an attractive form.

Characteristics: Leaves 3–6 inches long, about 2 inches wide, narrowly elliptical in outline; yellowish green to dark green above and silvery below, giving trees a two-toned appearance in a breeze. Flowers smaller than other native magnolias with up to about 15 creamy white tepals but not exceeding about 3 inches across the open blossom; appearing after new leaf development, April–July. Fruit a globular 2-inch aggregate of follicles, appearing July–October; follicles splitting at maturity to reveal attractive red-coated seeds.

Sweetbay magnolia, *left* and *above*.

Culture: A wetland tree of acidic soils in nature but adaptable in the garden to surprisingly dry sites. Not sensitive to root rot, unlike other magnolia species.

Typical Use: Used as a specimen shrub or tree. Especially useful in wetland restoration or to decorate the margins of wetland depressions and drainages.

Best Features: The two-toned leaves are very attractive. Multistemmed plants make attractive shrubs along large walkways or woodland borders.

Companion Plants: Inkberry, Jenkins' fetterbush, loblolly bay, netted chain fern, red maple, swamp azalea, titi, Virginia chain fern, Virginia sweetspire.

Similar and Related Species: This is one of only two native evergreen magnolias. Several cultivars are available in the trade, but species trees are more often used in gardening. See Chapter 8 for more information about growing all of our native magnolias.

Wax Myrtle

Morella cerifera (Linnaeus) Small

Family: Myricaceae (Bayberry)

Native Range and Habitat: Coastal plains. Numerous habitats from pine flatwoods to sandy pinelands, swamp and marsh edges, dune swales, and maritime forests. Widely planted and potentially naturalized beyond its typical habitats and native range. Coastal Virginia, south to southernmost Florida, west to eastern Texas.

Zones: 6–10, 10–6.

Form and Size: Typically a large, evergreen, multistemmed shrub but potentially forming a small tree to more than 35 feet tall. Dioecious, with

Southern wax myrtle.

male and female flowers borne on separate plants. The lower portions of older plants may lack foliage.

Characteristics: Leaves alternate, reverse-lance-shaped in outline, 1–6 inches long, less than 1 inch wide, with toothed margins. Flowers individually tiny but borne in conspicuous catkins at the leaf axils; typically appearing in April. Fruit a knobby, bluish, rounded ⅛-inch drupe; borne in erect clusters and appearing August–October.

Culture: One of the most adaptable and widely used southern native shrubs. Easy to grow, tolerant of abuse, and widely used in shady and sunny situations. Prefers acidic to neutral soils.

Typical Use: A popular landscape shrub for woodland borders, hedges, and foundation plantings, and to obscure the borders of backyard decks. Widely used in commercial plantings, for roadside beautification, and for landscaping highway rest areas.

Best Features: Evergreen habit and easy cultivation.

Companion Plants: American beautyberry, Georgia calamint, inkberry, live oak, Shumard oak, yaupon; underplanting with yaupon or inkberry will serve to mitigate wax myrtle's tendency to lose its lower foliage.

Similar and Related Species: Many reference books still list this species as *Myrica cerifera*. Several cultivars are available in nurseries. A smaller form, *M. pumila*, which does not exceed about 3 feet tall, is recognized by some authorities. Other dwarf selections are also available, many of which grow to about 6 feet tall. Zone 6 gardeners may want to try the very similar northern bayberry (*M. pensylvanica*).

Purple Muhly Grass

Muhlenbergia capillaris (Lamarck) Trinius

Family: Poaceae (Grass)
Native Range and Habitat: Coastal plains, Piedmont, mountains. Savannas, dry woodlands, grasslands. Widespread in the east, New York south to southern peninsular Florida, west to Texas and Kansas.
Zones: 7–10, 10–6.
Form and Size: A robust perennial bunchgrass to at least 3 feet tall and 3 feet wide with long, very narrow leaves and a conspicuous show of purplish fall flowers.
Characteristics: Leaves inrolled and rounded, similar in shape to a pine needle but up to about 3 feet long; gray-brown in winter, greenish in summer. Flowers individually tiny but borne in long, very showy purplish panicles above the leaves from late August to October. Fruit a tiny, inconspicuous grain.
Culture: Robust and easy to grow in slightly acidic to alkaline soils in full sun to very light shade. Drought and salt tolerant; does best with at least a little moisture. In the Piedmont, purple muhly prefers clayey or thin rocky soils.
Typical Use: Excellent in massed plantings, along walkways and foundations, as a backdrop for mixed perennial beds, along roadsides, in ditches, along woodland borders, or as an element in mixed beds of ornamental grasses.
Best Features: Evergreen habit and attractive fall flowering period.
Companion Plants: Best when massed or planted in isolated beds but may be augmented with other native grasses such as broomsedges, bluestems, lovegrass, and wiregrass. Longleaf pine makes an effective overstory.
Similar and Related Species: There are numerous species of native grasses, of which purple muhly is one of the more popular and widely used.

Alabama Snow-Wreath

Neviusia alabamensis A. Gray

Family: Rosaceae (Rose)
Native Range and Habitat: Piedmont and mountains. Moist, limestone-studded woods. Spottily distributed in six eastern states, including Alabama, Arkansas, Georgia, Mississippi, Missouri, and Tennessee.

Alabama snow-wreath, *left* and *above*.

Zones: 4–8, 8–1.

Form and Size: A sprawling deciduous shrub to about 6 feet tall and 6 feet wide; often with a pale appearance.

Characteristics: Leaves alternate, 1–3 inches long, with doubly toothed margins. Flowers white, lacking petals, produced in showy inflorescences of several headlike clusters composed of numerous stamens all radiating from a central point. Fruit a tiny achene.

Culture: Prefers well-drained neutral to alkaline soils in full sun to light shade; benefits from the addition of lime to acidic soils. Can be pruned following flowering to maintain size and shape.

Typical Use: Used mostly as a specimen or as part of a naturalistic hedge.

Best Features: Flowers often appear in great masses, making this species very attractive during its spring flowering period. Sought by native plant enthusiasts as a collector's item.

Companion Plants: Carolina rose, flowering dogwood, coastal witch-alder, hawthorns, ninebark, redbud.

Similar and Related Species: This is one of several native roses used in southern gardening. Ninebark (*Physocarpus opulifolius*) is similar. See Chapter 11 for more information about this and other native roses.

Blackgum, Sour Gum

Nyssa sylvatica Marshall

Family: Nyssaceae (Tupelo)

Native Range and Habitat: Coastal plains, Piedmont, mountains. Moist upland forests, rich woodlands, pine savannas. Widespread in the east, Maine to Wisconsin, south to north-central Florida and eastern Texas. Blackgum is an important component in the colorful autumn tapestry that clothes the southern Appalachian Mountains.

Zones: 4–9, 9–2.

Blackgum, *left* and *above*.

Form and Size: A large deciduous tree with a straight trunk, grayish bark, and laterally spreading branches that diverge at nearly right angles from the bole; very attractive in form and shape; mature trees can be at least 100 feet tall; the heights of very large trees can exceed 140 feet; cultivated trees grow relatively slowly and are often well under 100 feet.

Characteristics: Leaves alternate, 3–6 inches long, often with one or two large teeth along the margins; turning bright red in autumn. Flowers tiny, borne in separate male and female inflorescences, some trees with both male and female flowers, others with only male flowers; appearing April–June. Fruit an ellipsoid, blue-black, ⅜-inch drupe; appearing August–October.

Culture: Performs best in moderately acidic, well-drained soils in full to partial sun. Intolerant of highly alkaline soils.

Typical Use: Typically used as a specimen tree in open landscapes or in naturalistic woodlands.

Best Features: The lateral branches and spreading crown make this one of our most attractive native trees. Valued in fall for its striking and vibrant color.

Companion Plants: Flowering dogwood, fringe tree, mountain laurel, native azaleas, Shumard oak, southern sugar maple, spruce pine, sugar maple, swamp chestnut oak, white oak, willow oak, witch-hazel.

Similar and Related Species: At least four species of *Nyssa* occur in the southeast (some authorities accept five species). Only blackgum is a predominately upland species. Swamp blackgum (*N. biflora*), water tupelo (*N. aquatica*), and ogeechee tupelo (*N. ogeche*) are also often seen in the nursery trade but are less commonly available than blackgum.

Cinnamon Fern

Osmunda cinnamomea Linnaeus

Family: Osmundaceae (Royal Fern)

Native Range and Habitat: Coastal plains, Piedmont, mountains. Bogs, wet edges, swamp margins, borders of freshwater marshes, floodplains, pocosins. Widespread across the eastern United States, Maine to Minnesota, south to southernmost Florida and eastern Texas.

Zones: 3–10, 10–1.

Form and Size: A large clump-forming fern with erect, pale to medium green fronds 2–5 feet tall.

Characteristics: Sterile fronds large with expanded blade tissue and spreading pinnae. Fertile fronds very showy, lacking blade tissue and covered with thousands of cinnamon-colored sori (clusters of spore cases) that contain the reproductive spores.

Culture: Does best in moist to wet acidic soils in full sun or shade. Adapts to typical garden conditions but often requires at least periodic irrigation.

Typical Use: Especially effective along wetland edges, pond margins, artificial and natural bogs, or in other wet areas. An interesting addition to moist mixed fern beds.

Best Features: The clump-forming habit, upright stature, and interesting fertile fronds are this species' more important attributes.

Companion Plants: Bluestem palmetto, climbing aster, dahoon holly, inkberry, Jenkins' fetterbush, needle palm, netted chain fern, red maple, river birch, sweetbay magnolia, royal fern, Virginia chain fern.

Cinnamon fern.

Similar and Related Species: Three species of *Osmunda* occur in the southeast. Royal fern (*O. regalis* var. *spectabilis*), another wetland species available in the trade, is also used in gardening where adequate moisture is available. Its fronds are sterile below and fertile above and divided into numerous pinnae (leaflets). Interrupted fern (*O. claytoniana*) is similar in form to cinnamon fern, except that the fertile pinnae are borne near the center of the blade rather than on a separate frond. Interrupted fern is seldom available in the nursery trade.

Hophornbeam

Ostrya virginiana (P. Miller) K. Koch

Family: Betulaceae (Birch)

Native Range and Habitat: Coastal plains, Piedmont, mountains. Moist to dry woodlands and forests. Widespread across the eastern United States from Maine to North Dakota, south to north-central Florida and eastern Texas.

Zones: 5–9, 9–2.

Form and Size: A small to medium-sized graceful deciduous tree with brownish, flaking and scaly bark; usually not exceeding about 35 feet tall in cultivation.

Characteristics: Leaves alternate, elliptic, 2–4 inches long, 1–2 inches wide, borne in a

Hophornbeam.

two-ranked, spraylike arrangement along the branch; margins doubly toothed (smaller teeth between larger ones). Flowers tiny and individually inconspicuous; male and female flowers borne in separate catkins; male catkins pendent, 1–2 inches long and dangling from the axils of newly developing leaves near the tip of the twig; female catkins small, about ¼ inch long and borne at the branch tips. Fruit hoplike, consisting of an overlapping collection of thin, papery sacs that contain the seeds.

Culture: Prefers moist to somewhat dry, well-drained, acidic soils. Tolerant of sun or moderate shade.

Typical Use: Appropriate as a specimen tree, overtopping shrub beds, or as a component of naturalistic woodlands. Attractive when planted in groups of three or five.

Best Features: The scaly bark, small size, interesting fruit, and graceful form make this an excellent tree for small gardens and landscapes.

Companion Plants: Flowering dogwood, fringe tree, native azaleas, red buckeye, redbud, southern sugar maple, sweetshrub, winged elm.

Similar and Related Species: This is the only species of *Ostrya* native to the east (another occurs in the southwest). Several closely related species of native birch and alder are used extensively in southern gardening and landscape design, including American hornbeam and river birch.

Sourwood

Oxydendrum arboreum (Linnaeus) Augustin de Candolle

Family: Ericaceae (Heath)

Native Range and Habitat: Coastal plains, Piedmont, mountains. Upland forests, oak-hickory woodlands, sandy woods, coastal and Fall Line sandhills. New York to Illinois and south to northwest Florida and Louisiana.

Zones: 5–9, 9–3.

Form and Size: A medium-sized to relatively large deciduous tree to about 75 feet tall; often shorter in the garden; bark dark brown, furrowed, and very attractive; typical trees display a characteristic leaning habit.

Characteristics: Leaves alternate, narrowly elliptic with a long tip and finely toothed margins; blades 3–7 inches long, to about 3 inches wide; turning bright red to somewhat burgundy in fall; one of the showiest autumn trees of southern Appalachian forests. Flowers

Sourwood, *right* and *above*.

white, bell-shaped, about ¼ inch long, borne along one side of an attractive cluster of long, curving racemes. Fruit a hard, 5-valved capsule, the remains of which are evident on the tree for an extended period.

Culture: Does best in moist to relatively dry, well-drained, acidic soils. Easy to grow.

Typical Use: Valued as a specimen tree or for naturalistic woodlands.

Best Features: The leaning form, fall leaf color (even in coastal plains settings), and attractive inflorescences are the most ornamental attributes.

Companion Plants: Blackgum, drooping leucothoe, highbush blueberries, hophornbeam, mountain laurel, native azaleas and rhododendrons.

Similar and Related Species: Sourwood is the heath family's only large tree. Although it is included within the same family as the blueberries, azaleas, and mountain laurel, recent evidence suggests that it is genetically isolated from other members of the family. See Chapter 7 for more information about the heath family.

Allegheny-Spurge

Pachysandra procumbens Michaux

Family: Buxaceae (Boxwood)

Native Range and Habitat: Coastal plains, Piedmont, mountains. Rich woods. Primarily a species of the mountains and Upper Piedmont, confined largely to south-central Kentucky and central Tennessee southward to northern Alabama, Mississippi, and northwestern Georgia. Disjunct populations occur in single counties in North Carolina, the Florida panhandle, and eastern Louisiana.

Zones: 5–9, 9–5.

Form and Size: A low, evergreen to partly deciduous, shrublike perennial groundcover spreading by underground stems; typical plants do not exceed about 12 inches tall.

Characteristics: Leaves alternate, 2–4 inches long, irregular in outline, coarsely toothed along the margins, green above with lighter mottling. Flowers small, creamy white to

Allegheny-spurge.

tan, borne in erect, 2–4-inch racemes arising from the base of the plant; appearing March–April. Fruit a capsule.

Culture: Occurs naturally in rich, moist, organic soil, sometimes in association with limestone; tolerates acidic to neutral soils and deep shade.

Typical Use: An excellent woodland groundcover; not overly aggressive but will spread in the garden, especially where shaded and protected in winter.

Best Features: The low, spreading form, interesting inflorescences, and evergreen habit make this a good groundcover for much of USDA zones 6–7.

Companion Plants: Best as a dominant planting intermixed with woodland spring wildflowers such as atamasco lily, blue phlox, trilliums, and yellowroot.

Similar and Related Species: No native garden species are similar. The less attractive Japanese spurge (*P. terminalis*) is comparable and has become a widely used groundcover in USDA zones 6–8. It typically does not expand into adjacent woodlands and is generally not considered invasive, but it is difficult to eradicate once established.

Blue Phlox, Woodland Blue Phlox

Phlox divaricata Linnaeus

Family: Polemoniaceae (Jacob's-Ladder)

Native Range and Habitat: Coastal plains, Piedmont, mountains. Rich, shaded woods and deciduous hardwood forests. Widespread in the east from Vermont west to South Dakota, south to the Florida panhandle and Texas.

Zones: 4–8, 8–1.

Form and Size: Perennial herb to about 15 inches tall and topped with an attractive inflorescence of blue flowers.

Characteristics: Leaves lance-shaped, opposite, 1–2 inches long, borne in well-separated pairs along the stem; remaining green and evident long after flowering. Flowers tubular below, flaring above into 5 blue, ½-inch lobes that are notched at the apex; typically appearing April–May. Fruit a ¼-inch, papery capsule.

Blue phlox.

Culture: Shady woodlands with morning sun are best; tolerates neutral, slightly acidic, or slightly alkaline soils.

Typical Use: Used most often as one component in a spring woodland wildflower bed or in a naturalistic woodland setting.

Best Features: The spring flowering period, very attractive blue flowers, and leaves that appear before the flowers and remain after flowers are gone make this an excellent garden perennial.

Companion Plants: Allegheny-spurge, American beech, American hornbeam, atamasco lily, foamflower, Indian pink, Shumard oak, southern magnolia, trilliums, Walter's violet, wild columbine.

Similar and Related Species: The genus *Phlox* is a taxonomically complicated group of plants containing numerous species, many of which are used in gardening and roadside beautification. About 20 species occur in the southeastern United States. Blue phlox is the only truly blue native species. Several cultivars of blue phlox are available, typically varying in flower color. The flowers of 'Dirigo Ice' are lavender, those of 'Fuller's White' are very pale blue to nearly white, and those of 'Louisiana' are deep purplish blue. See Chapter 14 for more on this and other early spring wildflowers.

Ninebark

Physocarpus opulifolius (Linnaeus) Maximowicz

Family: Rosaceae (Rose)

Native Range and Habitat: Coastal plains, Piedmont, mountains. Stream banks, cliffs, calcareous rock outcrops. Predominantly a Piedmont and mountain species from Maine west to the Dakotas, south to a single population in northwest Florida, west to extreme eastern Oklahoma. Uncommon in Georgia and Alabama.

Zones: 3–8, 8–1.

Form and Size: Large, spreading, multistemmed deciduous shrub to about 10 feet tall and wide; forms a compact, densely fo-

Ninebark.

liated shrub with erect shoots in full sun; bark of older stems peeling and shredding but often obscured by the numerous branches and dense foliage.

Characteristics: Leaves alternate, 1–3 inches long, up to 2 inches wide, toothed along the margins, with 3 main veins arising from the base. Flowers long stalked, borne in showy, several-flowered umbellike clusters (actually a raceme) at the tips of new branches; individual flowers small, with 5 tiny, white to pinkish petals; appearing May–July. Fruit a ¼-inch, 2-valved pod.

Culture: Tolerant of acidic and alkaline soils, drought, and full sun or light shade; a tough plant adapted to a variety of uses. May be severely pruned in late fall to maintain size, or allowed to grow to maximum dimensions.

Typical Use: Effective in naturalistic borders and hedges, shrubby edges, along slopes to control erosion, or for screening.

Best Features: The dense, tangled form and numerous flowers are the chief attributes. Perhaps less often used in gardening and landscaping than it should be.

Companion Plants: Typically used alone. Companions might include Alabama snow-wreath, Ocala anise, and several of the St. John's-worts.

Similar and Related Species: Numerous species of the rose family are used in landscaping. None are similar to ninebark except Alabama snow-wreath, which is comparable in form but not in flowers. The cultivar 'Nanus' is a dwarf form of ninebark that grows to about 6 feet tall and wide and has become a popular choice for this species. Although several references suggest USDA zone 7 as ninebark's southern limit, plants perform well in gardens in the Florida panhandle. See Chapter 11 for more information on native roses.

Spruce Pine

Pinus glabra Walter

Family: Pinaceae (Pine)

Native Range and Habitat: Coastal plains. Rich slopes, bottomland woods, temperate hardwood forests. Confined to the southeast from southeastern South Carolina south to north-central Florida and west to Louisiana; absent in our region of coverage only from Virginia and North Carolina.

Zones: 8–9, 9–8.

Spruce pine, *right* and *above*.

Form and Size: Medium to large, single-trunked evergreen tree to about 120 feet tall; bark divided into very small blocky plates and on mature trees often resembling the bark of hardwoods rather than pines. An attractive and relatively fast-growing pine.

Characteristics: Leaves needlelike, 2–4 inches long; borne 2 per fascicle. Male cones purplish yellow, less than ⅜ inch long; inconspicuous and largely unnoticed. Female cones typical of the pines; small, brown at maturity, usually less than 4 inches long.

Culture: Prefers rich, moist soil but is adaptable to typical residential landscapes. Shade tolerant; not drought tolerant.

Typical Use: As a specimen pine or as a component in rich, naturalistic woodlands.

Best Features: The attractive bark, short needles, and small cones combine as this species' most ornamental characteristics.

Companion Plants: American beech, American hornbeam, native azaleas, red buckeye, sourwood, southern magnolia, southern sugar maple, tulip poplar, two-winged silverbell.

Similar and Related Species: At least 11 species of pine trees are native to the southeast, several of which are used in residential and commercial landscaping, as well as in habitat restoration.

Carolina Laurelcherry

Prunus caroliniana (P. Miller) Aiton

Family: Rosaceae (Rose)

Native Range and Habitat: Coastal plains, Piedmont, mountains. Open woods, roadsides, dry forests, maritime hammocks. Confined largely to the southeastern United States from extreme southeastern North Carolina south to south-central Florida and west to Texas; more common in the coastal plains.

Zones: 4–10, 10–1.

Carolina laurelcherry, *right* and *above*.

Form and Size: A large shrub or erect single-trunked evergreen tree to about 35 feet tall. Characteristics: Leaves alternate, leathery, dark green, 2–5 inches long, to about 1½ inches wide; margins with or without teeth. Flowers small, white, borne in numerous short-stalked racemes in the leaf axils; appearing March–April; fully flowered trees can be very showy. Fruit an oval or rounded, blackish, ½-inch drupe; usually appearing in late summer and fall, but flowers and fruit may be present simultaneously.

Culture: Extremely adaptable and easy to grow. Prefers moist, well-drained sites in nature but is somewhat weedy and tolerates a range of situations from sunny to shady exposures and acidic to mildly alkaline soils; may be pruned to maintain a shrubby habit.

Typical Use: Excellent as a screening shrub on large landscapes and along residential lot lines; may also be grown as a specimen. Will reproduce from self-sown seeds in most situations. Should be located away from porches and high-traffic areas due to fruit fall.

Best Features: Valued for its evergreen habit, profuse flowering, dense foliage, and for its attractiveness to wildlife.

Companion Plants: American ash, American beautyberry, American beech, red buckeye, southern magnolia, sweetshrub, wax myrtle.

Similar and Related Species: At least a dozen native *Prunus* occur in the southeast, several of which are used in gardening and landscaping (see Chapter 11). An equal or perhaps larger number of non-native *Prunus* are also regularly planted in residential and commercial landscapes. Carolina laurelcherry is one of the few black-fruited species.

Mexican Plum

Prunus mexicana S. Watson

Family: Rosaceae (Rose)
Native Range and Habitat: Coastal plains, Piedmont. Stream banks, upland woods, disturbed sites. Distributed mostly in the central United States from about South Dakota and Texas southeastward to North Carolina; not present in Florida or Virginia, rare in Georgia.
Zones: 6–8, 9–6.
Form and Size: An erect, deciduous, somewhat thorny tree to about 30 feet tall and nearly as broad; with an open crown and

Mexican plum. Courtesy of Ron Lance.

attractive, grayish to black, furrowed bark that peels off in plates at maturity; may have single or multiple trunks.

Characteristics: Leaves alternate, oval to elliptic in outline, 2–4 inches long, toothed along the margins; turning orange and becoming showy in autumn. Flowers white, 5-petaled, fragrant, to about 1 inch wide; borne in abundance and making plantings very showy during the spring flowering period. Fruit a 1-inch, rounded, yellow to purplish red, juicy, tasty drupe; maturing late summer to fall; used in making jams and jellies.

Culture: Prefers well-drained soils and full sun. Tolerant of acidic to alkaline soils. Moderately drought tolerant once established. May be trained to either a tree or multistemmed shrub.

Typical Use: Excellent small tree for smaller residential landscapes. Should be located away from porches and high-traffic areas due to fruit fall.

Best Features: Valued for its showy flowers, edible fruit, striking fall color, and value as a wildlife food. Does not form colonies as do some species of *Prunus*.

Companion Plants: American ash, American beautyberry, American beech, red buckeye, southern magnolia, sweetshrub, wax myrtle.

Similar and Related Species: At least a dozen native *Prunus* occur in the southeast, several of which are used in gardening and landscaping (see Chapter 11). An equal or perhaps larger number of non-native *Prunus* are also regularly planted in residential and commercial landscapes.

White Oak

Quercus alba Linnaeus

Family: Fagaceae (Oak)
Native Range and Habitat: Coastal plains, Piedmont, mountains. Rich deciduous forests. Widespread across the eastern United States from Maine to Minnesota, south to northern Florida, and west to eastern Texas.
Zones: 5–9, 8–1.
Form and Size: Large single-trunked deciduous tree with lateral branches, a broadly

White oak, *right* and *above*.

spreading crown (especially when open-grown), and very attractive, pale grayish to whitish bark that peels and flakes at maturity. A member of the white oak group.

Characteristics: Leaves alternate, 2–6 inches long, 1–4 inches wide, divided along the margins into 5–9 relatively narrow, rounded lobes; variable in size and shape on a given tree. Male flowers borne in pendent catkins from the point of origination of new shoots. Female flowers borne in small, inconspicuous catkins in the axils of developing leaves. Fruit a ¾–1¼-inch, shiny, brown acorn resting in a comparatively shallow, bowllike cup; maturing in one year.

Culture: Performs best in moist, well-drained acidic soils in full sun, but often occurs in relatively dry woods in nature and adaptable in the garden. Mulch to keep roots cool and protected.

Typical Use: Best as a specimen. Can obtain large dimensions but grows slowly; 20-year-old trees are typically less than 30 feet tall.

Best Features: Appreciated for its attractive bark and foliage. Acorns are useful to wildlife. An excellent southern landscape tree.

Companion Plants: American holly, American hornbeam, flowering dogwood, fringe tree, hophornbeam, native azaleas, Shumard oak, swamp chestnut oak, sweetshrub, southern magnolia.

Similar and Related Species: More than 50 native oaks occur in the eastern United States, a large number of which are used in landscaping and gardening. Bluff oak (*Q. austrina*) is similar to white oak and equally useful in the garden. Burr oak (*Q. macrocarpa*), which has scaly, very attractive acorn cups, is also a good companion for white oak.

Swamp White Oak

Quercus bicolor Willdenow

Swamp white oak. Courtesy of Ron Lance.

Family: Fagaceae (Oak)
Native Range and Habitat: Coastal plains, Piedmont, mountains. Depression swamps and bottomland woods. Maine to Minnesota, south to northern and central Alabama; absent in our region from Florida, Georgia, Mississippi, and Louisiana.
Zones: 4–8, 8–1.
Form and Size: Large, erect, deciduous tree to about 100 feet tall with dark gray, scaly bark. A white oak.

Characteristics: Leaves alternate, up to 7 inches long and 4 inches wide, with shallowly lobed margins; two-toned, dark green above, grayish white below (hence the scientific name *bicolor*); turning yellow to yellowish brown in autumn. Male flowers borne in pendent catkins from the point of origination of new shoots. Female flowers borne in small, inconspicuous catkins in the axils of developing leaves. Fruit a 1¼-inch, dark brown acorn resting in a comparatively deep, bowllike cup at the tip of a long stalk; maturing in one year.

Culture: Occurs naturally in wetlands but is surprisingly drought tolerant once established; full sun to partial shade; needs acidic soil.

Typical Use: Most valued as a specimen or shade tree for residential landscapes, parks, and parking lots.

Best Features: Large size, attractive foliage and bark.

Companion Plants: American hornbeam, burr oak, chestnut oak, flowering dogwood, native azaleas.

Similar and Related Species: More than 50 native oaks occur in the eastern United States, a large number of which are used in landscaping and gardening. The leaves of swamp white oak are superficially similar to those of white oak (*Q. alba*) but are less deeply and more numerously lobed.

Georgia Oak

Quercus georgiana M. A. Curtis

Family: Fagaceae (Oak)

Native Range and Habitat: Piedmont. Dry slopes, especially in association with granite outcrops. South Carolina, Georgia, and Alabama.

Zones: 6–8, 8–6.

Form and Size: A relatively small, deciduous, low-growing tree 25–75 feet tall; crown compact; bark grayish to light brown. A red oak.

Characteristics: Leaves alternate, 1–5 inches long, to about 3½ inches wide; deeply divided along the margins into several sharp-pointed, bristle-tipped lobes; turning red to orange in autumn. Male flowers borne in pendent catkins from the point of origination of new shoots. Female flowers borne in small, inconspicuous catkins in the axils of developing leaves. Fruit a ½-inch, shiny, brown acorn resting in a moderately shallow, bowllike cup; maturing in two years.

Georgia oak.

Georgia oak. Courtesy of Ron Lance.

Culture: Drought tolerant. Adaptable to acidic or neutral sandy soils. Grows taller on rich sites.

Typical Use: Rare in nature but an excellent specimen tree in residential landscapes or parking lots. Useful in decorating corners and commercial entryways.

Best Features: Valued for its small size, upright habit, fall foliage, and dense crown.

Companion Plants: Chestnut oak, blackjack oak, post oak, turkey oak.

Similar and Related Species: More than 50 native oaks occur in the eastern United States, a large number of which are used in landscaping and gardening. Other dry-site oaks include blackjack oak (*Q. marilandica*), bluejack oak (*Q. incana*), post oak (*Q. stellata*), sand post oak (*Q. margaretta*), and turkey oak (*Q. laevis*).

Swamp Chestnut Oak

Quercus michauxii Nuttall

Family: Fagaceae (Oak)

Native Range and Habitat: Coastal plains, Piedmont, mountains. Bottomland woods, floodplain forests, river terraces. Virginia to Missouri, south to north-central Florida, west to Texas.

Zones: 5–9, 9–6.

Form and Size: Large, relatively fast-growing deciduous tree with a spreading crown and attractive, shaggy, exfoliating bark that flakes off to show brownish gray inner bark. A white oak.

Characteristics: Leaves large, dark green above, 4–9 inches long, 3–6 inches wide; margins adorned with large, blunt teeth. Male flowers borne in pendent catkins from the point of origination of new shoots. Female flowers borne in small, inconspicuous catkins in the axils of developing leaves. Fruit a ½–1¼-inch, shiny, light to dark brown acorn resting in a bowllike cup that covers about ½ of the nut; maturing in one year.

Swamp chestnut oak.

Culture: Occurs naturally on wet to moist soils but is adaptable to surprisingly dry, sunny sites; prefers acidic soils, but often occurs in nature in thin soils over limestone.

Typical Use: Best as a specimen or shade tree.

Best Features: Valued for its large, attractive, coarsely toothed leaves, relatively fast growth rate, and attractive, scaly bark.

Companion Plants: American hornbeam, green ash, needle palm, Shumard oak, water oak, white oak, winged elm, winterberry, witch-hazel.

Similar and Related Species: More than 50 native oaks occur in the eastern United States, a large number of which are used in landscaping and gardening. Swamp chestnut oak is most similar in appearance to chestnut oak (*Q. montana*), chinkapin oak (*Q. muhlenbergii*), and to a lesser extent dwarf chinkapin (*Q. prinoides*) and swamp white oaks (*Q. bicolor*). All have coarsely toothed leaves and are used in gardening.

Willow Oak

Quercus phellos Linnaeus

Family: Fagaceae (Oak)

Native Range and Habitat: Coastal plains, Piedmont, mountains. Bottomland woods, river terraces, upland depressions, wet lake margins. New York and Illinois south to northern Florida, west to eastern Texas.

Zones: 6–9, 9–3.

Form and Size: Medium to large, fast-growing deciduous tree with an attractive, rounded crown, dense foliage, and ridged and furrowed bark. A red oak.

Characteristics: Leaves very narrow, lance-shaped, 2–5 inches long, less than 1 inch wide, with smooth margins. Male flowers borne in pendent catkins from the point of origination of new shoots. Female flowers borne in small, inconspicuous catkins in the axils of developing leaves. Fruit a ½-inch, brown, vertically flattened acorn resting in a bowllike cup that covers about ⅓ of the nut; maturing in two years.

Culture: An easy-to-grow tree; found in moist, well-drained soils in nature but is highly adaptable to almost any situation in the garden.

Typical Use: Used as a specimen or shade tree, or to accent corners or courtyards; may grow to relatively large proportions and should be sited accordingly.

Best Features: Valued for its fast growth rate, dense twiggy crown, and narrow leaves.

Companion Plants: American hornbeam, cucumber magnolia, green ash, needle palm, northern red oak, pin oak, scarlet oak, Shumard oak, southern magnolia, southern red

Willow oak.

Willow oak. Courtesy of Ron Lance.

oak, southern sugar maple, winged elm, winterberry, witch-hazel, umbrella magnolia. Similar and Related Species: More than 50 native oaks occur in the eastern United States, a large number of which are used in landscaping and gardening. Willow oak is most similar to the Darlington or laurel oak (*Q. hemisphaerica*) and the diamond leaf or swamp laurel oak (*Q. laurifolia*). The former is a widespread, somewhat weedy species that volunteers in residential landscapes throughout the south. The latter is a wetland species that has found great favor as a landscape tree and is a much better choice for gardeners than Darlington oak.

Shumard Oak

Quercus shumardii Buckley

Family: Fagaceae (Oak)
Native Range and Habitat: Coastal plains, Piedmont, mountains. Moist to dry woods, rich slopes and bottomlands. Pennsylvania to Kansas, south to north-central Florida, west to eastern Texas.
Zones: 5–9, 9–6.
Form and Size: A medium to large, relatively fast-growing deciduous tree to about 150 feet tall in nature, perhaps somewhat shorter in the garden and not exceeding about 75 feet; bark grayish, shallowly and finely fissured. A red oak.
Characteristics: Leaves 4–8 inches long, 2–6 inches wide, with 5–9 bristle-tipped lobes;

very ornamental; developing purplish spots in the leaf tissue as the leaves fall. Male flowers borne in pendent catkins from the point of origination of new shoots. Female flowers borne in small, inconspicuous catkins in the axils of developing leaves. Fruit a ½–1¼-inch, shiny, brown acorn resting in a comparatively shallow, bowllike cup; maturing in two years.

Shumard oak.

Shumard oak. Courtesy of Ron Lance.

Culture: Occurs naturally in well-drained soils. Adapts well to a variety of soils from acidic to neutral or mildly alkaline; performs well in full sun or partial shade; drought tolerant.

Typical Use: Preferred as a fast-growing shade or specimen tree that quickly (within 20 years) reaches relatively large proportions.

Best Features: Relatively fast growth; attractive ornamental foliage; shade.

Companion Plants: American holly, Ashe magnolia, Carolina laurelcherry, green ash, hophornbeam, native azaleas, needle palm, redbud, southern magnolia, swamp chestnut oak.

Similar and Related Species: More than 50 native oaks occur in the eastern United States, a large number of which are used in landscaping and gardening. Shumard oak is closest in form, foliage, and garden use to black oak (*Q. velutina*), northern red oak (*Q. palustris*), scarlet oak (*Q. coccinea*), and to a lesser extent southern red oak (*Q. falcata*).

Live Oak

Quercus virginiana Miller

Family: Fagaceae (Oak)

Native Range and Habitat: Coastal plains. Maritime forests, xeric and moist hardwood hammocks. Extreme southeastern Virginia south along the coast to and throughout Florida, west to southeastern Texas, including all of Louisiana.

Zones: 8–10, 10–7.

Form and Size: Potentially a massive evergreen tree with wide-spreading crown; typically branching low to the ground when open-grown, more erect in natural hammocks or closed forests; young trees are relatively fast-growing (2 feet or more per year), but growth rate slows with age. A white oak.

Characteristics: Leaves dark green above, grayish beneath, 1–4 inches long, up to 2

Live oak.

Live oak. Courtesy of Ron Lance.

inches wide. Male flowers borne in pendent catkins from the point of origination of new shoots. Female flowers borne in small, inconspicuous catkins in the axils of developing leaves. Fruit a ⅝–1-inch, dark brown acorn resting in an elongated, bowllike cup that encloses nearly ½ of the acorn; maturing in one year.

Culture: Extremely tough and adaptable; tolerant of a wide range of soils and difficult situations from very moist to xeric sites.

Typical Use: Widely used as an evergreen shade or specimen tree.

Best Features: Evergreen habit, moderately fast growth when young, upright form, dense foliage, and adaptability to a wide variety of conditions; salt and drought tolerant.

Companion Plants: American holly, American hornbeam, basswood, bluestem palmetto, hophornbeam, flowering dogwood, needle palm, redbud, saw palmetto, southern crabapple, witch-hazel.

Similar and Related Species: More than 50 native oaks occur in the eastern United States, a large number of which are used in landscaping and gardening. Sand live oak (*Q. geminata*), considered by some to be only a variety of live oak, is similar in appearance and use. The two hybridize in nature, and both are excellent for residential and commercial landscapes.

Needle Palm

Rhapidophyllum hystrix (Pursh) H. Wendland and Drude ex Drude

Family: Arecaceae (Palm)

Native Range and Habitat: Coastal plains. Moist woods, lower slopes bordering major rivers, moist calcareous woodlands, moist to wet hammocks. Georgia, Florida, Alabama, Mississippi.

Zones: 7–10, 12–7.

Form and Size: A large, evergreen, shrublike palm 3–8 feet tall and equally as wide, with

Needle palm.

numerous fronds radiating from a short, thick aerial trunk that is copiously covered with very sharp, needlelike spines that are piercing to the touch.

Characteristics: Leaves fan-shaped, 2–3 feet long and wide; borne on a long stalk. Flowers tiny, inconspicuous, borne among the trunk spines in a brownish inflorescence. Fruit small, purplish to reddish brown, inconspicuous among the trunk spines.

Culture: Prefers rich, moist soils in nature; adapts to, but grows more slowly in, drier sites; tolerant of full sun but performs best in at least moderate shade.

Typical Use: An excellent landscape palm; used as a specimen shrub, to obscure backyard decks, in foundation plantings, or as spaced individuals in shrub beds.

Best Features: Needle palm's evergreen habit, low stature, screening foliage, and attractive form are its best attributes.

Companion Plants: American holly, American hornbeam, bluestem palmetto, flowering dogwood, fringe tree, Indian pink, Jenkins' fetterbush, red buckeye, witch-hazel, yaupon.

Similar and Related Species: The two other shrubby palms used in southern gardening include the somewhat similar bluestem palmetto (*Sabal minor*), which has long, arching, conspicuous inflorescences, and saw palmetto (*Serenoa repens*). The latter produces conspicuous flowers and fruit and has sawlike teeth along the leaf stalk.

Florida Flame Azalea

Rhododendron austrinum (Small) Rehder

Family: Ericaceae (Heath)

Native Range and Habitat: Coastal plains. Rich woods and moist slopes. Georgia, Florida, Alabama, Mississippi.

Zones: 6–9, 9–6.

Form and Size: A large, multistemmed deciduous shrub to about 10 feet tall and 8 feet wide, often smaller.

Characteristics: Leaves alternate, 1–4 inches long, widest above the middle, often borne in a crowded, whorl-like arrangement at the tips of the branches. Flowers 1–2 inches long, tu-

Florida azalea, *left* and *above*.

bular below, flaring into 5 lobes at the apex; yellow to nearly orange; very showy and borne profusely before or as the new leaves emerge; fragrant; appearing mostly from March to May. Fruit a small, brown, linear capsule containing tiny, dustlike seeds.

Culture: Requires acidic soil; prefers moist, well-drained sites; flowers best in sun or high shade; also performs well (but flowers less prolifically) in partial shade.

Typical Use: Sometimes used as a specimen; more often massed with other native azaleas in single- or multiple-species azalea beds to allow for the progression of flowering across species and season. It has been used to decorate parking lot medians. May be pruned immediately after flowering before new buds form but achieves a more naturalistic and attractive form without pruning.

Best Features: Prized for its showy yellow to orange flowers and spring flowering period.

Companion Plants: Carolina jessamine, flowering dogwood, fringe tree, hophornbeam, Indian pink, mayapple, mountain laurel, needle palm, other native azaleas, redbud, sweetshrub, trilliums, wild columbine.

Similar and Related Species: At least 15 species of deciduous azaleas occur in the southeastern United States, all of which have been co-opted by gardeners. Several cultivars are available, varying mostly in flower color. See Chapter 7 for more information about native azaleas and other members of the heath family.

Piedmont Azalea

Rhododendron canescens (Michaux) Sweet

Family: Ericaceae (Heath)

Native Range and Habitat: Coastal plains, Piedmont, mountains. Swamps and swamp margins, wet flatwoods, savannas. Confined largely to the coastal plains and Upper Piedmont from southeastern North Carolina south to northern Florida, and west to easternmost Texas.

Zones: 6–10, 9–4.

Form and Size: A large, sometimes leggy, multistemmed deciduous shrub; old plants can exceed 12 feet tall, but garden plants are often smaller.

Piedmont azalea.

Characteristics: Leaves alternate, 1–4 inches long, elliptical or wider toward the tip, often borne in a crowded, whorl-like arrangement at the tips of the branches. Flowers 1–2 inches long, tubular below, flaring into 5 lobes at the apex; fragrant; pink to white flushed with pink; very showy and borne profusely before or as the new leaves emerge; appearing from late February to April, predominately March, often just ahead of Florida azalea. Fruit a small, brown, linear capsule containing tiny, dustlike seeds.

Culture: Occurs in flatwoods and along swamp margins in very acidic soil; prefers moist, well-drained sites but tolerates considerable moisture; flowers best in sun or high shade, but also performs well in partial shade. May be pruned immediately after flowering before new buds form but achieves a more natural, attractive, and pleasing form without pruning.

Typical Use: Sometimes used as a specimen; more often massed with other native azaleas in single- or multiple-species azalea beds to allow for the progression of flowering across species and season. Excellent for naturalistic woodlands and woodland borders.

Best Features: Enjoyed for its showy pink flowers and early spring flowering period.

Companion Plants: Florida leucothoe, fringe tree, highbush and lowbush blueberries, loblolly bay, other native azaleas, saw palmetto, sweetbay magnolia, Walter viburnum.

Similar and Related Species: At least 15 species of deciduous azaleas occur in the southeastern United States, all of which have been co-opted by gardeners. See Chapter 7 for more information about native azaleas and other members of the heath family.

Oconee Azalea

Rhododendron flammeum (Michaux) Sargent

Family: Ericaceae (Heath)

Native Range and Habitat: Coastal plains, Piedmont, mountains. Upland forests, ridges, slopes, sandhill woodlands. Essentially restricted to the Georgia Piedmont and extreme southwestern South Carolina.

Zones: 6–9, 9–7.

Form and Size: A low to moderately sized multistemmed deciduous shrub to about 8 feet tall.

Characteristics: Leaves alternate, dark green, more or less elliptic. Flowers 1–2 inches long, yellow to orange or red; tubular below but flaring into 5 lobes above; without glandular hairs; not fragrant; appearing as the new leaves emerge, April–May. Fruit a small, brown, linear capsule containing tiny, dustlike seeds.

Culture: Prefers acidic, well-drained soils; flowers best in high shade.

Oconee azalea, *left* and *above*.

Typical Use: Sometimes used as a specimen; more often massed with other native azaleas in single- or multiple-species azalea beds to allow for the progression of flowering across species and season. Perhaps less often used in gardening than some other native azaleas, but deserving of more attention.

Best Features: Valued for its showy spring flowers and its variable flower color.

Companion Plants: Bigleaf magnolia, bottlebrush buckeye, drooping leucothoe, flowering dogwood, fringe tree, highbush and lowbush blueberries, mountain laurel, other native azaleas, redbud.

Similar and Related Species: At least 15 species of deciduous azaleas occur in the southeastern United States, all of which have been co-opted by gardeners. This species is similar in flower color and general appearance to flame azalea (*R. calendulaceum*) but lacks gland-tipped hairs on the flowers. Several cultivars are available, including double-flowered forms and those accentuating various flower colors. See Chapter 7 for more information about this and other members of the heath family.

Great Rhododendron, Rosebay

Rhododendron maximum Linnaeus

Family: Ericaceae (Heath)

Native Range and Habitat: Coastal plains, Piedmont, mountains. Moist slopes, boggy stream banks and swampy areas in the mountains; north-facing slopes in the Piedmont; extending into the coastal plains only in north-central Virginia. Maine southward along the eastern seaboard, west to Ohio and Kentucky, south to northern Georgia.

Zones: 4–7, 7–1.

Form and Size: A large, evergreen, multi-stemmed shrub to at least 15 feet tall and nearly as wide; forms dense thickets—sometimes called "rhododendron slicks"—in the southern mountains.

Characteristics: Leaves alternate, leathery, 4–8 inches long, up to about 3 inches wide; elliptic, dark green above, paler below, very attractive;

Rosebay rhododendron.

those at the tip of the branch often whorl-like. Flowers with five petals, white with a pinkish blush, sometimes tinged yellowish, occasionally pinkish; about 1 inch long, 1–2 inches wide when fully open and borne in large, showy clusters at the branch tips; appearing in late spring and summer. Fruit a ½-inch, hard capsule.

Culture: Performs best in acidic soils in moderate shade; requires cool summer root temperatures and well-drained sites.

Typical Use: Size makes this species most appropriate for larger landscapes and naturalistic woodlands. Sometimes used in commercial landscapes, especially at inns and restaurants; best where not crowded by paved surfaces.

Best Features: Most prized for its large clusters of showy flowers, evergreen habit, and large size.

Companion Plants: Basswood, cucumber magnolia, drooping leucothoe, large witch-alder, Shumard oak, silverbell, umbrella magnolia, wild hydrangea, winterberry, witch-hazel.

Similar and Related Species: Five evergreen rhododendrons occur in the southeastern United States, of which the present species and purple rhododendron (*R. catawbiense*) are the more common in mid to higher elevations. These two species probably constitute the more widely known and recognized rhododendrons of the southern mountains. See Chapter 7 for more information about rhododendrons and other members of the heath family.

Pinxterbloom Azalea

Rhododendron pericly-menoides (Michaux) Shinners

Pinxterbloom azalea.

Family: Ericaceae (Heath)

Native Range and Habitat: Coastal plains, Piedmont, mountains; more characteristic of the mountains than the coastal plains. Slopes and stream banks, mostly in drier sites; to about 4,000 feet in elevation. New Hampshire west to Ohio, south to Georgia and Alabama.

Zones: 4–8, 8–1.

Form and Size: A multistemmed deciduous azalea to about 12 feet tall but often smaller; spreading by underground runners.

Characteristics: Leaves alternate, 1–4 inches long, to about 1½ inches wide, widest toward the tip; those at the end of the branches often whorl-like in arrangement. Flowers 1½–2 inches wide with 1-inch tubes; flaring at the apex into 5 lobes; fragrant; white to pink or pinkish purple and borne in showy, 6–12-flowered clusters; appearing April–May just before or as the new leaves emerge. Fruit a hard capsule.

Culture: Does best in dry, rocky sites; site in partial sun to high shade for best flowering.

Typical Use: Sometimes used as a specimen; more often massed with other native azaleas in single- or multiple-species azalea beds to allow for the progression of flowering across species and season.

Best Features: Valued for its showy pink flowers and spring flowering period.

Companion Plants: Bigleaf magnolia, bottlebrush buckeye, drooping leucothoe, flowering dogwood, fringe tree, highbush and lowbush blueberries, Indian pink, mountain laurel, other native azaleas, red buckeye, redbud, trilliums.

Similar and Related Species: At least 15 species of deciduous azaleas occur in the southeastern United States, all of which have been co-opted by gardeners. Pinxterbloom azalea is perhaps most similar in flower color and general appearance to Piedmont azalea (*R.*

canescens). See Chapter 7 for more information about native azaleas and other members of the heath family.

Plumleaf Azalea

Rhododendron prunifolium (Small) Millais

Family: Ericaceae (Heath)

Native Range and Habitat: Coastal plains, Piedmont. Mesic woodlands, steep slopes, stream banks. Occurring naturally only in a relatively small region on the Georgia and Alabama border near Pine Mountain, Georgia, but valued in the garden and more widely planted.

Zones: 6–9, 8–6.

Form and Size: Multistemmed deciduous shrub with irregular branching; to at least 15 feet tall; spreading slowly by underground stems.

Characteristics: Leaves elliptic, 1–4 inches long, less than 2 inches wide. Flowers red to crimson, with 1-inch tubes; borne in showy clusters well after the new leaves; typically appearing in mid to late summer. Fruit a hard, ¾-inch capsule.

Culture: Prefers rich, acidic, moist to quite dry soils. High shade produces the most abundant flowering.

Typical Use: Sometimes used as a specimen; more often massed with other native azaleas in single- or multiple-species azalea beds to allow for an extended flowering period among other, largely spring-flowering azaleas. Also valued along woodland edges.

Best Features: Valued for its red or reddish orange flowers and typically late July to early September flowering period.

Companion Plants: Bigleaf magnolia, bottlebrush buckeye, drooping leucothoe, flowering dogwood, fringe tree, highbush and lowbush blueberries, hophornbeam, mountain laurel, other native azaleas, red buckeye, redbud, sourwood.

Similar and Related Species: At least 15 species of deciduous azaleas occur in the southeastern United States, all of which have been co-opted by gardeners. Plumleaf azalea is

Plumleaf azalea, *right* and *above*.

the only brightly flowered species (other than the white-flowered swamp azalea) to bloom in mid to late summer. Several cultivars are available varying primarily in flower color. See Chapter 7 for more information about deciduous azaleas, rhododendrons, and other members of the heath family.

Black-Eyed Susan

Rudbeckia hirta Linnaeus

Family: Asteraceae (Aster)

Native Range and Habitat: Coastal plains, Piedmont, mountains. Roadsides, pinelands, fields, pastures, disturbed sites. Widespread across nearly the entire United States (when all varieties are taken into account). At least three varieties are limited primarily to the eastern United States, mostly in the coastal plains.

Zones: 2–10, 10–1.

Form and Size: An erect, more or less hairy, and multistemmed annual, short-lived perennial, or biennial; 18–40 inches tall.

Characteristics: Leaves alternate, coarsely toothed, variable in size, and rough to the touch. Flowers borne at the tip of the stem, with a dark central disc and numerous ¾–1¾-inch, yellow rays; appearing in late spring and throughout the summer. Fruit a tiny achene produced at the base of the disc florets.

Culture: Easy to grow and adaptable to varying conditions; full sun to light shade is best for abundant flowering; perhaps performing better with regular irrigation but a tough plant that is tolerant of poor care. Reseeds and spreads.

Typical Use: Often massed as a single species under mailboxes or along walkways. An excellent addition to mixed perennial beds and wildflower meadows.

Best Features: Valued for its abundant, showy flowers and extended flowering period.

Companion Plants: Blazing stars, goldenrods, ironweed, Joe-Pye-weed, milkweeds, other rudbeckias, purple coneflower, starry rosinweed.

Similar and Related Species: Numerous native asters occur in the southern United States—including at least 11 species of *Rudbeckia*—many of which are used in gardening and many of which resemble black-eyed Susan. The orange coneflower (*R. fulgida*) is also very popular. Several cultivars of black-eyed Susan are available, varying mostly in the form, color, and number of flower heads. See Chapter 12 for more information about this and other plants of the aster family.

Black-eyed Susan.

Sabal Palm

Sabal palmetto (Walter) Loddiges ex J. A. & J. H. Schultes

Family: Arecaceae (Palm)

Native Range and Habitat: Coastal plains. Maritime forests and the edges of salt marshes. Extreme southeastern North Carolina south throughout Florida and west to Louisiana, primarily along the coast (except widespread in Florida).

Zones: 8–11, 12–8.

Form and Size: An erect, moderately slow-growing, single-stemmed fan palm to at least 60 feet tall; trunk grayish on old trees; trunks of young trees are often covered by the bases of fallen leaves (which are often called "boots").

Characteristics: Leaves large, more or less circular and fan-shaped, 3–5 feet wide, reflexed and V-shaped from the central axis; the numerous leaf segments are lined with conspicuous, threadlike fibers. Flowers white and individually tiny, but borne in conspicuous, 3-foot-long, branching, spraylike clusters just below the leaves; appearing in spring and summer. Fruit rounded, black, ½ inch in diameter.

Culture: Very adaptable; does best in fertile, sandy soils with at least some irrigation. Salt tolerant. Intolerant of extended flooding. Can be purchased and planted when of tree stature.

Typical Use: An often-used palm in residential landscapes; also used along highways and to beautify parks and commercial buildings. Adaptable to difficult situations. Often planted in isolated groups.

Best Features: Valued for its erect stature, attractive fan-shaped leaves, and long life. Fruit is eaten by wildlife. Provides nesting habitat for birds.

Companion Plants: American beautyberry, live oak, loblolly bay, purple muhly grass, red maple.

Sabal palm.

Sabal palm. Courtesy of Donna Legare.

Similar and Related Species: This is our only tree-sized palm with V-shaped leaves. Bluestem palmetto (*Sabal minor*) is a closely related shrub that is also used in gardening.

Saw Palmetto

Serenoa repens (Bartram) Small

Family: Arecaceae (Palm)
Native Range and Habitat: Coastal plains. Flatwoods, maritime forests, sandy pinelands. Extreme southeastern South Carolina south throughout Florida, west to eastern Louisiana.
Zones: 8–11, 12–9.
Form and Size: A low, extremely long-lived evergreen shrub with fan-shaped leaves; trunk typically prostrate to nearly buried but sometimes growing erect to at least 10 feet tall.
Characteristics: Leaves fan-shaped, to about 3 feet wide, divided into multiple segments; leaf stalk to about 3 feet long, laterally flattened and armed with sharp, sawlike teeth along the opposing margins. Flowers small, creamy white, borne in a conspicuous, branched inflorescence arising from near the base of the plant; appearing in spring and summer. Fruit ellipsoid, about ¾ inch long, yellowish orange at first, maturing to bluish black.
Culture: Well-drained to poorly drained, acidic to neutral, organic or sandy soils; adaptable to varying situations. Performs well in full sun or partial shade. Drought tolerant once established.
Typical Use: Often massed in groups of three or more or as part of a shrubby background; may be used in foundation plantings; commonly seen in highway medians or decorating parks and commercial buildings. A versatile and very attractive shrubby palm.
Best Features: Evergreen habit, long life, wide adaptability, tolerance of difficult situations.
Companion Plants: Deerberry, Elliott's blueberry, highbush and lowbush blueberries, live oak and sand live oak, post oak, purple muhly grass, sparkleberry, starry rosinweed, tarflower, turkey oak, wild rosemary, wiregrass.
Similar and Related Species: Two other shrubby palms are native to the southeast. Needle

Saw palmetto.

palm has a short trunk copiously covered with piercing, needlelike spines. Bluestem palmetto (*Sabal minor*) produces an elongated flower stalk that far exceeds the length of the leaves. Both are regularly used in gardening and landscaping.

Starry Rosinweed

Silphium asteriscus Linnaeus

Starry rosinweed.

Family: Asteraceae (Aster)
Native Range and Habitat: Coastal plains, Piedmont, mountains. Flatwoods, roadsides, open pine woods, glades. Virginia south to west-central Florida, west to Missouri and Louisiana.
Zones: 8–10, 10–8.
Form and Size: An erect, herbaceous perennial with several 3–4-foot-tall flowering stems subtended by a mass of basal leaves.
Characteristics: Leaves on the stem opposite to alternate, long-elliptic, with or without marginal teeth, coarse, rough to the touch, 2–6 inches long, up to 2 inches wide. Flowers borne in a terminal inflorescence and consisting of a central disc surrounded by several ¾–1½-inch, yellow rays subtended by comparatively large floral bracts; showy; highly attractive to bees and other pollinators; appearing May–September. Fruit a tiny achene, produced at the base of the disc florets.
Culture: Adaptable to a wide variety of conditions. Performs well in typical garden conditions in sun or light shade; prefers acidic soils and minimum irrigation. Reseeds and spreads.
Typical Use: Valued as a moderately tall perennial in mixed wildflower and perennial beds; most attractive when planted in groups of three.
Best Features: Starry rosinweed's best features include its numerous showy flower heads, easy cultivation, tall size, long flowering period, and attractiveness to pollinators.
Companion Plants: Black-eyed Susan, blazing stars, coreopsis, goldenrods, ironweed, Joe-Pye-weed, milkweeds, rudbeckias, purple coneflower.
Similar and Related Species: At least ten species of rosinweed occur in the southeast, several of which are used in gardening. See Chapter 12 for more information about this and other members of the aster family. The present species might also be seen in the garden trade as *S. simpsonii*.

Blue-Eyed Grass

Sisyrinchium angustifolium P. Miller

Family: Iridaceae (Iris)
Native Range and Habitat: Coastal plains, Piedmont, mountains. Wet meadows, moist roadsides, ditch edges, woodlands. Widespread throughout the eastern United States, from Maine and Minnesota south throughout Florida and west to Texas.
Zones: 5–11, 11–5.

Blue-eyed grass.

Form and Size: A low, evergreen perennial; similar to a bunch grass in form; leaves linear and interspersed with numerous elongated flowering scapes, each terminated with an attractive blue flower.

Characteristics: Leaves very narrow and grasslike, 1–2 feet long, erect or spreading from a central cluster. Flowers blue (occasionally white) with a yellow center; with 3 petals and 3 sepals, all of which are similar to each other; borne in abundance and appearing in spring and summer, March–June. Fruit a small, ⅜-inch capsule.

Culture: Grows naturally in moist sites, adapts well to typical garden soils in surprisingly dry sites. Full morning sun produces the best flowering response. Tends to die back in the center with age and should be divided and replanted at least once every two years to ensure that plants remain healthy and attractive. Seeds into and spreads in the garden.

Typical Use: May be used as a single plant in a perennial bed, but better in groups of three or more; excellent as a perennial border along walkways or shrub beds.

Best Features: Highly valued for its cheery countenance, abundant spring flowers, and evergreen foliage.

Companion Plants: Atamasco lily, black-eyed Susan, cardinal flower, coreopsis, Florida anise, irises, purple coneflower.

Similar and Related Species: Several species of *Sisyrinchium* occur in the southeastern United States, of which the present species is the only one used regularly in gardening. See Chapter 14 for additional information about this species and other perennial groundcovers.

Indian Pink, Pinkroot

Spigelia marilandica (Linnaeus) Linnaeus

Family: Loganiaceae (Logania)

Native Range and Habitat: Coastal plains, Piedmont, mountains. Rich woodlands, temperate deciduous forests, moist slopes. Confined mostly to the southeast from southwestern North Carolina west to Illinois and Missouri, south to northern Florida and eastern Texas.

Indian pink.

Zones: 5–9, 9–2.

Form and Size: An upright leafy perennial herb, 12–30 inches tall and topped with a bright cluster of showy flowers; often forming small colonies in nature.

Characteristics: Leaves opposite, lacking stalks, egg-shaped in outline, 2–6 inches long; dark green and very attractive; appearing well before flowering and remaining well after the flowers have gone. Flowers very showy, with 5 petals that are fused and tubular below, bulging above, and flaring at the apex into conspicuous, yellowish lobes; appearing March–June. Fruit a ⅜-inch capsule with blackish brown seeds.

Culture: Prefers at least partial shade and moist, well-drained, neutral to mildly acidic or alkaline soils.

Typical Use: Excellent for shady spring ephemeral gardens, shady mixed wildflower beds, and naturalistic woodlands. A relatively recent and much-appreciated addition to the native plant trade.

Best Features: Prized for the showy flowers (which are also attractive to hummingbirds), relatively long flowering period, and attractive, opposite, long-lasting leaves. Parts of the plant are poisonous and should not be consumed.

Companion Plants: Atamasco lily, bird's-foot violet, blue-eyed grass, Christmas fern, foamflower, heartleaf, lady fern, mayapple, trilliums, Virginia sweetspire, yellowroot.

Similar and Related Species: Only the exceedingly rare gentian pinkroot (*S. gentianoides*) and Florida pinkroot (*S. loganioides*)—neither of which has red flowers nor is available in the trade—are closely related. See Chapter 14 for more about this and similarly used species.

Stokes' Aster

Stokesia laevis (Hill) Greene

Family: Asteraceae (Aster)

Native Range and Habitat: Coastal plains, Piedmont. Moist to wet pinelands and roadsides, carnivorous plant bogs. Essentially restricted to the coastal plains from South Carolina to northern Florida, west to Louisiana; more common in the western part of our region. Nowhere common in nature but widely planted in gardens.

Zones: 5–9, 9–5.

Form and Size: A leafy, low-growing perennial herb with a distinctive cluster of thick basal leaves; individual plants are usually 1–2 feet wide and up to about 2 feet tall when flowering.

Characteristics: Leaves alternate, fleshy, toothed, and lance-shaped to long-elliptic in outline; those along the upper stem are often clasping at the base; dying back briefly in early fall but returning and sometimes present throughout the winter, especially in USDA zones

Stokes' aster.

8B–9. Flower heads large, 1–2 inches wide, solitary but plants produce many heads; heads with spreading, very showy, raylike flowers that are cleft at the tip and surround creamy white disc flowers; heads vary from white to blue, lavender, or purplish; appearing June–August. Fruit tiny achenes produced at the base of the disc flowers.

Culture: An easy-to-grow garden perennial; flowers best in full sun and moist, moderately acidic soils but is surprisingly adapted to drier sites.

Typical Use: Best when planted in mass in groups of five or more; an excellent addition to sunny or partly sunny perennial gardens.

Best Features: Most valued for the large, complicated, showy flowers and lengthy flowering period; flowering can be extended considerably by regular deadheading.

Companion Plants: Blazing stars, coreopsis, purple coneflower, rudbeckias, sunflowers, yellow coneflower.

Similar and Related Species: Numerous members of the aster family are found in the southeast, none of which have flowers that closely resemble those of Stokes' aster. This is a popular garden perennial with about a dozen cultivars that vary mostly on flower color. White-flowered forms, or plants that produce at least some white flowers, are not uncommon. See Chapter 12 for more about this species and other members of the aster family.

American Snowbell

Styrax americanus Lamarck

Family: Styracaceae (Storax)

Native Range and Habitat: Coastal plains, Piedmont, mountains. Swamps, wet woods, often in standing water. Largely restricted to the coastal plains and lower Piedmont in our region; Virginia to southeastern Missouri, south to south-central Florida and eastern Texas.

Zones: 6–10, 10–6.

Form and Size: A moderately large shrub to very small tree with a rounded crown of ascending, spreading, zigzag branches; potentially to about 15 feet tall.

Characteristics: Leaves 1–3 inches long, alternate, soft green; margins smooth or with

American snowbell, *right* and *above*.

blunt teeth. Flowers showy, superficially bell-shaped but with 5 white, recurved petals that bend strongly backward to expose a conspicuous mass of showy, yellowish anthers. Fruit ¼ inch in diameter and grayish green; more or less rounded in outline and resembling a capsule.

Culture: Occurs naturally in wet, acidic soils but adapts to the garden with regular irrigation.

Typical Use: Excellent for wet, naturalistic woodlands or as a backdrop for shrub beds; may also be used as a specimen plant.

Best Features: The numerous bright white flowers constitute this species' major attribute; also valued for its use in wetland habitats.

Companion Plants: Bluestem palmetto, buttonbush, loblolly bay, lizard's tail, red maple, swamp tupelo, sweet pepperbush, sweetbay magnolia, titi.

Similar and Related Species: Several species from the storax family are closely related, almost all of which are used in gardening. The two-winged and mountain silverbells are similar but do not have reflexed flower petals. Bigleaf snowbell (*S. grandifolius*) is an upland species with divided, but not recurved, petals; it is not widely available in the trade.

Baldcypress

Taxodium distichum (Linnaeus) L. C. Richard

Family: Cupressaceae (Cypress)

Native Range and Habitat: Coastal plains, Piedmont. Floodplains of alluvial and blackwater rivers, usually in flowing rather than ponded water. Eastern United States from southern New York and Illinois southward throughout Florida, west to eastern Texas.

Zones: 5–11, 12–5.

Form and Size: A tall, straight, relatively fast-growing tree with a buttressed base, conical crown, large branches, and reddish brown bark that peels off in thin strips; very old trees—which can surpass 1,000 years in age—exceed 120 feet tall and 16 feet in diameter at breast height. Garden trees are typically much smaller. Cypresses of the genus *Taxodium* are among the very few deciduous conifers; they turn a beautiful bronzy color in fall and

Baldcypress, *right* and *above*.

add much ornamentation to the landscape.

Characteristics: Leaves ½–¾ inch long, more or less needlelike, often (but not always) spreading from short shoots in a single plane and giving a featherlike appearance to the twig; turning golden or rusty brown in fall and very attractive. Cones rounded, leathery, about 1 inch in diameter and changing from green to brown as they mature.

Culture: Although baldcypress occurs naturally primarily in wetlands, it adapts well to most conditions and is surprisingly drought tolerant, especially if irrigated during establishment. Prefers acidic soils (pH 4.5–6) and is tolerant of oxygen-poor soils. Roots and lower trunk can remain inundated for extended periods.

Typical Use: Widely used as a street and parking lot tree and as a specimen in residential and commercial landscapes; very attractive when planted in groups of three with overlapping crowns (where space permits). Probably should not be planted in continually moist lawns where it can produce knees that protrude from the ground and can damage mowing equipment.

Best Features: Valued for its upright habit, attractive reddish brown bark, colorful fall foliage, delicate spring foliage, ease of cultivation, and adaptation to both wet and dry sites.

Companion Plants: Blackgum, cardinal flower, Florida anise, inkberry, Jenkins' fetterbush, loblolly bay, red maple, sweetbay magnolia, Virginia willow.

Similar and Related Species: Pond cypress (*T. ascendens*) is similar and is also available in the trade. It occurs naturally in the coastal plains and is found naturally mostly in ponded water. These two species have similar growth forms but may be distinguished (though often with some difficulty) by characters of the leaves, bark, and young twigs.

Winged Elm

Ulmus alata Michaux

Family: Ulmaceae (Elm)

Native Range and Habitat: Coastal plains, Piedmont, mountains. Dry forests, moist woodlands, bottomlands, temperate hardwood hammocks, fields, disturbed sites. Virginia west to extreme eastern Kansas, south to central Florida and eastern Texas.

Zones: 3–9, 9–1.

Form and Size: A moderately fast-growing, medium- to potentially large-sized deciduous tree with an erect form, rounded crown, and attractive spreading branches that are often lined with corky, winglike outgrowths (hence the common name); can exceed 100 feet in height but is usually much shorter.

Characteristics: Leaves alternate, lance-shaped to elliptical in outline, 1–4 inches long, less than 1½ inches wide, doubly toothed along the margins; those at the tip of the twig larger than those below. Flowers tiny and individually inconspicuous, appearing in late winter and very early spring; imparting a delicate countenance to fully flowered trees. Fruit a hairy, elongated, waferlike samara about ¼ inch long.

Culture: A tough, drought-tolerant tree adaptable to a wide array of soil types from rich to more or less sandy, and from mildly acidic to mildly alkaline. Tolerates partial shade and full sun. Probably performs best in rich, organic soils with adequate moisture.

Winged elm. Courtesy of Ron Lance.

Typical Use: Used as a specimen or shade tree in residential landscapes; also used in parks as well as for roadside and parking lot beautification; particularly effective for small spaces. The shallow roots should be protected with heavy mulch.

Best Features: Valued for its relatively fast growth, erect form, interesting corky branches, and fall color.

Companion Plants: American ash, American holly, basswood,

green ash, needle palm, Shumard oak, sourwood, southern magnolia, swamp chestnut oak, sweetbay magnolia, white oak, witch-hazel.

Similar and Related Species: At least six species of elms occur naturally in the southeastern United States. Although several have found use in gardening and landscaping, winged elm is by far the more easily obtained.

Sparkleberry

Vaccinium arboreum Marshall

Family: Ericaceae (Heath)

Native Range and Habitat: Coastal plains, Piedmont, mountains. Dry, sandy woods, often in fire-maintained habitats; occasionally in moist sites. Virginia west to southern Missouri, south nearly throughout Florida, west to eastern Texas.

Zones: 7–10, 10–7.

Form and Size: Single-trunked shrub or small tree; more nearly evergreen in USDA zones 9–10, deciduous late in the year farther north; potentially exceeding 30 feet tall in nature with an attractive reddish brown, somewhat mottled trunk; grayish bark peeling off in relatively large and attractive plates to reveal reddish inner bark. Produces flowers and fruit when of a low, shrublike stature.

Characteristics: Leaves dark green above, shiny, averaging ¾–1½ inches long and 1 inch wide; sometimes showing a purplish to pinkish autumn color, even in plants that retain most of their leaves. Flowers bell-shaped, about ¼ inch long, borne profusely in conspicuous, showy sprays near the tips of the branches; appearing in spring. Fruit black, hard, about ³⁄₁₆ inch in diameter; not tasty.

Culture: Found in more or less acidic soils, but also common in thin sands and calcareous woodlands; more adaptable to alkaline soils than other members of the blueberry genus. Drought tolerant. Flowers more prolifically in full sun.

Sparkleberry, *right* and *above*.

Typical Use: Valued as a specimen tree or as part of a mixed heath bed. Also used in naturalistic woodlands and to decorate sandy borders.

Best Features: A very attractive, nearly evergreen blueberry with prolific flowering, attractive bark, and a more or less twisted trunk; very easy to grow and should be much more widely used in gardening and landscaping, especially in xeric sites.

Companion Plants: American beautyberry, deerberry, fringe tree, native azaleas, saw palmetto, wax myrtle, yaupon.

Similar and Related Species: Sparkleberry is one of several species of blueberries used in gardening. See Chapter 7 for more information on this and other blueberries, and other members of the heath family.

Highbush Blueberry

Vaccinium spp.

Family: Ericaceae (Heath)

Native Range and Habitat: Coastal plains, Piedmont, mountains. Dry to moist woods, swamp and pond margins, hammocks. The highbush blueberries are a complicated complex of several species. Some experts consider all members of the group to be part of a single, quite variable species, whereas others divide the group into several distinct species. As a result, a variety of scientific names appear in retail nurseries—*V. corymbosum*, *V. elliottii* (Elliott's blueberry), and *V. ashei* (rabbiteye blueberry) are three of the more common—but these are inconsistently applied, making the identity of nursery plants difficult to determine. As a group, these plants are excellent for the garden. Purchasing from local retailers who sell from locally grown stock will alleviate the need for nomenclatural precision and ensure greater success.

Zones: 5–10, 10–1.

Form and Size: Moderate to relatively large multistemmed deciduous (occasionally nearly evergreen) shrubs with long, slender, arching branches and flaking bark; variously 3–12 feet tall and nearly as wide.

Characteristics: Leaves typically oval in outline, thick and leathery, variously hairy beneath (depending upon species), grayish to pale green above; averaging 1–3 inches long and about 1½ inches wide. Flowers cylindrical, bell- or urn-shaped, white, typically hanging or pointing downward from the branch; less than ½ inch long; appearing in early to mid spring. Fruit a juicy, edible, blue-black to nearly black, ⅛–½-inch berry.

Culture: Blueberries prefer well-drained acidic soils with pH 4.5–5.5. Flowers best in full sun. Tolerates standing water for short periods.

Highbush blueberry. Courtesy of Ron Lance.

Typical Use: Excellent as part of a shrubby border or in a naturalistic woodland, but may also be planted as a specimen shrub. Highbush blueberry is the blueberry of choice for fruit production.

Best Features: Valued for its early spring flowers, excellent fruit, and attractiveness to wildlife.

Companion Plants: American beautyberry, Chapman's rhododendron, flowering dogwood, fringe tree, honeycups, inkberry, Jenkins' fetterbush, loblolly bay, lowbush blueberries, native azaleas (especially Piedmont azalea), sweetbay magnolia, titi.

Similar and Related Species: Elliott's blueberry (*V. elliottii*) is one of the easier-to-identify entities in the highbush blueberry complex and has gained increased popularity in the retail nursery trade. Its leaves are finely toothed and smaller than other members of the group (typically about ¾ inch long and ⅜ inch wide), and the one-year-old branches are typically green. Deerberry (*V. stamineum*) is another large blueberry that has proven attractive to gardeners. Although not part of the highbush complex, it grows to similar proportions. Its flowers are more bell-like than urn-shaped with an attractive mass of protruding stamens; the leaves are silvery white beneath. See Chapter 7 for more information on the blueberries and other members of the heath family.

Lowbush Blueberries

Vaccinium spp.

Family: Ericaceae (Heath)

Native Range and Habitat: Coastal plains. Flatwoods, wet to moist pinelands, margins of swamps. Extreme southeastern South Carolina south to and throughout Florida, west to eastern Louisiana (exact natural range depends upon species). The lowbush blueberries comprise two species with similar habitat preferences. Shiny blueberry (*V. myrsinites*) has the longer gardening history, but Darrow's blueberry (*V. darrowii*) is gaining rapidly in popularity.

Zones: 8–10, 11–9.

Form and Size: Low, rounded, evergreen shrubs usually not exceeding 2 feet (shiny blueberry) or 3 feet (Darrow's blueberry) tall.

Characteristics: Leaves relatively small, usually less than ⅝ inch long and ⅜ inch wide; shiny green above at maturity in shiny blueberry, often grayish pink to dull green at maturity in Darrow's blueberry. Flowers typical of the blueberries, urn-shaped, about ¼ inch long, borne in 2–8-flowered clusters; appearing in mid spring. Fruit a rounded, blue-black, ⅜-inch berry.

Lowbush blueberry.

Culture: Prefer acidic soils in full sun. Darrow's blueberry is a xeric species that can easily be overwatered; shiny blueberry occurs mostly in moist, acidic soils but adapts well to typical garden soils and is surprisingly drought tolerant.

Typical Use: Often used along walkways, to border beds of larger shrubs, and in butterfly and wildlife gardens; essential for flatwoods and upland pineland theme gardens. Fruit is preferred by wildlife; hummingbirds nectar on the flowers.

Best Features: Valued for its low stature, dense form, evergreen habit, numerous flowers, and tasty fruit. The foliage of Darrow's blueberry changes colors throughout the year from grayish pink to dull green to reddish purple and is very attractive.

Companion Plants: Black-eyed Susan, gopherweed, longleaf pine, other blueberries, purple muhly grass, saw palmetto, turkey oak, white wild indigo, wiregrass.

Similar and Related Species: Lowbush blueberries constitute two of several species of blueberries regularly used in gardening. See Chapter 7 for more information on these and other blueberries, and other members of the heath family.

Arrowwood

Viburnum dentatum Linnaeus

Family: Adoxaceae (Moschatel)

Native Range and Habitat: Coastal plains, Piedmont, mountains. Stream banks, moist to dry woods, margins of clear-water rivers. Maine to Missouri, south to central Florida and eastern Texas.

Zones: 3–9, 9–2.

Form and Size: A moderately fast-growing, deciduous, multistemmed shrub varying widely in height, form, and leaf; some plants distinctly shrubby, others more nearly arborescent; typically less than 10 feet tall.

Characteristics: Leaves opposite, egg-shaped in outline, quite variable in size and hairiness

Arrowwood, *left* and *above*.

from plant to plant; 1–5 inches long, to about 3 inches wide; coarsely toothed along the margins; in autumn varying from yellow to nearly burgundy. Flowers individually small, creamy white, borne in numerous more or less flat-topped, 4-inch-wide cymes; appearing March–April. Fruit a ¼-inch football-shaped drupe; appearing July–September.

Culture: Tolerant of a wide range of well-drained soils, from acidic to mildly alkaline. Does well in shade but flowers best in full to partial sun. Occurs naturally in wet to moist soils but readily adapts to drier sites.

Typical Use: Excellent as a background shrub, in massed plantings, in mixed shrub borders, intermixed in naturalistic woodlands, or overtopping lower shrubs.

Best Features: A tough and adaptable native that is tolerant of widely divergent soils, variable moisture regimes, and virtually any exposure. Valued for its showy flower clusters, attractive fruit, and coarse leaves. May be pruned to form a hedge. Attractive to wildlife.

Companion Plants: American hornbeam, buttonbush, Carolina jessamine, dahoon holly, Elliott's blueberry, needle palm, oakleaf hydrangea, possumhaw holly, winterberry.

Similar and Related Species: Several species of *Viburnum* occur in the southeast, most of which are used in gardening and landscaping. Two of the more important are treated in the following accounts. Rusty blackhaw (*V. rufidulum*), a small tree or large shrub with shiny green leaves and smaller but very showy inflorescences, is also an excellent garden plant. Several cultivars of arrowwood are available, varying mostly in leaf size, form, and the color of fall foliage.

Possum Haw

Viburnum nudum Linnaeus

Family: Adoxaceae (Moschatel)

Native Range and Habitat: Coastal plains, Piedmont, mountains. Floodplains, seepage areas, bogs, swamp margins. Maine to Wisconsin, south to south-central Florida, west to eastern Texas.

Zones: 5–9, 9–4.

Form and Size: A deciduous shrub or small tree to about 16 feet tall.

Characteristics: Leaves opposite, to about 6 inches long, shiny above, often folded upward and V-shaped from the central axis; margins smooth; changing from green to red in autumn. Flowers creamy white, individually small, borne in numerous showy clusters at the branch tips; appearing April–May. Fruit a ⅜-inch, mostly egg-shaped drupe; changing successively from whitish to pink to deep purple with maturity; appearing August–October and often persisting well after the leaves have fallen.

Culture: Occurs naturally in moist to wet soils but is adaptable to drier sites. Full sun produces best flowering, especially if the root zone is not subject to excessive drying.

Typical Use: Excellent in naturalistic woodlands and along streams or other wet margins. Adapts to average garden conditions; not drought tolerant.

Best Features: The showy flowers, attractive fall foliage, and long-lasting fruit are important attributes.

Companion Plants: Buttonbush, Carolina jessamine, climbing hydrangea, coastal witch-alder, highbush blueberries, inkberry, sweet pepperbush, Virginia sweetspire, winterberry.

Possum haw.

Possum haw 'Winterthur.'

Similar and Related Species: This is one of several native *Viburnum* used in southern gardening. It is most closely related and similar to witherod viburnum (*V. cassinoides*) and black haw (*V. prunifolium*), both of which are readily available and regularly used in southern landscaping. A few cultivars of possum haw have been introduced, of which 'Winterthur' (pictured) and 'Pink Beauty' are the more popular.

Walter Viburnum

Viburnum obovatum Walter

Family: Adoxaceae (Moschatel)

Native Range and Habitat: Coastal plains. Alluvial forests and calcareous woodlands. South Carolina south throughout Florida, west to extreme southeastern Alabama.

Zones: 6–9, 9–6.

Form and Size: A small deciduous tree or multistemmed shrub with stiff, often ascending or spreading branches and a leaning trunk; potentially to 30 feet tall but more often taking the form of a low, dense shrub in the garden; may be pruned to maintain size and shape.

Characteristics: Leaves opposite, without stalks, ¾–2 inches long, to a little more than 1 inch wide; margins smooth or bluntly toothed; typically widest above the middle. Flowers white, individually tiny, borne in numerous small, tight cymes a little more that 2 inches wide; appearing March–April; flowering individuals are very showy. Fruit a small, laterally flattened drupe to about ⅜ inch long; changing from red to black with maturity; appearing September–October.

Culture: Adapts to a wide range of soils and conditions with moist, well-drained situations optimal; tolerant of acidic to alkaline conditions; flowers best in full sun.

Typical Use: An excellent specimen shrub or tree; performs well in roadside and highway plantings and in parking lot medians. Useful for screening as a pruned or unpruned

Walter viburnum, *right* and *above*.

hedge. Larger plants serve well as small shade trees. Also used to provide food and cover for birds.

Best Features: Highly valued for its profuse spring flowering, compact foliage, dense habit (in certain cultivars), attractive fruit, and use by birds and other wildlife.

Companion Plants: Bluestem palmetto, dahoon holly, Elliott's blueberry, Florida leucothoe, needle palm, possumhaw holly, red maple, winged elm, witch-hazel.

Similar and Related Species: Several *Viburnum* are used in southern landscaping. Walter viburnum's small leaves set it apart from most species. Several selections are useful in the garden, the more popular of which form low, rounded, dense shrubs; 'Densa' is the best example.

American Wisteria

Wisteria frutescens (Linnaeus) Poiret

Family: Fabaceae (Bean)
Native Range and Habitat: Coastal plains, Piedmont, mountains. Wet margins of swamps and drainages, wet woodlands. New York west to Illinois, south to central Florida and eastern Texas.
Zones: 6–9, 9–6.
Form and Size: A high-climbing, twining woody vine (often trained to a vinelike shrub in the garden) to at least 30 feet long; sometimes running along the ground in natural areas.
Characteristics: Leaves alternate, 4–8 inches long, compound with up to 15 leaflets 1–3 inches long. Flowers purple to blue, borne in congested, headlike, racemose clusters to about 6 inches long; appearing April–May. Fruit a laterally flattened, several-seeded, linear, 4-inch pod with conspicuous constrictions between the seed cavities; appearing June–September.
Culture: Performs best in well-drained acidic soils. Occurs in wetlands and moisture-retentive soils in nature but is adaptable to quite dry sites in the garden.
Typical Use: An excellent replacement for the Chinese and Japanese wisterias, both of

American wisteria.

which have become troublesome invasive weeds (see Chapter 3). May be used as a specimen shrub or vine. Will grow as a stand-alone shrub or can be trained to trellises, fences, trees, and other upright structures.

Best Features: Valued for its attractive clusters of bluish flowers that appear late in the spring.

Companion Plants: Buttonbush, highbush blueberries, inkberry, Jenkins' fetterbush, loblolly bay, netted chain fern, sweetbay magnolia, sweet pepperbush, Virginia sweetspire, wax myrtle.

Similar and Related Species: Two species of wisteria have enjoyed long use in southern landscapes, neither of which is native to the United States. Japanese wisteria (*W. floribunda*) and Chinese wisteria (*W. sinensis*) have proven to be difficult-to-control weeds that have escaped into and disrupted natural areas. Kentucky wisteria (*W. macrostachya*) is also native to the United States and is sometimes used in gardens within our coverage area. American wisteria has given rise to several cultivars of which 'Amethyst Falls,' which flowers in both spring and late summer, is one of the more popular. 'Alba' is a selection with white flowers. See Chapter 14 for more about this and other native vines, and Chapter 13 for information about other species from the bean family.

Yellowroot

Xanthorhiza simplicissima Marshall

Family: Ranunculaceae (Buttercup)

Native Range and Habitat: Coastal plains, Piedmont, mountains. Stream banks, often along low embankments just above water level. Maine southward to a few populations in the Florida panhandle, west to extreme eastern Texas; mostly spottily distributed south and west of Alabama.

Zones: 3–9, 9–2.

Form and Size: A low, 2–3-foot deciduous shrub, spreading by belowground stems and forming small colonies along streams and small rivers. The wood of both stem and roots is yellow, hence the common name.

Characteristics: Leaves alternate, compound, divided into 3–5 deeply incised and delicate 4–5-inch leaflets; often clustered umbrella-like at the top of the short, straight stem. Flowers with several maroon to lavender lobes, borne in delicate, 2–6-inch racemes that curve downward and droop below the leaves. Fruit a small, one-seeded pod (follicle).

Culture: Performs best in moist, well-drained soils in partial shade or full sun.

Typical Use: Excellent in shady spring perennial gardens, along natural and human-made streams, especially in somewhat sandy soils; effective along foundations and for bordering walkways.

Yellowroot.

Best Features: The delicate leaves held near the top of the erect stem produce an attractive high groundcover. Will spread in the garden, especially in rich, moist soils.

Companion Plants: Allegheny-spurge, atamasco lily, blue phlox, bottlebrush buckeye, Elliott's blueberry, Indian pink, mayapple, trilliums, two-winged silverbell, wild columbine.

Similar and Related Species: Numerous species in the buttercup family occur in the southeastern United States, none of which are closely similar to yellowroot.

Honeycups, Zenobia

Zenobia pulverulenta (Bartram ex Willdenow) Pollard

Family: Ericaceae (Heath)

Native Range and Habitat: Coastal plains. Swamp and pocosin margins, wet edges of sandhill ponds and depressions. Southeastern Virginia south to southwestern Georgia, often within a few miles of the coast; also in portions of the Fall Line Hills bordering the Piedmont.

Zones: 5–9, 9–5.

Form and Size: An upright, multistemmed, deciduous shrub to at least 20 feet tall in nature; may be pruned to maintain a more shrublike form in the garden.

Characteristics: Leaves alternate, oval in outline, 1–3 inches long, dark green on some plants, bluish on others; plants from coastal locations generally all have green

Honeycups.

leaves, whereas plants of inland locations generally occur in mixed colonies, some plants with bluish foliage and others with green foliage; autumn colors yellow, orange, or red. Flowers broadly urn-shaped, similar to the blueberries, to about ½ inch long, nearly round in outline with a truncated apex; appearing in showy, branched clusters, April–June. Fruit a ¼-inch, brownish capsule.

Culture: Occurs in wet sites in nature but is adaptable to dry sites and surprisingly drought tolerant. Flowers best in full sun and well-drained soils.

Typical Use: Excellent in single-species shrub beds or in conjunction with other heath plants. Mixes well with coastal witch-alder, especially some of the blue-leaved cultivars.

Best Features: Most valued for its bluish leaf color, drought tolerance, and attractive and abundant flowers. Highly attractive to bees and other insects.

Companion Plants: Coastal witch-alder, fringe tree, inkberry, Jenkins' fetterbush, lowbush and highbush blueberries, native azaleas, red chokeberry.

Similar and Related Species: Honeycups is one of numerous woody shrubs in the heath family and is superficially similar to many of its closest relatives. It is easily distinguished by its leaves. This is an excellent and probably underutilized native shrub with wide applicability far beyond its native distribution. Though restricted in nature to the coastal plains, it performs very well in the Piedmont as well as south and west of its typical range.

Sources for Native Plants

The increased use of native plants in residential and commercial landscapes has resulted in a concomitant increase in the number of retail, wholesale, and mail-order nurseries that sell or specialize in indigenous species. A large number of retail nurseries now carry native plants, including many large-scale nurseries that do not ordinarily advertise themselves as native plant vendors. While some large retail nurseries continue to designate special display areas that house their native plant inventories, the rapid rise in the number of native species that have found their way into the mainstream retail market has made this approach increasingly untenable. Most retail nurseries now incorporate natives within their mainline inventory, often—but by no means always—labeling them as native to make them easier to find.

Although numerous nurseries now offer native plants, several vendors specialize in them, some of which have had long histories in the industry. The list below is organized by state (but includes numerous vendors that ship plants widely) and contains some of the southeastern United States' better-known or up-and-coming native plant vendors. The list includes retail, wholesale, and mail-order businesses, as well as a few botanical gardens that also sell plants. Given the number of outlets in the trade today, the list is certainly not exhaustive, and many additions can be found on the Web sites of state and local native plant societies. Nevertheless, the following list provides an excellent starting point for adding natives to your garden.

Sources of Information about Native Plants

Several southeastern states are served by native plant societies, all of which are valuable resources for native plant information and sources. Several of these organizations, including the Louisiana Native Plant Society, Virginia Native Plant Society, South Carolina Native Plant Society, and the Georgia Native Plant Society, maintain nursery lists on their Web sites. Most of these organizations sponsor local, regional, or statewide conferences and workshops. In addition, the annual Cullowhee Conference for Native Plants in the Landscape (http://www.wcu.edu/5033.asp), held each year near the end of July on the campus of Western Carolina University, continues to be one of the most important gatherings of native plant enthusiasts in the eastern United States. Now more than twenty-five years old, the Cullowhee Conference offers a variety of workshops, presentations, field trips, and native plant vendors. Following are native plant societies serving the southeast. *continued*

Society	Contact	Website
Alabama Wildflower Society	Maryalys Griffis, Treasurer 2021 10th Ave. South Apt. 720 Birmingham, AL 35205 membership@ alabamawildflower.org	http://www. alabamawildflower.org/
Florida Native Plant Society	FNPS P.O. Box 278 Melbourne, FL 32902-0278 info@fnps.org	http://www.fnps.org/
Georgia Native Plant Society	GNPS P.O. Box 422085 Atlanta, GA 30342-2085 (770) 343-6000 webmaster@gnps.org	http://www.gnps.org/
Louisiana Native Plant Society	Jackie Duncan, LNPS Treasurer 114 Harper Ferry Boyce, LA 71409	http://www.lnps.org/
Mississippi Native Plant Society	Mississippi Native Plant Society, Inc. c/o Dr. Debora Mann Millsaps College Box 150307 Jackson, MS 39210	http://www.nrims.org/ mysite2/
North Carolina Native Plant Society	North Carolina Native Plant Society c/o North Carolina Botanical Garden CB#3375, Totten Center UNC–Chapel Hill Chapel Hill, NC 27599-3375 tom@ncwildflower.org	http://www. ncwildflower.org/
South Carolina Native Plant Society	South Carolina Native Plant Society P.O. Box 491 Norris, SC 29667	http://www.scnps.org/
Virginia Native Plant Society	Virginia Native Plant Society 400 Blandy Farm Lane, Unit 2 Boyce, VA 22620 vnpsofc@shentel.net	http://vnps.org/

Sources of Native Plants for the Southeastern United States

Alabama

Biophilia Nature Center
Location: 12695 C.R. 95, Elberta, AL 36530
Phone: (251) 987-1200
Web site: http://www.biophilia.net/
Distribution: Retail, occasional mail order

Dodd and Dodd Native Nurseries
Address: P.O. Drawer 439, Semmes, AL 36575
Phone: (251) 645-2222; Fax (251) 645-2723
Web site: http://www.doddnatives.com/
Distribution: Wholesale only

Wildflower
Location: 234 Oak Tree Trail, Wilsonville, AL 35186
Phone: (205) 669-4097; Fax: (205) 669-4097
Distribution: Retail (by appointment), wholesale

Florida

Association of Florida Native Nurseries
Phone: Toll-free: (877) 352-2366
Web site: http://www.afnn.org/
Distribution: Retail, wholesale, mail order

Mail Order Natives
Location: P.O. Box 9366, Lee, FL 32059
Phone: (850) 973-6830; Fax (850) 971-5416
Web site: http://www.mailordernatives.com/
Distribution: Mail order, but visitors are welcome

Maple Street Natives
Location: 7619 Henry Ave., West Melbourne, FL 32904
Phone: (321) 729-6857; Fax (321) 729-6857 (call first)
Web site: http://www.maplestreetnatives.com/
Distribution: Retail

Native Nurseries
Location: 1661 Centerville Rd., Tallahassee, FL 32308
Phone: (850) 386-8882
Web site: http://www.nativenurseries.com/
Distribution: Retail

Sherman Natives
Location: 1329 Cattail Dr., Madison, FL 32340
Phone: (850) 973-4550
Web site: http://www.shermannatives.com/
Distribution: Wholesale

Superior Trees
Location: 12493 E. U.S. Hwy. 90, 4.5 miles east of Lee, Florida; P.O. Drawer 9400,
Lee, FL 32059
Phone: (850) 971-5159; Fax (850) 971-5416
Web site: http://www.superiortrees.net/
Distribution: Wholesale

The Natives
Location: 2929 J. B. Carter Rd., Davenport, FL 33837
Phone: (863) 422-6664; Fax: (863) 421-6520
Web site: http://www.thenatives.net/
Distribution: Primarily wholesale

Trillium Gardens
Location: 3532 Trillium Ct., Tallahassee, FL 32312
Phone: (850) 893-5757
Distribution: Wholesale, retail, seasonal mail order

Georgia

Callaway Gardens
Location: 17800 U.S. Hwy. 27, Pine Mountain, GA 31822
Phone: (706) 663-2281
Web site: http://www.callawaygardens.com/

Garden Delights Garden Center
Lazy K Nursery, Inc.
Location: Garden Delights Garden Center, GA Hwy. 27,
Downtown Pine Mountain, GA
Lazy K Nursery, 705 Wright Rd., Pine Mountain, GA 31822
Phone: Garden Delights, (706) 663-7964
Lazy K Nursery, (706) 663-4991; Fax (706) 663-0939
Web site: http://www.lazyknursery.com/
Distribution: Wholesale, retail, mail order

Georgia Perimeter College Native Plant Garden
Location: 3251 Panthersville Rd., Decatur, GA 30034
Phone: (678) 891-2668
Web site: http://www.gpc.edu/~decbt/
Distribution: Retail

Nearly Native Nursery
Location: 776 McBride Rd., Fayetteville, GA 30215
Phone: (770) 460-6284; Fax: (770) 460-7050
Web site: http://www.nearlynativenursery.com/
Distribution: Retail, mail order

Thyme after Thyme, Inc.
Location: 550 Athens Rd., Winterville, GA 30683
Phone: (706) 742-7149
Web site: www.thymeafterthyme.com
Distribution: Retail, wholesale, mail order

Louisiana

Coyote Creek Herbs and Useful Natives
Location: 9382 Island Rd., St. Francisville, LA 70775
Storefront: Main Street Market, 5th and Main, Baton Rouge, LA
Phone: (225) 635-6736; Fax: (225) 784-2222
Web site: http://www.coyote-creek.net/
Distribution: Retail, mail order

Jenkins Farm and Nursery, LLC
Location: 62188 Dummyline, Amite, LA 70422
Phone: (985) 748-7746; Fax: (985) 748-8219
Distribution: Wholesale

Louisiana Growers
Location: 63279 Lowery Rd., Amite, LA 70422
Phone: (985) 747-0510; Toll-free: (866) 747-0510; Fax: (985) 747-5850
Web site: http://www.louisianagrowers.com/
Distribution: Wholesale only

Prairie Basse Native Nursery
Location: 217 St. Fidelis St., Carencro, LA 70520
Phone: (337) 896-9187
Distribution: Retail (nursery visits by appointment only)

North Carolina

Carolina Native Nursery
Location: 1126 Prices Creek Rd., Burnsville, NC 28714
Phone: (828) 682-1471
Web site: http://www.carolinanativenursery.com/
Distribution: Retail, wholesale

Cure Nursery
Location: 880 Buteo Ridge Rd., Pittsboro, NC 27312
Phone: (919) 542-6186
Web site: http://www.carenursery.com/
Distribution: Wholesale

Elk Mountain Nursery
Location: P.O. Box 599, Asheville, NC 28802
Phone: (828) 683-9330
Web site: http://www.elk-mountain.com/
Distribution: Mail order

Growing Wild Nursery
Location: 193 Murphy Rd., Burgaw, NC 28425
Phone: (910) 259-6361
Web site: http://www.growingwildnursery.net/
Distribution: Retail

Meadowbrook Nursery/We-Du Natives
Location: 2055 Polly Sprout Rd., Marion, NC 28752
Phone: (828) 738-8300; Fax (878) 287-9348
Web site: http://www.we-du.com/
Distribution: Mail order, retail (call for hours), wholesale (to retailers only)

Mellow Marsh Farm
Location: 1312 Woody Store Rd., Siler City, NC 27344
Phone: (919) 742-1200; Fax (919) 742-1280
Web site: http://mellowmarshfarm.com/
Distribution: Wholesale

Niche Gardens
Location: 1111 Dawson Rd., Chapel Hill, NC 27516
Phone: (919) 967-0078; Fax (919) 967-4026
Web site: http://www.nichegardens.com/
Distribution: Retail, mail order

North Carolina Botanical Garden
Location: Old Mason Farm Rd., Chapel Hill, NC 27514
Phone: (919) 962-0522; Fax: (919) 962-3531
Web site: http://ncbg.unc.edu/

South Carolina

Fern Gully Nursery
Location: 2586 Hwy. 11 West, Chesnee, SC 29323
Phone: (864) 461-7146
Web site: http://www.ferngullynursery.com/
Distribution: Mail order, retail by appointment

Woodlanders
Location: 1128 Colleton Ave., Aiken, SC 29801
Phone: (803) 648-7522
Web site: http://www.woodlanders.net/
Distribution: Mail order

Tennessee

East Fork Nursery
Location: 2769 Bethel Church Rd., Sevierville, TN 37876
Phone: (865) 453-6108; Fax (865) 908-8761
Distribution: Retail

Native Gardens
Location: 5737 Fisher Ln., Greenback, TN 37742
Phone: (865) 856-0220, Fax: (865) 856-0220
Web site: http://www.native-gardens.com/
Distribution: Mail order, retail (by appointment), wholesale

Sunlight Gardens
Location: 174 Golden Ln., Andersonville, TN 37705
Phone: (865) 494-8237
Web site: http://www.sunlightgardens.com/
Distribution: Primarily mail order, but visitors are welcome

Virginia

Meadowview Biological Research Station
Location: 8390 Fredericksburg Tnpk., Woodford, VA 22580
Phone: (804) 633-4336
Web site: http://www.pitcherplant.org/
Distribution: Mail order, retail (by appointment)

Nature by Design
Location: 300 Calvert Ave., Alexandria, VA 22301
Phone: (703) 683-4769
Web site: http://www.nature-by-design.com/
Distribution: Retail

Pinelands Nursery and Supply, Inc.
Locations: 323 Island Rd., Columbus, NJ 08022; 324 County Route 112, Bleeker, NY 12078; with a retail location at 8877 Richmond Rd. (Route 60), Toano, VA 23168
Phone: (609) 291-9486, (800) 667-2729; Fax (609) 298-8939
Web site: http://www.pinelandsnursery.com/
Distribution: Wholesale, retail

Reference List of Names Used in the Text

Common Name	Botanical Name
Alabama snow-wreath	*Neviusia alabamensis*
Allegheny-spurge	*Pachysandra procumbens*
American ash	*Fraxinus americana*
American beautyberry	*Callicarpa americana*
American beech	*Fagus grandifolia*
American holly	*Ilex opaca*
American hornbeam	*Carpinus caroliniana*
American yellowwood	*Cladrastis kentukea*
arrowwood	*Viburnum dentatum*
Ashe magnolia	*Magnolia ashei*
atamasco lily	*Zephyranthes atamasca*
baldcypress	*Taxodium distichum*
basswood	*Tilia americana*
bergamot	*Monarda didyma; M. fistulosa*
bigleaf magnolia	*Magnolia macrophylla*
bird's-foot violet	*Viola pedata*
black locust	*Robinia pseudoacacia*
black titi	*Cliftonia monophylla*
blackgum	*Nyssa sylvatica*
black-eyed Susan	*Rudbeckia hirta*
blackjack oak	*Quercus marilandica*
blazing stars	*Liatris* spp.
bloodroot	*Sanguinaria canadensis*
blueberries	*Vaccinium* spp.
bluestem grasses	*Andropogon* spp.
bluestem palmetto	*Sabal minor*
blue-eyed grass	*Sisyrinchium angustifolium*
blue mistflower	*Conoclinium coelestinum*
blue phlox	*Phlox divaricata*
bottlebrush buckeye	*Aesculus parviflora*
box elder	*Acer negundo*
broomsedges	*Andropogon* spp.
burr oak	*Quercus macrocarpa*
bushy St. John's–wort	*Hypericum densiflorum*
buttonbush	*Cephalanthus occidentalis*
Carolina laurelcherry	*Prunus caroliniana*
Carolina jessamine	*Gelsemium sempervirens*
Carolina rose	*Rosa carolina*

Common Name	Botanical Name
Chapman's rhododendron	*Rhododendron chapmanii*
chestnut oak	*Quercus montana*
Christmas fern	*Polystichum acrostichoides*
cinnamon fern	*Osmunda cinnamomea*
climbing aster	*Ampelaster carolinianus*
climbing hydrangea	*Decumaria barbara*
coastal witch-alder	*Fothergilla gardenii*
common pawpaw	*Asimina triloba*
coontie	*Zamia pumila*
coral honeysuckle	*Lonicera sempervirens*
coralbean	*Erythrina herbacea*
coreopsis	*Coreopsis* spp.
cucumber magnolia	*Magnolia acuminata*
dahoon holly	*Ilex cassine*
Darlington oak	*Quercus hemisphaerica*
deerberry	*Vaccinium stamineum*
diamond leaf oak	*Quercus laurifolia*
dimpled trout lily	*Erythronium umbilicatum*
drooping leucothoe	*Leucothoe fontanesiana*
Elliott's blueberry	*Vaccinium elliottii*
Florida anise	*Illicium floridanum*
Florida leucothoe	*Agarista populifolia*
flowering dogwood	*Cornus florida*
foamflower	*Tiarella cordifolia*
fringe tree	*Chionanthus virginicus*
Georgia calamint	*Clinopodium georgianum*
goldenrods	*Solidago* spp.
gopherweed	*Baptisia lanceolata*
green-and-gold	*Chrysogonum virginianum*
green ash	*Fraxinus pennsylvanica*
green haw	*Crataegus viridis*
haws	*Crataegus*
heartleaf	*Hexastylis shuttleworthii*
highbush blueberry	*Vaccinium* spp.
honeycups	*Zenobia pulverulenta*
hophornbeam	*Ostrya virginiana*
Indian pink	*Spigelia marilandica*
inkberry	*Ilex glabra*
iris	*Iris* spp.
ironweed	*Vernonia* spp.
Jenkins' fetterbush	*Leucothoe axillaris*
Joe-Pye-weed	*Eupatorium fistulosum; E. purpureum*
lady fern	*Athyrium filix-femina*
lance-leaf coreopsis	*Coreopsis lanceolata*
large witch-alder	*Fothergilla major*
laurel oak	*Quercus hemisphaerica*
little brown jug	*Hexastylis arifolia*
live oak	*Quercus virginiana*
lizard's-tail	*Saururus cernuus*
loblolly bay	*Gordonia lasianthus*
longleaf pine	*Pinus palustris*
lovegrass	*Eragrostis* spp.

Common Name	Botanical Name
lowbush blueberries	*Vaccinium* spp.
mayapple	*Podophyllum peltatum*
mayhaw	*Crataegus aestivalis*
milkweeds	*Asclepias* spp.
mock orange	*Philadelphus* spp.
mountain laurel	*Kalmia latifolia*
native azaleas	*Rhododendron* spp.
needle palm	*Rhapidophyllum hystrix*
netted chain fern	*Woodwardia areolata*
New Jersey tea	*Ceanothus americanus*
ninebark	*Physocarpus opulifolius*
northern red oak	*Quercus rubra*
Ocala anise	*Illicium parviflorum*
oakleaf hydrangea	*Hydrangea quercifolia*
parsley haw	*Crataegus marshallii*
partridgeberry	*Mitchella repens*
Piedmont azalea	*Rhododendron canescens*
pin oak	*Quercus palustris*
poppy mallow	*Callirhoe* spp.
possumhaw holly	*Ilex decidua*
post oak	*Quercus stellata*
purple coneflower	*Echinacea purpurea*
purple muhly grass	*Muhlenbergia capillaris*
red basil	*Calamintha coccineum*
red buckeye	*Aesculus pavia*
red chokeberry	*Aronia arbutifolia*
red maple	*Acer rubrum*
redbud	*Cercis canadensis*
river birch	*Betula nigra*
rosemary	*Conradina* spp.
royal fern	*Osmunda regalis* var. *spectabilis*
rudbeckias	*Rudbeckia*
sand live oak	*Quercus geminata*
saw palmetto	*Serenoa repens*
scarlet oak	*Quercus coccinea*
serviceberry	*Amelanchier* spp.
Shumard oak	*Quercus shumardii*
silver maple	*Acer saccharinum*
smooth sumac	*Rhus glabra*
southern crabapple	*Malus angustifolia*
southern magnolia	*Magnolia grandiflora*
southern maidenhair fern	*Adiantum capillus-veneris*
southern red oak	*Quercus falcata*
southern sugar maple	*Acer floridanum*
sourwood	*Oxydendrum arboreum*
sparkleberry	*Vaccinium arboreum*
spicebush	*Lindera benzoin*
spotted Joe-Pye-weed	*Eupatorium fistulosum*
spruce pine	*Pinus glabra*
St. John's–worts	*Hypericum* spp.
starry rosinweed	*Silphium asteriscus*
Stokes' aster	*Stokesia laevis*

Common Name	Botanical Name
sugar maple	*Acer saccharum*
sundial lupine	*Lupinus perennis*
sunflowers	*Helianthus* spp.
swamp azalea	*Rhododendron viscosum*
swamp chestnut oak	*Quercus michauxii*
swamp dogwood	*Cornus foemina*
swamp laurel oak	*Quercus laurifolia*
swamp rose	*Rosa palustris*
swamp tupelo	*Nyssa biflora*
sweet birch	*Betula lenta*
sweet pepperbush	*Clethra alnifolia*
sweetshrub	*Calycanthus floridus*
sweetbay magnolia	*Magnolia virginiana*
tarflower	*Bejaria racemosa*
threadleaf bluestar	*Amsonia ciliata*
tickseeds	*Coreopsis* spp.
titi	*Cyrilla racemiflora*
topel holly	*Ilex × attenuata*
trilliums	*Trillium* spp.
tulip poplar	*Liriodendron tulipifera*
turkey oak	*Quercus laevis*
two-winged silverbell	*Halesia diptera*
umbrella magnolia	*Magnolia tripetala*
Virginia chain fern	*Woodwardia virginica*
Virginia sweetspire	*Itea virginica*
Walter viburnum	*Viburnum obovatum*
Walter's violet	*Viola walteri*
Washington thorn	*Crataegus phaenopyrum*
water oak	*Quercus nigra*
wax myrtle	*Morella cerifera*
weeping yaupon	*Ilex vomitoria* 'Pendula'
white oak	*Quercus alba*
white wild indigo	*Baptisia alba*
wild blue indigo	*Baptisia australis*
wild columbine	*Aquilegia canadensis*
wild ginger	*Asarum canadense*
wild hydrangea	*Hydrangea arborescens*
wild rosemary	*Conradina canescens*
winged elm	*Ulmus alata*
winterberry	*Ilex verticillata*
wiregrass	*Aristida stricta*
witch-hazel	*Hamamelis virginiana*
yaupon	*Ilex vomitoria*
yellow coneflower	*Ratibida pinnata*
yellowroot	*Xanthorhiza simplicissima*

Bibliography

Allen, Charles M., Dawn Allen Newman, and Harry H. Winters. 2002. *Trees, Shrubs, and Woody Vines of Louisiana*. Pitkin, LA: Allen's Native Ventures.

Armitage, Allan M. 2006. *Armitage's Native Plants for North American Gardens*. Portland, OR: Timber Press.

Austin, Daniel. 2004. *Florida Ethnobotany*. London: Taylor and Francis Group.

Bailes, Christopher. 2006. *Hollies for Gardeners*. Portland, OR: Timber Press.

Birr, Richard E. 1992. *Growing and Propagating Showy Native Woody Plants*. Chapel Hill: University of North Carolina Press.

Braun, E. Lucy. 1950. *Deciduous Forests of Eastern North America*. Reprint, 2001. Caldwell, NJ: Blackburn Press.

Burrell, C. Colston. 2006. *Native Alternatives to Invasive Plants*. New York: Brooklyn Botanic Garden.

Cappiello, Paul E., and Lyle E. Littlefield. 1994. *Woody Landscape Plant Cold-Hardiness Ratings, Lyle E. Littlefield Ornamentals Trial Garden, University of Maine, Orono, Maine*. Technical Bulletin 156. Orono: University of Maine Agricultural and Forest Experiment Station.

Case, Frederick W., Jr., and Roberta B. Case. 1997. *Trilliums*. Portland, OR: Timber Press.

Cerulean, Susan, Celeste Botha, and Donna Legare. 1986. *Planting a Refuge for Wildlife*. Tallahassee: Florida Wildlife Conservation Commission.

Chafin, Linda G. 2007. *Field Guide to the Rare Plants of Georgia*. Athens: State Botanical Garden of Georgia.

Cullina, William. 2002. *Native Trees, Shrubs, and Vines*. New York: Houghton Mifflin.

Del Tredici, Peter. Lost and found: *Elliottia racemosa*. Arnoldia 47(4): 2–8.

Dirr, Michael A. 1998. *Manual of Woody Landscape Plants*. 5th ed. Champaign, IL: Stipes Publishing.

———. 2004. *Hydrangeas for American Gardens*. Portland, OR: Timber Press.

Dirr, Michael A., and John H. Alexander. 1991. *Ilex glabra*—The inkberry holly. Arnoldia 51(2): 17–22.

Dormon, Caroline. 1958. *Flowers Native to the Deep South*. Baton Rouge, LA: Claitor's Book Store.

———. 1965. *Natives Preferred*. Baton Rouge, LA: Claitor's Book Store.

Dozier, Hallie. 1999. Plant introduction and invasion: History, public awareness, and the case of *Ardisia crenata*. Ph.D. diss., University of Florida, Gainesville.

Fontenot, William R. 1992. *Native Gardening in the South*. 2nd ed. Carencro, LA: Prairie Basse.

Fordham, Alfred J. 1969. *Elliottia racemosa* and its propagation. Arnoldia 29(1): 17–20.

Galle, Fred. 1997. *Hollies: The Genus* Ilex. Portland, OR: Timber Press.

GAO. 2000. *Invasive Species: Federal and Selected State Funding to Address Harmful, Nonnative*

Species. United States General Accounting Office Report to Congressional Committees, August 2000.

Harrison, Mary. 2000. Mary Gibson Henry, plantswoman extraordinaire. Arnoldia 60(1): 2–12.

Henry, Mary G. 1941. *Elliottia racemosa*. National Horticultural Magazine 20(3): 223–26.

———. 1947. A new lily from southern Alabama and northern Florida. Bartonia 24: 1–4.

———. 1950. Mary Gibson Henry: An autobiography. Plant Life 6(1): 9–30.

Honigsbaum, Mark. 2001. *The Fever Trail*. New York: Farrar, Straus and Giroux.

Hume, H. Harold. 1953. *Hollies*. New York: Macmillan.

Isely, Duane. 1990. *Vascular Flora of the Southeastern United States: Volume 3, Part 2 Leguminosae (Fabaceae)*. Chapel Hill: University of North Carolina Press.

Jaynes, Richard A. 1997. *Kalmia: Mountain Laurel and Related Species*. Portland, OR: Timber Press.

Jensen, Jens. 1990. *Siftings*. Baltimore: Johns Hopkins University Press [reprint of 1939 edition].

Johnson, Fran Holman. 1990. *The Gift of the Wild Things: The Life of Caroline Dormon*. Lafayette: University of Southwestern Louisiana.

Kuenzler, Edward J. 2004. *Time and the Piedmont*. [Chapel Hill, NC]: Chapel Hill Press.

Lawrence, Elizabeth. 1991. *A Southern Garden*. Chapel Hill: University of North Carolina Press [reprint of 1942 edition].

Loewer, Peter. 2004. *Native Perennials for the Southeast*. Nashville, TN: Cool Springs Press.

Marinelli, Janet, ed. 1996. *Going Native: Biodiversity in Your Own Backyard*. New York: Brooklyn Botanic Garden Publications.

Mickel, John. 1994. *Ferns for American Gardens*. New York: Macmillan.

McClelland, Linda. 1993. *Presenting Nature: The Historic Landscape Design of the National Park Service 1916 to 1942*. Online book. National Park Service, http://www.cr.nps.gov/history/online _books/mcclelland/mcclelland.htm.

Midgley, Jan A. W. 2006. *Native Plant Propagation*. Wilsonville, AL: Jan A. W. Midgley.

Miller, James H. 2003. *Nonnative Invasive Plants of Southern Forests: A Field Guide for Identification and Control*. Asheville, NC: Southern Research Station.

Miller, Wilhelm. 2002. *The Prairie Spirit in Landscape Gardening*. Amherst: University of Massachusetts Press [reprint of 1915 edition].

Nelson, Gil. 2003. *Florida's Best Native Landscape Plants: 200 Readily Available Species for Homeowners and Professionals*. Gainesville: University Press of Florida.

———. 2005. *East Gulf Coastal Plain Wildflowers*. Guilford, CN: Globe Pequot Press.

———. 2006. *Atlantic Coastal Plain Wildflowers*. Guilford, CN: Globe Pequot Press.

———. 2008. America's magnolias. American Gardener 87(5): 38–43.

Nowak, David J., Miki Kuroda, and Daniel E. Crane. 2004. Tree mortality rates and tree population projections in Baltimore, Maryland, USA. Urban Forestry and Urban Greening 2(3): 139–47.

Osorio, Rufino. 2001. *A Gardener's Guide to Native Plants*. Gainesville: University Press of Florida.

OTA. 1993. *Harmful Non-Indigenous Species in the United States*. Washington, DC: Office of Technology Assessment, United States Congress.

Pelczar, Rita, and William E. Barrick. *American Horticultural Society Southeast Smart Gardening Regional Guide*. New York: DK Publishing.

Phillips, Harry R. 1985. *Growing and Propagating Wild Flowers*. Chapel Hill: University of North Carolina Press.

Pimentel, David, L. Lach, R. Zuniga, and D. Morrison. 2000. Environmental and economic costs of nonindigenous species in the United States. BioScience 50(1): 53–65.

Pimentel, David, Rodolfo Zuniga, and Doug Morrison. 2005. Update on the environmental and economic costs associated with alien-invasive species in the United States. Ecological Economics 52(3): 273–88.

Ranney, Thomas G., and Paul R. Fantz. 2006. ×*Gordlinia grandiflora* (Theaceae): An intergeneric hybrid between *Franklinia alatamaha* and *Gordonia lasianthus*. HortScience 41(6): 1386–88.

Rehmann, Elsa. 1933. An ecological approach. Landscape Architecture 23(4): 239–45.

Ricketts, Taylor, Eric Dinerstein, David M. Olson, and Colby J. Loucks. 1999. *Terrestrial Ecoregions of North America: A Conservation Assessment*. Washington, DC: Island Press.

Roberts, Edith A., and Elsa Rehmann. 1996. *American Plants for American Gardens*. Athens: University of Georgia Press [reprint of 1929 edition].

Small, John K. 1972. *Manual of the Southeastern Flora*. New York: Hafner Publishing [reprint of 1933 edition].

Smith, Gerald L., and Mark Garland. 2003. Nomenclature of *Hymenocallis* taxa (Amaryllidaceae) in southeastern United States. Taxon 52(4): 805–17.

Smith, Gerald L., and Walter S. Flory. 1990. Studies on *Hymenocallis henryae* (Amaryllidaceae). Brittonia 42(3): 212–20.

Sorrie, Bruce A., and Alan S. Weakley. 2001. Coastal plain vascular plant endemics: Phytogeographic patterns. Castanea 66(1–2): 50–82.

Stein, Sara. 1993. *Noah's Garden: Restoring the Ecology of Our Own Backyards*. New York: Houghton Mifflin.

Sternberg, Guy, and Jim Wilson. 1995. *Landscaping with Native Trees*. Shelburne, VT: Chapters Publishing.

Tallamy, Douglas W. 2009. *Bringing Nature Home: How You Can Sustain Wildlife with Native Plants*. Portland, OR: Timber Press.

Towe, L. Clarence. 2004. *American Azaleas*. Portland, OR: Timber Press.

Van Doren, Mark, ed. 1955. *Travels of William Bartram*. New York: Dover Publications.

Wasowski, Sally, with Andy Wasowski. 1994. *Gardening with Native Plants of the South*. Dallas: Taylor Publishing.

Waugh, Frank A. 1917. *The Natural Style in Landscape Gardening*. Boston: Richard G. Badger [reprinted by Kessinger Publishing].

Weakley, Alan. Flora of the Carolinas, Virginia, Georgia, and surrounding areas. Working draft, 11 January 2007. http://www.herbarium.unc.edu/flora.htm.

Wells, B. W. 2002. *The Natural Gardens of North Carolina*. Rev. ed. Chapel Hill: University of North Carolina Press.

Wilcove, David S., David Rothstein, Jason Dubow, Ali Phillips, and Elizabeth Losos. 1998. Quantifying threats to imperiled species in the United States. BioScience 48(8): 607–15.

Wilson, James R., ed. 2001. *The Fire Forest: Longleaf Pine–Wiregrass Ecosystem*. Natural Georgia Series 8(2) Georgia Wildlife Press.

Yinger, Barry. 2007. When the magnolias don't freeze. Magnolia: The Journal of the Magnolia Society International 42(81): 1–6.

Index

Gil Nelson is a writer, naturalist, and field botanist specializing in the south-eastern United States. He is the author of a dozen successful gardening and botanical field guides, including *Florida's Best Native Landscape Plants*.